The Christian Moral Life

THE CHRISTIAN MORAL LIFE

Directions for the Journey to Happiness

JOHN RZIHA

UNIVERSITY OF NOTRE DAME PRESS
NOTRE DAME, INDIANA

University of Notre Dame Press
Notre Dame, Indiana 46556
www.undpress.nd.edu
All Rights Reserved

Published in the United States of America

Library of Congress Cataloging-in-Publication Data

Names: Rziha, John (John Michael), author.
Title: The Christian moral life : directions for the journey to happiness / John Rziha.
Description: Notre Dame : University of Notre Dame Press, 2017. | Includes
bibliographical references and index. | Description based on print version record and
CIP data provided by publisher; resource not viewed.
Identifiers: LCCN 2017001231 (print) | LCCN 2017011694 (ebook) |
ISBN 9780268101831 (pdf) | ISBN 9780268101848 (epub) | ISBN 9780268101817
(hardcover : alk. paper) | ISBN 9780268101824 (pbk. : alk. paper) | ISBN 0268101825
(pbk. : alk. paper)
Subjects: LCSH: Christian ethics—Catholic authors.
Classification: LCC BJ1249 (ebook) | LCC BJ1249.R955   2017 (print) | DDC 241—dc23
LC record available at https://lccn.loc.gov/2017001231

∞ *This paper meets the requirements of*
ANSI/NISO Z39.48-1992 (Permanence of Paper).

CONTENTS

ACKNOWLEDGMENTS

I wish to thank my colleagues, especially Andrew Salzmann and Michael Sirilla, who not only used earlier versions of this manuscript as textbooks in their classes but also gave me valuable feedback on it. Recognition must also be given to Benedictine College, which granted me a sabbatical so I could write a large portion of this book. I especially wish to thank my wife, Jeanne Rziha, who read through the manuscript more than once and gave many suggestions regarding both style and content. Raising nine children with her has also helped me better understand the nature of love. I further want to acknowledge one of my former students, Rachel Nofke, for proofreading a large portion of the text. Finally, I want to thank all the different saints who have helped me better understand moral theology—in particular Matthew, John the Evangelist, the Apostle Paul, Augustine, Gregory the Great, Thomas Aquinas, Thérèse of Lisieux, Teresa of Calcutta and John Paul II. Last of all, I want to thank our wise and loving God, who orders all of humans to happiness.

ABBREVIATIONS AND TRANSLATIONS

The books of the Bible are abbreviated as follows:

OLD TESTAMENT

Genesis (Gn)
Exodus (Ex)
Leviticus (Lv)
Numbers (Nm)
Deuteronomy (Dt)
Joshua (Jos)
Judges (Jgs)
Ruth (Ru)
1 Samuel (1 Sm)
2 Samuel (2 Sm)
1 Kings (1 Kgs)
2 Kings (2 Kgs)
1 Chronicles (1 Chr)
2 Chronicles (2 Chr)
Ezra (Ezr)
Nehemiah (Neh)
Tobit (Tb)
Judith (Jdt)
Esther (Est)

1 Maccabees (1 Mc)
2 Maccabees (2 Mc)
Job (Jb)
Psalms (Ps)
Proverbs (Prv)
Ecclesiastes (Eccl)
Song of Songs (Sg)
Wisdom (Wis)
Sirach (Sir)
Isaiah (Is)
Jeremiah (Jer)
Lamentations (Lam)
Baruch (Bar)
Ezekiel (Ez)
Daniel (Dn)
Hosea (Hos)
Joel (Jl)
Amos (Am)
Obadiah (Ob)

Jonah (Jon)   Haggai (Hg)
Micah (Mi)   Zechariah (Zec)
Nahum (Na)   Malachi (Mal)
Habakkuk (Hb)
Zephaniah (Zep)

NEW TESTAMENT

Matthew (Mt)   1 Timothy (1 Tm)
Mark (Mk)   2 Timothy (2 Tm)
Luke (Lk)   Titus (Ti)
John (Jn)   Philemon (Phlm)
Acts of the Apostles (Acts)   Hebrews (Heb)
Romans (Rom)   James (Jas)
1 Corinthians (1 Cor)   1 Peter (1 Pt)
2 Corinthians (2 Cor)   2 Peter (2 Pt)
Galatians (Gal)   1 John (1 Jn)
Ephesians (Eph)   2 John (2 Jn)
Philippians (Phil)   3 John (3 Jn)
Colossians (Col)   Jude (Jude)
1 Thessalonians (1 Thes)   Revelation (Rv)
2 Thessalonians (2 Thes)

The following works from Thomas Aquinas are abbreviated throughout the text:
Summa Contra Gentiles   SCG
Summa Theologiae   ST

All translations of the Bible are from the *New American Bible* (Iowa Falls, IA: World Bible Publishers, 1970).

INTRODUCTION

Some years ago I was asked to give a lecture on moral theology at a parish. As I prepared my speech, I assumed that my audience would believe that moral theology was all about laws one must follow in order to attain heaven and to avoid hell. Although I knew that these laws were important, I also knew that moral theology was so much more than laws. I was extremely excited to tell them that God was inviting all of them to be his friends for all eternity and that God wanted to share his own happiness with them. I wanted them to see how grace, virtue, wise mentors, and even laws worked together to help people attain this happiness. I did end up giving a lecture on the nature of true happiness to a receptive crowd of *five* people. Unfortunately, this was not the only time I spoke on moral theology to a relatively empty room. However, other lectures on more controversial or trendier theological issues often attracted much greater crowds. What I learned from these experiences is that many people either did not understand the subject matter of moral theology enough to want to come or they simply did not care.

I found the lack of knowledge and interest in the principles of moral theology to be particularly troubling, for the message of moral theology is one of the primary themes of the good news of Christ: we have a wise and loving God who wants us to be happy. Humans are created in such a way that they are fulfilled through loving relationships with God and other people, and the way to develop and cultivate these relationships has been revealed to us by Christ. Over the centuries, many great Christian thinkers, such as Augustine, Gregory the Great, Thomas Aquinas, Therese of Lisieux, and John Paul II, have contemplated the moral truths of the gospel and elucidated many concepts necessary for authentic happiness. This book seeks to build upon the insights of these and many other great Christian thinkers to uncover the moral wisdom of Sacred Scripture and show people how to be truly happy, both in this life and the next.

In order to build upon these insights, a more precise definition of moral theology would be helpful. Since moral theology is a branch of theology, I will begin with the word "theology." The word "theology" comes from the Greek words *theos* and *logos*. *Theos* is the word for "god." The word *logos* does not easily translate into English; however, in this context it is sufficient to simply translate it as "the study of." Theology is the "study of God."

Within the Christian tradition, theology has been divided into a number of sub-disciplines. One way of categorizing these subdivisions is based on the belief that all things come forth from God and are created with a natural inclination to return to God by performing their proper actions. Hence, a distinction is made between dogmatic (or systematic) theology, which studies God and all that comes forth from God (such as creation and revelation), and moral theology, which studies how humans return to God by performing their proper action.[1] Thus, moral theology can be defined as "the study of how humans attain eternal happiness through loving union with God by performing their proper actions with the aid of God's grace."

To better understand the nature of moral theology, an analogy is helpful. A traditional biblical analogy that helps explain the moral life is that of the pilgrim who is journeying to God.[2] The response of humans to God is like a journey to eternal happiness. In order to embark on a journey, people must know three things: where they are, where they are going, and how to get there. For example, imagine that you are visiting a large zoo for the first time. You only have a limited amount of time, and you really want to see the pandas. Upon entering the zoo, you come upon a large map. Although you could first look for the panda exhibit, knowledge of its location will not help if you do not know where you are in the zoo. Before you can do anything else, you must first figure out where you are on the map. So you look for the red "X," which says, "You are here." Once you know where you are, you can find the location of the pandas in relation to your current location. Finally, you can begin to plan your route of how to reach the pandas and begin your journey. Without knowledge of where you are, where you are going, and how to get there, you could wander aimlessly for hours and perhaps never find your destination.

Moral theology, as our journey to God, requires knowledge of the same three truths as does navigating your way around the zoo. First, we must know where we are—we must determine what type of being we are as human persons. Furthermore, we must determine what type of actions we are created to perform. Second, we must know where we are going—we are seeking a loving friendship with God, who offers us eternal happiness. Third, we must know how to get there: by performing actions ordered to this divine goal with the aid of grace, law, and the virtues. Part I of this book will follow this format.

First, we will briefly analyze human nature. Because this is a theology book, humans will be studied in relation to God and within salvation history as revealed in scripture. I will begin by analyzing humans as created in the image of God before the effects of original sin took hold. Humans are created to perform the actions of knowing and loving that allow them to enter into loving relationships with God and others. Then we will analyze the effects of original sin and the effects of Christ's redemption to see where we begin on our journey to God.

Next, we'll look at the goal—eternal happiness with God. I will show that humans are only perfectly happy when they are united to God by performing their most perfect action: knowing and loving God as he is.

Finally, the bulk of the first part of the book will cover how we get from our current state to perfect happiness by covering the moral principles essential for attaining eternal happiness. First, a brief analysis of the Bible will help determine a proper moral methodology. Then, using many of the best insights within the Christian philosophical and theological tradition, we will construct a more systematic moral theology. Building upon the earlier insight that humans are made to enter into loving relationships with God and others, yet are incapable of doing this without the aid of others, we will demonstrate how natural and human law guides humans to perform their proper actions. Through repetition of these proper actions, humans can form good habits, called "virtues." Virtues perfect the ability of humans to know and love, allowing them to be naturally happy. However, humans do not just desire natural happiness, they desire eternal happiness. But eternal happiness is not an action in accord with human nature; hence, humans need to participate in divine nature through grace to attain eternal happiness. Grace gives humans the theological virtues that allow them to be guided by the divine law to perform divine actions. These divine actions help to perfect the infused cardinal virtues, which allow humans to have supernatural happiness on earth and ultimately attain eternal happiness in heaven.

Whereas the first part of this book studies moral theology in general, the second part looks at the individual virtues and laws. In this part we will analyze the virtues of faith, hope, charity, prudence, justice, temperance, and fortitude. Along with each virtue, the corresponding laws and gifts of the Holy Spirit will also be examined.

Although this is an introductory text for moral theology, the order of the subject matter assumes that the reader is seeking a deeper understanding of moral theology than can be found in a mere explication of obligations. For beginners, laws (especially the human laws of parents and teachers) cause them to perform good human actions that will, we hope, gradually develop into virtues. In this early stage of the moral life, the person is primarily concerned with following the law and avoiding sin and temptation. Thus, a moral theology that is focused on beginners is primarily concerned with explaining in detail the law and how to avoid sin. For example, in the case of young children, parents may proclaim the law that their children are not to fight. Only after many times of choosing not to fight will the child finally obtain the virtue of promptly and joyfully avoiding fighting without being asked (or threatened). As people grow in virtue and seek a more profound understanding of morality, they no longer need the law to constantly guide and motivate them, nor are they plagued constantly with temptation. Hence, they can instead focus on growing in virtue. The law is still necessary, but with their growing virtues of faith, understanding, and prudence, people can determine the law through their reason enlightened by grace, and they are now motivated by their love and proper emotional desire. Consequently, although I recognize the clear importance of the law in the moral life, this book focuses primarily on helping the reader understand how to grow in virtue and treats the law as an aid for this growth.

This text is not meant to be a summary of all the contemporary debates and discussions in moral theology. Rather, it presents a traditional Christian anthropology and moral theology rooted in scripture and developed by the Thomistic tradition, with insights from recent papal writings (especially those by Leo XIII, John Paul II, and Benedict XVI) and further insights from spiritual guides such as St. Thérèse of Lisieux. Consequently, in order to present a more concise moral guide, I will not cover some contemporary discussions within the Catholic tradition that would distract from the overall scheme of the book. Study questions for this book can be obtained by contacting John Rziha at jrziha@benedictine.edu.

Part I

MORAL THEOLOGY IN GENERAL

This first part of the book will study moral theology in general by explaining the various components of moral theology and showing how they all relate to each other. The organizing principle will be the analogy of a journey to God. In the journey to God, travelers must know the beginning point (human nature), where they are going (to share in God's eternal happiness), and how to get there (by entering into a loving relationship with God). Chapters 1 and 2 will study human nature and the natural inclinations that proceed from it. Chapter 3 will study the end of the journey: happiness, and especially the perfect happiness found in God. Chapter 4 will further examine the Bible to help determine the way to proceed on our journey. The important roles of good actions, grace, laws, virtues, and the guidance of the Holy Spirit can be found in the Bible. These foundational concepts for the moral life will be covered in chapters 5 through 9. Chapter 10 will examine the impediments to this journey: sin, temptation, and vice. Chapter 11 will cover how all of these components fit together and discuss the proper meaning of freedom.

1

IN THE IMAGE OF GOD

Imagine that a family in a remote part of the world received a coffeemaker for a gift in the mail. They had never used a coffeemaker before or had ever seen one used, and, unfortunately, the instructions were lost in the shipping process. After only a little inspection they conclude that it is made to do something. But what is it made to do? And how do they get it to do this? Because they have no Internet access and cannot ask someone else for instructions, they must determine the purpose of this unfamiliar machine by their own investigation. They begin by examining the strange contraption. They look at all its parts and how they fit together. After a thorough analysis, they determine that the machine must heat some type of liquid, cause the liquid to absorb something for flavor, and then pour the flavored liquid into a pot. When they receive coffee beans and a grinder in the mail the next day, they are able to understand the function well enough that after a few tries they succeed in making coffee. Before they were able to figure out how to make coffee, they first had to examine the coffeemaker itself. In other words, to determine the function of the machine, they first studied its nature.

The analogy of the coffeemaker helps identify the starting point for moral theology. When intelligent beings make something, they make it for a purpose; they make it to do something. For example, the manufacturers of the coffeemaker construct it to make coffee. Because God is an intelligent being, he makes humans for a purpose, to do a particular type of action. Chapter 3 will explain how when humans fulfill their purpose, they are happy, but at this point it is sufficient to see that humans are made to perform certain types of actions. Just as the nature of the coffeemaker was examined to determine its purpose, human nature must be examined in order to determine the purpose of humans (i.e., their proper actions). On a primarily physiological level, in medical school students study the human body in order to determine how it works. However, humans are made to do more than just be physically healthy. They are also made to perform the spiritual actions of knowing and loving. Consequently, we will study the whole person—composed of both a body and a soul. This analysis will give us our starting point in our journey to happiness.

In the coffeemaker analogy, there are two ways to determine its function. One way is to look at the nature of the parts and how they fit together (which is what they did). The other way is to look at the instruction manual (which in the example was lost). When determining the purpose of humans, the philosopher "looks at the nature of the parts," but the theologian has the "instruction manual" (from divine revelation) given by the "manufacturer," namely, God.[1] Often, when people have to use a complicated machine or assemble something they buy, they both look at how the parts fit together and use the instruction manual. For example, if a bicycle is purchased with "some assembly required," one might need to look at how the parts fit together and also at the printed instructions in order to assemble it. Since the moral life can be complicated, a proper understanding of it involves studying both what can be known through philosophy (reason) and also what can be known from theology (divine revelation). Since this is a book on moral theology, the first focus will be on what is found in the Bible (divine revelation), and then some of the best insights of philosophy will be gathered to help explain these biblical truths. Since this chapter seeks to understand the starting point of moral theology—the nature of humans—a good place to start is with the creation stories found in Genesis 1 and 2.

These stories in Genesis 1 and 2 seek to answer some of the most fundamental questions asked by all human cultures: Where do we come from? What is our purpose? In other words, what does it mean to be human? The first story shows that humans, like all creation, come from God and have been wonderfully created. However, unlike the rest of creation, only humans are proclaimed to be created in the image of God (Gn 1:26–27). Hence, to understand how humans are unique and what they are made to do, we will investigate what it means to be "in the image of God." By analyzing this notion as interpreted within the Christian tradition, a robust answer to the question "What does it mean to be human?" can be found. Since in order to understand an image something must be known about the original, we will first briefly speak about some pertinent attributes of God, and then show how these divine attributes help us to understand what it means to be human.

GOD: THREE PERSONS IN ONE DIVINE NATURE

I once heard a story about Marco Polo's father and uncle presenting a crucifix as a gift to Kublai Khan upon first meeting him. Without an understanding of the Christian religion, Kublai Khan was extremely puzzled as to the significance of a dead man nailed to a cross. He simply could not understand why anyone would want to own a statue or a picture of someone being gruesomely executed. A crucifix is an example of an *image* of an actual event. However, unless someone knows the story of God sending his Son into the world to die so that humans can be saved, it can be difficult to understand what the crucifix means. Once someone knows this story, the crucifix becomes an image of the love that God has for all humans and an invitation to enter into a loving friendship with him. The story about the actual event helps us to properly understand the image. Likewise, to better understand what it means to be in the image of God, it is worthwhile to study God, even if briefly.

In the Old Testament, the Lord reveals that there is only one God (e.g., Dt 6:4). However, the New Testament proclaims that the Father is God, the Son is God, and the Holy Spirit is God, yet there is only one God. By the guidance of the Holy Spirit, the Church Fathers decreed that the one God is a trinity. They explained that God is *three persons in one divine nature*.[2] To better understand this statement, the terms "nature" and "person" need to be defined. Nature is what something is, and it determines the type of actions that something can do. For example, human nature gives people the ability to perform actions such as reading, writing, and laughing. Although dog nature does not give dogs these abilities, it does give them the ability to do other things, such as finding objects with their acute sense of smell.

Whereas nature is what something is, a person is *who someone* is. Persons are knowing and loving subjects who are *agents* of actions. In other words, although nature determines what types of actions something can do, it is a person who actually does them. For example, Kate (the person) reads a book (an action flowing from human nature). Thus, in reference to God, the divine nature determines the type of action that God does, while the individual persons of the Father, Son, and Holy Spirit actually perform the action. (However, because God is pure act and each of the persons is the fullness of the divine nature, it is more proper to say that each of the persons is the divine action.)

The Divine Nature

To properly understand how humans are in the image of God, we will examine both the divine nature and the divine persons. The divine nature will be examined first. The divine nature can be described as one infinite act of being. In explaining this description, I will begin by explaining the notion that God is *pure act*. Unlike God, created beings are not pure act; rather, they are a combination of *potency and act*. Potency (or potential) refers to the power that a created being has to act. This power comes from the being's nature (since nature determines the type of actions something can do). Although potency determines the type of actions something can do, it is not yet an action. For example, all humans are in potency to numerous different actions that they have not yet performed. As they perform more and more actions flowing from human nature, their potency turns into action. As they fulfill their potency by performing more and more good actions, they are perfected. For example, St. Teresa of Calcutta (Mother Teresa) was more perfect than most other people because she fulfilled her potency by performing the actions of loving God and others. However, God, by his very nature, is and always has been perfect; hence, he cannot move from potency to act. Rather, he is pure act, and he has no potency.[3] In other words, since things are perfect to the extent they perform their proper actions, God, who is the fullness of perfection, is also purely action. Unlike created beings, which are perfected when they perform their proper actions, God's very nature is action.

Because God is pure act, he is also infinite. Something is infinite if it is unlimited. When something performs an action, on the one hand, its potency gives it the ability to perform the action, but, on the other hand, its potency limits the greatness of the action. For example, dogs by nature have the potency to do actions greater than those of trees but not as great as those of humans. Dogs can do wonderful actions, such as showing great devotion to their owners, but they cannot perform actions such as writing books or solving complex algebra problems. Angels have a much greater potency, but even their nature ultimately limits their actions. Consequently, they cannot perform actions such as creating things from nothing and knowing everything. Only God is not a combination of act and potency; rather he is unlimited action itself and is thus infinite.

But what does this infinite action consist of? It consists of all pure perfections that exist or even could exist. Because human knowledge is so limited, we cannot know all the different perfections in God, but we can know about some of them because these perfections are found in a limited fashion in creation. Whenever you have a cause and an effect, the effect is always in some way like its cause. For example, children are always in some way like their parents. I have many children, and frequently when my wife was pregnant, we would be asked, "What are you having?" I could always say with certainty that we were having a baby human. Not only could I say with certainty that we were having a baby human, if I knew the genetic structure of my wife and me, I could narrow down the possible traits that my child would have. This ability to predict the nature and certain characteristics of a child is possible because of the assumed principle that an effect is in some way like its cause.[4] Thus, if there are perfections in creation, these perfections must also exist in God, but in an unlimited manner since God is pure act. For example, if love exists in creation, then God must be a pure act of love. If order exists in creation, then God must be the wisdom that causes this order. The same goes for truth, power, life, happiness, and any other perfection that can be found in creation.

Rather than enumerating all the perfections that are found in God, these perfections can be summed up in the term "being." The word "being" comes from the verb "to be" and refers to the act of existing in a particular mode. In other words, my being refers to my act of existing as a human and all the additional acts (and perfections) that I have attained. For example, Teresa of Calcutta is not only a human *being* but also a being who knows and loves God.[5] Since God exists as an infinite action, his mode of being refers to all that *is*. Thus, when God tells Moses his name in Exodus 3:14, he says that he should be called "I AM." Unlike all created things, which have certain perfections in accord with their nature, God IS. God is all perfections. It is proper to say that "I have love" or "I have being," but God *is* love, and God *is* being.

If God is an infinite act of being, then by necessity there can only be one God, for there can only be one infinite act of being. A circle can be used as an analogy. Imagine that there is a circle that contains all that exists and all that could exist. Since it contains all that could exist, it would have to be infinite (which would technically make it no longer a circle, but no analogy is perfect). Any other finite circle that I draw would have to be inside this infinite circle since the infinite circle contains all that exists. Even if there was another infinite circle, it would have to be identical to the infinite circle that I already had, for both would contain all that is (in this sense the analogy also prefigures the Trinity, where three persons are one). Hence, there can only be one infinite act of being, for all other acts of being are part of this one infinite act. Thus, there can only be one God. So, although there appear to be many different acts in God, they are really all different aspects of the one eternal act of being. Consequently, God's nature can be described as one infinite act of being (i.e., truth, love, power, or any other perfection).

THREE PERSONS IN ONE GOD

Although the above description of divine nature is drawn primarily from the Christian theological and philosophical tradition, one does not need to be a Christian to recognize that God is one infinite act of being. What is distinct about Christianity is the belief that this one God is three persons. The divine Son became human in order to reveal this truth to us. This truth is the most foundational tenet of the Christian faith—the truth that all other mysteries of the faith build upon.[6] God revealed this fundamental truth to humanity for the sake of our own happiness and fulfillment. Hence, studying how humans are in the image of the Trinity illuminates the types of actions humans are made to perform in order for them to ultimately be happy.

At the same time that God is one infinite act, God is also three persons: the Father, the Son, and the Holy Spirit. A person is a subject, the one that performs an action; it is *who* someone is. The Father, Son, and Holy Spirit is *who* God is. Persons exist within a particular nature. For example, there are billions of different human persons that all share in human nature. However, the way that humans are part of human nature is very different from the way that the divine persons are divine nature. Unlike humans, where each person is a part of human nature, each of the divine persons is the fullness of the divine nature. Since God's divine nature is one infinite act of being, the three persons are fully one infinite act of being. In other words, all three have the same infinite knowledge. All three have the same love, the same life, the same power, and so on.

If all three are alike in all of these ways, how are they distinct? Why are they not the same person? They are distinct based upon their relations.[7] The Father is distinct from the Son because the Father begets the Son. The Father and Son are distinct from the Holy Spirit because they breathe forth the Holy Spirit.[8] Before I give a detailed explanation of how they are distinct based upon their relations, an analogy is helpful to better understand how they are one but distinct. A famous analogy for the Trinity is the shamrock. There are three leaves, yet one shamrock. However, this analogy is not particularly helpful, for each of the leaves is only part of the shamrock, but each divine person is the fullness of God. Any material analogy like the shamrock will not really help explain the interior actuality of the Trinity, since it compares each divine person to a part of something, and each divine person is the fullness of the divine being. Thus, in order to find a good analogy, it is necessary to look for a spiritual analogy.[9]

One place that a spiritual analogy can be found is within loving, human relationships. These relationships contain a spiritual union that is based on knowledge and love. Imagine that Joe and Kate are united in a loving relationship. Their knowledge of each other begins when Joe and Kate acquire sense knowledge of each other. Joe sees that Kate is beautiful, and Kate is intrigued by Joe. They seek to get to know each other better by spending time together. By observing and listening to each other they begin to know each other.[10]

However, in a good relationship, the knowledge of the other person is not just shallow sense knowledge; rather, it is knowledge extending to the very depths of the other's soul. Although the soul cannot be directly sensed, the actions that stem from it reveal some of its inner contents. Hence, by observing each other's actions, Joe and Kate are able to reason to some knowledge of each other's souls. For example, by observing the way Joe interacts with children, Kate is able to determine whether he has the qualities of a good father. Likewise, by seeing how Kate interacts with her friends, Joe is able to determine that Kate is faithful to others. As Joe and Kate spend time together, they are able to observe many actions, and their knowledge of each other grows from sense knowledge to intellectual knowledge. Each person's sense knowledge of the other is united to intellectual concepts, such as "good," "faithful," "responsible," "joyful." Over time they begin to know the very depths of each other's souls.[11] They know each other's deepest goals, desires, sufferings, joys, strengths, weaknesses.

When humans know something, generally the knowledge is caused by something outside of them. This knowledge comes *into* their mind through their bodies (the senses). Furthermore, concepts within the mind are considered true when what is in the mind corresponds to reality (generally what is outside of them). For example, suppose Joe observes Kate easily understanding complex theories of quantum physics. Joe quickly reasons to the conclusion that Kate is intelligent. The knowledge that she is intelligent comes into Joe from the outside. And, if she actually is intelligent, then Joe's knowledge is true. The concepts in Joe's mind are both caused by reality and judged to be true by this reality. In reference to Joe and Kate's growing relationship, both Joe and Kate now have an elaborate concept of the other in their minds—one could even say that in a spiritual way Joe is in Kate's mind, and vice versa.

Knowing someone is just the beginning of the relationship. When humans know something as good, they begin to love it.[12] For example, when Joe begins to know Kate as someone good, he begins to love Kate. Knowledge comes into a person, but love goes *out* and attaches to whatever one loves. This attachment is generally seen in cases of loving other humans; however, it can also be seen in loving other things. For example, many people are attached to their coffee, or their favorite sports team, or their pet. Although this attachment can be physical (as for those who drink coffee), the attachment is primarily a spiritual unity. Among persons, this unity takes place because love causes one person to make the needs, goals, sufferings, and joys of the other person one's own. For example, if Joe knows that Kate has the goal of doing well in biology class, he also now has the goal of Kate doing well, and because of his love he will do whatever he can to help her attain her goal. What was in Kate's soul (her goal) is now also in Joe's soul. The goal is transformed from *her* goal into *their* goal. Because of his love for Kate, Kate has become Joe's other self, and vice versa.[13] They now share the same goals, sufferings, and joys and are spiritually united.[14] This principle that knowledge causes love that causes unity will come up many more times within the course of this book.[15] It is another way of expressing the biblical exhortation of St. Paul: "Be of one mind and heart."[16]

Having shown the development of the human relationship, the analogy can be applied to the Trinity. Imagine that Joe and Kate are married and are spiritually united to the point that they both have the same goal of helping each other, their children, and others get to heaven. You could now say that they share a single action. Although they are both performing the same action, each performs the action in his or her appropriate way based on the relation between the two. They are related to each other as husband to wife, and within this one action, one person acts as a husband, the other acts as a wife. Thus, like in the Trinity, Joe and Kate are persons who are united and are performing a single action. However, unlike the Trinity, the acts of humans are not the fullness of who they are, and hence there is never a complete unity between humans.[17] But imagine if we removed the bodies of Joe and Kate and looked at the overlap of their souls (the spiritual union between them). Their souls contain their knowledge, love, goals, joys, and so on. Hence, to the extent that their love makes the other's characteristics common to both of them (i.e., they share the same knowledge, love, goals, joys), their souls would be united. Of course, even for humans who know and love each other a great deal, there are many things in their souls that are not shared, because of their finite nature.

Continuing this imaginative exercise, suppose the souls of three persons contained infinite knowledge and love, and these acts of knowledge and love are the fullness of who they are. These souls would contain the same knowledge and love and would be numerically one (because there can only be one infinite act). Yet, the persons would still be distinct based on their relations, just as Joe and Kate are distinct. In other words, the Father, Son, and Holy Spirit are one infinite act of being, but they are three distinct persons. There are certainly deficiencies to this analogy, but it is helpful in emphasizing that God is one perfect act of knowledge and love, yet three distinct persons.

To further understand what makes the three divine persons distinct, it is necessary to look deeper into the eternal act of God. To be Trinity is of the nature of God.[18] In other words, within the one act of God is the act of the Father begetting the Son, and the Father and Son breathing forth the Holy Spirit. To "beget" is literally to "give birth." However, the term is traditionally applied to fathers begetting sons. For example, Abraham begat Isaac.[19] Unlike in humans where a child is born and then the action is over, God is pure act, so the Father is eternally generating the Son. Another way of saying this is that the Father is eternally giving the divine nature to the Son. Since each person is the fullness of the divine nature, the Father is eternally giving all that he is to the Son. Likewise, the Son is eternally receiving the divine nature of the Father. The same can be said in reference to the Holy Spirit, who is eternally receiving the fullness of the divinity from the Father and the Son. Inasmuch as the Father begets the Son, he is distinct from the Son.[20] Likewise, the Father and Son are distinct from the Holy Spirit as the source of the Holy Spirit. In other words, through the act of giving and receiving the divine nature, the individual persons are distinct from each other. For it is from these acts of giving and receiving that they are related to each other as Father to Son and Father and Son to Spirit, and their distinction as persons comes from their relation to each other. The three persons in the Trinity are one infinite act of love, and they are distinct from each other because of their giving or receiving of the divine nature (depending upon the person).

CREATED IN THE IMAGE OF GOD

Just as in God there are three persons who are perfectly united, humans are made to be united through knowing and loving each other. Furthermore, because the persons in God are distinct based on their relations, humans do not lose their individuality by being united to others through loving relationships, rather, they discover their true identity. As the three persons are made distinct through a complete giving and reception of the fullness of the divinity, humans also discover their true self by completely giving and receiving others in loving relationships. As the Second Vatican Council states, "Man can fully discover his true self only in a sincere gift of self."[21] Like the Trinity, we define who we are by a sincere gift of self. In other words, *because God is a loving relationship, and we are made in His image, we are fulfilled by loving relationships.*

This notion that humans are made to be fulfilled by loving relationships with God and others can be expanded upon by looking more deeply into what it means to be in the image of God. Just as God is three persons that are one loving community, humans are in the image of God both as individual persons and as a community.

In God's Image as Persons

As persons, humans are in the image of God because they are created to know and love God and others. An image is a copy of the original. Since all things are in some way like their cause, all things in creation are in some way a copy of the original. By looking throughout creation, we see all things are like God in that they have being. In other words, they exist in their own particular way. Even things like soil and rivers are like God by participating in his being.[22] Some things are even more like God in that they have both being and life (they are living beings). Plants are examples of living beings. Some things have being, life, sense knowledge, and emotions (e.g., animals). However, humans are especially like God in that they have being, life, sense knowledge, emotions, intellectual knowledge, and love. Intellectual knowledge gives them the ability to know and love God and others. Thus, the way that humans are distinctively in the image of God is through their ability to know and love God and others.

Just as each of the members of the Trinity eternally gives the fullness of the divine nature and/or receives the fullness of other members of the Trinity, humans are likewise made to give of themselves to others by knowing the needs, goals, and sufferings of others and lovingly making these their own. By making the needs of others their own, humans give of themselves to others. The Apostle Paul confirms this when he exhorts the Philippians to be of the same mind and love, "united in heart, thinking one thing . . . each looking out not for his own interests, but everyone for those of others." Paul then gives the actions of Christ as an example of someone who made the needs of humans his own: "Who though he was in the form of God, did not regard equality with God something to be grasped. Rather he emptied himself . . . coming in human likeness" (Phil 2:2–6). In other words, humans have a desire to share in God's love and happiness but are unable to attain this goal on their own. Hence, God manifests his love for us by sending his Son to become human, die for us, and become exalted, so that we can share in his love and happiness. Humans are fulfilled when they follow this example by entering into loving relationships with others through a giving of themselves.

By entering into these loving relationships with others, humans discover their true identity. Every human has a unique role in bringing God's plan for the fulfillment of the universe to perfection, and each discovers this role by entering into loving relationships with others. Although the way that humans love others will vary based on their distinctive roles, every human shares in God's plan by loving others. Hence, just as the members of the Trinity are made distinct through their relation to the other members, the personal identity of humans is found in relationships.[23] For example, if I am going to describe who I am as a person (not just that my nature is human), all of the most important elements of my description will refer to the relationships I have with others. I am first of all a child of God; second, a husband of my wife; third, a father of my children; fourth, a teacher of my students—these and other loving relationships describe who I am as a person.[24]

Another aspect of being made in the image of God as persons is that humans are free. Unlike the animals, humans have the ability to know and love. This ability to know and love gives them freedom. More precisely, humans are able to freely choose something because they can know an end (goal), know at least one way of attaining this end, and out of love for the end they can choose a way of attaining it. For example, Joe has the goal of attending a good college and has learned about many different options. Based on his love for one of these colleges, he freely chooses to attend it. His freedom is based on both his knowledge and love but especially his knowledge. If Joe does not know what a good college is, he cannot freely choose it. (He could accidentally choose it, but then it would not really be a free choice.) Likewise, if Joe does not know his options, he is also not able to choose one of them. Finally, if Joe does not love the idea of going to college and the options presented to him, he will also not choose them. Because freedom comes from our ability to know and love, which is received from God, true freedom to govern oneself and the rest of creation will be in accord with God's divine plan.

Because humans are in the image of God, they are created with the ability to know and love God and others. However, this ability must be perfected by God's aid and the development of virtues. The image of God is especially perfected in people when they are able to know and love God as he is in heaven. Much of the rest of this book explains how the image of God is perfected within us.

CREATED IN GOD'S IMAGE AS A COMMUNITY

Not only are humans in God's image as persons, but they are also in God's image as a community. Just as God is three persons who are united, humans are made to be united within loving relationships. Humans are social by nature and can only properly develop within a community. The second creation story in Genesis 2 explains this truth by noting that Adam was incomplete until the creation of Eve. Once Eve is created, Adam is fulfilled, for he has now found a suitable partner. The passage then notes, "That is why a man leaves his father and mother and clings to his wife, and the two of them become one body."[25] Because humans are made to be one with God and others, the goal of human life is unity with God (which includes unity with all others united to God). This goal will be explained more completely in chapter 3 of this book.

The means of attaining this unity with others has already been explained. Humans are united to others when they know and love them. Knowledge causes love, which causes unity. The same applies to our union with God. By getting to know God and his goals for each individual, humans can make God's goals their own and participate in the one infinite action of God.

HUMANS WERE CREATED BODY AND SOUL

The ability to know and love God and others is what makes humans distinct from the rest of creation (not including the angels). However, humans are like the rest of creation in that they also share in God's life and being as bodily creatures. A proper understanding of what it means to be human must include an analysis of humans as body and soul. Thus, to fully understand human nature, a deeper investigation of the soul and the body and how they are related is necessary.

Sometimes in popular movies the body is seen as simply a storage container for the soul; whereas the soul is the real you. This "storage container" can be completely changed without actually affecting your soul.[26] For example, in the 1959 Disney movie *The Shaggy Dog*, Wilby Daniel's body is replaced with the body of a sheepdog. Despite having the body of a sheepdog, Wilby is able to continue to think and act in the same manner as before his transformation. Although it can seem like one's particular body is not essential to personal identity, in reality, the body is an essential part of one's identity. The body and soul are so closely united that a particular soul is only suited to a particular body and vice versa. In other words, if it were possible to replace a human body with that of a dog, the soul would not be able to function as a human at all. This close union between the body and the soul has traditionally been explained using the philosophical terms "form" and "matter." The soul is considered to be the form, the body the matter.[27] A brief explanation of the terms "form" and "matter" can help illuminate what it means to say that "the soul gives form to the body (the matter)."

The philosophical terms of "form" and "matter" have been useful in explaining the nature of reality since the time of Aristotle. Aristotle believed that things are a composite of form and matter. The matter referred to the material that something contained; the form referred to the way that the material was organized. Since matter is interchangeable, the form determines the nature of the entity (i.e., what the thing is). For example, suppose a tree dies and is eaten by termites. Inasmuch as the termites take on the matter of the tree, both the tree and the termites contain the same matter, yet the way the matter is arranged varies between the two. If the matter is arranged in the form of a tree, then the object is a tree; if the matter is arranged in the form of a termite, then the object is a termite. In both cases, the existing thing is a combination of form and matter. So also with the body and soul, since the soul is the form of the body, it uniquely organizes the matter of the body and causes one to be a human. A particular human soul always organizes the matter into a particular human body.

Furthermore, since the form determines the nature of the thing and the nature determines what type of actions something can do, the form also determines the type of actions something can perform. For example, the form of an oak tree gives it the ability to grow in its proper way and produce acorns. So also, the human soul gives the body life, the ability to have emotions and sense knowledge, and the soul works through the body in knowing and loving. Calling the soul the form of the body emphasizes the intrinsic unity of the body and soul. However, as long as this unity is acknowledged, the soul and body can be examined separately for a more detailed understanding of human nature.

The Soul

The soul is the spiritual element within humans. Because it works through the body in all that it does, it is the first cause of all human actions. The capacities within the soul to cause actions are called "powers." Although there are numerous powers within the soul, the three most pertinent to human actions are the *intellect*, the *will*, and the *emotions*.[28] The *intellect gives humans the ability to know the truth*, the *will gives us the ability to love and choose things*, and the *emotions give us the ability to desire the bodily good*. Because these powers are within the soul, an understanding of them will require that humans reflect on the sources of their own actions within their soul. Therefore, before explaining these powers in greater detail, let me give an example manifesting all three powers in an action.

Imagine that Joe, like many other college students, has a great deal of trouble waking up early. However, Joe has an 8:00 a.m. class. Before going to bed (at 2:00 a.m.) the night before class, Joe sets his alarm for 7:15 a.m. By the power of his intellect, Joe knows the truth. The truth is that he needs to attend class to get good grades in order to graduate so he can get a job and support a family. He further knows that he needs forty-five minutes to get ready and get to class on time. However, when his alarm goes off at 7:15 a.m., Joe does not *emotionally* want to get up. Humans have emotions to keep the body alive. Hence, we emotionally desire things that are generally good for the body and dislike things that are bad. For example, humans emotionally desire things like food, drink, shelter, and companionship. Because sleep is necessary for the functioning of the body, humans emotionally desire sleep. However, the emotions are not rational (unless they are trained) and, hence, only desire the bodily good in general. What is good for the body in general is not always good for the body in a particular situation. For example, drinking water is good for the body in general, and the proper emotional response to dehydration is to desire to drink water. However, if someone was stranded on a boat in the ocean with no fresh water, the emotional desire to drink ocean water would go against what the intellect knows to be best. To return to our example of Joe, because Joe has a body, and in general it is good for Joe to get adequate sleep, his emotions desire to stay in bed even though his intellect knows he should get up.

There is now a conflict in Joe's soul. He knows that he should get up for class, but he really wants to stay in bed. To solve this conflict, the role of the will must be taken into consideration. The will loves the good and always chooses based upon what it loves the most. This might seem to be an easy decision. Surely, Joe loves sleep more than class. However, recall that Joe knows he must attend class to graduate and eventually get a job to support a family. Hence, the real choice is between the good of getting a job to support a family and the good of more sleep. Of course, the decision can become much more complicated. For example, the emotions can influence the intellect to think that maybe missing one class will not be so bad or to think that maybe Joe can sleep another thirty minutes and still make it to class. However, the example sufficiently shows that the intellect, the will, and the emotions are all involved in human actions by their respective powers to know the truth, love the good, and seek the bodily good.

A good way to further explain the different powers of the soul is by looking at their *natural inclinations. A natural inclination is an interior drive that a being has to perform its proper action.* Because God made everything for a purpose, all things have a natural propensity to do certain things. For example, spiders have a natural inclination to spin webs. Humans are made by God to attain unity with God and others based on knowledge and love. Therefore, humans have a natural inclination to these loving relationships and the natural inclinations to all things that are necessary to attain these relationships. To attain these loving relationships, all the powers of the soul must function properly. For example, the intellect must know God and other people. The will must love God and other people, and the emotions must aid the intellect and will in performing these actions. Because the proper functioning of these powers is essential to form a loving relationship with God and others, each of the powers of the soul is naturally inclined to a particular action.[29]

The intellect is naturally inclined to know the truth. By the power of the intellect humans can know much about the world, intimately know others, and even know God in a limited manner. The human intellect is not powerful enough to immediately know things (like God does), rather, humans must gradually learn about the world by means of sense knowledge. Although intellectual knowledge begins with sense knowledge, because the intellect can reason and understand abstract concepts, it can understand spiritual things (that cannot be sensed) and material things. Furthermore, once the intellect knows the needs and goals of others, it can determine what actions illustrate love of other people. Likewise, it can determine which actions can be done out of love of God and how to perform these actions.

Intellectual knowledge is not the same as sense knowledge. In general, sense knowledge refers to knowledge of particular material things; intellectual knowledge refers to knowledge of universals (abstract or general knowledge of things).[30] For example, a toddler, who is still learning about trees, might only have sense knowledge of a particular tree. An adult, who understands what trees are in general, would have intellectual knowledge of trees (and also have sense knowledge of particular trees). Since the adult has intellectual knowledge of a tree (or the general concept of a tree), she can identify any particular tree as being a tree. Although sense knowledge is generally of particular material things that can be sensed, it is much more than just sense data.[31] It might be described as already-interpreted sense data. For example, sense knowledge of a friend can include the sense data contained in many different experiences. This sense knowledge could be thought of as an "image," but an image that also includes sense data from hearing, seeing, touching, and smelling. Sense knowledge also includes images that are imagined and those of past memories. Although a distinction is made between sense knowledge and intellectual knowledge, humans use both simultaneously when they think.[32] Hence, an understanding of the notion of sense knowledge is very important since intellectual concepts are derived from it, sense knowledge is used in thinking, and the emotions follow sense knowledge.

The will is naturally inclined to love the true good. Once the intellect knows something as good, the will is able to love it. This love causes a person to seek this good by intending to attain it and by choosing to perform actions in order to obtain the good that it loves. To reflect on the example of the unity between Joe and Kate, Joe's intellect knows the goals of Kate. His will then loves her and attaches to her by making her goals his own. Based on his love of her, he then chooses a particular action to help her fulfill her goals.

The emotions (also called the "sense appetites" or "passions") are naturally inclined to desire the bodily good in accord with reason (or are repulsed by the bodily evil that violates reason).[33] As seen in the example of Joe waking up, the emotions are naturally attracted to goods that benefit the body that are known through sense knowledge. The emotions are necessary to keep the body alive and to ensure the propagation of the human race. However, the emotions are not rational, and although they seek the good of the body in general, they can seek something that is bad for the person in a particular instance. Thankfully, the emotions can be trained to seek what is determined to be good by the intellect. (They can also be trained to seek evil.) Because animals also have emotions (to keep their bodies alive), a good example of how emotions can be trained is seen in animals. Imagine a wild alley kitten is injured, and you want to help it. The kitten's emotional response to you will be either fear or anger, even though you are trying to help it. However, over time you can tame the kitten, and its emotions will no longer have fear of you. The kitten could eventually even be trained to have emotional love for you. Because good parents train the emotions of their children from a very early age, most people's emotional impulses drive them to do good things (although all humans have some unruly emotions that rebel against what they know is best).

We will give much more detail about the emotions throughout this book. However, to get a better beginning grasp of the emotions, it is helpful to have a list of them. Traditionally, the emotions have been divided into two categories: the *concupiscible* emotions and the *irascible* emotions. The concupiscible emotions desire bodily pleasure in and of itself (or recoil from bodily pain). These particular emotions are love and hate, desire and aversion, and joy (also called "delight") and sorrow. For example, some people have emotional love for hamburgers. This love causes them to desire hamburgers, and when they are eating them, they have joy. Conversely, others hate public speaking. They have an aversion to speaking in public, and when they must speak in public, they experience sorrow.

The irascible emotions seek the difficult and distant bodily good. The concupiscible respond to the pleasurable good itself, but the irascible seek the means to attain the good sought by the concupiscible appetite. To go back to the example of the hamburger, perhaps before being able to consume the hamburger, the person has to finish working. The hamburger is now a distant good. The irascible emotions could motivate the person to work hard in order to have the hamburger. The irascible emotions are hope and despair, fear and daring, and anger. There are two categories of emotions because sometimes people have conflicting emotions toward the same object. For example, someone might emotionally love having a major project completed but despair of actually doing the work to complete it.

Because the primary movement of both the emotions and the will is to love, it can be difficult to understand the difference between the emotions and the will. The difference is that the love of the will follows intellectual knowledge, but the love of the emotions follows sense knowledge. Food can be a good example for helping to understand the difference between love of the will and love of the emotions. Suppose that Kate loves the taste of bananas (following sense knowledge) and knows that they are good for her (intellectual knowledge). Inasmuch as she loves them because they are good for her, she has love of the will for them. Her will desires what her intellect knows to be true. Inasmuch as she loves them for their taste (or any other good feelings they cause), she has emotional love for them. Because the emotions follow sense knowledge, the act of recalling memories of time spent with friends, vacations with family, or even eating one's favorite food can elicit emotional joy. Likewise, memories of being treated unjustly can produce emotions of anger.

The Body

Thomas Aquinas believed that humans bridge the gap between the material and spiritual world and, hence, have both bodily and spiritual inclinations.[34] In other words, because on earth the body is essential for the proper functioning of the soul, the body's proper functioning is essential to the spiritual life. Thus, an elementary understanding of the body and what it is inclined to is essential to understand the moral life.[35]

The body is the material element of human nature and participates in the image of God through the soul. Because of the union between the body and the soul, the soul works through the body in all that it does. Hence, the body has an essential role in all actions, and because it is formed by a human soul, it is naturally inclined to stay alive and to remain healthy for the benefit of the human person. Because of its natural inclination, the body does not have to be taught to stay alive—it naturally seeks to stay alive, which is its proper end.[36]

The Relation between the Body and the Soul

In this chapter, we are studying human nature in order to better understand what type of actions cause humans to be fulfilled. The powers of the soul are the primary causes of these actions, but these powers work through a body when acting. For example, Joe's soul works through his body to both know and love Kate. Ultimately, both the body and the soul are causes of human actions, and both must be taken into consideration in determining what actions humans are created to perform. When acting, the soul is the primary (or first) cause of all actions, and the body is the instrumental (or secondary) cause of all actions.[37] A good example to help explain primary and instrumental causality is that of a piano player and a piano. The player is the primary cause of the music, and the piano is the instrumental cause of the music. Both causes are necessary for the music, but the primary cause moves the instrumental cause and determines what musical notes are actually played. Even though the player moves the piano, the piano also has its proper effect within the action, for the instrument also determines the quality of the music. A piano only makes piano music (not woodwind music), and a tuned piano makes better music than an out-of-tune piano. This analogy illuminates the roles of both the soul and the body. The soul moves the body and determines the type of actions that are to be performed. Nonetheless, the soul can only perform actions that the body is capable of performing, and a defect in the body (e.g., brain damage, hormonal and chemical imbalances, etc.) can greatly impair the functioning of the person.[38] For example, even humans with an educated and intelligent soul cannot think properly if they are tired or sick. To more clearly see the role of the body in human actions, let's analyze the relation between the body and the intellect, will, and emotions.

The intellect requires the body for two reasons. First, whenever we think, the intellect uses the brain as an instrumental cause of its thoughts. This truth is demonstrated by the fact that some people are genetically disposed to a higher intelligence than others and that people with brain damage are unable to perform certain intellectual exercises. For example, I once tutored a woman who, because of a car accident, was unable to perform certain logic exercises that she could have easily done before the accident.[39] The accident did not cause a change in her soul but rather a change in the body that her intellect worked through.

The second reason that the intellect works through the body is that all knowledge begins with sense knowledge. Unlike angels, who do not need a body to think, the human intellect is weak and requires many experiences and much repetition in order to come to knowledge.[40] The body, through the senses, provides the experiences that are necessary for the intellect to function. For example, because Helen Keller was unable to see and hear, her ability to learn was seriously impaired. Anne Sullivan taught Helen how to interpret the sense knowledge coming from the sense of touch. Had

Anne not taught Helen words through the sense of touch, it is very unlikely that Helen would have become the educated person that she was. The necessity of sense knowledge is especially seen in the way God reveals himself to humans. The Son came as a human, and he performed actions and proclaimed teachings that could be sensed. The Church continues to hand on this revelation in ways that can be sensed, such as through scripture and the sacraments.

The will also requires the body for two reasons. First, just as the intellect requires the body to think, the will requires the body (especially the brain) to love. Second, although knowledge comes in through the body, love goes out through the body. Humans cannot read each other's minds. The only way that love can be expressed is through bodily actions. These actions can be kind words, hugs, or even serving others. The Willie Nelson song "You Were Always on My Mind" describes how a woman failed to recognize the love that a man had for her because he never showed her that he loved her through physical signs. She may have always been on his mind, but because humans have bodies, authentic love is expressed through physical signs. For humans, love that is not shown through bodily signs is always somewhat incomplete. For example, Joe may say that he loves the poor, but unless he actually does bodily actions of serving the poor, his love is incomplete. Even in relation to God, who can read human hearts, we must still perform bodily acts that manifest love (for our own benefit, not God's).

Since the divine image in humans inclines them to enter into loving relationships through acts of knowing and loving that require the body, the body also shares in the image of God. In fact, the body is the physical element of the sincere gift of self through which humans discover their true self. John Paul II wrote extensively on how the body operates as a gift in his sermons on the "Theology of the Body." Only through the body, both male and female, are humans able to give and accept each other and discover their true selves.[41]

The fundamental unity between the body and the soul is especially seen in the emotions. Unlike the intellect and will, which are primarily powers of the soul, the emotions are powers of both the body and the soul. Hence, whenever an emotional response happens in the soul, a corresponding chemical change occurs in the body. For example, a great deal of psychological research has been done on the emotion of love. These studies have shown that multiple chemicals and hormones can be found in the body when someone is in love. Some of the predominant chemicals are adrenaline (which can increase your heart rate and cause you to sweat), dopamine (causing the feeling of great pleasure or ecstasy), serotonin (low levels cause one to focus on one's beloved), and oxytocin (giving feelings of attachment).[42] In fact, according to the biological anthropologist Helen Fisher, the dopamine-induced pleasurable feeling that people have when they are in love is the same feeling that people have when they take cocaine, nicotine, or morphine. All of these drugs elevate the levels of dopamine in the body.[43] The extremely close relation between the body and the soul is seen in the fact that the emotions cause a chemical change in the body, and a chemical change in the body can cause an emotional response in the soul, such as in cases of drug use or hormonal imbalances.

Another way that the body affects the soul is through the emotional response to sense knowledge. In the example of Joe waking up early, the emotions were able to influence his intellect and will. The emotions have this power because of the close relation between intellectual knowledge and sense knowledge in our soul. Not only does all knowledge begin with sense knowledge, but without sense "images" that correspond to intellectual knowledge, it is also impossible for humans to think.[44] In other words, humans must associate a sensible sign with a particular concept. For example, the word "bird" could be associated with the concept of "bird." Humans can then string together multiple sense "images" and form sentences. For example, if someone thinks in words (either spoken or written), they might take the word "bird" and place it with the words "have feathers."[45] The key point is that sense knowledge is always involved in our thinking.

Emotions are responses to sense knowledge. Hence, whenever we think, we also have emotional responses. For example, when you think about someone you deeply loved earlier in your life, you immediately have an emotional response within you. (The same thing can happen when you think of someone that made you angry—but with a different emotional response.) The emotions are powerful drives and can sometimes cause the intellect to focus on certain truths and neglect others. In extreme cases they can even blind the intellect. For example, an angry person might only think about how to get revenge or may even act without thinking much at all. The human intellect is very creative, and when under the influence of the emotions, it can find reasons to support nearly any evil action. The will when presented with these false reasons can also be influenced by the emotions to choose the evil act. However, the emotions can also aid the intellect and the will to perform good when the emotions desire the action that has been determined to be good by the intellect. Ultimately, the relation between the emotions and the intellect and the will can be complex because they can sometimes help, hinder, cloud, or even blind these higher powers. The key is that because the soul works through the body in all that it does, the composition of the body also determines what is in the soul. Your body, through physiological structures, chemicals, and sense knowledge, influences your thoughts and loves. Consequently, your body also determines your identity as a knowing and loving person made in the image of God.[46]

By looking at the biblical notion that humans are in the image of God, we find the starting point of our journey to eternal happiness. Humans as made in the image of God are created to know and love God and all others. Because knowledge causes love, which causes unity, humans are also like God when they enter into loving relationships with others. Furthermore, they find their true identity when they give of themselves in these relationships and become one in mind and heart with each other, just as the Father, Son, and Holy Spirit have the same knowledge and love. Because the soul works through the body when it knows and loves, the body also shares in the image of God and is an essential element in human relationships. The best insights of philosophy help further explain human nature by noting that the human soul has the powers of the intellect, will, and emotions. These powers give humans the ability to know and love God and others and, eventually, attain true happiness.

2

THE HISTORY OF HUMAN NATURE

Although humans are made to enter into loving relationships with God and others, they do not always seek these friendships. In fact, a quick glance at the news shows that many humans are often rather selfish. They frequently use other people to fulfill their own needs, rather than making the needs of others their own. Some people believe that their own desires are so important that they are willing to kill and hurt others in order to attain what they want. These malicious actions are contrary to the loving relationships that humans are made to attain. So if humans are made to enter into loving relationships with others, why do so many people commit evil actions? The early Israelite community asked the same question, and they found the answer in the very ancient story of Adam and Eve's disobedience to God. The first two chapters of Genesis tell the story of creation in order to answer the question of what it means to be human, but the third chapter seeks to answer the next logical question: If creation is good, where does evil come from? The author of the book of Genesis answers this question by telling the story of the original sin of Adam and Eve. God did not create evil, humans caused evil by sinning. Consequently, to find the beginning point in the journey to God, we must analyze the story of the original sin and its effects in creation (fallen nature). However, the human story does not end with the introduction of evil into society. The New Testament shows how this evil can be overcome through the grace of Jesus Christ. In order to fully understand where humans begin on their journey to God, it is necessary to take into consideration the effects of Christ's redeeming actions in addition to the effects of original sin. This chapter will give a brief history of human nature, beginning with a description of the original state of humanity as created by God (this state is also referred to as the "state of original holiness"). Then, we'll see a description of the effects of the original sin of the first humans (fallen nature).

Next, we will consult the New Testament to provide a brief description of the full inheritance that humans receive from the grace of God. Finally, we will describe the state that humanity is currently in—the *down payment of the full inheritance*.

THE ORIGINAL STATE OF HOLINESS

The "original state of holiness" refers to the condition of humans as they were created by God before any sins were committed (the state of humanity in Gn 1 and 2). As we saw in chapter 1, humans were created in the image of God. Furthermore, they were created good (Gn 1:31), and with the help of God's grace (a sharing in God's loving power), they were made to live in harmony with God and each other. More specifically, the goodness of the original state of holiness consisted of five harmonious relationships: (1) between humans and God, (2) within the soul, (3) between humans and other humans (e.g., Adam and Eve), (4) between the body and soul, and (5) between humans and creation. The harmonious relations further explain how humans were made in the image and likeness of God.

The first harmonious relationship is between humans and God. Adam and Eve were made to be in loving union with God by means of their knowledge and love of him.[1] Because they were made good, their intellect and will were made to function properly by knowing and loving God. Additionally, God also gave them grace to further perfect these powers. However, a properly functioning human intellect (even with the grace of original holiness) is not the same as a perfectly functioning angelic or divine intellect. In other words, these first humans did not know everything as God does, or even know things without the use of their senses, as angels do. Rather, they still had to learn through sense knowledge. Nonetheless, because their intellect was made to function properly, their ability to know things would have been much more perfect than natural human understanding today. They would have had a detailed understanding about God as he is revealed in creation.[2] Since the will was also made to function properly, this understanding of God would have resulted in the will loving God, causing union with him. In other words, Adam and Eve were made to discover God's plan for them and to choose to make it their own because of their love of God. Consequently, with help of God's grace, the first humans would have been in a harmonious, loving union with God.

This first harmony was the cause of the second: harmony within the soul. Because the intellect and will were made to be focused on God, they were in harmony with each other. Furthermore, the emotions were made to desire the true bodily good as determined by the intellect and loved by the will. The emotions in all animals seek the bodily good, but because humans can specifically know the proper bodily good through their intellect, the emotions were created to follow the guidance of the intellect. Hence, with the help of God's grace, the emotions followed the will, which followed the intellect, which was focused on God. Unlike after original sin, when the emotions often desire apparent or false goods that contradict the true good as determined by the intellect, the emotions of the first humans were made to seek the true good. For example, Joe's emotions rebelled when it was time for him to get up early in the morning. The action of getting up was very difficult to perform because of the emotional rebellion within his soul. However, because Adam's intellect would have recognized the true bodily goodness of waking up, his emotions would have immediately followed, causing the action of getting up to be easy and pleasurable.

Since all the powers of the soul were made to function properly, the first two humans were also in harmony with each other. The fully functioning intellect of Adam would have had great knowledge of Eve's goals, needs, and joys, and Eve would have had the same knowledge in relation to Adam. The fully functioning will would have allowed both of them to completely share in each other's goals and needs, resulting in a profound union. Furthermore, the emotions would have constantly sought the good of the other as determined by the intellect. In other words, unlike today when the emotions can dislike other people or can dislike helping those we love, because of God's grace, Adam and Eve were completely, emotionally in love with each other and always desired to do what was best for each other. Their relationship would have been filled with great emotional joy.

Not only was there interior harmony within the soul, but the body was also in harmony with the soul. Because of the power given to the soul by God, the soul was able to preserve the body from corruption.[3] As Thomas Aquinas explains, "For as long as the soul was subject to God, the flesh was so subject to the spirit that it felt no corruption, whether of death or of sickness or of other passions."[4] In other words, not only could the soul command the body to move, but the soul could also command the body to live forever and to avoid suffering.[5] However, this power of the soul over the body did not do away with the natural activities of the body. Even with this harmony, the body would still require air, water, and food. Furthermore, the aid of God would be necessary to preserve it from extreme injury.[6] Nonetheless, because of the harmony between the body and soul, humans could live forever and avoid suffering.

Finally, all creation was in harmony with humans. God created humans to be the bridge between the spiritual and the material world. As long as the body and soul were in harmony with each other, God ruled the material world through humans. As divine governor, God moves all of creation to its proper perfection. By sharing in this divine governance, humans were given dominion over the animals, plants, and material world. These created beings fulfilled all the needs of these first humans, and humans were made to perfect the rest of creation by their actions.[7] Consequently, in the original state, creation was subject to humans, the body was subject to the soul, the emotions followed the intellect and will, and the intellect and will followed God and entered into a loving union with him.[8]

A good analogy for the relation between the different harmonies can be found in the way that a magnet affects paper clips.[9] When a powerful magnet touches a paper clip, the paper clip is not only attracted to the magnet, but the paper clip also becomes magnetic. Hence, other paper clips are attracted to the magnetized paper clip, and a chain of paper clips can be formed where all are attracted to each other by participating in the power of the magnet. If the magnet is lifted off the table, the chain will also be lifted up. However, if the first paper clip is removed from the magnet, the entire chain loses its magnetic capabilities, and the entire chain falls to the table. This image can be applied to the relationship between humans and God in the original state. God is like the magnet: he is the source of the power of all the harmonious relationships. As long as the intellect and will are united to God, the emotions, the body, and creation all follow (in that order). Hence, as long as Adam and Eve loved God, all the harmonies were maintained, and life was wonderful, since Adam and Eve were performing their proper actions.

THE STATE OF FALLEN NATURE

When the first paper clip in the chain is removed from the magnet, all the rest of the paper clips fall to the table. So also, when Adam and Eve committed the first (original) sin and no longer loved God above all things, all the other harmonies were corrupted. The ensuing corrupted state is called the "state of fallen nature." In this state, humans often have great turmoil in their lives, hate others, and will eventually die. Because they are not performing the actions they were made to perform, they are unhappy. However, before looking at the effects of the original sin, it is necessary to analyze this first sin in more detail and to answer how it is possible that Adam and Eve were able to commit sin at all if they were created good. To discover the answer, the story in Genesis, chapter 3, must be consulted.

This story describes how Adam and Eve commit the sin of disobeying God. They are free to eat the fruit of all the trees in the garden except for the fruit from the tree of knowledge of good evil. They know that they were not allowed to eat the fruit of this tree. However, the serpent tempts Eve by telling her that she will be like gods, who know good and evil. Eve finds the fruit good for food, pleasing to the eyes, and desirable for gaining wisdom. Thus, because of the temptation of the serpent, she eats it and shares some with Adam, who also eats it (Gn 3:1–6). This story (as does Gn 2) uses figurative language to describe an ancient event that took place at the beginning of human history.[10] In the story, the eating from the trees is symbolic of performing actions. Adam and Eve are free to eat of the fruit of any of the trees in the garden except for the fruit of the tree of knowledge of good and evil. This freedom to eat of all the other trees is symbolic of Adam and Eve performing good actions in harmony with God.[11] However, eating of the fruit of the tree of knowledge of good and evil is symbolic of Adam and Eve determining moral norms apart from God. In other words, they now "know" good and evil in the sense that they create their own moral truths ("the knowledge of good and evil").

Because God created humans to be fulfilled when they perform their proper actions of knowing and loving God and others, he knows which actions cause humans to be truly happy (and are thus good) and which actions destroy true happiness (and are thus bad).[12] Thus, God's wisdom is the source of the *true* knowledge of what is good and evil—the understanding of all those actions each person should (or should not) do in order to share in God's happiness. Because God created humans to be fulfilled when they perform a particular type of action, humans can then discover what is good and evil through knowledge of what fulfills them. When humans discern which actions they are made to perform, their intellect shares in God's wisdom. For example, because God made humans to enter into loving relationships with each other, he knows that murder is wrong because it contradicts the act of loving others. When humans determine that murder is wrong, because it destroys the loving relationships they were made to attain, their knowledge that murder is wrong shares in God's knowledge. In the original state, Adam and Eve were given this ability to share in God's wisdom and to determine which actions would ultimately make them happy.

However, Adam and Eve were not created to independently and arbitrarily invent moral truths. When they created their own moral truths ("know good and evil"), they decided to proclaim a particular action to be good, despite the fact that God knows it to be evil. In knowing good and evil they became "like" God in a certain deficient sense.[13] Although they were like God from the perspective that they created moral norms (God also creates moral norms), they were in reality less like God because they no longer shared in his wisdom. The goals in the mind of Adam and Eve were now less like the goals in the mind of God. This exercise of declaring something to be good that is in reality evil happens within the mind of all people when they freely choose to commit a serious sin they know they should not commit. Because the Genesis story uses symbolic language, it does not tell us the actual sin that was committed (other than it was some form of disobedience), but we can determine that it stemmed from pride. Adam and Eve decided that their self-created goals were more important than God's goals and chose to act accordingly.

The next question to answer is this: Why were Adam and Eve able to sin if they were created to be in harmony with God? The answer is that Adam and Eve, like all of creation, were made in a perfect state of imperfection. They were perfect in reference to their nature but imperfect in terms of their action.[14] In other words, everything in terms of its nature is created good, yet it must still perform its proper action to be more like God (who is pure act).[15] For example, an acorn is good in terms of its nature. However, to be perfect in terms of its action, it must still grow into a magnificent oak tree. Likewise, God created all humans to be good by nature. Yet, they must still perform the actions to which they are naturally inclined in order to be more like God. To be good in an absolute sense, humans must perform actions of knowing and loving God and others.

Being created imperfect in terms of action has both good and bad aspects. On the good side, humans, and the rest of creation, can be even more like God than if God had created them already performing their proper action.[16] In other words, as made in God's image and given dominion over creation (Gn 1:26–28), humans are given greater responsibility and, hence, greater dignity because God works through them to bring the world to perfection.[17] God could have created all humans as full-grown adults already knowing and loving God and all others (in other words, already performing their most perfect actions). God certainly does not need the help of humans to procreate and raise children. However, one of the most fundamental attributes of God is that he causes goodness through his love. When humans procreate, take care of children, educate others, and help others, they are more like God in that they cause goodness in themselves and others. If all humans were created in a state of perfection in terms of action, they would not have this opportunity to be more like God by causing goodness in themselves and others.

Because there are degrees of perfection in the universe, humans can aid God in helping others attain perfection. For example, some children have great difficulty learning to read. In teaching these children, parents and teachers must spend countless hours trying numerous different pedagogical techniques. This process can be very frustrating for both the students and the teachers. Had God simply made these children full-grown and perfectly knowing and loving him, the parents and teachers would not have had to spend countless hours teaching them how to read. The children would immediately know how to read, for God would have created them perfect in terms of action. However, if God created them this way, parents and teachers would not have the opportunity to help these children learn. They would not have the chance to use their creativity, patience, and love to help these children. They would miss the happiness of seeing these children succeed. Likewise, I, as a parent, would not be able to help my children learn to walk, talk, play football, and do many other things. All these activities bring joy because we humans are like God when we perform them. In other words, because God causes goodness in others, I am more like God when I help others to be perfected. Consequently, humans were created to be perfected by actions so that they would become more like God by causing goodness in themselves and others.

The good effect of being created in a perfect state of imperfection is that ultimately humans can be more like God and thus share even more perfectly in his happiness, but the bad effect is that humans can fail to perform good actions (and be very unhappy). In other words, humans are created to be like God by knowing and loving. As we saw in chapter 1, actions that come from knowledge and love are free actions. Thus, humans must freely choose to perform these actions of knowing and loving. If humans are free to choose these actions, they also have the opportunity not to choose them. Some humans do not choose to perform these actions and fail to attain their created potential. Hence, although Adam and Eve were created to know and love God and to live forever, they still had to perform these actions in order to be perfect in the absolute sense. When Adam and Eve committed the sin of pride, they failed to perform their proper act of knowing and loving God. Instead, they loved the lesser good of themselves more than God and committed the original sin.

When Adam and Eve committed original sin, all five harmonies were damaged. The Genesis account notes that the "tree was good for food, pleasing to the eyes, and desirable for gaining wisdom. So she took some of the fruit and ate it; and she also gave some to her husband . . . and he ate it" (Gn 3:6). Notice that all the pertinent powers of the soul were involved in the sin. The intellect sought the wisdom. The will sought the goodness of the fruit. The emotions sought the fruit as pleasing to the eyes. Eating the fruit is symbolic of the body performing the action, and both Adam and Eve were involved in the sin. Consequently, the natural inclinations of all the powers became corrupted because of the sin.

Within the sinful action, the intellect was no longer focused on knowing God and his plans for human happiness but became focused on itself and its "creation" of truth. The participation in divine wisdom was traded for imperfect human wisdom, which was quite weak. Furthermore, since the intellect sought to define the world by its own standards, error became mixed with truth. Consequently, the natural inclination to know the truth was tarnished, and the intellect became subject to ignorance. Although the natural inclination to know the truth was not completely destroyed, humans have only to look into their experiences to see that their intellect does not always reason correctly. Excellent examples of this can be seen in the fact that vast numbers of people disagree on fundamental moral issues, such as abortion today and slavery in the past.

Furthermore, in this first act of pride, the will replaced love of God with love of self. The goals of God were replaced by the goals of Adam and Eve. Since the will now had inordinate self-love, it became subject to concupiscence (an inclination to do evil). In other words, the natural inclination to the good was corrupted, and an inclination to do evil accompanied the natural inclination. Again, a short look within our experiences shows times when we knew something was wrong but willed to do it anyway.[18] Because the intellect and will were no longer focused on knowing and loving God, the first harmony between man and God was broken. In other words, the grace giving humans the ability to be united to God through knowledge and love was removed, damaging the original unity.

The emotions, which in sinning no longer followed the truth of the intellect, became unruly and desired all sorts of bodily goods: some were truly good, some only appeared to be good. Because the emotions were unruly, they caused humans to perform many evil actions and caused great turmoil within the soul. The Genesis story highlights the corruption of the emotional desire for sex. Before original sin, Adam and Eve did not need clothes because their sexual desire was always within a relationship of complete unity.[19] In other words, because of their love for each other, they always made the needs and goals of the other their own and, therefore, would never use each other as sexual objects. After original sin, sexual desire could be separated from true love, and the other person could now become primarily an object to bring pleasure (cf. Gn 3:10–11). The sexual action, which was created to unite Adam and Eve, could now be used to cause pain and suffering and could drive humans apart.[20]

Because of the corruption of the natural inclinations, the intellect, will, and emotions no longer always work together. The harmony within the soul is now damaged. The intellect is often unsure of what to do, the will does not always follow the guidance of the intellect, and the emotions can become completely unruly. Great turmoil can now reign in the soul, destroying interior peace and causing pain and unhappiness. The harmony between humans is also wounded. Adam and Eve no longer always share in each other's actions by means of a loving union. As Genesis notes, man dominates woman (3:16). Quite frequently through human history, men have lorded over women as if they were slaves or beasts of burden. However, women are not completely off the hook; just a few chapters later, in the story of Jacob and Rebecca (Gn 27), we see that women can also dominate men by being conniving. The key point is that as long as either a man or a woman is seeking to control the other person, either by force or deception, he or she is not participating in a loving relationship, and the unity of true friendship is flawed.

The harmony between body and soul was also damaged. The body that was made to express love of others was used to commit sin. Consequently, the body will now suffer and die.[21] Although death is seen as a punishment, it also shows God's mercy. What could be worse than living forever in a world without union with God and others? Death keeps people from living forever in the state of misery caused by original sin.

Last of all, the harmony between humans and creation was corrupted.[22] This corruption is symbolized by Adam and Eve being banished from the Garden of Eden and forced to till the ground, which would only be fruitful with much toil and effort (Gn 3:17–19). Throughout history, the natural world has often been a brutal world of famine, disease, and natural disasters.

Not only were these five harmonious relationships injured, but their effects on human nature were passed on to future generations. Every sin has its effect on the soul and sometimes even the body. Sins can also affect future generations. For example, if a mother is on drugs when she is pregnant, the child will suffer from the effects of the drugs. If the child is raised in a drug culture, it is likely that the child's children (and maybe even grandchildren) will likewise suffer from the effects of the original mother's sins. The more serious the sins are, the more likely they are to harm the soul, body, and future generations. Because Adam and Eve were given the grace to have complete harmony in the soul, the subjective seriousness of their sin was greater than anything we could ever commit. In other words, when humans sin today, because of their corrupted inclinations, they are often influenced by ignorance or unruly emotions. These factors diminish their culpability. Adam and Eve did not have corrupted inclinations. They had to become prideful to the point that they countered their natural inclinations, and then their human nature became corrupted. Their sin was so serious that it caused their nature to be fallen.[23] All things, when they procreate, pass on their particular nature. Since humans now have fallen nature, fallen nature is what is passed on to the next generation.[24] Consequently, humans inherit the effects of original sin: corrupted inclinations, a loss of grace, and, worst of all, a destruction of their harmony with God.

REDEMPTION FROM ORIGINAL SIN

If the state of fallen nature was the end of the story, then the proper reaction should probably be despair. Having the goal of a relatively permanent happiness in this life (let alone eternal happiness) would be out of the question because of the difficulty of entering into loving relationships with God and others. In reflecting on this fallen state, the sage would recommend that his disciples lower their goals in order to be content. The sage would say that happiness is unrealistic and that the sooner disciples realize this and stop working for this illusory goal, the better. However, this gloomy message is not the message of Christianity. The good news of Christianity is that Christ has redeemed us so that we can be eternally happy. Through the Incarnation, Crucifixion, and Resurrection, Christ has not only restored the five harmonious relationships to their natural perfection, but he has also elevated human nature, giving humans the ability to form new harmonious relationships even beyond those experienced by Adam and Eve.[25] This gift of grace can be referred to as *the inheritance bestowed by the Father upon his adopted children.*[26]

Humans are able to share in this inheritance because the Father sent the Son to earth to save humanity. The Son returned to the Father but sends the Holy Spirit to continue the process of salvation through the Church. The Holy Spirit then transforms humans into a new creation (2 Cor 5:17), giving them the ability to have supernatural knowledge (faith) and supernatural love (charity) of the Son. Since knowledge causes love, which causes unity, humans are then united to the Son and become one with him (as part of the one body of Christ). Through this union with the Son, they become adopted children of the Father, "and if children, then heirs, heirs of God and joint heirs with Christ" (Rom 8:17; cf. Eph 1:1–10). In other words, those united to Christ share in the inheritance that the Father eternally gives to the Son. What is this inheritance? It is a share in the fullness of the divine nature that the Father eternally gives to the Son. Adopted children of God are given the gift of being able to participate in the relation between the Father and the Son. The full inheritance is when humans share in the divine nature and can know and love God as he is (sharing in the one act of knowing and loving God).[27] In meditating on how love is the greatest gift from God, St. Paul describes the full inheritance in the following way: "At present we see indistinctly, as in a mirror, but then face to face. At present I know partially; then I shall know fully as I am fully known."[28] In other words, because we are God's children, "we shall be like him, for we shall see him as he is" (1 Jn 3:2). When humans are able to know and love God as he is, all the harmonies are restored and elevated. Humans will be completely united to the Trinity and share in God's happiness for all eternity.

However, if Christ has given humans the capacity for perfect harmony, why do Christians still have the effects of original sin? In other words, why is there still tension in our relations with God and others, and why does the body still die? The answer is that although Christians will ultimately receive the full inheritance at the second coming of Christ, right now they only have the *down payment of the inheritance.*[29] Until the second coming of Christ, the degree to which Christians can share in the divine nature is limited—they have some access to God's transforming grace but not the complete access they will one day receive. As an analogy to help explain this notion of the *down payment,* imagine that you have a benevolent billionaire uncle who has no children, but he does have many nieces and nephews. This wise uncle plans to leave all of his fortune of $50 billion to one of his nieces or nephews. However, to make sure that the niece or nephew will use the money wisely, he is going to give each one $50 *million* as a test to see which one uses the money to do the most good on earth. The test will show both the wisdom and love of each of his nieces and nephews. You take your $50 million and go to a small, poor country in Africa in an attempt to assist the country as a whole. However, even with $50 million, many problems cannot be addressed, so you start with the most important problems, hoping that by fixing them the rest of the country will be aided. In the analogy, the rich uncle stands for God. But God is not just giving you $50 billion; he is giving you something infinitely more valuable: eternal happiness.[30] However, eternal happiness is not obtained until you can know and love God as he is, which does not happen in this life. Right now you only have the down payment of the full inheritance, a portion of the grace that you will ultimately receive (like the $50 million in the example). Even this portion of grace gives you the ability to be wiser and love God and others more perfectly. Hence, even in this life you can begin to participate in God's happiness. Although this grace of the down payment begins restoring and even elevating the different harmonies, it is not enough to completely restore all of them. Hence, Christians are currently in a state of tension. On the one hand, they still have the effects of original sin, yet on the other hand, they have the grace of God to help them perform even greater acts than those of Adam and Eve. A more detailed explanation of both the state of the full inheritance and the state of the down payment will help to show where humans are on the journey to eternal happiness.

THE FULL INHERITANCE

Recall from chapter 1 how the nature of something determines the type of actions that something can do. For example, kangaroo nature allows kangaroos to do kangaroo actions. Because the full inheritance is a participation in the divine nature, humans are able to act by the power of God's nature and share in God's actions. In other words, their natural inclinations to action are perfected by inclinations beyond their natural powers. The intellect is able to share in the divine knowledge by knowing God as he is. God is the fullness of all truth; hence, to the extent that they know God, humans can know everything. They will be able to know all other humans perfectly to the very depths of their souls. Likewise, the will is able to share in the divine love by loving God as he is. Humans will likewise be able to love all other humans perfectly. By means of this knowledge and love, humans are able to share in the divine unity: first, by being united to the Father, Son, and Holy Spirit, and then, to the extent they are united to God, they will be united to all other humans. Within these loving relationships that fulfill their natural inclinations, humans will be perfectly happy by participating in God's infinite happiness. We will see more on sharing in this divine happiness in chapter 3.

The emotions will be given the grace to intensely desire God and the good of all others. They will always follow the intellect and will. Hence, the soul will once more be in complete harmony.

Although the full inheritance begins when we die, it is not completed until the resurrection of our bodies. With the resurrection of our bodies, we will once more live as bodily beings forever. Furthermore, just as the body of Jesus after his resurrection took on spiritual attributes (it could pass through walls, appear and disappear, etc.), so also our bodies will take on spiritual attributes. They will also be beyond space and time and will be able to "sense" spiritual things, such as the thoughts and love of others. These spiritual powers allow the bodies to be proportionate to the elevated soul, so that we can still learn and express love through our bodies.[31]

In our current state, our ability to enter into deep, loving relationships is always restricted because of the limitations of the body and soul. Because we can only know people by observing their actions, and our intellect is limited in what we can know, we can really only become truly close friends with a few people. In other words, we only have the time and ability to know a few people to the depths of their souls. Furthermore, since loving relationships require humans to make the greatest goals and needs of others their own, time and ability also limit the number of close relationships we can have. However, with the perfections of the body and soul, we will be able to immediately know all others to the depths of their souls and will have the time and ability to make their needs, goals, and joys our own. The best analogy for the state of the full inheritance is the loving relationships that humans have with family and friends. If you take the happiest relationship that you have and multiply the depth of this relationship many times and extend this relationship to all others, this is what the full inheritance will be like. Of course, the cause of all of these relationships will be our relationship to God.

Last of all, creation will be in complete harmony with humans. The resurrected bodies will live on the new earth, and God will once more rule creation through humanity. The nature miracles found in the Gospels (such as the calming of the storm) foreshadow the relation between creation and humanity.

Because the full inheritance is a supernatural participation in the divine nature, it not only heals all the corruptions inflicted upon human nature, but it also elevates human nature beyond the perfections of the natural level. For example, the intellect in the full inheritance not only functions properly (the natural perfection found in the original state), it also knows God as he is (a supernatural perfection only attainable by grace). The will surpasses its natural ability to love God by loving God as he is. Even the body, which would have lived forever in the original state, is supernaturally perfected by taking on spiritual attributes. In other words, the perfections of the full inheritance are substantially greater than those of the original state.

THE CURRENT STATE OF THE DOWN PAYMENT

Now that we have analyzed the full inheritance, we can determine a proper understanding of the starting point on the journey to God. For those given God's grace through baptism, the starting point is this state of the down payment of the full inheritance.[32] As we saw in the description of the analogy of the rich uncle, humans have only a share of the grace of the full inheritance, and this share is not sufficient to fully reconstruct all of the harmonies that were broken by original sin. The intellect is still subject to ignorance, but it has been given the light of faith to help it to know not only natural truths but also supernatural truths about God and how to attain him. The will is still subject to concupiscence (the natural inclination to love is corrupted), but it has also been given the gift of charity to love God and others. Hence, through faith and charity the harmony between humans and God has been restored, even if only partially. Humans now have the ability to avoid sin, but because of the lingering effects of original sin, all humans (with the exception of Jesus and Mary) do sin occasionally (and often frequently). Even though the harmony with God has been restored, tension still often exists in our relationship with God, and the harmony can be lost.

The emotions are still unruly and desire sense goods that are not truly good for the person. However, the emotions are aided by the movement of the Holy Spirit to desire God and the good of others as determined by the intellect and will. Consequently, sometimes the soul has great harmony, but at other times there is still turmoil.

Because of the harmony with God and the soul, the harmonious relationships that humans were created to have with each other have also been restored and even elevated. Through God's grace, marriage allows humans to supernaturally participate in the unity of God. Also, as members of the body of Christ, the Church, humans are united to each other through their union with Christ. These two institutions offer a foretaste of the complete unity of the full inheritance. However, at the same time, because of the effects of original sin in the soul, tension is still found between humans. Even among those united by God's love, people sometimes seek to pursue their own interests at the expense of others. Even though it should be the most natural thing in the world based on how humans are made, forming and maintaining loving relationships with others requires perseverance and hard work.

The body will still suffer and die. However, before the incarnation of Christ, suffering was often thought of as a meaningless punishment. Now this suffering has acquired meaning. In this state of the down payment, making the needs of others our own will require humans to sacrifice and suffer for others. The ability to suffer for others can be a proof of our love for them.[33] Hence, it was fitting that God chose to redeem humans through Christ's suffering on the cross. Through his crucifixion Christ teaches us the way to be truly happy by sacrificing for others. Furthermore, Paul teaches us that through our suffering we are able to share in the suffering of Christ (see Col 1:24–29). Earlier, we quoted Romans 8:17 to show how Christians are adopted children of the Father and heirs of the full inheritance. Paul continues by noting that we will receive this inheritance "if only we suffer with him so that we may also be glorified with him." Suffering and death now become a means to being glorified with God. If we truly love others, their sufferings become our sufferings. Many saints, such as Francis of Assisi, welcomed suffering because they loved Christ so much that they wished to share in his sufferings. Because their suffering was endured out of love for God, it became an occasion for great happiness.[34] A proper understanding of suffering can make a significant difference in the happiness of the lives of many people.

Finally, the harmony between humans and creation is still damaged. Nonetheless, since humans are body and soul, the divine plan of bringing humans to eternal life incorporates the use of material things. For example, bread becomes the body of Christ in the Eucharist, and water is an instrumental cause of grace in the sacrament of baptism.

In some ways the ability to properly function in the current state of the down payment is greater than that of the original state, and in other ways it is significantly less. Inasmuch as humans can more perfectly share in the perfections of the full inheritance, they can perform actions beyond the ability of Adam and Eve. However, inasmuch as humans are still subject to the effects of original sin, their nature falls short of the perfections of the original state. For example, following the Incarnation, by means of faith humans can know truths about God as Trinity beyond the ability of Adam and Eve. But at the same time, the human intellect is still subject to ignorance. It can be a real struggle to believe, and its comprehension of revealed truth is often limited.

Having analyzed the history of human nature, we can now understand the starting point of human nature. We humans were created to be in loving communion with God and others. However, our nature is fallen, causing us to seek goods that are not proportionate to our calling. Yet, because humans are redeemed, God gives us the ability to fulfill our supernatural vocation. But, we only have the down payment of the inheritance in this life, and striving for eternal happiness is very difficult. A spiritual battle between the gifts of the Holy Spirit and the effects of fallen nature is constantly being waged within us. Humans yearn for communion with God and true and lasting friendships with others, yet this unity can be challenging to attain, even with the aid of God's grace. Thus, in order to attain the goal of eternal happiness, humans need the aid of God and help from other humans. The intellect, will, and emotions will all need to be perfected by grace, and likewise with the virtues. Consequently, after discussing the nature of the ultimate goal (eternal happiness in loving union with God), we will explain how to attain this goal by means of law, virtue, grace, and other moral principles necessary to aid humans on their journey. Table 2.1 summarizes the history of human nature.

Table 2.1. History of Human Nature Chart

Original State	Fallen State (The natural inclinations are corrupted.)	Down Payment of the Inheritance (The starting point on the journey.)	The Full Inheritance
Humans are in union with God.	Unity with God is broken.	Unity with God is restored but still subject to tension.	Perfect unity with God.
Intellect knows God and others.	Intellect is subject to ignorance.	Intellect is subject to ignorance but perfected by faith.	Intellect knows God as he is.
Will loves God and others.	Will is subject to concupiscence.	Will is subject to concupiscence but perfected by charity.	Will loves God as he is.
Humans are in union with each other.	There is tension in the relationships between humans.	Humans have grace to unite them, but there is still tension.	All humans participate in the unity of the Trinity.
Emotions follow the intellect and will.	Emotions become unruly.	Emotions are unruly but can be moved by the Holy Spirit.	Emotions fully desire God and others.
Body is completely subject to the soul causing it to live forever.	Body will suffer and die.	Body still suffers and dies, but these now have meaning.	Body lives forever and takes on spiritual attributes.
Creation is subject to humans.	Creation is no longer subject to humans.	Creation is still not subject but is used in bringing humans to salvation.	Creation is completely subject to humans.

3

HAPPINESS

God's Goal for Humans

People want to be happy. They might not know what happiness is or how to attain it, but they want to be happy. A quick search on Amazon for books about how to be happy reveals hundreds of titles written by psychologists, philosophers, journalists, business leaders, theologians, biologists, and even historians. Many of these titles are rather straightforward, such as *The Secret to True Happiness*; others are rather humorous, such as *The Antidote: Happiness for People Who Can't Stand Positive Thinking*.[1] Some even present happiness as something rather hidden or esoteric, such as *Living the Quaker Way: Discover the Hidden Happiness in the Simple Life*. The key point is that many people in many different disciplines are searching for happiness, and the fact that there are so many diverse books on happiness (and that people are buying them) shows that for some people happiness can be fleeting and hard to understand. However, multiple times in the first two chapters of this book I stated that humans are made to share in God's happiness. I further noted that happiness is connected with the actions that humans are created to perform: entering into loving relationships with God and others. In other words, the destination of the journey to God ends in true happiness. In speaking of the full inheritance, I presented how the New Testament shows that the destination consists of humans sharing in divine nature and spending eternity in a loving union with God. However, given the diversity of approaches in seeking happiness in popular culture, it may not be clear that the New Testament concept of knowing and loving God for all eternity is the greatest act of human happiness. Therefore, this chapter will analyze the ultimate end of the journey in greater detail, showing that the acts in the full inheritance are the most perfect acts of happiness.

Before giving the general definition of human happiness, three background points must be covered in order to build the underpinnings for understanding this definition. The first point is that *all created beings are happy when they perform their proper action.* Christians believe that God is intelligent and good. Intelligent beings make things for a purpose. Hence, when humans make something, they have a reason or goal for whatever they make. For example, if they make an airplane, the airplane is not perfect in the absolute sense until it performs its proper action of flying. Likewise, when an intelligent God creates a thing, he creates it to perform its proper action. Creatures must perform their proper actions to be fulfilled, because by performing actions they are more like God, who is pure act. Furthermore, God is also pure goodness. Since God is good, he wants all of creation to be happy. Consequently, God created all creatures to be happy when they perform the action that they were made to perform. In other words, God imprinted all things with a natural inclination to happiness.[2] This natural inclination is fulfilled when a created thing performs its proper action.

Although the term "happiness" is usually only applied to humans, it can also apply to plants and animals. If I say, "That is a happy tree," nearly everyone would know what I mean. The tree is flourishing and doing exactly what trees are supposed to do. In other words, the tree is performing its proper action. Another example can be seen in reference to animals. One of my sons used to really love frogs. When he was four or five, he would catch little ones when we went to a pond or stream. He would bring these frogs home and hold them in his hand. However, my wife would inform him that eventually he had to let them go because the frogs were not happy. The frogs were not happy because, if they spent the rest of the day in his hands, they would die. Being "loved" to death by a small child is not the proper action of a frog. Had my son been playing with a puppy all day, the puppy may have been very happy because dogs are social animals. Consequently, even nonhuman creatures are happy when they perform actions in accord with their nature (even though this action might not make a human happy). Since humans are created to know and love God (and all others) and to enter into communion with God and others, the type of acts that must ultimately make us happy are acts of knowing and loving God and others.

The second foundational point is that *God wants all humans to be happy.* This point has actually already been shown in the paragraphs above, yet it must be further explained. Happiness is not just for a few privileged souls—it is for everyone. However, just because everyone is made to be happy does not mean that it is immediately evident to everyone that knowing and loving God is the ultimate act of happiness. The problem is that many other things bring limited and temporary happiness (a false happiness, as opposed to authentic happiness). Hence, some people seek happiness in things like wealth, health, pleasure (e.g., drugs and sex), honor, or power. The problem with these things is that since they only bring limited happiness, they always leave these people unsatisfied. As we saw in chapter 1, humans have multiple natural inclinations, including some that they share with other created beings (like the inclination to bodily pleasure) and some that are exclusive to persons. Fulfilling any of these inclinations can bring some happiness (sometimes authentic and sometimes false).[3] However, because God wants humans to have an extremely intense and everlasting happiness, he created them to be in a loving relationship with an infinite God. Thus, he gave them a natural desire for the infinite good.[4] Nothing short of God will ultimately satisfy the depths of human desire.[5] Many examples of this unquenchable desire can be found in every generation: the wealthy person who loves money more than anything else can never get enough money; the person who loves bodily pleasure will often try stronger and stronger drugs in order to get a greater emotional high, and so on. In their deluded pursuit of happiness people often reject the very things that can bring them greater happiness, such as God and other humans. Hence, in the end, these limited and false forms of happiness can leave one very unhappy. Because God wants all humans to be truly happy (and not to simply have the fleeting and illusory forms of false happiness) he has given them a natural inclination to the infinite good. Consequently, in the end, only a loving relationship with God will bring complete and permanent happiness for humans.

Although God has created each individual human with a natural inclination to happiness, the happiness of individuals always affects the happiness of others. The Southern saying "If momma ain't happy, ain't nobody happy" is meant to be humorous, but it points to a profound truth about humanity. Humans are social beings made to share in the joys and sufferings of others, and the happiness (or unhappiness) of one person always affects the happiness of others. In other words, humans are happy when they perform their proper actions of loving God and others. If humans are not performing their proper actions, then they are not loving others. Since humans are made to be loved and to love, a failure to love generally results in unhappiness for both the one failing to love and the one who is not loved. Because humans are created in the image of the Trinity, happiness is found in communal relationships, and the unhappiness of some members of the community affects the happiness of the rest of the community (cf. 1 Cor 12:26). Because the happiness of individual humans is intertwined with the happiness of others, the performance of actions resulting in our own unhappiness also affects the happiness of others.

The third background point is that *every human action is done in order to ultimately attain happiness.* Every act is done for an end (a goal or reason for acting). Usually this end is only an intermediary end, which is ordered to another end and so forth until the ultimate end is reached.[6] For example, if I asked Joe why he was getting up, he might respond, "To go class." If I asked him why he was going to class, he might respond, "To graduate with good grades." If I further asked him why, he might say, "To get a good job." If I continued to interrogate him, he might answer, "To use the money to support a family." Eventually Joe would come to the thing that he considers to be the most important goal in his life. Since all humans want to be happy, they will seek this happiness in their most important goal.

For many people, the ultimate reason they do something is because they love God. However, numerous other ultimate ends could be given, such as wealth, power, bodily pleasure, and honor. For example, perhaps Joe is coming to class because he sees it as a step toward becoming the richest person in the world. Or, perhaps it is because Kate is in the class, and he wants to admire her beauty from his seat in the classroom. No matter what the reason, Joe goes to class because he believes it will ultimately make him happy. If Joe did not think his goal would make him happy, he would not have gotten up in the first place (assuming he is cogent enough to reason at this early hour). Consequently, every human action is performed in order to ultimately attain happiness, even if the act does not bring immediate satisfaction. Humans must seek this goal of happiness in general because they are naturally inclined to happiness.

Because every act is done in order to attain happiness, a different understanding of happiness can change the type of actions that are done. In other words, like any journey, a different destination results in traveling a different route. For example, if the ultimate end is wealth, a different action might be taken than if the ultimate end is knowing and loving God. Whereas the goal of wealth might cause someone to work for eighty hours a week, to the detriment of those around him, having God as an ultimate end might cause someone to spend only forty hours working, allowing him to spend the rest of his time with his family, praying, worshipping in church, and so on. The action may not always be changed, since often two journeys to two different destinations will cover the same route at the beginning, but eventually the two paths will divide. Recall that Joe could pursue either the ultimate end of wealth or the ultimate end of God by going to class, but eventually the goal of wealth would cause Joe to perform drastically different acts than the goal of loving God. However, Joe can properly have an intermediary goal of wealth, as long as it can logically be ordered to love of God (who should always be the ultimate goal). Because our actions affect others, a proper understanding of happiness is essential both for the benefit of the individual and for the benefit of the rest of society. Simply having the proper concept of happiness is half the battle. Even if humans do not always know what actions to perform to attain their goal, they are at least trying to do actions that will result in true happiness. If these actions are truly ordered to God, they will also be acts of love of others.

Because God is intelligent and good, he wants humans to be happy by performing their proper actions. Consequently, all humans have a natural inclination to be happy, and they always seek happiness. However, they do not always know how to attain authentic happiness and, hence, often seek a false happiness that is ultimately unsatisfying (but can be very satisfying in the short term). Any definition of happiness must take into consideration all of these different points.

THE NATURE OF HAPPINESS

The definition of happiness must include the proper actions of humans; hence, it must include the act of knowing and loving. Furthermore, it must be broad enough to take into account the fact that sometimes people are not always happy when they perform loving actions of sacrificing for others, and people are sometimes happy when they are doing improper actions. Finally, it must allow for the most perfect state of happiness to be an act of eternally knowing and loving God. The following definition is in conformity with all of these points: *happiness is the **act** of contemplating (thinking about) the goods that we know, love, and possess* (although hope of attaining something gives limited happiness). I will now explain all the components of this definition. First, happiness is an act. It is not a feeling or a state of being. The feeling of happiness (emotional joy) often accompanies true happiness, but it is not the act of happiness itself.[7] Because emotional joy can come from things that are ultimately bad for you, many people can have a great deal of emotional joy but be very unhappy (e.g., drug addicts). Happiness is also not a state of being. However, if humans are living a life of virtue, they can attain great happiness by contemplating the state of their life because their life is very good. This can cause people to believe that happiness is a state of being, but the happiness in this situation is the act of contemplating this state.

Second, happiness is an act of contemplation. By contemplation, I only mean that a person is actively thinking about something. There are many things humans know that are seldom thought about. For example, most people know that Jupiter is the fifth planet, but they rarely think about it. However, the astronomer who loves studying Jupiter may attain great happiness by thinking about it. The key is that one must think about the good in order to be happy.

Third, that which is contemplated must be good (or at least believed to be good).[8] All things have some goodness because they share in the goodness of God. However, the more like God something is, the greater the goodness it has. The greatest goodness is divine goodness itself. Because God created humans to know and love Him, the more a created thing shares in God's goodness, the greater happiness it can bring to the human contemplating it.

Fourth, in order to contemplate the goodness of something, we must know what it is. In other words, it is not just enough to have a good thing, we must also recognize that thing as good, or it will bring no happiness.[9] For example, many students do not realize the privilege that they are receiving when they get a good education. They take a good education for granted. Consequently, thinking about school may make them unhappy when it should bring them great happiness.

Fifth, the good must be loved, or it will never make a person happy. Although happiness is primarily an act of the intellect, love of the will is absolutely necessary for it to occur. The act of the will loving the good comes both before and after the act of contemplation. It comes before because something must first be loved in order for it to make someone happy. For example, if people do not love their roommate, thinking about their roommate will not bring happiness. The act of the will comes after contemplation because the joy of the will further perfects the act of contemplation.[10] The good that was desired is finally attained, and the will delights in this good.

A few examples will demonstrate that happiness truly is an act of contemplating something that is known and loved. Imagine a young boy, Fred, who badly wants a bicycle for Christmas. Upon waking up on Christmas morning, he finds a bicycle waiting for him. Fred is very happy. Why? First of all, he knows what the bicycle is and what he can do with it. All people have experienced getting a gift and asking, "What is it?" Although these people may be happy that someone loved them enough to give them a gift, the gift itself will not make them happy until they know what it is. Second, Fred loves the bicycle. This is clearly seen in his great longing to have one. I can remember a time when one of my sons was three years old, and he got a big dump truck from his godfather. Upon opening the package, he burst into tears because he wanted frogs. In other words, he did not love the gift and was unhappy. Third, as long as Fred is thinking about the good of his bicycle (including thinking about all the fun times he will have with it), he is performing the act of happiness.

For a while Fred is very happy. In fact, if he continues to use the bicycle for a long time and continues to love it, the bicycle may make him happy for a year or so, until he outgrows it. However, many times I have seen my children get toys on Christmas morning, and by afternoon they are ready to go to their grandparents' house and get more presents. Material things, by their nature, are a limited good, and therefore only bring limited happiness. To better understand happiness, a nonmaterial analogy is also helpful. Imagine that Fred grows up, goes to high school, and finds a girlfriend. I can remember when one of my friends found his first girlfriend. His entire disposition changed for a while as he walked around in a daze just thinking about the good of his girlfriend (or at least the good of having one). His parents even noticed that his attitude had improved because he was so happy. Fred acts the same way, and as long as he is thinking about this girl he knows and loves, he is performing the act of happiness. Another human can bring more happiness than a material good because humans are a much greater good. However, in my friend's case, the relationship only lasted so long, and the happiness from it diminished.

An even greater good would be a relationship with another human that is permanent. Marriage is made permanent by the bonds of divine love uniting two people as one. Because of the greatness of the relationship, a spouse can bring even greater happiness than a boyfriend or girlfriend. Consequently, many people have wedding pictures and other reminders of their spouse so that they can think about him or her on a regular basis. Children are another great good. Parents often have picture albums, refrigerator artwork, or crooked clay pots that remind them of the good of their children so that they can think about this goodness and be happy. In other words, when spouses know and love each other or parents know and love their children, contemplating these loving relationships brings great happiness.

These examples also show that the greater the goodness of the thing, the greater the potential it has for causing happiness. I say potential for happiness, because many people fail to appreciate the goodness of things or others around them, or they fail to love them. When they do not know and love these goods, they cannot attain happiness from them. Nonetheless, since goods that are more perfect can bring greater happiness, it follows that God who is infinite goodness brings the most perfect happiness.

However, even in relation to God, if he is not known and loved, thinking about him will not bring happiness. For example, at Mass, Catholics are united to God through the sacrament of the Eucharist. The great saints were made very happy by attending Mass. However, someone could go to Mass and not understand what is going on and, hence, not be made happy by it. Another person could go to Mass and understand its goodness but not love it; he will likewise not be happy. Mass only makes the person happy who knows how good it is and loves it.

Consequently, four things are necessary for an act of happiness to take place.[11] First, humans must contemplate the goods that they have. Often the difference between happy people and unhappy people is that happy people regularly think about the good things they have been blessed with, while unhappy people take these things for granted. Because God wants humans to be happy, he requires that on one day a week we abstain from work and contemplate him and the gifts that he gives us.[12] Furthermore, in the United States there is even a holiday to help us "count our blessings" called Thanksgiving. Second, humans must know the goodness of the things they have. Generally, this means learning more about God and regularly entering into meaningful conversations with those we love. Third, humans must love the goods they have. This point cannot be overemphasized. Unless humans enter into loving relationships, they will never really be truly happy. Fourth, humans must have goods to love. On a natural level this may be impossible. Some people may simply have too many misfortunes in their lives to have any significant goods to contemplate. Long before the time of Christ, Aristotle wrote extensively on happiness. Many of the basic ideas about happiness that I am presenting can be traced back to him. Yet, he also noted that happiness requires that one have external goods, such as good birth, good looks, and prosperity.[13] These external goods are often beyond one's control, and the one without these goods is simply out of luck. In other words, if you were born a slave or a member of the lower class, Aristotle would say that you could never really be happy. On the natural level, Aristotle may to be right—happiness is only for the lucky and the elite. However, the good news of Christianity proclaims that with the supernatural grace of God even the poor and misfortunate are able to be happy because they can be united to God through knowledge and love. Everybody can have goods to contemplate if they know and love God.[14]

Three Degrees of Happiness

A good definition of happiness needs to take into consideration the natural happiness humans regularly experience, the ultimate goal of sharing in God's happiness, and even false happiness. To better understand that happiness is the act of contemplating the good that is known, loved, and possessed, it is helpful to make a distinction between three degrees of happiness: *perfect happiness, supernatural happiness in this life*, and *natural happiness* (which also includes false happiness). Since humans are generally most familiar with natural happiness, it will be treated first.

Natural happiness is obtained through contemplating the natural goodness contained in the goods that are loved. Recall that nature determines the type of actions that something can do. The proper actions of human nature result in natural happiness. Hence, natural happiness is simply the happiness that can be attained through the powers of the soul that are not aided by grace. Because humans are naturally inclined to their proper actions, the satisfaction of any of the natural inclinations brings some happiness. For example, even bodily health and proper emotional pleasure can cause limited happiness since humans are naturally inclined to these actions. However, true happiness is found in the acts of the intellect and will since this is the way that humans are most like God. Because greater goods cause greater happiness, the greatest examples of natural happiness can be found in knowing and loving friends and family and especially in knowing and loving God through our natural powers (i.e., without the aid of divine revelation and grace).

Although natural happiness is the lowest of the three degrees of happiness, it is still a wonderful thing. It is the happiness that comes from contemplating goods ranging from a good meal, to a beautiful sunset, to a life-long friend. All of these goods can bring happiness when they are known and loved. Because natural happiness comes from goods to which humans are naturally inclined, the highest degrees of natural happiness always correspond to what is truly good for humans (i.e., their proper actions which perfect them). Nonetheless, low levels of natural happiness (false happiness) can be obtained through false goods that are not ultimately good for humans, such as illegal drugs, premarital sex, overconsumption of material goods, greed, sloth, and so on. False happiness can be defined as "the happiness that comes from contemplating the false goods resulting from immoral actions." Because all things come from God, these false goods still have some goodness in them. Consequently, even things that are bad for humans can result in a limited happiness when humans know and love them. For example, a greedy person might find happiness in taking advantage of poor people because he is contemplating the money he is making. The jealous person might find joy in spreading harmful gossip because he contemplates how much better he is than others. Although both of these actions keep these people from the friendships that will result in true happiness, they both bring happiness because they are a contemplation of a good that is loved. False happiness is a type of happiness, yet in the end it diminishes or even destroys true happiness by hindering people from performing their proper actions. Furthermore, because the immoral actions underlying false happiness often hurt others, false happiness also generally causes others to be unhappy.

So why do people seek false happiness? For two reasons. First, all people seek happiness, and if they do not know where to find true happiness, they will try to find it in these false goods. In other words, because of the effects of fallen nature, humans do not always know where to find true happiness.[15] I have known people that were raised without any religion or stable relationships in their lives. They were never taught where to find true happiness (either explicitly, by example, or by experiencing it), so they sought happiness in whatever limited forms they could attain it. Since humans are made to be in union with others, this happiness usually was sought by trying to fit into a group that often did pleasurable things together but never really loved each other as true friends. Because these actions brought some limited happiness, they continued to seek more and more. However, along the way they strayed farther and farther from the loving relationships that bring true happiness. Second, true happiness takes work, effort, and sacrifice, and many are willing to settle for a lesser happiness. They do not always love the true good that will cause this happiness, and their emotions often seek bodily pleasure that does not lead to true happiness. They may know where to find true happiness but are often not strong enough to attain it.

Humans who seek happiness in false goods are like a wasp at a closed window. If a wasp gets into a house, it tries to get out by going to the light source, often a closed window. Even if someone opens a door, the wasp will continue to bang against the glass rather than go to the open door. False goods are like the light of the window. All people want happiness, and as long as they are getting some happiness, they will not look for the greater goods that will bring them true happiness. For example, people who love material possessions too much will receive some happiness every time they purchase some new item because they know and love that material good. As long as they keep purchasing more things, they are distracted from the goods that will make them truly happy. Like the wasp that ends up enslaved by the glass of the window, these people are ultimately restricted from finding true happiness. Because God wants people who are "enslaved by false happiness" to be truly happy too, he allows them to grow more and more unhappy until they "hit rock bottom" and turn to seek happiness in other more legitimate sources.[16]

These warnings about the potential dangers of natural happiness may lead a person to think that natural happiness is to be avoided. But this is not true; natural happiness is a wonderful thing! All humans were made to be naturally happy, and by nature they desire it. All things should be loved in proportion to their goodness, and if they are truly good, they should result in great happiness. Consequently, humans should contemplate the goodness of things, such as good food, good music, good work, and good friends.[17] They should share in the happiness of others, and let others share in their happiness. Yet, even these wonderful things will never fully satisfy humans because they were ultimately made to supernaturally share in God's happiness.

Although supernatural happiness is the next most perfect type of happiness, to understand it better, it is helpful to analyze perfect happiness first, just like before when the full inheritance was analyzed before the down payment stage. The supreme happiness for any particular thing is when that thing is performing its greatest action. In chapter 1 we noted the different ways things are like God. Some things have only being; others are living beings. Still others are sensing, emotional, living beings, and humans are understanding, loving, sensing, emotional, living beings. The proper action of each thing stems from its highest perfection (the way that it is most like God). For example, it is not enough for a tree (a living being) to just exist, it must grow and produce fruit to perform its proper action. Likewise, for apes to be happy, they cannot just live, they must have sense knowledge and the emotional joy that comes from it. So also, the proper act of humans as humans is to know and love the highest thing that can be known and loved: God.[18] And furthermore, because the intellect seeks to know things as they are, humans must know God as he is (not just by looking at the effects of God in creation or divine revelation). Thus, perfect happiness is the highest act of the highest power: the act of knowing and loving God as he is.[19] This act is beyond the power of human nature and is only possible after humans die and receive the full inheritance from God. Chapter 2 described the state of the full inheritance, where humans know and love God and all others perfectly by sharing in his divine nature in heaven. Because God is a pure act of knowing and loving his infinite divine truth and goodness, he is happiness by nature. To the extent that humans share in God's divine nature through grace, they also share in his happiness. This infinite and eternal happiness is the goal that all humans desire, even if they do not know that it is possible to attain it. This supreme action completely fulfills all human desires and is the goal of our journey to God, and it can only be fully attained in the next life.

Like perfect happiness, supernatural happiness on earth is only attained by means of God's grace. Consequently, it is also a share in God's happiness; however, it is limited because it stems from the grace of the down payment, which is not as great as the grace of the full inheritance. Although it is only a share of perfect happiness, it is much greater than natural happiness. In fact, the difference between supernatural happiness in this life and eternal happiness in heaven is only a difference of degree, as both stem from God's power working within us. This share in eternal happiness is in contrast with natural happiness, which is different in type in that it stems solely from human power.[20] In other words, supernatural happiness is a foretaste of the happiness in heaven and a participation in eternal happiness even while on earth. For those with supernatural happiness, heaven has already begun. Supernatural happiness on earth exists in two closely related forms. First, it comes from the knowledge and love of God obtained through faith and charity. Second, it comes from the contemplation of created goods that we love on account of our love of God.

The first of these two forms takes place whenever one contemplates the goodness of God as known through faith and loved through charity. In other words, through divine revelation, God has revealed many wonderful truths about himself to humanity. The fullness of this revelation can be found in the actions and words of Jesus Christ, the divine Son, who came to earth so that we could be united to God.[21] Through the gifts of faith and charity, humans can enter into an intimate relationship with God. Within these loving relationships, contemplation of God brings the most perfect happiness that can be found on earth. Practically speaking, this contemplation usually takes place in times of formal prayer, but it can take place anytime someone reflects on the glorious gifts God has given them.

The second form of supernatural happiness is found when we contemplate God through created goods that are loved out of love of God. Because earthly goods are limited, the amount of happiness that they can cause is also greatly limited. However, if our love for them is ordered to our love of God, these earthly goods can bring much greater happiness, since they are loved on account of the infinite good, God himself. A good analogy can be found in doing sacrificial acts for other people. Imagine that Kate is so busy one weekend that she has trouble taking time to get a nutritious meal. Joe recognizes this and decides to cook a meal for Kate. Joe does not particularly like to cook, and, additionally, he will be cooking the meal instead of watching his favorite team play football. Nonetheless, after slaving for hours on a meal of macaroni and cheese with all the fixings, Joe is very happy. Not because he loves the macaroni and cheese and fixings in and of themselves (although they are good) but because he loves Kate. In other words, because the meal is ordered to the greater good of Kate, Joe can contemplate the greater good of Kate, and it brings Joe much greater happiness.

Just as acts done out of love of others can bring great happiness, acts done out of love of God can bring even greater happiness. For example, after being flogged for preaching about Christ, Peter and the apostles were "rejoicing that they had been found worthy to suffer dishonor for the sake of the name" (Acts 5:41). The beatings and dishonor attached to it caused great happiness because they were endured out of love of God. Beatings, in and of themselves, should not make anyone happy, but because these were accepted out of love of God, they became a means to unity with God and, as such, they were a wonderful good. Peter and the apostles were contemplating the goodness of God, their friend whom they loved, even as they were being beaten.

Because all good actions can be done out of love of God, every good action can bring supernatural happiness. The greater the love of God that is involved in the action, the greater the amount of happiness that can be obtained. There is a famous quotation from Teresa of Calcutta: "Do little things with great love." She understood that to be happy humans do not have to do great things, but they only have to do little things with great love for God. Even mundane actions, such as studying, helping your neighbor, donating to the poor, or sleeping, can bring supernatural happiness if the action is truly ordered to God and done with great love for him.

Great suffering can also bring happiness if it is endured out of love of God. As we saw in chapter 2, even suffering and death can now have meaning in our lives and can help us to be happier. This notion that true happiness can be attained by giving of ourselves to the point of suffering is somewhat counterintuitive. In other words, because of their fallen nature, humans tend to seek happiness by serving themselves and not others. Consequently, in order to show humans how to truly be happy, Christ publicly died in a horrific manner.[22] Christ's death reveals the complete giving that takes place within the Trinity and teaches humans that true happiness consists in a true gift of self. It further teaches that every human, even those not blessed with material goods, can be happy by giving of themselves to God in a loving relationship.

Great supernatural happiness can be found by loving good things out of love of God. Even things that bring great amounts of natural happiness can bring even more happiness if loved out of love of God. For example, loving a spouse or a child can bring great natural happiness, but loving them out of love of God can bring additional supernatural happiness. Furthermore, because they are loved out of love of God, the relationship is much more permanent.[23] The key to all supernatural happiness is that when earthly goods are loved out of love of God, the goodness of God is also contemplated. This contemplation of the goodness of God is a taste of the eternal happiness of heaven and should give great hope for the future.

The analysis of the three degrees of happiness helps clarify how happiness is the act of contemplating the goods that are known and loved. The study of natural happiness shows us why humans can even have limited happiness in things that will ultimately cause them to be unhappy, because all things have some goodness that can be contemplated. However, actions that are truly good for humans have the potential to bring much greater happiness. Our study of supernatural happiness shows that every good act on earth can cause happiness if it is done out of love of God. Finally, perfect happiness is the most perfect action that a human can perform: knowing and loving God for all eternity.

Unhappiness

Just as happiness consists of contemplating the good that we have, intellectual sorrow (unhappiness) consists of contemplating the lack of goodness, or the evil, that we have. For example, if a woman has cancer and thinks about the evil of not being healthy, she will be unhappy. In general, if any one of the four necessary elements of happiness is missing, humans will be unhappy. First, those who think about the evils in their lives rather than the goods will be unhappy, as seen in the cancer example just given. Second, those who do not understand the goodness of the things they have or fail to understand what really makes humans happy will also lack happiness. Third, those who do not love the greater goods in life, such as God and others, will also ultimately be unhappy. Finally, those who have no great goods in their life will have nothing to love and contemplate. Furthermore, since unhappiness comes from not performing one's proper actions, it will also often negatively affect the happiness of others. However, since God wants humans to be happy, he offers his grace to all humans, and all people have the opportunity to have supernatural happiness.

HAPPINESS IN THE JOURNEY TO GOD

Because humans are made in the image God, they are made to be one with God and to share in the unity of the Trinity. The way humans attain this unity is by knowing and loving God as he is through the gift of the full inheritance. With God's grace, humans will be able to contemplate the infinite goodness of God, whom they know and love. Happiness is the act of the contemplating the good that is known and loved, and the greatest happiness is the highest act of the highest power. Consequently, knowing and loving God by means of the full inheritance is eternal happiness. Inasmuch as humans are united to God, they are also united to all others. Furthermore, the body will live forever and take on spiritual characteristics, as we saw chapter 2. This state of union with God is the end of the journey and the goal of the moral life.

However, this goal is not attained immediately. A long journey takes many steps over the course of a long time. Likewise, to maintain a loving relationship with someone requires many loving actions and virtues. With the help of God's grace, humans can remain in a loving relationship with him, but only with vigilance and effort on their part. More specifically, eternal happiness requires many good human actions stemming from faith and charity over the course of a lifetime.[24]

In order to strengthen a loving relationship on earth, actions must be ordered toward love of the other person. For example, if a husband uses his wife for his own benefit (rather than making her needs his needs), his action harms the relationship. It is not ordered to the love of the other person. Likewise, in order to attain eternal happiness, all of a person's actions need to be ordered to the love of God. If the actions are not ordered to the love of God, then they harm or even destroy the relationship, which can cause a person to forfeit the full inheritance. Since the ultimate end consists in knowing and loving God, human actions on earth must also consist of knowing God (through faith) and loving God (through charity). To go back to the journey analogy, if each step is not toward the ultimate goal, then it is toward some other end that will not bring eternal happiness.

IN CHAPTERS 1 AND 2, we analyzed the starting place of the journey, and in this chapter, we studied the end of the journey. The rest of the book will look at the journey itself. In the first three chapters, we consulted the Bible to determine both the beginning and the end of the journey. Now we will examine the Bible to find guidance for the journey itself. In order to attain the end of the journey, humans must do actions of loving God. However, there are different ways of determining what actions should and should not be done. In other words, there are many different moral methodologies. Chapter 4 will further examine the Bible in order to discover the parameters of a proper moral methodology. This analysis of scripture will show the importance of grace, laws, and virtues in completing the journey. Later chapters will then discuss these points in more detail.

4

MORAL METHODOLOGY
IN THE BIBLE

What is the essence of the journey to happiness like? Is it primarily a life of following external rules to avoid punishment (such as in hell) or is it about being transformed into the type of person that easily and joyfully loves God and others? Sometimes in the past the moral life has been especially equated with following lots of different rules. About thirty years ago, Servais Pinckaers wrote an insightful book (*The Sources of Christian Ethics*) lamenting the fact that over the last several hundred years moral theology has been overly preoccupied with laws, sins, and external rewards and punishments.[1] He argues that following the fourteenth century, important concepts like happiness, virtue, grace, and inspirations of the Holy Spirit were mostly replaced with concepts such as obligation, laws, external actions, and rewards. As an example, he points to the textbooks used to teach moral theology to seminarians for the last few hundred years. He notes that these textbooks were primarily concerned with sin and the obligations stemming from the Ten Commandments.[2] He contrasts these "moralities of obligation" with the moral theology of Thomas Aquinas and the early Church Fathers, who especially focused on happiness, the infused virtues, and the guidance of the Holy Spirit (the new law).[3] However, the Bible is certainly full of laws, obligations, punishments, and rewards. Is Pinckaers right in criticizing a "morality of obligation" focused primarily on these points? I have already shown in the first couple chapters the importance of being in a loving relationship with God, so it is already evident that the focus cannot primarily be on laws. Nonetheless, to fully understand a proper moral methodology (how the most important parts of the journey to happiness relate to each other), I will contrast the moral methodology of the Old Testament with that of the New Testament. We will see that even though laws and external rewards and punishments are very important, ultimately they exist to help humans become people capable of entering into and maintaining permanent, loving relationships with God and others.

MORAL THEOLOGY IN THE OLD TESTAMENT

The biblical concept of morality stems from the Jewish understanding of the covenant. Basically, all moral passages in the Bible are an exposition of the covenant with God. Hence, in order to understand the notion of moral theology in the Bible, it is necessary to understand the notion of covenant. Today, people associate covenants with the Bible and God's adoption of the Jewish people. However, in the ancient biblical world, covenants were common business and political practices (not just for the Israelites, but for many different people throughout the Middle East).[4] Because ancient people often could not appeal to a higher judicial authority to enforce treaties and contracts, they relied on covenants to maintain peace and support commerce.

A covenant was an unbreakable contract where both parties would swear before God (or gods, for those who were not Hebrew) that they would keep the terms of the contract. It was generally sealed by the killing of an animal, and all participants in the covenant believed that God (or gods) would do the same thing to them as happened to the animal if they broke the covenant.[5] For example, in Jeremiah 34:12–20, the Hebrew people make a covenant with their servants and swear before God. To seal the covenant they slaughter a calf and pass between its parts. However, they then break the covenant, and therefore God states that he will "make [them] like the calf which they cut in two, between whose two parts they passed . . . [God] will hand over all of them to their enemies, . . . their corpses shall be food for the birds of the air and beasts of the field" (Jer 34:18–20). Just as the calf was slaughtered to seal the covenant, the Israelites who broke the covenant will also be killed. Throughout the Bible the words "cut off" are used to describe what happens to someone who breaks the covenant.[6] Because most people during this time period believed in God (or gods), covenants were very effective ways to ensure that people would keep their treaties or contracts.

Since covenants were an important part of the ancient Middle Eastern culture and since God comes to his people and speaks to them in terms that they understand, he makes a covenant with the Israelites. God wants the Israelites to understand both that he is faithful to them and that they must be faithful to him. When God forms a covenant with them, they are assured that God will keep his promises, and they are also challenged to be faithful to God. For example, when Abram questions whether or not God will keep his promise of giving the land of Canaan to him (Gn 15:8), God responds by making a covenant with him and promises him the land of Canaan.[7] Later,

God will promise Abraham (by now his name has been changed) many descendants and that Abraham will be the father of many nations (Gn 17:3–8). In return, Abraham and his male descendants must be circumcised (Gn 17:9–14). Because of the cultural belief in the indissolubility of covenants, Abraham can confidently trust that God will keep his promises, and, furthermore, Abraham and his descendants are obligated to be faithful to God (or be killed).

Although God made various covenants with the Israelites, Old Testament morality is especially derived from the covenant with Moses. In this covenant God promises the Israelite people that they will be his chosen people (Ex 19:5). The nature of this promise is further explained throughout the first five books of the Bible (called the Pentateuch): God would bless the Israelite people with great material benefits and a long and prosperous life.[8] In return the Israelites agreed to follow the commandments (Ex 24:3). During this time period, when a king made a covenant with a tribal leader (or other vassal), the obligations would often consist of a general obligation to be faithful above all to the king, along with several specific obligations explaining how to be faithful.[9] For example, a king might require a vassal to first be faithful to him above all and then would require that the vassal show his faithfulness by not harboring his enemies and by other acts of loyalty. So also, when God makes the covenant with the Israelites, he first requires them to be faithful to him alone ("You shall not have other gods beside me.") and then expounds on this first commandment by giving them other commandments (traditionally numbered as nine other commandments).[10] Since the nine commandments were specific ways to remain faithful to God, breaking any of these commandments was a violation of the covenant and would result in the person or nation being "cut off." In other words, the same thing would happen to those who violate the covenant that happened to the bulls slaughtered to seal the covenant (Ex 24:3–8).[11]

Under this moral system, the Israelites understood that if they followed the Ten Commandments, they would live a long and materially prosperous life. However, if they broke the commandments, they would be punished by God. This theme is repeated multiple times throughout the Old Testament. For example, in Leviticus 26, God promises rewards, such as good crops, abundant food, peace, victory over enemies, and his abiding care to those that keep the commandments. However, to those that break the commandments, God threatens to inflict them with pestilence, severe famine, defeat by their enemies, and horrible deaths of intense suffering (cf. Dt 28). Thus, the terms of the covenant with Moses reveal the basic schema of moral theology in the Old Testament: the goal is material prosperity and the avoidance of physical pain and death. The way to attain this goal is by keeping the commandments. If the commandments are not kept, then God will punish the perpetrators. However, if God truly killed everyone who violated the covenant, there would be very few people left. Hence, God instituted a way to have transgressions of the covenant forgiven: the offering of sacrifices for sin (see Lv 16). Even though under the terms of the agreement violators of the covenant deserved death, God would allow for an animal (such as a sheep or goat) to be sacrificed in place of the sinner.

This moral system is very legalistic and obligation-based. It can be described as a *deontological* moral system. Ethicists will often differentiate between two types of moral systems: deontological and teleological systems. The word "deontological" comes from the Greek word for "duty" (*deon*). It is a moral system where actions are considered to be right or wrong based on whether or not they correspond to the will of the lawmaker. For example, in a deontological system, acts of murder are considered wrong because they violate a law made by a society and made by God. There are many different types of deontological systems.[12] The Old Testament system is based on God's divine commandments. In this system, the rules are primarily about external actions (as opposed to internal dispositions) and are based on the will of God. The rewards and punishments are also primarily external. The motivations for doing good actions are primarily fear of punishment and desire for material rewards. For example, in Joshua 24, Joshua tells the Israelites that they must fear God, for God is a jealous God who will destroy them if they serve other Gods. Notice how the Israelites are motivated to act out of fear of God's punishments.

Another example can be found in Psalm 73, where the psalmist questions why the wicked are prospering (for under the terms of the covenant, only those doing good should prosper; the wicked should be punished). The psalmist laments, "Such, then, are the wicked; always carefree, while they increase in wealth. Is it but in vain I have kept my heart clean and washed my hands as an innocent man?" Because the psalmist believes that the covenant benefits are bestowed by God on those that do good, he questions why he is struggling to do good when the wicked are prospering and he is suffering "chastisement with each new dawn" (Ps 73:12–14). However, as the psalm proceeds, he finds the answer to his question, "You [God] set them [the wicked], indeed, on a slippery road; you hurl them down to ruin" (v. 18; cf. v. 27). In other words, God is allowing them to prosper now so that their punishment will be even greater. On the other hand, God will eventually bring the innocent psalmist to his glory (v. 24). Here the deontological nature of the moral system can once more be seen: the wicked disobey the commandments and will eventually be physically punished, and the innocent will be rewarded.[13] Another example is Psalm 119, which spends 176 verses praising God's law and acknowledging God's "kindness" and "salvation" upon those who follow it.[14] An excellent short summary of the system can be found in the conclusion to Ecclesiastes: "Fear God and keep his commandments, for this is man's all; because God will bring to judgment every work" (12:12–23). Many other examples of the deontological nature of the moral system can be found in the Old Testament.[15]

Even in the New Testament, this deontological system still permeates the understanding of the Jewish people. See, for example, John 9:2, where the disciples ask Jesus about a blind man: "Who sinned, this man or his parents, that he was born blind?" In other words, blindness was considered to be a physical punishment resulting from sin.

See also Matthew 19:25, where the disciples are astounded that it will be difficult for the rich to enter the kingdom of heaven. The disciples are astounded because they believe that being rich is a material reward for keeping the covenant. Since these people are rich, they must be particularly faithful to God, and if the rich cannot enter the kingdom of heaven, then "who can be saved?" Both of these cases show the deontological understanding of the moral system, because the people's observance of external commands causes either physical punishment or material rewards. In both of these cases, Jesus corrects the disciples' understanding by stating that sin did not cause the blindness and that material wealth is a distraction, not a blessing. Jesus is introducing them to a different type of moral system, which we will explain below.

The primary moral system in the Old Testament was an external, deontological system based on following God's law and receiving material rewards and punishments. However, throughout the centuries before Christ another type of moral system based on an interior transformation of the person slowly begins to evolve. As early as the book of Job, the deontological nature of the system is questioned. Job is suffering, yet he has done no evil. The book implores, why is Job suffering if he has not broken the covenant? However, no satisfactory answer is yet given as God responds to Job in poetic words asking, if Job is so smart, does he understand how God created the world? (Jb 38). In other words, this is a mystery that the Israelites are not yet prepared to understand, God's greater plan. As God reveals more to the Israelites throughout the centuries, he begins to require them to cultivate interior dispositions and also follow external commands, and the reward becomes more and more focused on the possession of God himself, in addition to material possessions. For example, already in Deuteronomy 6, shortly after emphasizing the deontological nature of the covenant, God tells them, "You shall love the Lord, your God, with all your heart, and with all your soul, and with all your strength." God is not only a "jealous God" who must be feared and obeyed, but he is also a loving God who should be loved in return.[16] In reference to the covenantal rewards, multiple Psalms speak of the happiness that comes from keeping the commandments (e.g., Pss 1, 4, 40, 119). Although this happiness is still often tied to material goods (e.g., the fulfillment of the covenant promises in Psalm 40 and 119), it is also equated with the spiritual benefits of singing the praises of God and being faithful to him (e.g., Pss 4, 73, 75, and 119). In other words, along with the deontological system, a system concerned with the interior development of the person is beginning to develop in the Old Testament.

This system of internal development is called a *teleological* moral system. The word "teleological" comes from the Greek word for "end" (*telos*), as in something's perfection or completeness. In other words, a teleological system is focused on what actions should be done in order to become a particular type of person.[17] Whereas the deontological system was focused on external actions and rewards and punishments, a teleological system is especially focused on internal transformation resulting in the ability to perform one's proper action. In this type of moral system, actions are determined to be good or bad based on whether or not they lead to true happiness. However, as we will later see, this internal transformation still requires that humans perform good external actions, only now these actions are ordered toward the happiness of loving union with God rather than toward an external material reward.

In explaining the nature of happiness, we stated in chapter 3 that because God is an intelligent and good god, humans are happy when they perform their proper actions. God wants the ancient Israelites to be happy, so he comes to them and gives them commandments that are necessary for human happiness. However, because many of the Israelites are not yet ready to understand the fullness of God's plan, he establishes a deontological moral system that appeals to their desire for material goods and to their fear of punishment. Because this moral system is instituted through a covenantal system, God is able to gradually add more and more teleological elements to the system as the Israelites progressively begin to understand God's loving faithfulness. In other words, they saw that even though they constantly broke the covenant, God remained faithful and that God is a good god worth loving in and of himself.[18] Thus, teleological elements like offering sacrifices to show love of God[19] and seeking happiness in faithful relationships with God begin to enter into the moral system.[20] A deontological moral system is incomplete, and as God prepares the Israelites for the coming of the Word Incarnate by revealing more truths, he also gradually reveals more and more elements of a more comprehensive moral system. However, it is not until the New Testament that the moral system becomes primarily teleological.

MORAL THEOLOGY IN THE NEW TESTAMENT

The word "testament" comes from a Latin translation (*testamentum*) of the Greek word for "covenant" (*diatheke*). Thus, whereas the Old Testament tells about the old covenant, the New Testament tells about the new covenant. Just as the moral system of the Old Testament is derived from the old covenant, the moral system in the New Testament is likewise derived from the new covenant. Although we could study many passages of the New Testament to understand the terms of this covenant, a sufficient understanding of it can be obtained by studying the Sermon on the Mount in the book of Matthew, John 15, and various passages from Paul's epistles. A study of these passages will reveal a teleological moral system focused on attaining a loving union with the Father through Jesus Christ.

Matthew seeks to present Jesus as the new Israel by presenting parallels between what happened to Israel as a nation and what happens to Jesus. For example, the old Israel went to Egypt to avoid death (Gn 46–47), crossed the Red Sea (Ex 14), and was tempted in the desert for forty years (Ex 15, 17; Dt 8). Likewise, Jesus went to Egypt to avoid death at the hands of Herod (Mt 2:13–18), was baptized in the Jordan River (Mt 3:13–17), and was tempted in the desert for forty days (Mt 4:1–11). Just as the old

Israel received the terms of the old covenant (the Ten Commandments) on Mount Sinai (Ex 20), Jesus goes up on a mountain and gives the terms of the new covenant (the Sermon on the Mount, in Mt 5–7). Hence, Matthew uses the Sermon on the Mount to explain the terms of the new covenant.

The sermon begins with the beatitudes. The word "beatitude" comes from the Latin word for "happiness" (*beatitudo*). Hence, from the beginning, the focus is on happiness. The genre of the beatitudes is a covenant genre. Just as the terms of the Old Testament covenants were composed of obligations and blessings, so also the beatitudes each have an obligation and blessing. For example, the first beatitude is "Blessed are the poor in Spirit, for theirs is the kingdom of heaven" (Mt 5:3). The benefit reflects back on the covenant benefit promised to David: his kingdom would last forever (2 Sm 7:16). However, this kingdom promised by Christ is not primarily a political kingdom but a spiritual kingdom that exists wherever Christ's saving grace brings people into a loving relationship with God.[21] To enter into this kingdom, humans must first be poor in spirit. In other words, they must be humble. Humility is necessary to enter into any loving relationship because only humble people can make the needs and goals of others more important than their own. Those who are prideful always consider their own needs and goals as most important and, hence, are incapable of entering into a true loving friendship with others. Thus, humility is necessary for Christians to make God's goals the most important aspect of their lives. By requiring humans to be humble, Jesus is requiring humans to have an internal disposition that is necessary for the happiness of loving relationships.

Because the beatitudes will be analyzed in the chapter on charity (chapter 14), it is not necessary to cover all of them now. However, a few more points need to be illuminated to fully understand the nature of the new covenant. Once humans have humility, they are able to make God's goals their own. This causes them to seek to share in the mission of Christ. Christ's mission is that of a suffering servant who teaches how to love others by sacrificing his own life. Hence, the second beatitude is "Blessed are those who mourn, for they will be consoled" (Mt 5:4). Sharing in Christ's suffering servant mission will require humans to be meek (5:5), to be merciful to others (5:7), to love God above all other things (5:8), and to spread the peace that comes from being part of the kingdom of heaven (5:9). In return, the new covenant reward will consist of being united to God as his children and sharing in God's happiness by seeing God as he is (5:8–9). These terms of the new covenant highlight the required internal dispositions necessary to perform the actions of knowing and loving God. Hence, whereas the old covenant was especially concerned with external actions, the new covenant begins with a focus on internal (spiritual) dispositions. Furthermore, the rewards for keeping the covenant are no longer material but are the internal, spiritual rewards of entering into a loving relationship with God (eventually, eternally).

However, the requirement for spiritual dispositions does not mean that the external obligations of the old covenant are jettisoned. Christ states that he did not come to abolish the old covenant law, or prophets, but to fulfill it (Mt 5:17). He emphasizes that the external elements of the law must still be kept; however, they must flow from proper internal dispositions. In other words, Jesus is extending the terms of the old covenant to include the dispositions necessary for loving others. For example, Jesus states that you have heard it said that you should not kill, "but I say to you, whoever is angry with his brother will be liable to judgment" (5:22). He also says that the old law stated not to commit adultery, but Jesus says not to lust (5:27–28). Jesus further teaches the importance of honesty (5:37) and not retaliating (5:39).

Then, to especially emphasize the nature of the new covenant, Jesus talks about loving one's enemies. He states that there is nothing exceptional about loving only one's friends, for even unjust people do this. Rather, Christians should be like God, who loves everyone: "For he makes the sun rise on the bad and the good and causes rain to fall on the just and unjust" (Mt 5:45). This statement further shows the transformation of the terms of the covenant. In the Old Testament, a common punishment for the unjust who broke the covenant was famine caused by drought (e.g., Dt 28:23–24). By specifically stating that God showers material benefits on both the just and unjust, Jesus shows that the primary benefits and punishments of the new covenant are no longer material but spiritual: being "children of your heavenly father" (Mt 5:45). As children of God, the way that Christians are most like their heavenly Father is by loving everyone, especially their enemies. In doing this, they are made perfect, as their heavenly Father is perfect (5:48). The word translated as "perfect" (*teleios*) is derived from the Greek word *telos*, which is also the source of the word "teleology." In Greek, something's *telos* is its proper end, that which fulfills it. In other words, Jesus is saying that the action that especially fulfills us as humans and makes us like God is the act of loving everyone, especially our enemies.

In the Sermon on the Mount, the teleological nature of the new covenant is emphasized. The goal of the moral life is to attain the dispositions and virtues that give humans the ability to enter into a loving union with God as his children. Virtues such as humility, meekness, and love are especially emphasized. The external actions of the commandments must still be kept, but these become secondary.

These teleological themes are further expanded in the Gospel of John. Although this entire gospel is filled with great moral insights, the passage that especially shows the nature of the new covenant is found in chapter 15. The chapter begins by calling Christ the vine, the Father the vine grower, and Christians the branches. This metaphor is used to explain the relationship between Christians and God. Only by being united to Christ and receiving power from him can Christians bear fruit (become Christ's disciples and perform proper actions). Those that are not united to Christ will be "thrown out and burned."

The passage then gives many of the essential elements of the new covenant moral life by further explaining the metaphorical bearing of fruit as Christ's disciples. The way that Christians share in God's power to bear fruit is by being united to Christ.

They are united to Christ through the love of the Father found in the Son: "As the Father loves me, so I also love you, remain in my love" (Jn 15:9). The way of maintaining this love is then explained: "If you keep my commandments, you will remain in my love, just as I have kept my Father's commandments and remained in his love" (15:10). Those that love others make the goals of the other people their own. Jesus shows that his love of the Father has caused him to keep the Father's commandments, and if we love Jesus, we will also keep his commandments. The role of commandments in a teleological system is elucidated in this passage: commandments are followed as acts of love resulting in loving union. Jesus then states the nature of the commandment, "love one another as I love you" (15:12). To make sure the disciples understand how intense this love should be, he states, "No one has greater love than this, to lay down one's life for his friends" (15:13). In other words, to perform our proper actions (bear fruit), humans must love others with their entire being, just as God is love by nature.

However, unlike the old covenant, where the motivation to follow commandments was fear or worldly desire, now the motivation is love guided by knowledge. Jesus states, "I no longer call you slaves, because a slave does not know what his master is doing. I have called you friends, because I have told you everything I have heard from my Father" (Jn 15:15). The commandments are not followed in blind obedience according to the will of a distant lawgiver, the commandments are followed because Christians understand that they co-workers in bringing God's plan to completion. They understand God's revealed goal and are driven by love to complete it. They are not just servants as in a deontological system; they are friends of God, for he loves them and allows them to share in his plan. By sharing in this plan, they perform their proper actions and bear great fruit.

When humans perform these actions that participate in God's love, they are happy, for they share in God's happiness. Jesus states, "I have told you this so that my joy might be in you and your joy might be complete."[22] The goal of the moral life is to be true friends with God, and if humans are friends with God, he will share his love and happiness with them. In other words, as we have seen in the first three chapters, God made humans so that they are happy when they perform their proper actions of loving God and others, and the deeper the love, the more intense this happiness will be. Thus, although the Christian moral life certainly contains laws and obligations, at its core it is about being open to God's transforming grace so that Christians can attain the dispositions necessary to cultivate enduring friendships with God and others.

These passages in Matthew and John show that the moral methodology of the New Testament is different from that of the Old Testament. Whereas the Old Testament method is primarily deontological, the New Testament is primarily teleological. In the Old Testament, the focus was on obeying laws in order to avoid punishments and to attain material goods. The people were primarily seen as servants of God who blindly obeyed God's will.[23] However, with Christ, the hidden plan (*mysterion*) of God is finally revealed (Eph 1:1–14). Humans are made to be united to God through Jesus Christ. Hence, the focus is on the internal dispositions necessary to enter into loving friendship with God. The commandments must still be obeyed, but now they are seen as guidelines given by a loving Father. These wise guidelines help humans love each other and attain happiness. Jesus is now our friend, and because of our love of him, we make his goals (our unique role in his saving mission), joys (supernatural happiness), and earthly sufferings our own. When humans fail to perform their proper actions and become friends with God, they are unhappy. The punishment for breaking the new covenant is this separation from God. Recall that in John 15, those that do not bear fruit are separated from the vine and burned (15:6). In the Sermon on the Mount, Jesus states that those who fail to keep the covenant will be thrown into Gehenna (the city dump).[24] Although the main point of these passages is to show the spiritual suffering that happens to those who do not love God (i.e., hell), they can also be interpreted in a more deontological way (as an external suffering) for those who need a more concrete motivation to begin growing in virtue. Nonetheless, the primary moral methodology in the New Testament is teleological.

Having seen the general moral methodology of the New Testament, we will now consult the epistles of Paul to explain further how the various components of the moral life work together. By studying Paul, we can construct the basic map for the journey to God's happiness. In analyzing Matthew and John, we noted that laws and virtues (internal dispositions) are necessary components of the moral life. John also especially emphasizes that without God's love working within humans (from grace), they are not able to share in God's happiness. Paul explains how all of these different components of the moral life fit together.[25]

Prior to the time of Christ, both the Jews and the Gentiles living in Rome had a sophisticated standard for morality. The Jews had the Old Testament law given to them by God. As long as they kept this law, they would receive benefits. A frequent theme in the Old Testament is how blessed the Jews are because God has given them the law (e.g., Pss 19 and 119). The Gentiles had Greek wisdom (the Stoics, Plato, and Aristotle). One of the high points of Greek wisdom was its moral philosophy, which contained an elaborate account of how the virtues perfected human nature. Both groups took great pride in their ethical systems.

These two groups were both part of the Church in Rome between 50 and 60 AD, and they argued about who was the best. The Jews claimed that they were the best because they had been given the Jewish law. The Gentiles claimed that they were the best because they had Greek wisdom. On account of their prideful boasting, a division arose between them, and St. Paul rebuked both sides firmly (see Rom 1–3). Paul noted that neither Greek wisdom nor the Jewish law had the power to save, but that all were saved through faith in Jesus Christ given to them by God's grace (Rom 3:30).

Later in his writings, Paul notes that true faith in Jesus also includes love of God (charity).[26] Paul frequently speaks of the necessity of love for salvation, but the role of love is especially emphasized when he states, "If I have all faith so as to move moun-tains, but do not have love, I am nothing."[27] Consequently, faith in Jesus Christ is perfected in charity. Faith and charity are essential to salvation because they unite Christians to Christ, forming them into his body, the Church (Eph 4:16). In other words, knowledge causes love, which causes unity. The faith gives supernatural knowl-edge of God, and charity (love) unites Christians to Christ, causing his mission to be their mission. As members of Christ's body, each has a particular role in building up the Church (1 Cor 12–14). United to Christ, Christians are a new creation (2 Cor 5:17), and the Holy Spirit becomes the primary source of their actions (Gal 5:24–25).

Because salvation is from the grace of Jesus Christ, neither the old law nor human virtues have the power to save. Through their prideful boasting, Christians in Rome were making the Old Testament law and human wisdom more important than the unity found in Christ. Consequently, Paul had to categorically deny that anything was more important than being united to Christ.[28] However, once Paul established that, above all else, faith and charity are necessary for salvation, he then made use of the Jewish law and the Greek virtues to implement faith and love.[29] In other words, once Christians are united to Christ through faith and love, the law guides them to actions that are truly in accord with the Christian faith. Likewise, the virtues are essential for applying charity to their life. I will further expound on these last two points.

The law has two roles in Paul's writings. First, as seen in the first chapters of Ro-mans, the law condemns people because they are unable to keep it. This condemna-tion drives them to seek the grace of Christ in order to be reconciled to the Father through faith and love. However, once they are reconciled to the Father, the law be-comes a guide. For example, in 1 Corinthians 6:9–10, Paul notes that the unjust will not inherit the kingdom of God. He then gives examples of those who are unjust: for-nicators, idolaters, adulterers, practicing homosexuals, thieves, greedy, drunkards, and so on. Although this list is aimed at promoting unity among the people of Corinth, the root of these condemnations can be found in the Old Testament law. Paul continues by noting that the Corinthians' bodies are members of Christ and that they must avoid immorality. Although the old law does not have the power to save, it still has the power to guide Christians to good actions because it is from God.[30] In addition to the guid-ance from the Old Testament law, Paul writes that humans are especially guided to good actions by the new law of the Spirit (Rom 8). Those who are not guided by the law of the Spirit cannot be saved.

The Greek virtues are also essential for salvation. Once someone has faith, hope, and charity, the Greek virtues can be utilized to build up the Body of Christ. In other words, these virtues are transformed by charity so that they are no longer ordered to natural ends but to spiritual ends. Paul notes, "Finally, brothers, fill your minds with everything that is good and pure, everything that we love and honor, and everything that can be thought virtuous (*arete*) or worthy of praise."[31] The term *arete* refers to the classic Greek virtues.[32] In other places, Paul speaks of virtues that are essential for Christians to live a life of charity.[33] In general, Paul's attitude towards natural wisdom or virtues can be summed up in 1 Thessalonians 5:21: "Test everything, retain what is good." If some natural "wisdom" or virtue violates Christianity, it should be removed. However, if some natural virtue helps someone to live a Christian life, it should be retained.

The classic Greek virtues of *prudence, justice, temperance,* and *fortitude* are all essential to living a life of charity. People with charity love God and seek to implement his goals in their lives by loving others. However, without prudence they will be unable to determine which actions are truly loving. Without justice they will have trouble giving others their due. Without temperance and fortitude they may lack the self-control and courage to perform loving actions. For example, since loving someone makes their friends your friends, loving God requires humans to love everyone. If we truly love the poor, their needs become our needs. However, prudence is needed to determine the best way to help the poor. Temperance is needed to consume in moderation so that there will be something to give to the poor. Fortitude is needed to help a person have the courage to give away money, even during difficult financial times. Giving to the poor is an act of charity, but it is implemented through the other virtues.

Paul's moral theology can be summarized in the following way: Paul notes that the natural law (Rom 2:14–15), natural virtues, and Old Testament law are all good (Rom 3:2 and Phil 4:8), yet, they do not have the power to save. Salvation requires the grace of God transforming humans into a new creation. Once humans are transformed by grace, they are given the gifts of *faith, hope,* and *charity.*[34] These gifts allow humans to perform actions by the power of the Holy Spirit. However, once humans have faith and charity, the old law and natural law help humans determine the proper actions. Furthermore, charity is applied through the virtues. Transformed by grace, the virtues and the law cause good acts leading to the ultimate act of eternal happiness.

An examination of both the Old and New Testaments shows that a complete moral methodology should be teleological. However, an examination of how God gradually led the Israelites from an incomplete moral system to a more complete one shows that in trying to teach someone moral theology, the pupil is not always mature enough to understand a teleological system. In other words, for beginners in the moral life, sometimes the deontological aspects need to be emphasized, and after they grow in knowledge and virtue, they will be ready for the full teleological system. For example, if a two-year-old is biting his sister, it is not particularly helpful to explain to him that he will not be as happy if he keeps biting his sister because he is harming his friendship with her. The two-year-old will not understand these points, and at this point he does not have the virtues that would allow him to be happy in controlling his anger. Instead, he must be told that if he bites his sister, he will receive some sort of punishment. Although parents have a teleological system in their mind (they want the two-year-old to be transformed to perform his proper actions), they present a deontological system to the two-year-old. In past centuries, the Catholic Church was often composed of uneducated members who were often preoccupied with attaining the necessities of life. It was sometimes prudent to simply command the laity to avoid certain actions because they were sometimes not educated enough to understand the more complete moral system. Hence, the emphasis was on laws and obligations, and heaven and hell were presented as basically external rewards and punishments. As the general population has become more and more educated, it is extremely important that moral theology be presented in its completeness: as a teleological system. Educated people will quickly deduce the contradiction between a good and intelligent God and deontological system built on fear and external rewards.

When forming those just beginning on the moral journey, laws and obligations might be primarily emphasized, but, in general, the map to eternal happiness should be structured around the notion that humans are fulfilled by performing a particular type of action. The starting place for the map is human nature and the ultimate goal is sharing in God's happiness as his friend. Also, as we see in Matthew, permanent internal dispositions (virtues) must be formed so humans are capable of entering into loving relationships. Furthermore, laws must still be kept to guide humans in properly loving others. Furthermore, as in Paul's epistles, actions flowing solely from human nature cannot save, that is, bring people into loving union with God. Hence, the transforming power of God's grace must have a prominent place in any moral system (as must faith and love).

Based on the New Testament, the map to the journey must therefore include human nature, natural inclinations, grace (and faith and love), good human actions, law, and virtues, and, of course, it must end with a participation in God's eternal happiness, where humans know and love God as he is (1 Cor 13:12). These are most of the basic components of the moral life; however, many individual parts of the system, along with the relation between the parts, have yet to be explained. At this point, we have covered in detail only human nature, the natural inclinations, and natural and eternal happiness. All the other elements and more on how they relate to each other will be covered in the following chapters.

5

THE INDIVIDUAL STEPS ON THE JOURNEY

Human Actions

In the Gospel of John, friendship with God is the goal of the journey. However, any truly good friendship takes time and effort. Humans are complex individuals who have been shaped into unique persons, both by their genetics and a myriad of different experiences. To become deeply acquainted with someone can involve years of observing her actions, listening to her stories, meeting her friends and family, and working together with her. Furthermore, because love is expressed through bodily actions, a deep and permanent love can only be communicated through an abundance of loving actions. In other words, to truly become friends with others requires one to do many different loving actions to attain knowledge of the other person and to express love of the other. And even when authentic friendship is achieved, because life on earth is constantly changing, friends must continue to spend time communicating with each other so that they learn these changes and can continue to make each other's needs, sufferings, joys, and goals their own and love each other accordingly. Just as human friendship requires many actions over the course of a lifetime, friendship with God also requires a multitude of actions, not only for one's earthly life but also for eternity. Thus, in the journey to happiness, the individual steps of the journey are composed of good human actions.

In later chapters we will look at the causes of these good actions (grace, laws, virtue, etc.), but this chapter will focus on the nature of the actions themselves. In a teleological system, every action should be ordered toward the end of loving union with God. Or, to speak in terms of the journey, since the destination is God, every step along the way (the actions) must be moving toward the goal of God. In order to help ensure that actions are truly ordered toward loving union with God, an analysis of human action is beneficial. First, this chapter will analyze the difference between "human actions" (freely chosen) and "actions of a human" (not freely chosen), then human actions will be broken down into various steps to help one understand how to make actions more perfect, and finally we will examine the different components of what makes an action good (versus evil).

HUMAN ACTIONS

Actions expressing love are important steps on a journey to friendship. Yet, for an action to truly express love, it must be freely chosen. If someone accidentally aids others in attaining their goals, the action is not considered to be a loving action. Or if someone is completely forced to help a person out, it is also not considered to be loving. For an action to truly express love, it must freely proceed from the will. These freely chosen actions are called "human actions." Ultimately, only through human actions are people able to progress closer to (or farther from) their goal of sharing in God's happiness as his friends. Thus, to better understand how to love God, we will study the nature of human actions.

In ordinary language, the term "human action" means roughly the same thing as the term "action of a human." However, in moral theology these two terms take on technical meanings to show the distinction between acts that are freely chosen (human actions) and all other actions (actions of a human). Only acts that are freely chosen are considered moral actions and can be ordered to loving union with God. The legal system makes a similar distinction between an act that is deliberately chosen (such as first-degree murder), an act that did not contain prior deliberation or planning (such as second-degree murder or voluntary manslaughter), and an act that was completely accidental. At the heart of these distinctions is a realization that humans are more accountable for some actions than for others because of the active role of the intellect and will within the action. Although moral theology is less concerned with the relation between civil punishment and accountability within an action, it is very concerned with how different types of actions affect our relationship with God and others in different ways. To bring to light these different types of actions, we make a distinction between human actions and acts of a human. This distinction is rooted in human nature as made in God's image.

In chapter 1, I talked about how all created things are in God's image in different degrees. All created things are in God's image as having being, while others, such as dogs, have being, life, and sense knowledge. Human nature contains these perfections that it shares with other creatures (such as being, life, and sense knowledge) and additional perfections that are specific to humans (the ability to know and love God and others). Thus, what is distinct about human nature is the ability to know and love God and others. Since the nature of something determines the type of actions that it can do, humans can both perform actions that are common to other things in creation (such as living, growing, sensing, etc.), and they can perform actions that are distinct to humans (those that come from the intellect and will). Those actions that both humans and other creatures are able to perform are called "actions of a human." Examples of these actions include breathing, growing, digesting food, and so on. Those actions that are distinctive in humans (as knowing and loving beings) are called "human actions."[1]

Because human actions proceed from the ability of humans to know and love, they are freely chosen. Chapter 1 explained how freedom comes from our ability to know a goal, know at least one option to attain the goal, and choose the action based on our love for the goal. Thomas Aquinas affirms this by noting that a human action proceeds from a "deliberate will."[2] The term "deliberate" refers to the fact that the intellect has determined the proper course of action to a goal. "Will" refers to the movement of the will loving a particular way of attaining the goal. Consequently, a human action only exists when someone knows the goal or purpose of the action and wills the action to attain this goal. These actions that come from a deliberate will are also called "voluntary actions." The word "voluntary" comes from the Latin word for "will" (voluntas). Thus, the very word "voluntary" denotes that something is deliberately willed. When humans perform human actions, they are considered the masters of their actions. In other words, they are responsible for their actions. All other actions humans perform that are not voluntary are actions of a human.

Some actions proceed from irrational powers and are not normally human actions, such as digesting food, snoring, or sleepwalking. However, other actions that normally proceed from the intellect and will (and are human actions) are sometimes not freely chosen because of some defect in the intellect, will, or emotions. For example, a loss of rationality in the intellect can cause an action that appears to be a human action to be only an act of a human. The more severe the defect, the more freedom is diminished. The defects that diminish freedom that I will analyze are those in the intellect, disordered passions, bad habits, and coercion.

Defects in the intellect can result from either ignorance or a lack of functioning within the intellect. Ignorance can diminish freedom when either someone does not know the relevant moral laws or someone does not know the relevant aspects of a situation. An example of the first type of ignorance is when someone does not know that drunk driving is wrong. He may freely choose to drink and drive, but he is not freely choosing an evil action because he does not know that drunk driving is evil. An example of ignorance of the situation is when someone becomes inebriated because he does not know that there is alcohol in the punch. He may freely choose to drink, but he does not freely choose to get drunk, and hence getting drunk was not a human action.

Not all types of ignorance remove voluntariness from an action. For example, suppose someone missed Mass on Sunday because he chose not to call to find out the Mass times. Although he was ignorant of the Mass times, the action of missing Mass is still voluntary because he could have easily learned the necessary information. Consequently, a distinction is made between *vincible* and *invincible* ignorance. Vincible ignorance exists when the pertinent information should have been known. In other words, it exists when someone is negligent in seeking the truth. This type of ignorance does not remove voluntariness (but it can diminish voluntariness). Perhaps the most common type of vincible ignorance is when people choose not to learn moral truths out of laziness or attachment to evil. Invincible ignorance exists when there is no practical way that someone could have known the pertinent truth. Since these people do not know what they are doing, invincible ignorance removes voluntariness from the actions.

The improper functioning of the intellect can also diminish or remove voluntariness. For example, if a man is under the influence of drugs, his intellect may be unable to properly determine the correct action. Voluntariness would then be removed (but he may still be considered accountable for his action if he willingly chose to misuse the drugs). Other examples of this type of defect in the intellect are extreme tiredness, mental illness, or even lack of development, as in the case of a young child.[3] Often in these cases, voluntariness is only diminished, but it can be completely removed, causing the action to be an action of a human and not a human action.

Disordered emotions can also diminish or destroy voluntariness. For example, I once heard a true story about a woman who was dreadfully afraid of snakes. The house she lived in had old stone walls that snakes liked to use to keep cool in the summer. One warm day she was bathing her toddler children when a bull snake slithered into the bathroom. A bull snake can be large, but it is not venomous and is not particularly dangerous to humans. Because of her fear, she crawled on top of a chair in a state of sheer panic. Meanwhile, the snake proceeded to find its way into the bathtub where the remaining young child helplessly sat. (The older children abandoned the tub.) Because of her fear, the woman was completely unable to move from the chair. In the end, the snake did not harm the child but slithered away. The woman's husband eventually came home and killed the snake. Although the story may seem anticlimactic, the point of the story is that because of the intensity of the emotion of fear, the woman lost all rationality and was not free to remove her children from the tub. If the woman had retained some rationality, then her voluntariness would have only been diminished and not removed. Voluntariness is diminished when, because of the influence of an emotion on either the intellect or the will, the correct action is extremely difficult to choose (but not impossible, as in the case of complete removal of rationality). The emotions of anger, fear, and lustful desire can especially diminish or remove voluntariness.

Bad habits can also remove or diminish voluntariness. When humans are in the habit of performing a particular action, they may perform it without thinking about what they are doing. For example, during times of stress, people in the habit of smoking cigarettes may begin smoking a cigarette without even thinking about what they are doing. However, if the people smoking do judge whether the act is right or wrong, then the act might be voluntary even if the freedom is diminished by the habit. Furthermore, like the cases of vincible ignorance, if the person with the habit is not actively trying to get rid of the habit, then the action can still be considered voluntary.

Last of all, coercion can also diminish or destroy voluntariness. If someone is physically forced to perform an action that goes against her will, then this type of coercion completely removes voluntariness. For example, if a bank teller is forced at gunpoint to empty the safe, the teller is not committing the act of theft. Other cases of coercion may diminish freedom but not remove it. For example, during the time of the Roman persecutions, the bishops of the Catholic Church varied the severity of the penances in accord with the different forms of the sin of apostasy (a denial of the faith) that were committed by the people. The Romans commanded all within their empire to worship the emperor or face the penalty of death. Since Christians only believe in one God, to worship the emperor was to deny the faith. After the persecutions, many of the Christians, who had apostatized, sought to be reconciled with the Church by confessing their sins to the bishop. Those who immediately denied the faith upon hearing the edict were given the most severe penance. However, those who only denied the faith after being tortured were given a lesser penance.[4] This example shows that the early bishops recognized that coercion and torture can diminish freedom.

For an action to be a human action, it must be freely chosen. Only human actions are moral actions and hence either take us toward our end of God or away from our end of God. Actions of a human may bring great evil into the world, but they do not directly affect the progress of humans on their journey to God. For example, if someone accidently kills someone else, he does not commit the human action of murder and is not morally responsible for this action. His love of God is not diminished by the action because the action was not freely chosen. However, he does hurt another person, and many lives are affected by the action. Many defects can diminish or remove voluntariness. If voluntariness is removed (i.e., the agent does not judge whether the action is right or wrong), then the act is not a human action. If voluntariness is diminished, then the act is still a human action, but the agent's responsibility is mitigated. As we can see in this analysis, there are various degrees of freedom. Some actions are freer than others based on the degree that the intellect and will are properly functioning when acting. As long some degree of freedom exists, the actions are considered to be human actions.

The distinction between a human action and an act of a human can be especially helpful because it shows the importance of the proper functioning of the intellect, will, and emotions in performing free actions. When these powers are not functioning properly, freedom is diminished. Hence, there is a need to develop these powers through virtues and guidance, as we will see in later chapters. Furthermore, because these powers use the body as an instrumental cause, a physiological deficiency can also result in a lack of freedom. For example, because of the effect that hormones have on the emotions, a hormone imbalance can diminish and even remove freedom in certain cases. Injuries to the brain or endocrine system can also diminish or remove freedom. The use of pharmacology (or other physiological treatment) might be necessary to help the body function properly so that a person can be free. There can also be environmental factors that result in neurosis or even psychosis. In these situations, psychological treatment might be necessary to aid the person in attaining a minimal level of freedom.[5] Without at least a minimal degree of freedom, humans are not responsible for their actions and are unable to progress (or even regress) on their journey to God. However, in most of the examples mentioned above, freedom is merely diminished and not removed. In these cases, humans are still able to progress (or regress), but it can be significantly more difficult to make headway. Because there are so many ways that people can lose freedom, humans should always refrain from judging other people's souls. When my students ask me about the degree of culpability a particular person has for his or her evil actions, I reply, "I'm in sales, not in management." In other words, because of my love for God and my desire to see that others are happy, it is my job to spread the faith to others, but it is not my job to determine whether or not others are guilty of sin. God can determine a person's accountability in acting.

THE TWELVE STEPS OF THE HUMAN ACTION

Now that a human action has been defined, we can analyze the action at a much deeper level. The goal of this analysis is to help people understand actions better so that they can perform their proper actions. It is easy see that a human action contains a number of steps. For example, everyone has intended to do something, then researched how to do the action, and yet chosen not to perform the action. Without much investigation of one's experiences, these three basic steps of intention, research, and choice can be determined. A more inclusive investigation might yield other steps, such as judging which action to perform or commanding oneself to do the action. Following the thought of Aquinas, moral scholars have put together a much more comprehensive and helpful list encompassing twelve steps in a human action.[6] These twelve steps flow from the natural way that humans think and love.

Are there really twelve steps in a human action? Anything with twelve steps seems like it should be complicated and lengthy. However, even young children can perform human actions without trouble. Furthermore, human actions often seem to happen quickly. For example, there is usually nothing complicated or lengthy about the process of deciding where to eat lunch. Yet, most people can think of a time when the decision to eat lunch was probably very complicated and long. Perhaps there were a number of different competing goals to the act of eating lunch: Should lunch be healthy, tasty, convenient, or fast? Even after deciding upon a particular goal (lunch should be fast) there may be many different options that could attain this goal: the cafeteria, fast food, a sack lunch. . . . And even after deciding the best option, it can be difficult to perform the action. The point is that even though some actions are simple and quick, other actions can be long and complicated. Within some of these longer actions, twelve distinct steps can be identified.

One reason that many actions are simple and quick is that the agent has already completed many of the twelve steps in previous similar actions and does not need to go through them again. For example, if Joe is always in the habit of eating at the same place for the same reason, he does not need to think through the entire twelve steps each time. Also, sometimes people simply fail to think about what they are doing, causing them to miss important steps in the decision-making process. Consequently, the twelve steps are for an ideal action that is traced from the very beginning of the action until the end. In point of fact, very few actions go through all twelve steps.

However, if some actions can be determined easily, why needlessly complicate the process by dissecting the action into twelve steps? An analogy borrowed from coaching athletes can be helpful in explaining why this dissection is essential. In many sports, actions that look extremely simple can be very difficult for someone without training. For example, the pros often make hitting a baseball look extremely simple. Yet, many young children struggle with learning to hit effectively because there are a number of different aspects of hitting that need to be perfected. Thus, a good coach will often break down the action of hitting into a number of different steps.[7] The goal of this process is to identify which steps of the action the batter is having trouble with so that the problem can be corrected. For example, if the batter is having trouble with bat control, the coach can think of an exercise that will correct this problem, such as constantly swinging the bat in a certain way. The same logic applies to the breakdown of the human action. Many people fail to perform actions that they would like to perform, or their performance is poor. By breaking down the action, the problem can be identified. Once the problem is identified, the person can work on a particular virtue to perfect the defect. Just as practicing the different steps of hitting a baseball causes one to be a good hitter, the formation of different virtues through the practice of the different steps of a human action cause one to be good at performing actions. Thankfully, divine aid is also available to help with human actions.

Since a human action stems from the intellect and will, the twelve steps are found in these two powers. Furthermore, within an action, the intellect and will always work together. *If there is a step in the intellect, there must be a corresponding step in the will.* They must work together because, on one hand, the intellect supplies knowledge of the things that the will loves. Without this knowledge, the will has nothing to love. On the other hand, the love of the will drives the intellect to set goals and to determine how to attain them. Without this love, the intellect will not pursue the completion of an action. One of the reasons for studying the twelve steps is to illuminate the essential collaboration between the intellect and the will. The different steps within the intellect correspond to the diverse ways humans naturally know things. Although the steps in the will have different names, ultimately they are all simply acts of love and are only differentiated because they are responses to the diverse acts of the intellect. Table 5.1 lists the twelve steps of the human action. We will then give a detailed description of each step.[8]

Table 5.1. The 12 Steps of the Human Action

Intellect	Will
1. **Simple Apprehension** of the things.	2. **Desire for the Good Apprehended**.
3. **Understanding of the End** (goal or law) to be pursued.	4. **Intention of the End** (goal or law).
5. **Counsel** (the acts of research and reasoning, moving from the universal to the particular).	6. **Consent** to the various activities of reason.
7. **Judgment** (judging the particular by the more universal).	8. **Choice** of the proper means.
9. **Command**.	10. **Execution**.
11. **Contemplation of the End Attained** (the act of happiness).	12. **Joy/Delight in the End Attained** (the secondary element of happiness).

STEP 1: SIMPLE APPREHENSION

Since the will can only love what is known by the intellect, the first step of the human action begins in the intellect. Simple apprehension is not only the first step of the human action, it is also the first act of the intellect in general.[9] In other words, all intellectual activities begin with this step. In this step, the intellect first begins to understand what things are by abstracting concepts from sense knowledge.[10] These concepts represent things that exist in reality, and these concepts are the building blocks of thinking, since thinking takes place when concepts are united together. For example, a baby has many sense experiences of various different foods before it understands the concept of an apple. Once the baby has the concept of an apple, the baby is able to link this concept to other concepts to form sentences, such as "An apple is good for eating." This step is called "simple apprehension," because it is only the beginning of the complete understanding of something. Because humans learn things gradually through sense knowledge, the first concepts they form are generally incomplete, and additional thinking is necessary to gain a more perfect understanding of something. For example, as the baby grows up, she will learn more about apples, such as that they can come in various sizes, colors, textures, and flavors. In the human action, multiple concepts are needed to set goals and to determine how to attain these goals.

Because an explanation of the twelve steps can be abstract, as I explain each step some concrete examples are needed. I will use the following three examples throughout my discussion: (1) the act of finding one's vocation (the state of life God calls you to), (2) the act of deciding to come to class, and (3) the act of driving safely. In order to perform these actions the intellect must have concepts of a vocation, of class, and of driving safely. In addition to these concepts, the intellect must understand all other concepts that will be related to these concepts in performing an action, such as the concepts of marriage, religious life, good grades, and so on. This first step is very important because a misunderstanding of an essential moral concept can lead to evil actions. For example, in regard to how to treat some of the most vulnerable members of society, if people do not understand what it means to be a person, they may mistakenly consider the unborn, mentally handicapped, or those who are unconscious to not actually be persons. A result of this error might be to cause them to think that neglecting or even killing these people is allowable.

Although people are constantly learning new concepts, most of the concepts that are used in moral reasoning were learned as children. Consequently, in the actual performance of an action, only rarely do people have to begin with this first step because they already have the necessary concepts. However, when it comes to difficult decisions, it is necessary to make sure that all the pertinent concepts are properly understood.[11] Sometimes new concepts must be learned in order to perform a different type of action.

Step 2: Desire for the Good Apprehended

In order for the intellect to take these concepts and form goals, the will must desire the good thing that is apprehended. Once the will desires the good, it moves the intellect to form goals, which is the next step. Usually this step takes place in the following way: people already have thousands of different concepts of good things in their mind. At any particular point, a situation will arise that reminds them of one of these good things, and they begin to desire it. This desire then sets the person in motion towards the end of completing an action. For example, Joe might be wondering about his future after college. These thoughts might cause him to think of graduating, which the will then desires. The desire of the will then sets the intellect into the motion of setting the goal of graduating (steps 3 and 4). The person can then begin to think of different ways to attain this goal (step 5).

Step 3: Understanding of the End (Goal or Law)

Because humans are intelligent beings, they do things for a purpose. Hence, human actions are always ordered to a particular goal or end. In other words, a human action by nature is teleological in that it is ordered to a particular end. In this step of understanding the goal, the different concepts are united together to form a goal or a law (the end of the action). For beginners in the moral life, other people must often determine the proper end of an action by dictating a law. For example, parents may set the law that their children must do well in school or the law that their children cannot date until they reach a certain age. At other times, the goal is self-determined. However, even in these cases, a goal acts as a self-imposed law in the sense that it directs one to a proper end.

This step of understanding the goal corresponds with the second act of the intellect.[12] The first act of the intellect was forming concepts by simple apprehension of things. Now that the intellect has concepts, it can understand things by joining or separating concepts into premises or sentences.[13] By uniting concepts with others or by dividing them, the thoughts in the intellect more properly reflect reality and give the person a more perfect understanding of the things themselves. For example, the baby with the concept of an apple can unite it with the concept of growing on trees.[14] Now the baby understands that the concept of apple includes the notion of growing on trees. Her understanding of apples is perfected. Humans are constantly understanding things by comparing new concepts to ones that are already in their mind. Every time teachers ask if a student understands something, they are asking if the student took the concepts given in class and united them to (or divided them from) concepts that were already contained in the students' minds.

In terms of the human act, the concepts that are desired are united together to form goals, such as "I am going to pursue my vocation," or "I am going to graduate," or "I am going to drive safely." Concepts could also be separated into laws, such as "I will not steal" or "I will not lie." These goals act as universal premises and must still be applied to a situation.[15] People that lack the ability to complete this third step of understanding are unable to determine the proper goals in life and fail to understand what actions are good or evil.

Step 4: Intention of the End (Goal or Law)

Once the end (goal or law) is determined by the intellect, the will must love it. An action is intended when, out of love for the end, the will moves the intellect to determine how to attain it. If the will does not love the end, then the means of attaining it will not be sought. For example, many people know that they should help the poor, but if they do not love this goal, they will not seek ways of actually helping the poor. In reference to the examples in this section, the will intends the goals of pursuing one's vocation, graduating, or driving safely, which causes the intellect to determine how to attain these goals. These first four steps determine the end of the action, and the next six steps apply this end to a particular situation.

Step 5: Counsel

There is an old adage: "The road to hell is paved with good intentions." Simply intending the action is not the same as choosing it. Hence, once the goal has been intended, the intellect and will must still apply this goal to a particular situation. The first step in this application process is called "taking counsel." It is also referred to as "deliberation." This step can be further split into two parts: research and reason. First, one must understand the particular situation by doing research, and second, one must be able to reason to a conclusion. Although the term "research" usually has connotations of late hours in a library, in this case the term means that someone inquires into all the aspects of a situation that are relevant to the intended action. So although research may mean going to the library, it usually means things like inquiring into the possible lunch choices or seeking the possible options that God is calling one to perform, or observing the current weather conditions to determine how fast to drive. It can even mean going shopping if the goal is to buy clothes. The goal of the research is to form a premise that properly reflects the situation. (This is called the "particular premise.") For example, in the case of the person shopping for clothes, the premise might be "These clothes are inexpensive and fit my body."[16]

Once the particular premise is determined, the universal premise (the goal or law determined in step 3) can be applied to the particular situation by means of reasoning. This act of reasoning corresponds to the next act of the intellect in general: discursive reasoning. In the second act of the intellect, the intellect joined or separated concepts into premises or sentences. In discursive reasoning, these premises are then combined or separated to yield a conclusion by means of a common middle term.[17] An example of this process can be seen in using an argument to separate the concepts of spiders from insects by use of the middle term "eight legs": all spiders have eight legs. No insects have eight legs. Therefore, no spiders are insects. The terms "spiders" and "insects" are separated via the middle term "eight legs." Thus, the mind is able to separate the terms "spiders" and "insects" in order to have a fuller understanding of reality, since in reality spiders are not insects.[18]

In the moral realm, conclusions are drawn from the universal premise and the particular premise by means of a middle term. For example, the universal premise "I will graduate" is combined with the particular premise "to graduate I will need to go to class" to form the conclusion "I will go to class." This form of reasoning is called the "practical syllogism." Although sometimes only a single syllogism is needed, often many syllogisms are interspersed between phases of research. For example, in order to graduate, students might reason to the conclusion that they need good grades. Yet, to get good grades they conclude that they must learn the material. To learn the material they must go to class. Ultimately, people taking counsel continue to reason until they come to an action that they can perform right now. (This can include determining that now they should do nothing.) Sometimes, the act of taking counsel will reveal that there are multiple good ways of attaining the goal. For example, a young man might determine that he could fulfill his vocational calling by either getting married or being a priest. In all cases of taking counsel, the reasoning process moves from the more universal to the more particular.

This step is not always necessary in performing a human action. For most actions, people have already taken counsel about the best action and do not need to take counsel again. For example, most people do not need to deliberate on how to get to work every day. After the first few times, they have already figured out the best route. Although taking counsel is not always necessary, for many actions it is essential. People who are not good at this step often know what they should do in general, but they are unable to determine how to properly apply this information to the particular situation.

STEP 6: CONSENT

Through all of these steps of research and reasoning, the love of the will must continue to drive the intellect. This act of loving the results of counsel is called "consent." Besides driving the intellect, consent has two very important functions. First, if there is only one option presented by the intellect, the will can love this option, causing the intellect to stop taking counsel and to begin judging the action. In this manner the will puts an end to the deliberation, which can otherwise go on indefinitely. Second, if the intellect determines that multiple actions will attain the end, the will can love one of these options more than the others. My own vocational discernment story is a good example of this second function.

I can distinctly remember, when I was nineteen, setting (*understanding*) the goal to determine my vocational calling and *intending* it. For the next three years I did research (took *counsel*). This research consisted of daily prayer, where I asked God what his plan was for me, and it also consisted of learning about the different states of life to which God calls people (single, married, or religious). At the end of the three years of research, I went on a retreat to help reach a conclusion. During this retreat there was a period of thirty minutes set aside where each person received vocational direction from a priest. Forty-three young men attended that retreat, and there were only fourteen priests available to give direction. Consequently, each priest met with three men. However, there was one person left over. I was the one person. Providentially, I was able to spend the entire hour and a half with the retreat master.[19] He had me write a list of all the reasons why I thought God was calling me to be a priest and all the reasons why I thought God was calling me to get married. (This continues the step of *taking counsel*.) At the end of this process, I could not make a decision, since both vocational states appeared to be good ways for me to attain my intended goal of following my vocation. Since the intellect alone was unable to determine the proper action, the retreat master then asked me to look into my soul and determine which vocational state I loved the most (*the act of consent*). The answer was easy, I had always loved the idea of getting married. My will consented to the idea of getting married that was presented by the intellect. Yet, were my reasons for getting married the right reasons? This question will be answered in the description of the next step, judgment.

Step 7: Judgment

Once a prospective action is loved, the intellect must judge whether or not the action is in accord with the law or goal. *Because of the teleological nature of the moral life, the action must be judged to be in accord with both the proximate end (the goal intended) and higher ends (including the ultimate end).* In other words, while taking counsel, a person moves from the more universal to the more particular. While in judgment, the person judges the particular by the more universal. The person makes sure that all ends (both intended and higher) are rationally ordered to the true ultimate end of God. For example, in the case of the goal of driving safely, suppose someone is transporting a woman who is about to give birth. The intellect takes counsel and determines that there are two options: the posted speed limit and a higher speed (as much over the speed limit as conditions will allow without seriously endangering oneself and others). The intellect then judges in accord with the intended end and determines that following the posted speed limit would indeed attain the end of driving safely. However, when it judges by the higher end of saving lives, the intellect determines that a prudently higher speed would be the proper action in order to save the lives of the mother and child. The goal of driving safely is ordered to saving lives; hence, it would be wrong to drive the speed limit if the higher goal of saving lives was not fulfilled. Although judgment is essential even if there is only one potential action, often the intellect must judge multiple actions to determine which action most perfectly fulfills both the proximate and the higher goals. In the example above, the intellect determined that moderate speeding was the best action.

Just as the other steps in the intellect corresponded to the acts of the intellect in general, judgment corresponds to the most perfect of the acts of the human intellect: acts of wisdom. Once the intellect is able to reason to higher principles (the third act of reasoning described in the section on counsel), it practices wisdom by judging how all things relate to these principles. For example, people who discover that God exists can determine how all the rest of their knowledge corresponds to this highest truth. Consequently, in the moral realm, the ability to judge well is also called "practical wisdom." When someone has a defect in the ability to judge, they often have good goals and know many possible options to attain these goals, but they then decide (*judge*) to do something foolish.

The higher principles that are used to judge actions are determined either by an act of practical understanding (like what takes place in step 3) or by logically deriving new principles from the principles already known through an act of understanding. For example, a person combines the concepts of action, good, and ordered to God to form the higher principle that an act is good if it is ordered to God. In the United States, a recent popularized way of judging by a different form of this principle is to ask, "What would Jesus do?" Another example of a higher principle is that murder is wrong. A principle that is logically derived from this principle is that abortion is wrong. Although humans generally have thousands of higher principles from which they are able to judge their actions, it is sometimes necessary to discover unknown higher principles in order to determine the proper action. For example, if a young pregnant woman is being pressured to have an abortion and has no idea what to do, she may need to research and reason in order to discover the higher principles that should guide her decision. Because in this step one determines whether or not an action is good or bad, completing this step is what is commonly referred to as "following one's conscience."[20]

Now, back to my example of determining my vocation: I had to determine if the reasons for wanting to get married were truly good reasons. In other words, I had to *judge* whether or not they were in accord with my goal of finding my vocation and whether or not they were in accord with the highest goal of loving God. I ultimately determined that they were good reasons, and I *chose* to get married (step 8). I still had to carry out the action (steps 9 and 10) by convincing someone to marry me, but I did eventually marry a wonderful woman, and we are the proud parents of nine children.

Step 8: Choice

Once the intellect has judged the correct action, the will chooses it based on its love of the end. For example, I chose the action of getting married. The student loves the goal of graduating and, hence, chooses to go to class. The driver chooses to drive faster to save the mother and the baby. Although this is the last step of the decision-making process, the action must still be performed.

Step 9: Command

The intellect commands the will to carry out the action. Sometimes this step is momentary; sometimes it takes a long time. For example, once I had decided to get married, I still had to find a wife, get engaged, and get married. This process took a couple of years. Throughout this process, the intellect has to stay focused on the goal to make sure the goal is attained. A good example of the focus needed is seen in the case of doing homework. The act of doing homework may take hours, and the intellect must stay focused to keep from indulging in other distractions.

Step 10: Execution

The will executes the command by moving the body to act. For example, the student actually goes to class, or the driver actually does the driving. For the action to be completed, the will must love the command given by the intellect. For example, even if the intellect commands the will to stay focused on homework, if the will does not love the end of the action enough, it will not carry out the action. Nearly every person can think of times when they intended to do something, actually choose to do it, but were distracted before completing the action. This inability to complete the action is because of a failure in the ability to command and execute the action. Finally, after completing this step, the action has been performed.

STEP 11: CONTEMPLATION OF THE END ATTAINED

Since the action is now completed, it would seem that there are only ten steps. Yet, humans are created to be happy, and contemplation of the good attained is the act of happiness. Although the action has already been performed, these last two steps of contemplation and joy are important since they allow humans to achieve the happiness that comes from attaining a good end. This contemplation completes the action and drives humans to continue to perform good actions. For example, I contemplate the good of being married and am happy. The student contemplates the good of graduating. The student's happiness pushes her to set more good goals and attain them.

Happiness is a fitting end of actions since happiness requires knowledge and love of a good. In a human action, a good end is intended. The intellect must have some knowledge of the good in order to attain it, and the will must love it, or else it will not cause the action. Consequently, much of the happiness in this life comes from contemplating completed human actions. Since more difficult actions require greater love, generally speaking, the more difficult the action, the greater the potential for happiness. Hence, although it may sound counterintuitive, humans should pursue difficult and significant actions in order to be happy. Of course, the greatest of these actions is the pursuit of eternal happiness. Just as contemplation of a good action causes happiness, contemplation of an evil action should cause one to be unhappy.

STEP 12: JOY/DELIGHT IN THE END ATTAINED

Once the good end is attained, the will rests in the good that it desired. This resting in the good is the act of joy. In other words, since love causes unity, the love of the will in carrying out the action causes a unity with the good. For example, suppose you help a friend because you want your friend to be happy. Your love makes the friend's needs your own and causes you to perform the good action. Your friend is made happy, and you share in your friend's happiness. The difference between happiness and joy is that *happiness is primarily in the intellect*, and *joy is primarily in the will*. However, because the intellect and the will work together, happiness and joy also come together.[21] Humans who are not good at these last two steps often do great actions but fail to have the proportionate happiness that corresponds to these actions. Happiness and joy are the natural ends of good actions, and they drive humans to continue to perform good actions. They are a foretaste of eternal happiness.

THE ROLE OF THE EMOTIONS

Because an action is a human action if it proceeds from the intellect and the will, there are no steps in the emotions. Nonetheless, because humans have bodies, the emotions are also causes of actions. So, where do the emotions fit into the twelve steps? As we have noted earlier in this chapter, the emotions can influence both the intellect and will. Consequently, although there are no steps in the emotions, the emotions can enter into any of the twelve steps because emotions follow sense knowledge.[22] In other words, any time that sense knowledge is used by the intellect within the steps of the action, the emotions are also present. Sense knowledge is necessary to form and think about concepts (steps 1 and 2). Furthermore, goals are always understood and applied in particular situations, and sense knowledge is required to know particular situations (steps 3 to 10). Finally, happiness and joy require that a person has sense knowledge that an action has been completed (steps 11 and 12). In short, the emotions can affect any of the steps. The effect of the emotions can be either positive (following the intellect and will) or negative (rebelling against the intellect and will). For example, emotional hope and love drove my intellect and will to intend the goal of finding my vocation. My emotional love of the goal helped my intellect stay focused and helped my will to avoid loving distractions that would keep me from attaining this goal. Furthermore, emotional joy accompanied my intellectual happiness and joy once I got married. Of course, the emotions can also hinder the intellect and will in any step. For example, emotional desire to engage in recreation can divert the intellect and will in the quest to do homework, or emotional desire for bodily comforts can hinder the intellect in attaining greater happiness by sharing one's possessions with the poor.

THE BENEFITS OF THE TWELVE STEPS

Very few actions go through all twelve steps and rarely are the steps followed in order. Humans often move back and forth through different steps in different orders depending upon the situation. Furthermore, the steps are only guides to help one find the best moral option; following them will not guarantee that the best action will be found. They should not be viewed as a "moral calculator" that always results in happiness. Nonetheless, in general, following these steps can help people maintain the teleological nature of the human actions and attain their proper end of friendship with God. Proceeding through these steps ensures that people have concrete goals, take into consideration the particular situation, and reason to conclusions. Furthermore, people avoid rash and foolish decisions by judging by higher principles, and they are reminded to stay focused within the action. In the end, their happiness should increase.

Because of the teleological nature of humans, knowledge of the twelve steps is also important since it can help humans diagnose problems that they are having within the performance of their actions. Humans are ordered to actions that are in accord with their nature, and by finding the way that humans naturally think and love, the proper virtues to improve human nature can be found. For example, suppose Joe has trouble carrying out the action of cleaning his refrigerator after deciding to clean it. The problem is in the steps of command and execution. Now that the problem is diagnosed, a particular virtue can be found that will help fix the problem. Consequently, the twelve steps of the human action serve as a foundation for the proper understanding of virtues and also the gifts of the Holy Spirit.

DETERMINING THE GOODNESS OF A HUMAN ACTION

Another benefit of studying the twelve steps is that it helps humans determine the goodness of actions. Although it is usually easy to determine whether an action is good or evil, there are times when it can be difficult. For example, suppose someone is dying of cancer and needs large amounts of painkillers to alleviate the pain. One effect of the painkillers is that it shortens the life of the patient. Is this a good action or not? On the one hand, controlling pain is a good thing; on the other hand, the person will die earlier.[23] Because it is not always easy to determine the goodness of an action, over the centuries moral theologians have developed a number of helpful distinctions and principles that we will examine. The first helpful distinction is between interior and exterior actions. An understanding of this first distinction aids one in understanding the next distinction between the three things that must be considered in determining the goodness of an action: the end, the object, and the circumstances.

INTERIOR AND EXTERIOR ACTIONS

Because sometimes people think they are doing something good but are actually doing something evil (or vice versa), a distinction is made between interior and exterior actions. The interior action refers to the act of the intellect and the will within the soul. The exterior action refers to the act as it is executed outside of the soul. In other words, the interior action refers to what people think they are doing, and the exterior action refers to what is happening in reality. Normally the two acts are the same type of actions. For example, if Joe chooses to study (the interior action) and actually does study (the exterior action), then the species of the interior act is the same as the species of the exterior act. However, because of defects in the intellect, the two acts can be different types of actions. For example, suicide bombers might believe that by killing innocent people they are preserving their faith from harmful influences. Because they believe that they are preserving their faith, the interior act would be preserving one's faith. However, the exterior act would be murder (what is really happening).

To better understand the relation between the interior action and the exterior action, the notions of form and matter are helpful. The interior action is the form of the action, and the exterior action is the matter. Just as the form determines the nature of something, normally the interior action determines the nature of the action performed. For example, if someone thinks that they are helping the poor, usually they actually are performing the act of helping the poor. However, in cases of form and matter, the matter must be proportionate to the form or else the form will not be able to inform it (in other words, the form will not be able to cause it to be a particular thing). For example, the matter of steel can be formed into a 1,000-foot-tall skyscraper capable of holding thousands of people, but the matter of marshmallows cannot be formed into a skyscraper of this kind. This type of matter (marshmallows) is simply unsuitable to receive this particular type of form (skyscraper form).[24] The same is true with actions. Generally what people intend (the interior action and the form) is what they are doing (exterior action and matter); however, if the matter of the exterior action is not proportionate to the intended form, then even though they may think they are doing a particular type of action, they will actually be doing something else. For example, suppose a researcher wants to find a cure for a deadly disease. But in order to find the cure, he tricks a bunch of healthy children so he can infect them with the deadly disease. In this case, the intended form of the action is finding a cure for a deadly disease, but the matter of intentionally infecting healthy children with a deadly disease does not correspond with the form. Hence, even though he thinks he is doing a good action, in reality he is committing the evil action of endangering children (or something similar).

The cause of the interior action being different from the exterior action is the failure of the intellect to properly determine the particular action. In other words, if the intellect fails in any of the steps of understanding the goal/law properly, taking proper counsel, or judging properly, then the exterior act can differ from the interior one and the person will be mistaken as to the nature of the action. For example, in the case of the suicide bomber given above, the bomber errs in either taking counsel or judging and, hence, erroneously believes that the object of the act is preserving his faith when in fact it is murder. Likewise in the case of the researcher, if he was judging properly, he would know that exposing healthy children to extreme danger is not the proper way to work for the cure of a disease.

Although the interior act can vary from the exterior, only the interior act causes people to progress on their journey to God or to falter on their journey. To explain this in a less sophisticated way, God judges people based on what they think they are doing (assuming invincible ignorance, for if they practically could have known better then they still falter on their journey). Two important points can be drawn from this distinction. First, humans can never fully know what is going on in the soul of other humans simply by looking at their exterior actions. Consequently, although the exterior act can be judged to be good or evil, the interior act, which determines a person's relation to God, should never be judged. Note that the inability to judge refers solely to the interior act, Christians can certainly judge whether or not the exterior act is wrong. Second, although the interior act determines the relation to God, the exterior act inflicts good or evil effects on other people. For example, if a medical professional fails to take proper counsel and gives contaminated blood to a patient, she may not be fully morally culpable for her action, but she still causes great evil because the patient may get sick or even die. Hence, it is of utmost importance that the intellect is perfected to make sure that the interior and exterior actions conform. The virtue of prudence, which we will cover in Part II of this book, is the virtue that ensures that the intellect properly functions so that the interior and exterior actions correspond.

THE THREE COMPONENTS OF A GOOD ACTION

The notion of the interior action as the form and the exterior action as the matter can be helpful in determining the nature of a particular action. However, because of the complexity of some moral actions, a further helpful distinction among *the end*, *the object*, and *the circumstances* has been developed. The end (or usually ends) refers to the ultimate end (and all higher goals) that an action is ordered to attain. The object is the moral species of the action (the best moral description of the action explaining what the action is). The circumstances change the degree of good or evil within an action. In order for a human action to be good, the end and the object must both be good. If either is evil, then the action is evil. To better understand these parts of an action, we will treat each one in detail.

The Ultimate End and Higher Ends

In a teleological system, the most important determinate of the goodness of an action is whether or not it is ordered to the ultimate end of God.[25] However, not only must the ultimate end be taken into consideration, but also all higher ends. The use of the term "end" can be somewhat confusing because the term can refer to the intended end, higher ends (intermediary ends between the intended end and the ultimate end), and the ultimate end. In a good action, the intended end is ordered to the higher ends, which are ordered to the ultimate end, God. For example, the intention to go to work might be ordered to the higher end of supporting one's family, which should be ordered to the ultimate end of God. In determining how the *ends* affect the goodness of an action, only the ultimate end and all higher ends are taken into consideration since the intended end is normally identical to the object of the action, which will be covered below. Hence, in the above example, the ends are supporting one's family and God. (Going to work is the intended end that determines what the act is—the object.) For an act to be good, all the higher ends must be good, which means they are properly ordered to the ultimate end of God (even if people are not consciously thinking of God when they perform the action).[26] If the ultimate end is something other than God, such as bodily pleasure, or if one of the higher ends is evil (and incapable of being ordered to God) then the action is evil. To use the work example given above, if someone works solely for money (this is his ultimate end—the thing he loves more than anything else), then the action is evil—even if the work in itself is good. Likewise, if he went to work to perform immoral actions (such as embezzlement), even if he mistakenly thought that he was doing the action out of love for God (he was going to give the money to the Church), then he would still be performing an evil action.[27] In this latter case, the embezzlement is an evil higher end but not the ultimate end. The point is that an evil higher end makes an action evil, even if the means to attain it are good.

Because every human act is ordered to an ultimate end (either God or something else), every act is either good or evil. Although an act can be morally neutral in the abstract, in reality every human act is done for a reason. For example, the act of driving a car is morally neutral in the abstract. However, in reality, driving is always ordered to an end. If someone drives a car to work, then the act is good (assuming that the work is ordered to God). If someone drives a car to run over someone, then the act is evil. Since human actions by definition are ordered to an end, then every human action is either good or evil. Even acts like eating or sleeping can either bring one closer to God or drive one farther from him. As seen in the example of driving, sometimes an act that is normally good can be evil because of a bad end. An extreme example might be going to Mass solely out of vanity. If someone goes to Mass primarily to look good (and not out of love of God), then this particular human action is evil.

THE OBJECT

The term "object" has a technical meaning in the realm of morals. The object of the act is its moral species.[28] Just as our species is what we are (humans), the object of the act tells what an action is. In other words, *the object of the act is the best rational moral description of the essence of the action*.[29] For example, the act of vacuuming a room could be described as the act of cleaning, or the act of making noise, or the act of exercise. Unless one is intentionally vacuuming to make noise or exercise, then the object of the act is cleaning because cleaning best describes what the action is. Likewise, the act of using a gun to threaten a bank teller in order to get money could be described as the act of redistributing money, getting money for college, raising the teller's blood pressure, or armed robbery. Normally in this situation the object of the act would be armed robbery, even if one was going to use it for the good end of going to college. Whereas the end tells *ultimately why* someone does the action, the object tells *what* the action is.[30] However, determining the object can be very difficult. For example, if someone takes some food to save the life of another person, is the object of the action stealing or saving the life of another?

The anatomy of the human action that was given above is extremely helpful in determining the object. When an act is considered teleologically, assuming there are good higher ends, *the object is the same as that which is intended (steps 3 and 4) if (and only if) that which is chosen (step 8) is essentially ordered to that which is intended.*[31] "Essentially ordered" means the same thing as "properly ordered" or "truly ordered": the reasoning is valid, the premises accurately reflect the situation, and the action is judged to be in accord with higher ends that are rationally ordered to the ultimate end—steps 5 and 7. In other words, if a person takes proper counsel and judges properly by higher ends, then what he intends is what the object is. For example, in the case of self-defense, the goal that is intended is to defend one's life (steps 3 and 4).[32] If the only way to save one's life is to mortally wound the attacker, and the intellect validly reasons and judges that this is the proper action (determined in steps 5 and 7), then the object of the act is the same as the intended goal: defending one's life in self-defense.[33] However, if the situation is such that one's life could be saved without the killing of the attacker, and the will chooses to kill the attacker anyway, then the object of the action is not the same as the intention. Rather, because killing does not logically follow the intention of saving one's life in this situation, the object is murder.

The reason that the object is not the same as the intention if the chosen act is not properly ordered to the end is because the action takes its species from both its form (the intended end) and its matter (the exterior action). In these cases where there is a failure in the intellect, the matter is not capable of being formed into a particular type of action, and the species of the action is not from the intention but from the matter itself. For example, if a woman gets an abortion (the matter) in order to get a college education (the intended end), the object of the action is getting an abortion and not getting an education. Abortions are not naturally ordered to a college education and, hence, the most relevant description of the action is getting an abortion and not getting a college education.

This description is somewhat complicated, but the knowledge of the twelve steps can help make the process easier to understand, for another way to describe this process of determining the object is *that the object is the same as the intended end if there are no defects in the acts of research, reasoning, and judgment.*[34] In other words, as long as the intellect prudently takes counsel and judges, then the act chosen is what the person intends.[35] However, if humans do not take counsel and judge correctly, then what they are trying to do is not the same as what they actually do. Hence, the object of the act would be different than the intention. (Likewise, the interior act would be different from the exterior act.) A key point here is that some people do evil acts but have good intentions. For example, suppose someone wanted to kill a handicapped person because he did not want that person to suffer ridicule in life. The intention of not wanting handicapped people to suffer ridicule is good, but the act of killing does not morally correspond to the intended end of avoiding ridicule. There are numerous defects in the research and reasoning, but the most important problem is that the action would not pass the judgment of the higher laws of conserving life and loving God. In other words, the *end* of the life of the person in general and the *end* of the way the person fits into God's divine plan take precedence over the *end* of removing suffering. Furthermore, there are numerous ways that suffering could be removed that are fully in accord with these higher ends, such as promoting loving interaction between the general population and handicapped individuals.

However, because either an evil end or evil object can make an act evil, the form and matter analogy does not work for determining the object of an action with a good exterior action but evil higher ends. If even one of the higher ends is evil, the object is the same as the evil end. If there are multiple evil ends, then the object is the same as the most fundamental higher end.[36] The embezzlement example given above illustrates this point. Although the matter is good (going to work), the best moral description is embezzlement (the higher evil end). Suppose the person was going to work to embezzle in order to make money to hire a murderer to kill his wife. In this case the object would be murder since murder is the most fundamental higher evil end. In other words, the best description of the action is that he is working toward murdering his wife. The action is evil even if the person does a good action in the process of attempting something evil.

There are some actions that are always wrong because they necessarily violate the higher ends of human nature. In other words, these actions violate the ends to which humans are naturally inclined by God. These actions are called "intrinsically evil," for they can never be ordered to love of God. Some examples of these actions are murder (but not killing), blasphemy, perjury, and adultery.[37]

Circumstances

Circumstances are the final thing that we must consider in determining the goodness of an action. In morals, the term "circumstance" is used in a technical sense and does not simply mean the situation. Within any situation, some parts of the situation are more significant in determining what an action is than other parts. For example, if someone picks up a large amount of money that is not his, the fact that the money does belong to him is more significant than the amount of the money. Although, in general, one might call both of these facts "circumstances," technically speaking, the fact that it does not belong to him determines the object (stealing), and the amount of money is a circumstance. A circumstance refers to the aspects of a situation that do not change the nature or species of an action. In the stealing example, whether someone steals a lot of money or a little money is a circumstance—in both cases the species of the action is stealing. A circumstance does not change the object of an action; it only changes the gravity of the action (i.e., the degree of good or evil in the action).[38] Although stealing a little money and stealing a lot of money are both stealing, stealing a lot of money is generally worse than stealing a little.

Whereas the object refers to what the action is, circumstances generally refer to who, where, when, and how. For example, when the object of the act is stealing, the gravity of the act is changed based on the type of person from whom the property is stolen. Stealing from a poor person is generally worse than stealing from a rich person. Circumstances can also refer to why the action was performed if the intention is not the same as the object. For example, if the intention is to get good grades and the action chosen is cheating, then the intention is merely a circumstance since the action is not morally in conformity with it. Although a disordered "good intention" does not change the object of the action, it can change the gravity of the action since the person was attempting to perform something good (even if the exterior act is evil). For example, the person that actively kills someone to remove suffering is still performing murder, even though the good intention might lessen the gravity of the evil. Circumstances are important in determining the goodness of an action because they help determine the degree of goodness within the action, even if they do not change the object.

Sometimes a thing that is normally a circumstance can in certain situations actually affect the object of an action.[39] For example, normally parents have an obligation to raise and educate their children. Most of the reasons why parents might not be involved in the raising and educating of their children would merely be circumstances. However, if the parents were not morally prepared to raise their children in a proper manner, then they could give up their newly born child for adoption. The state of not being able to properly raise children is such an important part of the situation that it is not just a circumstance but actually affects the object of the action.[40] The object of the action is not neglect of children but giving the child up for adoption.

An action is good if it has a good end and a good object. Although circumstances do not change the object of an action, they determine the degree of goodness or evil within an action. Understanding the role of circumstances is particularly helpful in understanding concepts we will examine later, such mortal sin. Although the object tells what kind of sin something is, the circumstances sometimes determine whether the sin is mortal or venial.

ACTIONS ARE LIKE individual steps on the journey to sharing in God's happiness. It is important that they are always ordered toward God (the ultimate goal). To help ensure that actions are good both interiorly and exteriorly, the action can be divided into twelve steps. Breaking down the human action into twelve steps has many benefits. It can help ensure that people intentionally attempt to set good goals and reason logically to attain them. It can also give people some concrete thinking skills that will help them determine whether or not the end and object of an action are good. Additionally, it serves as the background for different virtues (especially those subordinated to prudence) and gifts of the Holy Spirit. Furthermore, it shows the important role of law in actions as the law is intended and then applied to a particular situation. Consequently, the information about the anatomy of the human action will be used repeatedly in later chapters that deal with virtues, laws, and the morality of particular actions.

6

THE TRANSFORMING
POWER OF GRACE

Difficult journeys that are inspired by devotion to God are often called "pilgrimages." One of the most popular pilgrimage routes in the world is the *Camino de Santiago* (the *El Camino*) across northern Spain, with a few starting points in France too. This trek of up to 500 miles to the tomb of St. James the apostle is very popular for both Christians and others seeking spiritual healing in their lives.[1] Although this particular pilgrimage route is quite developed, with many modern conveniences along the way, it can be used as an analogy to help explain the ultimate journey in our lives: the journey to share in the eternal happiness of God. To hike the *El Camino*, pilgrims first need to know where they are starting from, where they are going, and how to progress on the journey. In relation to the journey to friendship with God, these points were already covered in the first five chapters of this book. However, in order to complete the *El Camino*, a number of other things are required. The pilgrims need guidance along the way in the form of signs, advice from others, and/or a map. They also need to be in good enough physical shape to walk nearly 500 miles on hard surfaces and have other helpful dispositions, such as good traveling skills. Attaining these abilities might require them to physically train and condition themselves before making the journey. Finally, they need the aid of others to help sustain them, rejuvenate them, heal them, and even physically transport them if necessary.

These three requirements for the journey to the tomb of St. James also apply to the journey toward union with God. Recall that the analysis of the moral theology of St. Paul (in chapter 4) indicated that laws, virtues, and especially grace were essential elements of the Christian moral life. Just as the pilgrim needs directions on the journey, Paul notes that Christians need guidance from natural law, the commandments, and the guidance of the Holy Spirit. Furthermore, just as the pilgrim needs to be in good physical condition to make this arduous trek and have other dispositions, such as "good traveling skills," Christians need virtues to perfect the powers of their souls to know and love God and others. Finally, humans need God's grace to sustain them, rejuvenate them, heal them, and carry them. However, the analogy is quite imperfect when it comes to the role of God's grace. God's grace not only sustains and heals, it also transforms humans, allowing them to share in God's power and attain an even greater end: friendship with God himself. Laws, virtues, and grace are all essential causes of the good human actions needed to attain a share in God's happiness. Following the methodology of Paul, who noted that without grace, law and virtue are unable to save, we will examine God's grace in this chapter, and in subsequent chapters I'll explain law and virtue.

THE NECESSITY OF GRACE

As I stated in chapter 2, God created humans perfect in terms of their nature, but imperfect in terms of their actions, so that humans can be more like God. They are more like God when they cause goodness in themselves and others. Consequently, God intentionally created humans with the natural inclination to the lofty goal of union with him and others, but he did not give them the ability to attain this end by their own power. In fact, humans do not even have the ability to attain true friendships with other humans without the help of others. Humans need the help of parents, teachers, grandparents, and other mentors to guide and motivate them to good actions through laws, customs, and expectations. For example, young children have to be taught how to share, how to treat others with respect, how to make the needs of others more important than their own needs, and so on. When children perform these good actions repetitively, they form virtues. For example, by serving the poor over and over, children can obtain the virtue of loving the poor. Once children have developed the virtues perfecting the different powers of the soul, they are then capable of entering into loving relationships with others by their own powers. They now have dispositions such as humility, mercy, kindness, and patience, which give them the ability to truly make the needs, goals, sufferings, and joys of others their own. With these virtues they can perform good loving actions and contemplate the goodness of their relationships. In other words, because of the guidance of others and the development of virtues, they can be happy. Their parents and mentors are now more like God because they help cause their children to become better people. The children themselves are likewise more like God in that they also participate in the development of their own virtues. God creates humans to be happy but only with the aid of others within a community.

Even with the assistance of others, the goal that God created humans to attain is beyond their ability. Humans need the further assistance of God's grace. God's grace is necessary both to heal the effects of fallen nature and to transform (elevate) human nature to attain the eternal happiness humans truly desire. As we saw in chapter 2, because of the effects of original sin, human nature is fallen. Hence, the natural inclinations to know and love have been corrupted, and humans have a tendency to commit sins. These sins lead to vices, which ultimately lead to unhappiness. To use the Pauline phrase, humans became "slaves to sin" (Rom 6:17). Although the inclinations have been corrupted by original sin, they are never destroyed, and even in the fallen state humans have the potential for limited natural happiness. With the help of others and the acquisition of virtues, the natural inclinations can be focused once more on good human actions and the ensuing natural happiness. However, the happiness available in the fallen state is always difficult to obtain and is always fleeting. With original sin, even the desire that humans have for natural happiness is often unfulfilled, and the concept of eternal happiness would be considered to be an unattainable dream. Humans need the help of God's grace to *heal* their fallen nature so that they can have a more permanent and intense natural happiness.

Although natural happiness is wonderful, humans have an infinite desire for the good. They seek to know and love the very essence of goodness itself, God.[2] Nothing short of knowing and loving God as he is will satisfy the heart and bring perfect happiness. Even permanent and intense natural happiness cannot fulfill the infinite desires God created in humans. Recall that all things act in accord with their nature. By their natural abilities, humans are able to perform human actions. The act of knowing and loving finite things is a human action that brings natural happiness. However, the act of knowing and loving the infinite good of God himself is not a human action. Only God has the natural power to know and love the divine essence as it is. Even the angels need the grace of God to "see" God as he is. The act of perfect happiness is a divine action that flows from God's infinite power. Consequently, in addition to having the effect of original sin healed, humans especially need God's grace to transform them so that they can participate in God's nature and perform the divine actions necessary for eternal happiness. This participation in divine nature is called "sanctifying (or deifying) grace" and will be one of the things we explain in this chapter. Additionally, grace in general will be defined, and different types of grace will be analyzed, such as uncreated grace and the supernatural movement of the Holy Spirit. Finally, we will examine the issue of grace perfecting nature and the relation between grace and nature in moral theology. This last section will show in more detail how God's grace transforms humans so that they can attain the lofty end to which they are inclined.

GRACE IS A GIFT FROM GOD

Grace is a gift from God. Often, the term is used to mean any gift from God at all, such as a beautiful sunset or a healthy baby. Although these are certainly gifts from God, they stem from nature and are not instances of grace in the technical sense of the term.

Technically speaking, grace refers to unmerited supernatural gifts that are given to us through Christ's death and resurrection: the gifts that cause persons to become and remain children of God.[3] This distinction between nature and grace is essential to manifest the uniqueness of the incarnation, death, and resurrection of Jesus Christ. In other words, Christians believe that the event of the divine Son becoming human in the person of Jesus Christ is unlike any other event in the history of the world. The Incarnation and the gifts that flow from it are substantially different than any of the "natural" gifts from God. Grace is essential for salvation, whereas the natural gifts will not save.[4] To further understand the role of grace in salvation and the moral life, we'll make a distinction between the two primary types of grace: uncreated grace and created grace.[5]

Uncreated Grace

There is only one thing that is uncreated, God himself. Hence, uncreated grace refers to the gift of God himself. All three persons of the Trinity give themselves as gifts to humanity. The Father gives of himself by sending the Son. The Son gives of himself by becoming human and dying for the sins of all humans. The Holy Spirit dwells in the hearts of humans and guides and moves them to unity with the Father through the Son.[6] The gifts of the three persons within salvation history manifest the interior love of God that draws humans to perform actions beyond their natural ability.[7] By observing this love, humans can understand the true meaning of love and the true road to happiness.

The uncreated grace of the three persons of the Trinity is the cause of all types of created grace. The Holy Spirit transforms humans through sanctifying grace and moves them to supernatural actions. By the power of this grace, humans are able to perform acts of faith and love that unite them to the Son. The Son unites them to the Father, making all one, as God is one (Jn 17:22). This unity with God, which begins on earth, is the beginning of eternal happiness.

Created Grace

Created grace refers to gifts that are created by God for the sake of our salvation. This type of grace either transforms humans to perform a particular type of action or moves humans to actually perform the action. Since grace perfects nature, God moves humans by grace in a similar manner to the way he moves humans naturally. On the natural level, God is the first cause of all human actions, and humans are the second cause. When God causes a human action, he first gives humans the ability to perform the action and then guides and moves them to perform the action. For example, if Kate performs the action of visiting a sick person, God first gives Kate the ability to know and love the sick person and then moves her intellect and will to actually know and love the person. By means of this knowledge and love, Kate makes the sick person's need for companionship her own. Likewise, in reference to the role of grace, God first transforms humans so that they have new abilities: divine abilities. God then moves them to perform actions in accord with these abilities. The grace that transforms humans is called "sanctifying" or "deifying grace," and the grace that moves humans is called "the supernatural movement of the Holy Spirit."[8]

Sanctifying/Deifying Grace

Sanctifying grace is the gift whereby God makes humans like himself by giving them the ability to participate in his divine nature.[9] All things act in accord with their nature. By nature humans are able to attain natural happiness, but they are *not* able to perform actions ordered to eternal happiness. However, with this ability to participate in divine nature, humans are able to perform actions in accord with God's nature: divine actions capable of attaining eternal happiness.[10] The principle that all things act in accord with their nature needs to be expanded to read as follows: *All things act in accord with either their substantial nature or their participated nature.* When humans perform human actions they act in accord with their substantial nature (i.e., their human nature), when they perform divine actions, they act in accord with their participated nature (their divine nature).[11]

How is it possible that humans are able to act by the power of divine nature and still retain their own nature? The answer to this question can be found in a deeper examination of the notion of "participation."[12] To participate in something is to share in the perfections that something else has by nature.[13] Furthermore, the thing doing the participating does not lose its individual identity when it attains these perfections. A good example to explain the nature of participation is the participation of water in the heat of fire.[14] Fire is hot by nature. In other words, the proper action common to all fire is the production of heat. Water is not hot by nature, as seen by the fact that there is cold water. However, water can become hot by *participating* in the heat of the fire. Once the water is hot, it can heat up other things (such as eggs), because the water participates in the proper action of the fire. In other words, water is able to perform actions of heating by the power of the nature of fire. The fire is analogous to God. God is divine by nature and capable of performing divine actions. The water is analogous to humans, and the water's act of heating is analogous to humans performing divine actions. Humans, like the water, are able to share in the perfections that God has by nature and are able to perform actions by means of God's power. Sanctifying grace is also called "deifying grace," because through it humans become divine by participation.

Although it is proper to say that grace recreates nature, it re-creates it by perfecting human nature and not by destroying it.[15] Just as the water retains its nature when heating the egg, humans remain humans when they perform divine actions. Furthermore, not only do humans retain their human nature when they perform divine actions, they also retain their personal identity. Recall from chapter 1 that nature determines the type of actions that something can do, but a person performs the actions. With sanctifying grace, a human person performs a divine action by means of divine nature. For example, all actions of faith and charity are caused by the participation in divine nature through grace. So, if Kate visits the sick because of her faith and charity, the primary cause of this action is the divine nature. However, the person who performs the action is Kate.

Since grace perfects human nature and does not destroy it, the acts stemming from grace are freely chosen.[16] The intellect and will are essential elements of human nature.[17] These powers are both perfected by grace to participate in God's knowledge and love. This participation enhances the intellect's ability to know the truth and the will's ability to love the good. Since greater knowledge and love result in greater freedom, grace increases freedom. In other words, just as God causes humans to act freely when humans act naturally, so also with grace God causes humans to act with even more perfect freedom. Acting by means of divine nature does not destroy freedom but enhances it.[18] Consequently, since these actions are still freely chosen, they are still human actions, even though they are done by the power of God.[19]

Sanctifying grace is a type of habit.[20] It is not a habit acquired by doing good actions, since grace is a free gift from God. Rather, it is a special type of infused habit. A good habit is a perfection of the soul that gives humans the ability to perform a particular type of action. Within the soul, good habits are situated in a position midway between nature and action. In other words, human nature causes actions through habits. Grace is a habit because it is also a perfection of the soul that causes a particular type of action. By means of grace, humans are able to perform divine actions. Because humans require habits on the natural level to perform their proper actions, it is only fitting that they also require habits on the supernatural level to perform their proper actions, since grace perfects nature.

With all types of habits, repetition of their proper actions increases their strength. For example, repetitively performing acts of courage increases the strength of the habit of courage. Since grace is a habit, further acts stemming from grace increase the participation of humans in divine nature. In other words, additional acts stemming from grace increase grace. However, how is this possible if grace is a free gift from God? Grace increases from further like actions because the cause of these supernatural actions is not human nature but *divine nature*.[21] In other words, even these further actions are gifts from God, since they stem from divine nature.

It is fitting that further acts of grace increase the degree of participation in divine nature, since grace perfects nature and does not destroy it. Just as the nature of water is not destroyed by participation in the power of the fire, human nature is not destroyed by grace. Rather, human nature is enhanced so that it can act by means of divine power. Likewise, just as habits in humans naturally increase through like actions, so also habits that stem from divine power increase through like actions. Consequently, although grace is always a gift from God, there are two normal instrumental causes of this grace on earth. Initially, the normal cause of grace is the sacraments.[22] Most people first receive the grace of God when they are baptized. This grace is then enhanced by the further reception of the sacraments, such as the Eucharist and confession.[23] The sacraments act as instrumental causes of grace. Because the sacraments give humans the ability to participate more perfectly in divine nature, receiving them is an important aspect of the moral life. Once humans have sanctifying grace, a second instrumental cause is humans themselves through their actions. When humans continue to perform actions stemming from a participation in divine nature, they are instrumental causes of grace.

Just as human nature works through virtues to perfect the natural inclinations and to cause actions leading to happiness, so also grace, which perfects human nature, works through virtues to cause divine actions. Consequently, sanctifying grace is the cause of all the infused virtues through which it works. These virtues include the theological virtues of faith, hope, and charity, and also the infused cardinal virtues of prudence, justice, temperance, and fortitude. All of these virtues will be explained in chapter 8.

The Supernatural Movement of the Holy Spirit

Because God is the first cause of all human actions (natural and supernatural), he not only moves humans to perform actions in accord with their nature but also moves them to perform actions flowing from divine nature. In order for humans to do an action beyond their nature, they must be moved in a manner beyond their nature. In other words, both the ability to be moved (sanctifying grace) and the movement to divine acts are gifts from God. This supernatural movement has also been called "actual grace," since it moves humans to act.

To show how the manner of movement to actions changes when a human is transformed by sanctifying grace, an analogy of a carpenter and a saw is helpful. Imagine that a carpenter is going to build a desk. He must first cut the wood. He has four saws: a new handsaw, a dull and broken handsaw, a dull power saw, and a new power saw. The motion that he uses to cut the wood with each saw is different. For the new handsaw, he takes long smooth strokes and makes a straight cut easily and quickly. With the broken saw, the saw blade frequently gets stuck, and the amount it can cut with each stroke is restricted. Hence, the carpenter's strokes are uneven, and many more strokes are needed to cut the wood. The carpenter can still make the desk but only with a great deal more difficulty, and the cuts are less beautiful. Even with a dull power saw, the carpenter can make straight cuts much more quickly and efficiently than with the handsaw. His motion changes from many strokes to a single steady stroke. Of course, with a new power saw the carpenter can make the most beautiful cuts most efficiently. With a single, smooth stroke the carpenter can move the saw to make a straight cut.

In the analogy, the carpenter is the first cause, and the saw is the second or instrumental cause. The carpenter represents God, and each of the saws represents a different stage in the history of human nature. The new handsaw represents the original state, where God moved Adam and Eve to good actions in accord with their nature (keeping in mind that Adam and Eve already participated in Christ's grace). The broken handsaw represents the fallen state. God can still move humans to good actions, but because the instrument acts in accord with its nature, the type of actions humans can perform are limited by fallen nature. Likewise, the manner by which God moves humans is also changed. The dull power saw represents the down payment of the full inheritance state. Just as a power saw can be moved to greater actions than a handsaw, so also humans can now be moved to actions beyond their nature. However, they are still subject to some effects of original sin. (Hence, the power saw is dull.) God can move humans to perform the most perfect actions in the state of the full inheritance (the new power saw). The point is that just as the movement of the carpenter changes, so also the divine movement changes with the addition of sanctifying grace.

Once humans are transformed by sanctifying grace, humans are constantly moved and guided by the Holy Spirit. The Holy Spirit inspires their intellects and moves their wills and emotions to love their proper actions. This movement and guidance of the Holy Spirit is the law of the spirit that is spoken about in the New Testament (e.g., Rom 8:2) and is a cause of actions leading to supernatural happiness.

Grace is a necessary cause of eternal happiness. The uncreated grace of the Holy Spirit dwells within human souls. The Holy Spirit transforms humans into a new creation by means of sanctifying grace. Sanctifying grace is a participation in divine nature and gives humans the ability to perform actions ordered to eternal happiness. Once humans are transformed, the Holy Spirit moves and guides humans to the divine actions of knowledge (through faith) and love (through charity) of the divine Son. This supernatural knowledge and love of the Son result in union with the Son. Unity with the Son causes humans to be united to the Father as his adopted children. As children of God, humans are also coheirs with Christ and participate in the divine nature that is eternally being given to the Son (2 Pt 1:4). This inheritance, which begins on earth with the down payment, causes humans to perform actions of knowing and loving God and others, and it results in the eternal happiness of the full inheritance.

GRACE PERFECTS NATURE

A common theme throughout this chapter is that grace does not destroy nature but rather perfects nature. As a participation in divine nature, grace allows humans to attain the greatest end that is logically possible without losing their personal identity. The greatest end that could be imagined would be that humans become God by nature, but that is impossible. However, the next greatest possible end is that by participating in divine nature, humans are able to perform divine actions while still remaining human beings. Humans with grace are able to know and love as God knows and loves and are able to share in the unity of the Trinity. They are able to perform the divine action of eternal happiness. They are able to do all these things while still retaining their personal identity. The good news of the gospel is that Christ became human so that humans could be coheirs of the inheritance from the Father (Rom 8:14–17). However, this end is only possible if grace perfects nature and does not destroy or replace it.

Although grace allows humans to fulfill their greatest inclinations, its effects are less tangible than those of nature, and hence it is less easily understood. However, because grace perfects nature, we can study the perfections of nature in order to better understand the perfections of grace.

For example, a study of the perfections of human relationships can teach us about the way humans should interact with God. Likewise, for every principle of happiness in the natural moral life, there is a corresponding principle that flows from grace. On the natural level, the journey begins with human nature. From human nature come natural inclinations to good human actions. However, in order to actually perform these actions, human guidance in the form of laws is necessary to guide and motivate humans. With the aid of law, humans perform good human actions repetitively. This repetition of good actions causes virtues, which give humans the ability to perform even better human actions. These actions are better because they are caused by greater knowledge and love and, hence, result in natural happiness.

For each of these natural principles of action, there is a corresponding principle caused by grace. Grace perfects human nature by causing a participation in divine nature. Just as human nature is followed by natural inclinations, so also grace is followed by supernatural inclinations. These supernatural inclinations are the theological virtues of faith, hope, and charity, which perfect the natural inclinations to know and to love.[24] Even with the theological virtues, humans must still be guided by the Holy Spirit and the written element of divine revelation (e.g., the Sermon on the Mount and Ten Commandments). Since humans now act by the power of divine nature, they are guided by the Holy Spirit to divine actions, which perfect human actions. However, the theological virtues must be applied through the cardinal virtues of prudence, justice, temperance, and fortitude. Since the natural virtues cannot cause supernatural actions, these cardinal virtues must be infused by God. These virtues perfect the natural virtues. By means of grace and the infused virtues, humans are able to perform divine actions of knowing and loving God and others. These actions cause supernatural happiness on earth and eternal happiness in heaven. Table 6.1 shows both the natural and corresponding supernatural principles of the journey to attain God.

Table 6.1 fills in most of the elements of the map for the journey to eternal happiness. As Paul noted in his epistles, all the moral elements discovered by Greek virtue (the principles on the natural level, such as human laws and natural virtues) cannot

Table 6.1.   The "Big Picture" of the Moral Life

Grace (participation in divine nature)→	Theological Virtues (supernatural inclinations)→	Divine Law→	Divine Actions by Participation→	Infused Cardinal Virtues→	More Perfect Divine Actions→	Eternal Happiness (participating in God's happiness)
Nature→	Natural Inclinations→	Natural and Human Law→	Good Human Actions→	Natural Virtues→	More Perfect Actions→	Natural Happiness

save (bring one into loving friendship with God). Only by the power of grace are humans able to participate in divine nature and share in God's perfections—including his knowledge (through faith) and love (through charity). Yet as Paul states, faith and charity still must be guided by the law (primarily the divine law consisting of the guidance of the Holy Spirit) and applied through virtues (the infused cardinal virtues). Once humans have grace, divine law, and infused virtues, they are able to share in God's happiness through supernatural happiness on earth. Ultimately, when they die their participation in divine nature will increase exponentially, and they will know and love God as he is.

BECAUSE GOD created humans to be happy, he gives us the gift of his Son. The Son gives us the gift of his life and, together with the Father, sends us the Holy Spirit. The Holy Spirit transforms humans through sanctifying grace and supernaturally guides and moves them to divine actions. Furthermore, grace aids humans in avoiding sin and keeps us from establishing vices. The actions caused by grace allow humans to be supernaturally happy in this life and to have eternal happiness in the next life. Because grace perfects nature, humans retain their personal identity while performing actions by the power of God. In addition, every element in the natural moral life has a corresponding element that flows from grace. More specifically, grace causes the supernatural inclinations of faith and charity, which are guided by law and applied through virtue. Hence, the next two chapters will cover law and virtue.

7

LAW

Guidance to Proper Actions

In most deontological systems, the law is seen as an obstacle to freedom. In these systems the commands are followed because of fear of external punishment or desire for some external reward. The law keeps people from being "free" to do whatever they want to do at any particular time. For example, in the Old Testament, the law said that children must honor their father and mother. If they did honor their father and mother, they would have a long life in the promised land.[1] Although this commandment is extremely necessary for the material and spiritual welfare of the community, children could also see it as an obstacle to their freedom.[2] In a teleological moral system, laws ultimately result in true freedom. In this type of system, laws are intentionally made to guide and move humans to their proper actions. They help the intellect by guiding humans to their proper actions and help the will and emotions to form virtues that result in greater love and proper emotional responses. With these perfected powers, knowledge and love are increased, giving humans greater freedom. In the end, laws cause happiness. In the teleological moral system of the New Testament, the law of the Holy Spirit is closely equated with true freedom. For example, the Epistle of James calls the obligations of the new covenant "the perfect law of freedom" (1:25; 2:12; cf. Rom 8). Although a teleological system is not primarily focused on laws (as in a deontological system), laws are nonetheless an extremely important part of this system because they cause humans to perform their proper actions. When humans get into the habit of performing these actions, they become virtuous and are then free to attain what they ultimately desire: happiness.

This chapter will show the function of law within the complete moral system. To show this function, we will examine the proper understanding of law and its relation to moral truth. To better understand the proper role of law, we will then analyze the different types of law: eternal law, divine law, natural law, and human law. Finally, because laws correspond to human rights, we will study the relation between human rights and moral truth.

THE NATURE OF LAW

Laws give direction to human actions. In other words, laws order people to a particular end. They cause humans to perform a certain type of action that will result in a particular goal being accomplished. Law is defined as "a command of reason ordering people to their proper end."[3] When a law governs a particular community, it must also be made by the proper authority and enacted. Under this definition, law is not simply based on the power or will of the authority, but it must rationally order human actions to their proper end.[4] For example, the proper end of a political state is the happiness of all its members (the common good). The leaders of the state must use their intellect to determine which actions their subjects should do or avoid in order for the common good of the state to be attained. A law that does not rationally order people to their proper actions is an unjust law and harms people rather than helps them. Those who enforce laws that are not rational (but stem solely from a leader's power) are called "tyrants."

Although often the term "law" is limited to laws made by regional or national states, in this book, law refers to the laws of every community and even to individuals inasmuch as their intellect directs them to their proper actions. For example, in the community of the family, parents must make good laws for their children. They must guide and motivate their children to do actions that are ordered to God. Individuals must also set good goals for themselves. For example, when monks or nuns take religious vows, they are declaring a law for themselves: they will always be committed to the religious state of life. Although usually laws are specifically stated, they can include unspoken expectations, customs, and traditions within a family or society that direct humans to their proper actions. For example, business customs, such as the power of a handshake, have traditionally been very important in the regulation of the workplace. When societal customs and traditions break down, they must often be replaced by state regulations, causing greater inefficiency and bureaucracy. Consequently, in this book, a law refers to *any ordinance of reason that guides humans to good actions, including goals, customs, and the expectations of others.*[5]

In a teleological system, law has three proper functions. First, and most important, laws guide humans to good actions. Humans are perfected in a community where wiser humans guide others in their moral development. When lawgivers participate in divine wisdom by guiding others to their proper actions, they are more like God. Second, laws help move the will and emotions to choose and desire the correct actions. In other words, even when humans know the right action, they often need motivation to actually perform it. The rewards and punishments that accompany law can help motivate one to choose the right action. For example, even though most people know that cheating on an assignment (or their taxes) is wrong, the possibility of being punished (either in this life or the next) can motivate them to not cheat. By guiding and motivating humans to good actions, the law causes people to become virtuous.[6] The primary function of law is to move humans to actions that will make them happy, but because those actions also affect the happiness of others, the third function of laws is to protect people from the unvirtuous. For example, there are laws against stealing that protect people's property from others. Ideally, people who follow the law would become virtuous and respect the property of others. Once they have this virtue, they would no longer need to be motivated by the law. However, since others do not have this virtue, the law is necessary to motivate them and protect the property of others from them. Laws are necessary to make sure that people have opportunities to attain true happiness. If people are murdered, abused, or neglected, they will be unable to perform their proper actions of knowing and loving God and others.

The primary role of law is to move and guide humans to perform their proper actions. For a law to be a good law, it must rationally order people to their proper end. Since humans also need to be motivated to good actions, laws must also include rewards or punishments that appeal to either the will or the emotions.

THE FOUR TYPES OF LAW

For a law to be a good or just law, it must order people to their proper actions. However, it can be difficult to determine whether or not a law orders people to their proper actions because of the complexity of the human person and the complexity of the society. In other words, how can someone know if a law is just or not? How can people know if they are making good laws? An explanation of the four principal types of laws and how they are related to each other can help people determine whether or not a law is good. The four types of laws are *eternal law, divine law, natural law,* and *human law.*

Eternal Law

The eternal law is the wisdom in God's mind moving and guiding all things to their proper end. When God creates things, he creates them to perform a particular action. When a human creates something, before she creates it, she has a plan (or blueprint) in her mind. This plan includes not only the form of the thing to be created but also the actions the created thing is made to do. For example, imagine that Anna is a great musician who also designs and builds musical instruments. Before she begins designing the instrument, she has an idea of the instrument in her mind. She has an idea of the form of the instrument and also an idea of the form of the songs she will play on the instrument. She then builds the instrument based on the idea in her head and plays the songs also based on her ideas. In philosophical terms, these ideas in her mind are called "exemplary causes" of the thing that is made.

This analogy of the musician can be extended to teach us about the eternal law. Like a musician that makes instruments, God is the exemplary cause not only of all existing things but also all of their actions. Furthermore, just as there are many instruments in an orchestra that are played differently yet make beautiful music when played in harmony with each other, God created many diverse creatures that he guides to their proper actions within an ordered universe. God's knowledge of the nature of all created things is called the "divine ideas"; his plan directing all things to their proper end is called the "eternal law." The eternal law is the plan that contains the proper actions of every creature. In reference to humans, since God perfectly moves humans to act, the eternal law includes all proper actions that humans must perform in order to attain their end of true happiness. Because the eternal law is God's plan for the fulfillment of each and every human, by learning the eternal law humans are able to discover their role in God's plan and their true identity. However, since humans do not perfectly know the eternal law, they participate in this plan in various degrees. In other words, although God guides humans to perfect actions, humans, because of their imperfections, do not always perform perfect actions.

Since the eternal law is God's plan of how all humans are to attain to their proper end, it is the cause and measure of *all* moral truth. Thus, the eternal law determines what actions lead to true happiness as fulfilling human nature (good actions) and what actions contradict human nature (evil actions). Because the eternal law is the source of all moral truth, when humans understand moral truths, their knowledge participates in the eternal law. For example, God created humans to live in loving harmony. Murder violates this loving harmony and, hence, it violates God's plan, the eternal law. When humans understand that murder is wrong, their knowledge participates in the eternal law. When they make a law stating that murder is wrong, this law receives its content and authority from the eternal law. Consequently, the eternal law is the cause of all laws to the extent that they are rational, for rationality participates in God's reason (the eternal law). To the extent that laws fall away from the eternal law, they are not true laws, but unjust laws that do violence to the human soul and cause unhappiness.

If humans could know the eternal law perfectly, then they would know what to do in every situation in order to perform actions that make themselves and all others happy. When humans know God as he is by the power of the full inheritance, they will also fully know the eternal law. However, on earth, God can only indirectly be known through his effects (such as creation), which can never fully manifest him. Likewise, the eternal law can also only be known in its effects. This knowledge of the eternal law is obtained either by means of the intellect naturally understanding the ends to which humans are naturally inclined (natural law), or by means of the intellect supernaturally understanding divine revelation (divine law).[7] Another way that humans can know the eternal law is through the wise guidance of others (human law). The eternal law is the ultimate rule of human reason; however, because it cannot be directly known on earth, it must be known through these other types of law.

Because there is an eternal law, there is an absolute truth by which every action can be judged. Even if as humans we cannot always fully know that truth, we can know with certainty that some actions are right or wrong because of our knowledge of eternal law, either through natural reason or through divine revelation (scripture, tradition, and Church teaching). Thus, although moral systems can vary from person to person based on the degree of participation of the person's intellect in the eternal law, moral relativism is false.[8]

The eternal law is God's wisdom ordering all things to their proper actions. It is the source of all moral truth and the foundation for all other laws. However, it cannot be known directly on earth and must instead be known through divine, natural, and human laws. A good analogy of how eternal law is known is the way a person knows the outside world through a window. Imagine that Julie is never able to leave a particular room because of health reasons. Her only knowledge of the outside world comes from looking out the window, which overlooks a little park. By looking out the window over a period of years, she can learn many things about the outside world. She can have limited knowledge of the weather, biology, astronomy, and so on. She can even observe things like erosion and can form theories that mountains and valleys could exist. However, there are nearly an infinite number of things that she will never know. In the analogy, the outside world is like the eternal law. Just as the outside world goes on and on and appears to have no limit, the eternal law is infinite, containing the knowledge of all acts that do happen and could happen. Just as Julie has a window to the outside world, humans have a number of windows into the eternal law. The largest window is the divine law. The divine law is all moral guidance given through divine revelation (the Bible and tradition). It contains everything, from the Ten Commandments to the guidance of the Holy Spirit within souls. Since the divine law stems from the word of God, it is a window into the eternal law. A smaller window located within the larger window of the divine law is the natural law. The natural law refers to all moral laws that can be known by the natural ability of humans to determine what fulfills their nature (i.e., leads to natural happiness). Since reason participates in the eternal law, the natural law is another window into the wisdom of God. Inside the divine and natural law is the smallest window, the human law—it refers to all those laws made by humans that guide humans to their proper actions. These three windows allow humans to participate in the eternal law and to be guided by divine wisdom to happiness. They are like the window to the outside world. They only give knowledge of a small part of the eternal law, but they do give true knowledge of it.

DIVINE LAW

The divine law is all moral guidance given to humans through the supernatural means of divine revelation (the Bible, Christian tradition, and the promptings of the Holy Spirit). It is the biggest window into the eternal law and the highest participation in it. It can be divided into two parts: the old law and the new law.

The Old Law

The old law was set forth in the old covenant. It tells the Israelites what they must do to keep the covenant (be justified) and is summarized by the Ten Commandments.[9] This law revealed the conditions necessary for them to remain faithful to God. In addition to guiding the Israelites to their proper actions, it also motivated them to act correctly. If the Israelites broke the commandments, they could expect to be punished by God; if they kept them, they could expect to be rewarded with temporal prosperity (cf. Dt 28).

Much of what is contained in the old law could be determined by natural reason alone, but God revealed these moral norms to the Israelites to make sure that they correctly knew how to achieve true happiness (since many would not figure this out without God's help). For example, one of the Ten Commandments is "You shall not murder." Natural reason alone can determine that murdering other people contradicts the peaceful community that is essential for true human happiness. However, some people, out of ignorance, cultural bias, or attachment to sin, might not discern the importance that respecting human life has for the community. Others might know that it is wrong but need some motivation to keep the commandment. God aids both of these groups of people by giving them this commandment.

The New Law

Just as the old law is the law of the old covenant, the new law is the law of the new covenant. It is also called the "law of the Spirit," "the evangelical law," or the "law of love." It is the law that flows from the revelation of Jesus Christ, the Word incarnate. There are two parts of the new law. The primary element is the grace of the Holy Spirit guiding the intellect and moving the will to perform actions of charity (Rom 8:2; Jer 31:31). The secondary element is the written law of the gospel.

In the primary element of the new law, Christ guides and moves humans to their proper actions by means of the Holy Spirit that dwells within their souls. This divine guidance is the supernatural movement of the Holy Spirit that we discussed in chapter 6 on grace. The Holy Spirit guides humans by inspiring the intellect to understand the proper end and to reason correctly how to attain it. The Holy Spirit also moves the will and emotions to love the proper end and the proper way to attain this end.

Unlike most laws that apply to humans in general, the movement of the Holy Spirit is individualized, for he is able to guide each individual to the actions that are most in accord with God's plan. Laws that pertain to *all* humans must necessarily be somewhat abstract because they still need to be applied to a particular situation. The result of this abstractness is that humans can still do a poor job applying the law and still only participate in the eternal law at a low level. For example, the law to love others can be misapplied. A person trying to follow this law might actually hurt another person. Suppose Kate attempted to love a friend who was allergic to peanuts by making peanut butter cookies for her. Although Kate loves her friend, she could seriously hurt her because she does not fully know all of the pertinent elements of a situation. Since the Holy Spirit knows the best actions of humans in every situation, he can move every human to the most perfect action in every situation.[10] Because this law contains the individualized plan of each human, it is the highest participation in the eternal law and also the biggest window into it.

The secondary element of the new law is the written words of the gospel that guide humans to their proper end. This element consists of all the physical components of the law that manifest the spiritual guidance of Christ. These components include the words of scripture (such as the Sermon on the Mount),[11] the moral guidance of tradition,[12] the teaching of the Church, and the sacraments.[13] This written element gives general laws and exhortations that apply to all human beings, such as the exhortation that all humans are to be "poor in spirit" (Mt 5:3).

If humans can be led individually by the grace of the Holy Spirit, why is this physical element of the new law necessary? The reason for this physical element is that discerning the guidance of the Holy Spirit is not always easy. Humans can mistake their own desires for the movement of the Holy Spirit. Hence, a physical sign is necessary to evaluate spiritual thoughts so that people are not deceived into doing something evil and blaming the action on the Holy Spirit. Furthermore, because humans are body and soul, the Holy Spirit reveals truth through the physical elements of the law. Just as God became man in Jesus to reveal his spiritual nature though a physical body, so also the guidance of the Holy Spirit is revealed through physical signs. For example, the Holy Spirit continues to guide humanity through the visible church. Consequently, when following the inspiration of the Holy Spirit, people must still judge to make sure that whatever they believe they are called to perform is in accord with the written element of the new law. For example, the Holy Spirit will not guide someone to get revenge, because revenge violates the written words of Jesus (see Mt 5:38–48).

Just as the guidance of the new law comes primarily from the interior inspiration of the Holy Spirit and secondarily from the written word, so also the motivation for acting comes primarily from the movement of the Holy Spirit. Unlike the old law, which motivated the Israelites with exterior rewards and punishments, the new law motivates people by giving them the power to love the right action out of love for God. For example, people can have two different types of motivations for going to Sunday Mass. They can be motivated by a reward or punishment, or they can be motivated by their love. Those who are motivated by their love choose to go to Mass because they *want* to go to Mass and not because they *have* to go to Mass. Of course, those who go because of their love are made happy by the action of going, since they know and love the good action. Consequently, the new law is also called the "law of love."

Because the new law stems from grace and motivates people to perform actions out of love for God, unlike the old law, the new law has the power to save. The new law causes people to perform actions that are ordered to eternal happiness. Furthermore, as the law of love, the new law transforms the moral elements of the old law, so that these elements also help guide people to salvation.[14]

The divine law guides humans to actions ordered to supernatural happiness. It also gives humans the ability (through grace) to perform these actions. Because it includes all actions that a person should do to attain eternal happiness and to help others attain it, the divine law is the biggest window into the eternal law.

Natural Law

The next largest window is the natural law. The natural law refers to reason's natural participation in the eternal law. It refers to all those moral laws that can be known by our natural ability to determine what fulfills human nature (e.g., what leads to natural happiness). Because humans are created by a wise God, they are created for a purpose. By our natural ability alone, we are able to identify that purpose and determine that some acts lead to true happiness and some acts do not. We can determine the morality of different actions by looking at how we are created to achieve certain ends and by looking at the way certain acts are ordered to these ends and how other acts are not. In other words, humans have natural inclinations to their proper actions, and good actions are ones in accord with these inclinations. For example, as humans we are naturally inclined to do good and avoid evil, to know, love, and live in society with others (be of one mind and heart with them), to be virtuous, to be happy, to continue the human species, and to remain alive.[15] A good action is in accord with these inclinations. Natural law is our natural knowledge that certain acts fulfill these inclinations and certain other acts do not. The Ten Commandments, and the Golden Rule, are all examples of laws that can be determined by natural reason.[16]

The natural law is understood in the third step of the human action: understanding the law or end.[17] These laws are then applied to a particular situation in order to cause good human actions. However, sometimes two inclinations can contradict. For example, what if an action necessary for the health of the body contradicts the inclination to love others. This problem is solved in the judgment stage (step 7) of the human action because some inclinations take precedence over others. In other words, in a teleological system the inclinations themselves are ordered and result in a hierarchy of laws, where the lower laws are ordered to the higher laws. As we saw in chapter 1, even on a natural level, humans are ultimately made to be happy by knowing and loving God. Hence, the highest natural inclination is to be happy by knowing and loving God. This inclination results in the obligation to know and love God. This law is the most universal, and all other laws are ordered by their relation to this law.

Because humans function fully only within a society, they are naturally inclined to live in society. Thus, natural reason then states that the common good of all individuals is the next highest good. Humans have an obligation to seek the good of all individuals within a society, but not in such a way that any individual can be unjustly sacrificed for the good of the whole. In addition, for the sake of the common good, humans have a natural inclination to procreate and raise virtuous children. In order to love God and others and to raise virtuous children, humans are naturally inclined to know the truth and love the good. This knowledge and love allows humans to fulfill their inclination to freely do good actions and avoid evil. This inclination is followed by the inclination to virtue, which is necessary for humans to perform all the above actions. Following this inclination is the inclination to seek the emotional good in accord with reason. Last of all is the inclination to health and bodily life and the material necessities that are essential for this life.[18] Table 7.1 lists some of the natural inclinations along with duties that flow from them.

This hierarchy of laws, where the lower laws are ordered to the higher laws, must be taken into consideration when determining the proper action in a particular situation. In addition to this hierarchy of laws, the degree to which an inclination pertains to a particular situation must also be considered. Some laws pertain more directly to a particular situation than others. A higher natural law that only slightly pertains to a situation does not overrule a lower natural law that pertains directly to a situation. For example, humans have a natural inclination to act freely—hence, normally, intentionally consuming a substance that removes freedom is morally wrong. However, this law does not pertain to cases where people use general anesthesia if they are having surgery. For, although failure to use anesthesia could severely impair health, it only temporarily removes freedom within a situation where free actions are not as essential. In other words, one needs to be able to act freely in situations where free decisions are essential for loving God and others, but in this case the more extensive contradiction of the inclination to health takes precedence over the inclination to freedom. Furthermore, an extensive impairment of health also removes the ability to freely love others.[19] This situation is different from a case where a man wants to prolong his life by harvesting the organs of a living homeless man, resulting in the death of the homeless man. Although this would prolong his health, it would egregiously violate the higher inclinations of living in society and of loving one's neighbor and would hence be wrong. In all of these cases, prudence (which will we cover in chapter 15) must be used to judge the proper action.

Table 7.1.   Examples of Laws Stemming from Natural Inclinations

Natural Inclinations	*Natural Law*
To God	Duty to worship God and seek God.
To natural happiness	Duty to seek true happiness (vs. false happiness).
To live in community	Duty to enter into loving relationships with others. Duty to respect the dignity of all humans, to avoid racism and unjust discrimination, to transform culture. Duty to work for just laws and good government.
To know the truth	Duty to seek wisdom. Duty to understand the truths of natural law. Duty to form conscience.
To love the good	Duty to do good and avoid evil. Duty to love all others.
To act freely (because of the intellect and will, humans are naturally inclined to free actions)	Duty to perfect the powers of the soul in order to act freely and to remove impediments to freedom.
To seek the true bodily good	Duty to properly train emotions. Duty to seek morally necessary activities that are pleasurable in the proper amount and way.
To procreate and raise children	Duty to raise holy children. Duty to only have sex within marriage between a man and a woman. Duty to be open to life. Duty to obey parents and proper authorities.
For the body to be alive and healthy	Duty to live a healthy lifestyle. Duty to take the medical treatment necessary to follow God's plan.
Material goods necessary for performing proper actions (and only those necessary)	Duty to use material goods in accord with Catholic social teaching. Duty to take care of the created world.

Natural law is a participation in the eternal law because it results from an understanding of the divinely planned order in human nature. The world and human nature are patterned after God's mind. Just as a sculptor puts order into a stone by making a statue, so also God ordered the world. Before the sculptor carves the statue, the sculptor has the pattern of the statue within his mind. If the sculptor is truly a skilled artist, then the statue will be a material image of the pattern within his mind. By looking at the statue, people can know the pattern within the mind of the sculptor. God has ordered humans so that certain actions fulfill humans and certain actions do not. By getting to know the order within human nature (natural law), humans are also able to know the pattern in the mind of God (eternal law). Hence, natural law is also a window into the eternal law. For example, God created humans to seek bodily health in order to perform the more spiritual activities of knowing and loving. When humans determine that they should take care of their bodies, their knowledge participates in God's plan for the universe.

Since human reason participates in divine wisdom, humans must obey their reason (assuming they tried their best to come to right judgment). This act is called "following one's conscience." The consciences of humans have the force of law because they participate in the voice of a higher reason, God's eternal reason. In other words, humans must always seek to know as much of the eternal law as possible (through human, natural, and divine law), and the more perfectly they follow the eternal law, the more they will share in God's happiness.

Because of the natural law, all humans have access to some moral truth even without divine law. This moral truth is determined by understanding what actions fulfill human nature and what actions violate human nature. Because the amount of knowledge that can be obtained by natural reason is less than what can be obtained by divine revelation, the natural law is a smaller window into the eternal law than that of the divine law. Nonetheless, the natural law is a true participation in God's wisdom.

HUMAN LAW

Human law is the smallest window into the eternal law. It refers to all laws made by humans to establish order on earth. Civil laws, parental laws, customs in the workplace, and even individual goals are examples of human laws. These laws are true laws if they are derived from the eternal law. However, since the eternal law cannot be known directly, human laws must be derived from the eternal law via the natural or divine law.[20] If a human law is not in conformity with the eternal law as known through the natural and divine laws, then it is an unjust law and can lead others astray rather than guide them to their proper end. Consequently, the way to tell the difference between a just law and an unjust law is by judging whether the law is in accord with the natural and divine laws. For example, the segregation laws in the United States from the time of the Civil War to the civil rights movement were unjust because they violated the natural law by violating the natural inclination to be united with others in society.[21] Furthermore, these laws violated the divine law's call to charity.[22]

Although all human laws should be derived from natural and divine law, not every natural or divine law should be made into a human law. Some divine and natural laws cannot be prudently enforced because enforcing them will cause more harm than good. For example, humans have a natural obligation to perform some type of work.[23] However, in order for a government to require that all people work, the government would have to implement a socialist system, which would more violently contradict the natural law.[24] Consequently, there will always be some morally wrong actions that are contrary to natural and divine law that nonetheless should remain legal. People of goodwill should still exhort others not to perform these types of actions, and they should work to form customs that discourage these types of actions. For example, businesses and individuals should act in such a way that the number of people employed with just labor is maximized.[25]

Because the human intellect is weak from ignorance and vice, in addition to the natural law, the divine law is necessary to form good human laws. However, because of the plurality of society, arguing from divine law principles in the political square will not be effective. Thus, Christian lawmakers will have to found laws on naturally known principles. Because these arguments are based on natural reason, humans in all traditions can potentially agree on them. Since natural law comes from the same source as the divine law, arguing by natural law principles alone still results in the formation of just laws. For example, in order to argue that infanticide is wrong, it is not necessary to quote the Ten Commandments. Nonetheless, because of the weakness of the human intellect, it will always be necessary to judge the precepts of our reason by the divine law.[26]

Human laws should help make people virtuous by guiding and moving them to good actions. In addition, they should protect people from the unvirtuous. As long as human laws are derived from the eternal law by means of natural and divine law, they will be good laws that will help people fulfill God's divine plan that all humans are happy.

HUMAN RIGHTS

Although the concept of individual rights has always been part of the Christian tradition, in the last century the use of "rights language" to express individual freedoms has become particularly common in society.[27] In fact, widespread use of this language and the worldwide acceptance of the UN's Universal Declaration of Human Rights (1948) caused Pope John XXIII in 1963 to devote a significant portion of his encyclical on world peace (*Pacem in Terris*) to a proper understanding of the notion of human rights.[28] However, already during the reign of John XXIII, rights language was being abused, and people were claiming to have rights to anything they wanted. Hence, John XXIII sought to place human rights within their proper context of natural and eternal law.[29] Despite the attempts of John XXIII and later popes, many people today believe that they have a right to whatever they passionately want, provided it does not take away the rights of another human. For example, many people wrongly believe that they have a right to have an abortion.[30] Others believe that their right to free speech means that they can say things that degrade other humans. In a democracy, a widespread misunderstanding of human rights means that at any one time a certain segment of the population might be legally abused or even killed. Consequently, a proper understanding of human rights is very important in our current society.

Like just laws, true rights have their foundation in the eternal law. Human rights come from laws. Each type of law has a corresponding type of right. *Human laws* cause civil rights. For example, the First Amendment to the U.S. Constitution protects the civil rights of freedom of religion, speech, and press. Natural rights come from the *natural law*. For example, the natural law requires that humans respect the lives of others and do not murder each other. Corresponding to this law is the natural right to life. Divine rights come from the *divine law*. For example, in the Sermon on the Mount, Jesus says that humans should not lust after other humans. Hence, humans have a divine right not to be seen as a sexual object. Finally, *eternal law* gives humans the right to all the things that are needed for their eternal perfection.

Just as human law must be in accord with the natural and divine law to be just, individual and civil rights must be in accord with natural and divine rights (stemming from natural and divine law) to be authentic rights. Rights that do not come from natural and divine law are false human rights. Consequently, humans do not have a right to do anything that they please but only that which is in accord with the eternal law. Natural rights include all those things that are essential for legitimate natural happiness, such as life, religion, work, health care, and culture.[31] Divine rights include rights to all those things that are necessary for eternal happiness, such as education in the faith, the sacraments of initiation, and so on.[32] Because the eternal law moves humans to true happiness, humans have true rights to all of those things essential for true happiness. Likewise, since false rights refer to things that are not in conformity with the eternal law, when humans pursue false rights, they end up with false happiness. States should not make laws that deny any of the natural or divine rights, nor should they promote rights that do not flow from natural or divine law.

Law is a dictate of reason participating in eternal law that causes humans to do good actions that lead to happiness. The eternal law is God's wisdom, and it orders humans to actions that make them happy. Because it is God's wisdom, it contains every moral truth. The way that we know the eternal law most perfectly is through the new law, which is the grace of the Holy Spirit. The Holy Spirit moves humans to do acts of charity that participate in the eternal law at the highest possible level, causing the greatest happiness. However, to make sure that humans are genuinely moved by the Holy Spirit and not by their own spirit, they must have written laws, such as the Ten Commandments (for it was the same Spirit who gave the old and new law) and other written laws found in the Bible, tradition, and Church teaching. Furthermore, humans can know the truth of eternal law through their natural reason. All human laws should be in conformity with eternal law as known through natural and divine law. Authentic human rights are also in conformity with the natural and divine laws. Because law participates in the eternal law, which is God's plan moving all humans to happiness, law guides and moves humans to good actions that cause happiness. Hence, laws make humans free to attain that which they really want: happiness.

8

VIRTUE

Good Habits Perfecting the Natural Inclinations

The last few chapters have frequently noted the importance of virtue in the moral life. On the natural level, virtues perfect the natural inclinations to know, love, and seek the bodily good. They give people the ability to enter into the loving relationships that are necessary for true natural happiness. On the supernatural level, the theological virtues of faith, hope, and charity act as supernatural inclinations. These supernatural inclinations give humans the ability to perform actions ordered to eternal happiness. Just as the natural inclinations are ordered to their proper actions through the natural virtues, the supernatural inclinations are ordered to their proper actions through the infused cardinal virtues. By means of these virtues, humans are able to enter into the loving relationship with God that is essential for supernatural and eternal happiness.

Virtues are extremely vital principles on the journey to God, and this chapter will cover them in detail. Since virtues are good habits, we first give a description of habits. Within this description of habits, we will cover the notion of virtues in general. After this general description, we will present the different types of virtues, beginning with the natural (acquired) virtues. These natural virtues will be followed by the theological virtues, and then the infused cardinal virtues will be covered last. Finally, we will study the role of virtues as the mean between the excess and the defect.

HABITS

The average human uses hundreds, if not thousands, of habits to perform everyday activities. Humans need habits to talk, to walk, to stand up, to think, to eat, and so on.

In addition to these habits common to nearly all humans, some humans have special-ized habits that correspond to their trade, such as being good at teaching, welding, farming, and building things. By nature, humans require habits to perform nearly all of their actions.

Humans are born relatively helpless. From even before leaving the womb, we begin forming habits by practicing particular activities over and over again. Even simple activities, such as focusing our eyes and grabbing objects with our hands require days of practice. In time, habits develop, and these activities become easier and are per-formed more perfectly. Eventually, more complex habits, such as the ability to walk and talk, are developed. With the addition of each habit, more habits can be built upon the preceding ones. For example, the habit of walking is built upon the habit of keep-ing one's balance. The habit of running is then built upon the ability to walk. The habit of being able to play soccer is then built upon the ability to run. The point is that humans are not able to perform their proper actions immediately. In every area of life, many actions are needed to form habits that are necessary for proper functioning. The moral order is no different.[1] Only after many acts of a particular type are the powers of the soul disposed to their proper actions. For example, if humans want to be good at loving others, they will need to form a habit by constantly performing acts of love.

In the English language, the word "habit" can refer to a qualitative change in hu-mans that perfects their natural abilities, allowing them to perform more perfect ac-tions, or the word "habit" can refer to a subconscious routine. Examples of the former meaning of habit can be found in the preceding paragraph. Other examples include the ability to accurately kick a soccer ball or the ability to be brave. Examples of the latter meaning of habit are the involuntary biting of one's nails or certain arbitrary speech mannerisms. Because the word "habit" contains more than just the notion of a qualitative perfection, some scholars like to differentiate between the word "habit" and the Latin word *habitus*. These scholars make this distinction in order to keep people from thinking that virtues are involuntary dispositions that remove freedom.[2] In reality, virtues increase freedom by making people free to perform greater actions. Despite the possibility for misunderstanding, this book will use the word "habit" when referring to those dispositions that give humans the ability to perform more perfect actions, and a precise definition will be given below to help the reader avoid under-standing it as a subconscious routine.

Aristotle defines a habit as a "lasting disposition whereby someone is disposed well or ill."[3] A "disposition" is a "firm and unchangeable tendency to always act in a certain way."[4] Hence, someone with a habit is able to consistently perform a particular type of activity. For example, someone with the habit of courage is able to easily per-form a courageous activity in any situation. Other people might be able to perform a courageous activity with the help of another person or by chance, but they do not have the habit of courage since they are not able to consistently act courageously by their own power. Because a habit is a *lasting* disposition, it is not easily changed. It takes a great deal of effort to either cause a habit or break a habit.

Habits perfect humans so that their actions are *easy, prompt, joyful, and done with greater perfection*.[5] An action is *easy* when a person is able to perform it with little or no internal struggle. An action is *prompt* when a person is able to perform it in every situation, and not just on good days. An action is *joyful* when intellectual and emotional joy accompany it. Finally, habits make people good at *performing* certain actions. An analogy can be found in walking through a field of tall, coarse grass. At first, walking through the field is very difficult and takes a great deal of effort and motivation. However, as one walks along the same path over and over the grass becomes trampled, and it becomes much easier to walk along the path. Eventually, the grass dies, and a true path emerges. At this point it is easy to walk along the path (both in terms of physical effort and motivation). Because of the ease of the action now, walking on the path is much more enjoyable, and there is no repulsion to walking, even when one is tired. Finally, one can walk much faster than before and can even run down the path (an action that would have been nearly impossible with the tall grass).[6] With the addition of a habit, the action can be done with much more perfection and is easy and enjoyable.

An example of these attributes of a habit can be found in the following scenario: suppose that Emily wants to acquire the habit of eating in moderation. At a Thanksgiving meal, she is tempted to eat her favorite dessert, pumpkin pie, even though she knows she has already eaten as much as she needs. After a difficult internal struggle, she reluctantly chooses not to eat the pie. Although she did the right action, she does not have a habit yet. The action was not easy. If she had been tired or was having a bad day, she would have given into her temptation, so the action was also not prompt. Although she would have had some satisfaction for not giving into the temptation, she did not have the joy that accompanies a strong habit. Finally, her ability to choose the right action needed to be perfected. However, over the course of the year, Emily continues to practice eating in moderation. When Thanksgiving comes again, she has developed a habit. Her temptation to eat too much is basically gone, and the action of eating in moderation is now easy, prompt, and joyful. She is also good at determining how much and how often she should eat.

A habit can be either good or evil. A good habit is called a *virtue*. An evil habit is called a *vice*. A habit is good if it corresponds to human nature.[7] In other words, a habit is a virtue if it corresponds to our natural inclinations to our proper actions. Because we were created to do things that lead to happiness, a virtue causes acts that lead to God. Since the intellect determines the proper actions, a virtue must be in accord with our reason's determination of actions that flow from love of God. A habit is evil if it goes against human nature. In other words, a vice contradicts our inclinations to know and love God and others.

Just as actions flowing from a virtue are easy, prompt, and joyful, so also actions flowing from a vice are easy, prompt, and joyful. For example, if an adolescent boy continually looks at pornography, in a matter of time he will come to the point where he no longer has to struggle against his conscience at all. This evil act becomes easy, prompt, joyful, and can be done with greater efficacy. With the help of others and practice of good actions, a vice can be overcome. A good example of overcoming the vice of lust can be found in the story of St. Jerome. Jerome was frequently tempted with lust as a young man. However, every time he was tempted, he went and studied Hebrew. Jerome became perhaps the greatest Hebrew scholar that ever lived, and he is famous for translating the Bible from Hebrew and Greek into Latin. Understanding Hebrew became easy, prompt, joyful, and he was very good at it.

Habits are necessary for perfecting human nature.[8] Because humans are created imperfect in terms of their actions, the help of others is necessary to aid the natural inclinations in performing their proper actions. Through the repetition of these good actions, virtues are then formed. These virtues further perfect the natural inclinations so that humans are able to perform the actions through their own abilities.[9] For example, when a toddler learns to walk, his parents first hold his hands as he learns to keep his balance with each step. However, once the toddler has the habit of walking, he is able to walk by his own ability. The habit gives the child a particular proficiency in acting, allowing him to act by his own power. So also in the moral life, habits perfect the natural inclinations so that humans are able to perform their proper actions with greater proficiency. For example, young children will generally need the guidance and motivation of their parents to learn not to hurt others. However, once these children acquire the virtue of justice, their own love of others (rather than their parents' love) keeps them from hurting others. The children now have a greater ability to love and can love with greater proficiency. Loving others is also now easy, prompt, and joyful. This proficiency allows the children to act by means of their own knowledge and love, leading them to happiness.[10]

This growth in virtue can be divided into four stages. In stage one, when beginning to form a virtue, beginners will usually need the help of others, such as parents, friends, mentors, and God, who guide and motivate them to perform the good actions. They need guidance to determine what actions to perform. Furthermore, in this stage emotional desire for contrary things is very strong, and it will cloud the intellect and influence the will to do contrary actions unless these mentors and friends motivate them to do their proper actions. With the help of others, they will be able to perform these virtuous actions repetitively, and a nascent habit begins to form. This emerging habit gives them the ability to perform the actions by their own power—but only through an interior struggle, where they must force themselves to go against contrary emotions (stage two). As they continue to struggle against these contrary emotions by forcing themselves to do the virtuous action, the power of the habit will continue to grow. As the habit develops, the intellect is perfected to easily determine the proper action, and the will is perfected to love the action. The emotions are now transformed enough that they have less desire for the contrary actions and begin to desire the virtuous action. Thus, in stage three, the emotions of these progressing humans are at first repulsed by the thought of the good action, but now humans can will their emotions to desire the virtuous action. In other words, through their intellect and will they have enough control over their emotions that they can will themselves to desire a particular thing. As they continue to do the virtuous action, the emotions are completely transformed so that they now only desire the good action and no longer desire the contrary action at all. At this point, the virtue is a full-fledged virtue, and the action is easy and joyful (stage four).

The process of growing in the virtue of sharing with the poor is a good example for illustrating these different stages. Suppose that when Joe was younger, he was very attached to the money that he made. He did not want to share any of it with others. However, his parents required him to give a certain percentage of the money to others. He gave the money to the poor, but only because his parents made him give this money away (stage one). As he continued to give the money to the poor, the virtue of sharing with the poor began to emerge. He intellectually knew that giving to the poor was the right action, and through his will he loved God and willed to help the poor. However, he was still emotionally attached to the things he could buy for himself with the money, and his disordered emotions still made it very difficult to choose to give any of the money away. Yet, through sheer willpower, he sent some of his paycheck to an organization helping poor children in Haiti (stage two). The action was not easy, but as he did this good action over and over, his emotions were slowly transformed. Now, when he first thinks of sharing his money, his emotions are initially repulsed by the thought and cause the intellect to think of all the other things he could buy with the money. However, they are no longer as unruly, and Joe can now transform his emotions to have compassion for the poor children and desire to help them. He causes this change by imagining the poor children without enough food and thinking about how he would feel in their situation. The mostly trained emotions respond by loving these children and desiring to help them (stage three). Finally, Joe's emotions are completely transformed so that he has a strong desire to help the poor, and they drive Joe to regularly give not only his extra income but also some of his essential income to those who need it more than he needs it.

This example also shows how habits help humans consistently perform good actions. Because humans are rational, they are capable of performing a wide variety of actions, some good and some evil.[11] Consequently, unlike nonrational beings, which by necessity perform their proper actions,[12] humans can perform actions that, in the long run, do not make them happy. Habits drive humans to perform a particular type of action, giving them the ability to always perform good actions. Since the intellect, will, and emotions are all involved in human actions, all three powers must be perfected by habits. By means of virtues, these powers of the soul can be perfected to perform good actions, leading to happiness.

However, if habits determine humans to a particular type of action, do habits remove freedom? It depends on whether the habit is a virtue or a vice. In general, virtues increase the ability of humans to perform good actions, making them free to perform actions they would not be able to perform without habits. For example, the habit of being a good reader gives children the freedom to read. This general notion of freedom extends to moral freedom (the freedom to choose a particular action). Moral freedom exists when the intellect, will, and emotions act properly. The perfection of these powers increases a person's freedom. For example, a lack of knowledge keeps people from properly understanding their choices and restricts the freedom of the will. So also, unruly emotions overwhelm the intellect and will, removing freedom. Good habits that perfect the intellect to know, the will to love, and the emotions to aid the intellect and will also increase freedom.[13] However, only good habits increase freedom. Bad habits decrease freedom.[14] Vices in the intellect, will, and emotions hinder their ability to act properly and restrict the ability of humans to choose freely.

Because habits are an essential part of human nature, *every single human action either causes a habit, increases a habit, or decreases a habit.* If the actions are good, they cause virtues; if they are bad, they cause vices. Since virtues and vices are opposites, often an action that decreases a vice also starts a virtue, and vice versa. This truth that every human action affects habits is very important to moral perfection and has many implications. For example, this truth explains why it can take many years to perfect a habit such as promptly and joyfully doing homework. Every time students do their homework, they are building a good habit. However, every time they procrastinate or choose to do some other less important activity instead of their homework, they decrease the habit. Since they are constantly performing contrasting types of actions, the habit does not grow, and the action does not become easy, prompt, and joyful. Consequently, in order to form good habits, an action must be done consistently, and all contrary actions should be avoided. Another closely related implication is that parents and teachers must consistently enforce good behavior at all times to form good habits. There is no such thing as not training children. If parents and teachers do not guide and motivate the children to virtue, their neglect will allow the children to be trained in vice. The key point is that *all* human actions shape one's moral character.

The Cause of Virtues

Virtues can be divided into two types, acquired and infused. Acquired (natural) virtues flow from human nature and are caused by the repetition of a certain type of action. Infused virtues (such as faith, hope, and love) are gifts from God. This section gives a more detailed explanation of how each of these types of virtues is attained and perfected.

Although the seeds of acquired virtues are in our nature (natural inclinations), these virtues are formed by constantly performing acts of a certain type and *intensity.* Not only must there be a repetition of like actions, but to truly increase a virtue, the actions must be done with a certain intensity.[15] A good analogy can be found in the coaching profession. Coaches will often tell their athletes to practice with intensity. If athletes go to practice and unenthusiastically go through the motions, their ability to play the sport may actually diminish, even though they are practicing. For example, suppose the players on a basketball team fail to practice with intensity. Their lack of effort could carry over to the game, and the basketball team could actually get worse. So also with the moral life—at the beginning of the formation of virtue, simply doing the same types of actions is sufficient to begin the habit. However, for the habit to continue to develop, people must perform the actions with greater intensity. For example, a husband might be in the habit of loving his wife. However, if he begins to take his wife for granted and fails to do loving actions with intensity, the love between them may diminish. It might diminish even if the husband is still doing loving actions for her. To rekindle the love, he must focus on intensely performing many loving actions.

What does it mean to act with intensity? Or to return to the analogy, what do coaches mean when they say "practice with intensity"? For an action to be intense, all three powers of the soul must be actively engaged. The intellect must be focused on the act being performed. The will must deeply love the goal and choose the right action, and the emotions must aid the intellect and will by acting with great passion. For example, when the basketball players practice with intensity, they stay focused on the practice drills, work as hard as they can to attain the goal, and act passionately throughout the entire drill. Likewise in life, to truly grow in perfection, humans must act with intensity. Teresa of Calcutta is credited with saying, "We cannot do great things, but only little things with great love." Virtues are increased, not necessarily by the external greatness of the action, but by the internal intensity from which the action flows. To continue to increase their love of God (or of any other person), humans must be focused on their actions, must deeply love God (or others), and must act with great passion.[16]

Since the infused virtues flow from grace, they are caused by God alone. Like grace, the normal instrumental cause of the infused virtues is the sacraments. However, once these virtues are infused, repetition of like actions can increase them because God causes these acts in a supernatural way. In other words, the infused virtues are habits, and since grace perfects nature, like all habits, the infused virtues are increased by like actions. When humans perform actions flowing from the infused virtues, they act by means of the power of the divine nature. Hence, God works within them and causes the virtue to increase. For example, after humans have the virtue of charity, they are able to do acts beyond their nature, such as loving God and others. These acts increase the habit of charity, allowing them to love even more. As with the acquired virtues, humans must act with great intensity for the infused virtues to continue to develop.[17]

ACQUIRED VIRTUES

Acquired virtues are naturally attained by repetitively performing acts of increasing intensity. These virtues give humans the ability to perform better human actions: actions flowing from their own knowledge and love. These actions cause natural happiness. Because human actions stem from the intellect, will, and emotions, all three of these powers must be perfected by virtues for humans to perform their proper actions. This section will specifically show how particular virtues perfect the intellect, will, and emotions.

INTELLECTUAL VIRTUES

Before analyzing the specific intellectual virtues, a distinction must be made between the *speculative intellect* and the *practical intellect*.[18] The speculative intellect is directed toward consideration of the truth, and the practical intellect is directed toward actions. In other words, knowledge within the speculative intellect is for its own sake; knowledge in the practical intellect is for acting. For example, David might know that the Ural Mountains are in Russia. However, unless David is planning on visiting the Ural Mountains, this knowledge is only speculative knowledge, knowledge for its own sake. If David actually does plan a trip to the Ural Mountains, then the knowledge is used to act and becomes practical knowledge. Chapter 5, in which we explained the twelve steps of the human action, presented both the steps of the speculative and practical intellect. Various virtues perfect these different steps.

Because of the weakness of the human intellect, humans do not understand the essence of things immediately; rather, they require many sense experiences and have to go through many different actions. In order to know the truth, the speculative intellect must first form concepts by apprehending things (step 1 of the human action); then it perfects the understanding of these concepts by joining or separating them into propositions or sentences (step 2); and finally it reasons to conclusions (step 3). Once the intellect is able to reason to the highest and most foundational truths, it judges the rest of its knowledge based on these truths (step 4). For example, young children begin to form concepts such as "cause" and "effect" (step 1). As they grow in the ability to understand, they combine different concepts to form the following statement: "An effect is always in some way like its cause" (step 2).[19] By using cause-and-effect arguments, humans can come to knowledge that God exists and that he has certain attributes (step 3).

The following argument is an example of this reasoning: Things exist. Nothing in this world has the power to cause its own existence and hence must be caused by something else. Eventually in the causal chain there must be something that necessarily exists, or else nothing would exist at all. This thing that necessarily exists must be the ultimate cause of all things that exist within creation. This uncaused cause can be referred to as God.[20] By means of this and other arguments, many attributes of God can be known, such as that God is one, perfect, infinite act of being. Once humans know something about God, they can judge everything else that they know by this truth in order to increase their understanding of what they know (step 4).[21] For example, the wise man knows that because God is good and creates a good world, then all existing things have some goodness. The greater the participation of something in the goodness of God, the greater the goodness of the thing and the more it should be loved. Consequently, in order for the intellect to fulfill its natural inclination to know the truth, it must go through several steps.

Intellectual virtues perfect this natural inclination to know the truth. However, since there are several steps involved in knowing the truth, there are also several virtues perfecting these various steps.[22] The first step of the speculative intellect, simple apprehension, does not require an acquired virtue since the natural inclination is sufficiently powerful to form concepts of things without the aid of virtues. Since virtues are formed by the repetition of actions, the intellect must be able to perform its first actions by its own power, or else it could not act at all.

The second step of the speculative intellect, understanding, is perfected by the virtue of *understanding*. People with this virtue are able to better understand the essence of things. By joining or separating concepts, the intellect can penetrate deeper into the underlying reality and determine how things relate to the rest of the world.[23] Parents and teachers are constantly increasing the understanding of their children and students by showing how different concepts relate to each other. For example, in geometry, the simply apprehended concept of a triangle is better understood when the students join to it to the concept that the sum of all the angles within a triangle equals 180 degrees. Another example is from the moral life itself. A person might have a basic understanding of the concept of happiness. Upon learning that happiness is the act of contemplating the good that is known and loved, a person can enrich his basic understanding by joining concepts to or separating concepts from his already-apprehended concept of happiness. For example, if he previously thought happiness was an emotion, he might separate the concept of emotion from that of happiness. Now that he *understands* that happiness is not an emotion, he can *understand* that it is the act of knowing and loving. The thoughts of people with the virtue of understanding correspond more perfectly to reality because they have a deeper perception of what things are and *understand* how different things relate to each other.

The third step of the speculative intellect, discursive reasoning, is perfected by the virtue of *knowledge* (*scientia* in Latin), also called *science*. People with this virtue are good at reasoning to conclusions. As with understanding, parents and teachers should push their children and students to reason logically. For example, students who understand that the sum of all the angles in a triangle equals 180 degrees can then reason to the conclusion that one angle is 45 degrees if the other two angles are 45 and 90 degrees.

The fourth step of the speculative intellect, judging by the highest truths, is perfected by the virtue of *wisdom*. The wise person understands the most important things and is able to determine the order of the rest of world in relation to these most important things. Traditionally, theologians and philosophers have sought to understand the highest truths and to judge all other knowledge as it relates to these truths. For example, in chapter 1 we analyzed the understanding of humans as related to the highest truth of God as Trinity. An analogy to another science can be helpful. Engineers who understand the theory behind engineering (the highest truths in their science) can judge whether any particular structure (such as a bridge) is stable based on their knowledge. Likewise, wise humans understand how all the different aspects of creation fit together. The virtue of wisdom gives humans the ability to be consistent in their thinking. Humans are inconsistent in their thinking if what they think in one discipline contradicts what they think in another discipline. For example, suppose someone believes that he needs to love the poor when he is at church, but he believes that he can hurt the poor in the realm of business because it is "good business." This man may know something about Christianity and something about business, but the man is not wise. If he properly judged all areas of his thinking by the higher truths of loving God and others, he would remove this inconsistency in his thinking. Wisdom is one of the most important virtues since it allows humans to recognize the ordered effects of God in science, art, culture, and all other areas of life. Since humans require habits to be good at thinking, the virtues of understanding, knowledge, and wisdom are essential for perfecting the speculative intellect's natural inclinations to know the truth.

The attainment of practical knowledge also takes several steps. These steps have already been covered in chapter 5, since they are the steps of the human action that take place in the intellect. Using the numbering given in chapter 5, we have step 1, simple apprehension; step 3, understanding of the end (goal/law); step 5, taking counsel; step 7, judgment; and step 9, command. (Step 11, contemplating the good attained, is actually an act of understanding or judgment by higher truths in the speculative intellect.) Each of these steps, except command, corresponds to an act in the speculative intellect. Simple apprehension in both the practical and the speculative refers to the apprehension of things by abstracting concepts from sense knowledge. The only difference is that these concepts in the practical intellect are ordered to action. Understanding the end in the practical intellect corresponds to speculative understanding. However, since practical understanding is ordered to action, it refers to goals or laws that guide the intellect in acting. Counsel includes both research and reasoning to a conclusion. Inasmuch as counsel includes reasoning to a conclusion, it corresponds to discursive reasoning in the speculative intellect. Finally, judgment in both the practical and the speculative intellect is by higher principles. However, in the practical intellect, actions are judged to be good or evil. Command has no corresponding step in the speculative intellect since its sole reason for existence is to cause actions.

Just as with the speculative intellect, each step has a different virtue that perfects it. Like in the speculative intellect, practical simple apprehension does not require an acquired virtue since the natural inclination of the intellect is sufficiently strong to apprehend concepts without a virtue.

The step of understanding in the practical intellect is perfected by the virtue of *practical understanding* (*synderesis*).[24] Practical understanding perfects the intellect's ability to join or separate concepts in order to form good goals and laws. The person with this virtue is particularly good at understanding the natural laws flowing from his natural inclinations and at understanding what goals are necessary to attain happiness. For example, someone with practical understanding might understand the importance of a good education and might set the goal of getting a good education.

The next three steps of counsel, judgment, and command are all perfected by the virtue of *prudence*.[25] The person with prudence is able to adeptly apply the goal or law to a particular situation and command it. In other words, humans with prudence are good at determining the best way to attain their goals or to follow the guidance of moral laws. For example, prudent people can properly apply the goal of eating the right foods to live a healthy lifestyle. They would first determine what foods are healthy and what foods are available. They would then reason to the conclusion of what available food best attains health. For example, they might reason to the conclusion that chicken and broccoli are the best option. They would then judge whether they should eat these foods or if there are other more important reasons for not eating them. Finally, they would be good at commanding the will to execute the action of eating the proper food (and not something less healthy). Prudence gives them the ability to easily and promptly perform the right actions in the right circumstances.

The intellect is naturally inclined to know and command good actions and requires virtues to perfect these natural inclinations. The virtue of practical understanding perfects the intellect's ability to determine laws and goals (the end of the action), and the virtue or prudence perfects the intellect's ability to apply these ends to the particular situation. See table 8.1 to see how these different acts and virtues are related.

Table 8.1.   Acts of the Intellect and Corresponding Virtues

Steps of the Speculative Intellect	Virtues	Corresponding Steps of the Practical Intellect	Virtues
Simple Apprehension	None needed	Simple Apprehension	None needed
Understanding	Understanding	Understanding of End	Practical Understanding
Reasoning	Knowledge or Scientia	Counsel: Research and Reasoning	Prudence
Judging by the highest truths	Wisdom	Judgment by intended and higher ends	Prudence
		Command	Prudence

The Virtues of the Appetitive Powers: The Will and Emotions

Although there are various steps that take place within the will (see chapter 5), fundamentally the will is doing the same action in each of these steps: loving the good presented by the intellect. In other words, any distinction in the different acts of the will comes from the fact that what is presented by the intellect varies, and not because the will is performing a different type of action. Consequently, because all the steps of the will are acts of loving the good, all the steps of the will are perfected by the virtue of *justice*.

Since the primary act of the will is to love, justice perfects the ability of humans to love others. In humans, the natural inclination to love oneself is generally powerful enough that humans do not need an acquired virtue to perfect it.[26] However, they do need a virtue to perfect their natural inclination to love God and others. Since love requires that we make the needs of others our own, justice is the virtue of making the natural needs of others our own and of giving God due honor. (God does not have any needs, but humans are naturally inclined to honor him.) Natural needs correspond to the natural rights that we covered in chapter 7. For example, all humans have a natural need for food, shelter, health care, and everything else essential to attaining natural happiness. Hence, those with the virtue of justice seek to make sure that the poor have enough food to eat because they love the poor. To summarize, through justice, humans seek the natural good of their neighbors and give due honor to God. Because all humans ought to have their natural needs met, justice can also be defined as giving to others what they deserve. However, this definition can lead people to believe that justice is all about retribution of past offences, when in reality justice is about loving others.

The emotions seek the bodily good as known through sense knowledge. The emotions can be split into two categories: the concupiscible and the irascible. The concupiscible emotions desire (or detest) the sensible goods (or evil) in general. In other words, they desire a sensible good as an end to an action. For example, they might desire the bodily good of the pleasure derived from food or sleep. Since attaining the bodily good can be difficult, the irascible emotions seek the difficult or distant good. In other words, they seek the means of attaining the pleasure. For example, humans might desire the pleasure of bodily health but realize they must exercise in order to attain it. The concupiscible emotions seek the end of the pleasure from bodily health, while the irascible seek the difficult good of bodily health obtained through exercise (or are repulsed by the difficult good if someone hates exercise).

Temperance is the virtue that perfects the concupiscible emotions. Temperance transforms the emotions so that humans have the appropriate amount of desire for the proper bodily good. In other words, humans should not have too much or too little desire for a pleasurable good, nor should they desire the wrong type of pleasurable good. The intellect must determine the proper amount of desire and the proper thing to be desired. Temperance forms the emotions so that humans automatically desire the good in accord with reason. For example, the person with temperance desires the proper type of food and also has the proper amount of desire for this food. Another example pertains to the moderation of sexual desire. The person with temperance only desires the proper type of sexual actions resulting in pleasure (the sexual act within marriage) and has the proper amount of desire for this bodily good.

Fortitude is the virtue that perfects the irascible emotions. Fortitude transforms the emotions so that humans hope for and pursue the difficult bodily good (or fear the distant bodily evil). Like with temperance, reason determines both the amount of intensity within the emotion and the proper object for the emotion. Fortitude perfects the emotions so that they automatically seek the proper means to attain a true bodily good. For example, the person with fortitude is able to overcome the fear of public speaking in order to attain the end of giving a speech. A good example that uses both temperance and fortitude is Joe having to finish his work before he can begin his vacation. The emotions perfected by temperance desire the pleasure that comes from the bodily good of proper recreation. They do not have so much desire that they distract Joe from his work, but they do have enough desire that they motivate Joe to work harder. Fortitude perfects the emotions to cause Joe to passionately persevere at his work, for he must finish his work to go on vacation (the difficult means to the end). Once Joe is done with his work, temperance causes Joe to have the proper amount of enjoyment of his vacation.

Prudence, justice, temperance, and fortitude have traditionally been called the *cardinal* virtues.[27] The term "cardinal" refers to the fact that they are foundational to other virtues. In other words, these four virtues perfect the powers of the soul involved in acting. Most other virtues can be subordinated to these four. For example, the virtue of honesty is a subvirtue under justice. Courage is a subvirtue under fortitude.

In order for someone to be truly virtuous, all four virtues must be present. Prudence is necessary to determine the proper action to be pursued. Justice is necessary to perfect the will to love it, and temperance and fortitude are necessary so that the emotions aid the intellect and will and do not rebel (causing the intellect and will to pursue a false good). A traditional analogy showing the necessity of both prudence and the moral virtues (justice, temperance, and fortitude) is that of a chariot driver and his horses. Prudence is the chariot driver. Justice, temperance, and fortitude are the horses. The chariot driver is necessary to direct the other virtues—both in terms of where they are going (determining the proper goal of the will and emotions) and in terms of how fast they can go (determining the proper intensity of the will and emotions). Without the chariot driver, the horses will blindly wreck the chariot, and so without prudence, the moral virtues will passionately lead the person astray. Aquinas compares strong moral virtues without prudence to a blind horse without a rider.[28] The faster the horse runs, the greater the damage when it crashes. The stronger the moral virtues without prudence, the greater the evil the person can inflict upon the world. However, the horses are also necessary, or the driver and chariot will not move. In other words, the moral virtues are needed to drive the person to the particular action determined by prudence. If one of the horses goes lame, the whole team is slowed down, and if one of the moral virtues is missing, completion of the good action is jeopardized.

Prudence perfects the practical intellect's acts of counsel, judgment, and command. Justice perfects the will to love God and others. Temperance and fortitude perfect the emotions to aid the intellect and will throughout the human action. Since all three of these powers are involved in performing good actions, all four of these virtues are necessary to perfect the soul so that humans can perform good actions.

THE THEOLOGICAL VIRTUES

The cardinal virtues perfect humans according to created nature, but because humans can participate in divine nature through grace, man can be ordered to a supernatural end: communion with God. Hence, supernatural virtues are needed to perfect the intellect and the will to perform the divine actions ordered to knowing and loving God as he is.[29] Just as nature causes human actions through natural inclinations, so also grace causes divine actions through supernatural inclinations. These supernatural inclinations are the *theological virtues*.[30] Like the natural inclinations, which incline humans to natural happiness, the theological virtues incline humans toward the goal of eternal happiness.

The theological virtues are *faith*, *hope*, and *charity*. Faith perfects the intellect, and hope and charity perfect the will. Since these virtues are supernatural inclinations, they each supernaturally perfect a natural inclination. Faith perfects the natural inclination to understand the truth. Hope perfects the natural inclination to love oneself, and charity perfects the natural inclination to love others.[31]

Faith is the habit of believing divinely revealed truths. It perfects the natural inclination to understand the truth because through faith humans are able to understand truths that are beyond their natural ability to grasp. For example, faith gives humans the ability to know that God is a Trinity, a truth that humans cannot know without divine revelation. Just as the natural inclination to understand the truth gives humans the ability to know natural truths that guide humans in the performance of human actions, faith gives humans the ability to know supernatural truths that can guide humans in the performance of divine actions. For example, as we recall from chapter 1, knowledge that God is a Trinity teaches us that humans only attain their true identity by a sincere gift of self.

Because faith perfects the natural inclination to know, it perfects all of the different steps in the intellect (see table 8.1), including simple apprehension. In order for humans to have faith, God must reveal divine truths through physical signs that can be sensed by humans. For example, the Father is revealed through the physical body of the divine Son. Also, God must give humans the grace to believe these truths. Since faith also begins with sense knowledge, it perfects the ability of humans to apprehend divinely revealed concepts (step 1). These concepts can be joined and separated to form the principles of the faith (step 2). From these principles humans can reason to conclusions (step 3), and judge the rest of their knowledge (step 4).

Hope and charity perfect the natural inclinations of the will. The natural inclination of the will in general is to desire the good, to love. However, this natural inclination can be separated into both a natural inclination to love oneself and a natural inclination to love others. The natural inclination to love oneself causes the act of *love of use*, and the natural inclination to love others causes the act of *love of friendship*. Love of use is when humans love something or someone else because they will receive some benefit from the thing or person that they love.[32] For example, suppose Joe loves his car. Joe does not love his car for its own sake; Joe loves his car for the benefit of transportation he receives from it. Love of friendship is when humans love someone else for that person's own sake. In other words, even if they did not receive any benefits, humans with love of friendship would make the needs of the other person their own needs. For example, Joe loves Kate for who she is in and of herself.

It would appear that the love of use for other humans should be wrong, since it causes people to make their own needs more important than those of other humans. Although love of friendship is certainly the more perfect type of love, love of use for other humans is only wrong when it is not accompanied by love of friendship.[33] In fact, relationships often begin with a person first loving another for a benefit to be attained. Then, after getting to know the other person, this love of use turns into love of friendship. For example, perhaps Joe first dated Kate because he saw her as a prospective spouse (love of use). However, over time Joe begins to love Kate for who she is, whether she becomes his spouse or not (love of friendship). Furthermore, as Joe's love of friendship for Kate grows, his desire to marry her also grows. In other words, love of friendship over time increases love of use. Nonetheless, relationships that are solely based on love of use are selfish. The love of use must either mature into love of friendship, or the relationship will never bring true happiness to either of the persons involved.

Hope is the habit of desiring God as the source of eternal happiness and trusting in the divine assistance that he provides. Hope perfects the natural inclination to love oneself and is a type of love of use of God.[34] In other words, when someone has hope, they love God because he will give them the benefit of eternal happiness. However, because humans cannot attain eternal happiness by their own power, the primary aspect of the virtue of hope is trusting in God's mercy. God desires that humans share in his happiness, and because of God's goodness, humans should have great hope that he will help them attain it. Thus, someone with hope performs actions ordered to the end of eternal happiness because they desire this happiness and trust that God will provide them with the grace to attain it.

Charity is love of friendship of God. It is the habit of loving God for his own sake and results in union with God. Charity perfects the natural inclination to love others. Humans with charity make God's goals their own goals and perform all of their actions because they love God.

On the natural level, knowledge causes love, which causes unity. Since love of use can precede love of friendship, knowledge frequently causes love of use, which causes love of friendship. For example, first Joe gets to know Kate. As his knowledge grows, he sees Kate as a prospective spouse (love of use). This love causes him to get to know Kate even better, and, over time, the love of use becomes love of friendship, which results in unity. Since grace perfects nature, the same order applies to the theological virtues. Faith (supernatural knowledge) causes hope (love of use of God), which causes charity (love of friendship of God), which causes union with God. A man hearing St. Paul preach around 50 AD would hear the good news that Jesus is God and that Jesus offers eternal happiness to his followers. The man would first believe the message (faith). Then, he would want eternal happiness (hope). Finally, he would come to love God as a friend (charity). The love of friendship would cause communion with God (salvation). Once the man loved God as a friend, he would want to know even more about God and would desire eternal happiness all the more. Hence, although faith causes hope, which causes charity, charity perfects both faith and hope.

Just as the natural inclinations give humans the ability to perform human actions, the theological virtues act as supernatural inclinations, giving humans the ability to perform divine actions. Faith causes a supernatural participation in divine knowledge, and hope and charity cause a supernatural participation in divine love.

THE INFUSED CARDINAL VIRTUES

Even though the natural inclinations cause humans to perform human actions, these inclinations must be perfected by the acquired virtues in order for humans to perform actions that will truly make them happy. For example, the natural inclination to love others is perfected by the virtue of justice to give others their natural needs. Since grace perfects nature, the supernatural inclinations of faith, hope, and charity must also work through other virtues in order to perform even more perfect divine actions. Because the acquired virtues can never cause actions in accord with eternal happiness, the virtues that faith, hope, and charity work through must be infused. These virtues are the *infused cardinal virtues*. These infused cardinal virtues are just like the acquired cardinal virtues, except that they are infused by God and ordered to eternal happiness. In other words, the infused cardinal virtues perfect the same powers of the soul as the acquired virtues; however, they perfect these powers to perform supernatural actions.

Recall the section on St. Paul's moral theology in chapter 4. There I stated that charity is applied through the Greek (cardinal) virtues. Both charity and the infused cardinal virtues are essential to the moral life. Charity requires the infused cardinal virtues in order to be applied to one's life, and the cardinal virtues need charity to be ordered to eternal happiness.[35]

Because charity is love of friendship of God, charity causes Christians to make God's goals their goals. Yet, goals must still be applied to the particular situation. The infused virtue of prudence is necessary to perfect the intellect to apply God's goals for Christians to a particular situation. The infused virtue of justice is necessary to perfect the will to love and choose the means of attaining these goals. The infused virtues of temperance and fortitude are necessary to perfect the emotions so they can aid the intellect and the will to act with intensity. For example, if David decides to do missionary work, charity causes the work ultimately to be done out of love for God. Prudence determines where and how David should serve. Using prudence, David decides to do missionary work in the Ural Mountains in Russia. Justice causes the will to love serving the people of Russia out of love for God and others. Fortitude perfects the emotions to persevere in the missionary work, and temperance perfects the emotions so that no emotional attachments keep him from doing the work.

The traditional way of explaining the relation between charity and the cardinal virtues is that *charity is the form of the virtues*. In other words, since the form determines the object of an action, all actions stemming from the infused cardinal virtues are acts of charity. For example, an act of martyrdom requires the infused virtue of fortitude, but it is essentially an act of love of God. Since acts from the infused cardinal virtues are also acts of charity, unlike the acquired virtues that are guided by the natural law, the infused cardinal virtues are guided by divine law and especially by the movement of the Holy Spirit. With the infused virtues, the Holy Spirit allows Christ to work through humans.

VIRTUE IS FOUND IN THE MEAN

The virtues that perfect the appetitive powers (will and emotions) exist as a mean (a middle position) between an excess and a defect. An analogy from the realm of health is helpful.[36] When seeking bodily health, some exercise and good food is essential. However, too much exercise and too much good food is harmful to health. On the other hand, no exercise and no good food destroy health. Consequently, to attain health, a mean must be found between the excess and the defect. Likewise, the virtues in the will and the emotions seek a mean between the excess and the defect. Too much or too little desire of a particular good is a vice. Examples from justice, temperance, and fortitude are helpful to illuminate this point.

The first example is from temperance. In reference to eating food, the temperate person desires the proper amount of food and the proper type of food. Those who desire too much food have the vice of gluttony (the excess). Those who desire too little food have a vice similar to the condition of anorexia[37] (the defect).

An example of fortitude can be seen in the case of courage, which is a subvirtue under fortitude. Courage moderates the emotions of fear and daring. The person with too little daring has the vice of cowardliness (the defect). The person with too much daring is a fool (the excess). For example, an Olympic swimmer who is afraid to jump into a deep pond to save a drowning person is a coward, because this swimmer has the ability to save the person. Conversely, someone who jumps into the pond but cannot swim is a fool, for both she and the other person will end up drowning.

Virtues under justice always hit the mean between loving others too much (resulting in the person who loves being treated unjustly) and not loving others enough (resulting in the person treating others unjustly). For example, the virtue of obedience is under the virtue of justice. The obedient person easily and joyfully obeys the commands of a proper authority. The person who does not love the authority enough does not obey and has the vice of disobedience (the defect). On the other hand, the person who loves the authority figure so much that they would follow an unjust law likewise has a vice (the excess).

The intellect, perfected by prudence, must determine the mean in every situation. In other words, in determining the proper action, prudence also determines what the will and the emotions should desire. In cases of temperance and fortitude, the mean is proportional to the subject and the situation. In other words, the mean for one person will be different from the mean for another person. For example, a professional swimmer could probably eat an entire pizza and still be eating in moderation because his lifestyle is so active. However, if a less active man ate that much food, he would be gluttonous. Another example can be found in the virtue that moderates consumption of alcohol: sobriety. The sober person only desires the appropriate amount of alcohol. Those who desire too much alcohol have the vice of drunkenness. However, some people for various reasons are unable to drink any alcohol. The mean for them could be to not drink alcohol at all. Because the mean can vary with each person, prudence must determine the proper mean for every person in every situation.

The intellect determines the mean when it applies the appropriate law or goal to a particular situation. For the acquired virtues, the mean must be in accord with the natural law. However, for the infused virtues, the mean must be in accord with the divine law. Because the divine law orders humans to a higher end, the mean will also be different. In other words, the different concepts apprehended through faith cause different goals, which result in different actions. Thus, the mean for someone with faith will differ from the mean for someone without faith. For instance, with the subvirtue of proper use of money (liberality) under justice, the mean for someone with faith is generally closer to self-sacrifice (being treated unjustly) than for those without faith. Jesus illustrates this truth when he praises the poor woman who gives from her necessities (Lk 21:1–4). Unless there was a catastrophe, natural law would only require that one give from their excess. An example under fortitude is a woman who is dying. Someone with faith will prepare for death differently than someone without faith. The anticipation of eternal happiness will cause the woman to endure the hardships of death joyfully for the sake of the glory to come (see Rom 8:17). Other examples might be found in how faith changes the mean in cases of fasting and celibacy.

The *theological* virtues of hope and charity do not have a mean.[38] Although humans should love finite things a particular amount (in accord with their goodness), there is no limit to how much humans should love God. Furthermore, since charity increases hope, there is no limit to how much humans should desire to be with God and trust in his divine assistance.

VIRTUES ARE GOOD HABITS that dispose a person to perform good actions. Because humans are not automatically disposed to the proper good in every situation, virtues are needed to ensure that humans are always performing actions ordered to happiness. Since human actions require various steps from various powers, multiple virtues are essential. Each of the different acts of the intellect requires a virtue to perfect it. By understanding the acts of the intellect, the corresponding virtue is also understood. An understanding of the steps of the speculative intellect provides the foundation for understanding the virtues of faith, understanding, knowledge, and wisdom. An understanding of the steps of the practical intellect allows humans to understand the virtues of faith, practical understanding, and prudence. As in the intellect, an understanding of the role of the will allows humans to understand the virtues of justice, hope, and charity. Finally, an understanding of the emotions helps humans understand temperance and fortitude. Although I didn't cover it in this chapter, the understanding of all these different steps and powers also helps humans understand the gifts of the Holy Spirit, such as understanding, knowledge, wisdom, and counsel.[39]

Although law gives humans the ability to perform good actions by moving and guiding them, virtues give humans the ability to perform even better actions. This greater ability comes both from the greater proficiency to act that comes from the virtues and from the fact that virtues cause humans to freely perform good actions with greater intensity. Since these actions stemming from virtues flow from more perfect knowledge and love, they cause happiness.

9

GUIDANCE FROM THE HOLY SPIRIT

As children develop, their parents must guide them to perform good actions. Parents should already have the virtues, which give them the ability to make and enforce laws, such as that children should not put their fingers in the electrical outlets or play with matches, that they should eat healthy meals and get plenty of sleep. Over time these human laws cause good habits, and eventually children acquire the virtues to perform good actions by their own power.

Just as children require the guidance of their parents to form the virtues that are essential for happiness, humans also require the guidance of our heavenly Father to form and perfect the virtues necessary for eternal happiness. The Father guides humans by means of the primary element of the new law: the grace of the Holy Spirit. The Holy Spirit dwells in human souls. He guides them to good actions and gives them the love to perform these actions.

The guidance of the Holy Spirit is especially essential in aiding humans in complex actions. Some actions are so complex that the weak human intellect can never know the nearly infinite possible outcomes. Thankfully, God already knows the best action and offers his guidance. Furthermore, since God is the first cause of every action, the Holy Spirit also guides humans in *every* action that flows from grace, not just in complex ones. For example, important life actions, such as finding the right spouse or determining what occupation to pursue, are complex issues that can depend on many future variables, which are unknown. These types of issues especially require the help of the Holy Spirit, who knows the future variables. At the same time, simple actions flowing from grace, such as deciding when to sleep or when to pray, also require the guidance of the Holy Spirit, who directs humans to actions ordered to eternal happiness.

Because the Holy Spirit knows the actions that will make humans most happy, his guidance is a great gift. Unfortunately, discerning the guidance of the Holy Spirit is not always easy. In fact, people can be completely mistaken in their discernment and do evil actions that they attribute to the guidance of the Holy Spirit. (This shows the need for the written element of the new law.) This chapter will give advice on how to better discern the guidance of the Holy Spirit. Before we can receive this advice, a couple of preliminary topics require our attention. First, we need to analyze the gifts of the Holy Spirit. The Holy Spirit gives humans these gifts so that they are more easily guided and moved by his inspirations. These divinely given dispositions make humans especially docile to the guidance of our divine friend, who shares his wisdom with us. Also, to properly understand how the Holy Spirit moves humans, it is also necessary to examine how God works through humans to cause actions. This study of the divine causality of human actions illuminates the role of humans within the divine plan.

GIFTS OF THE HOLY SPIRIT

Because humans participate in divine nature (through grace) and have the supernatural inclinations of the theological virtues, the Holy Spirit can move humans to divine actions that are substantially greater than natural human actions. However, even with the theological virtues, humans need the gifts of the Holy Spirit to be moved even more perfectly by the Holy Spirit. The Holy Spirit's gifts aid the theological virtues by further perfecting the natural inclinations of the intellect, will, and emotions. The gifts perfect the natural inclinations so that humans have a spiritual "instinct," a participated divine inclination to actions ordered to eternal happiness.[1]

Thomas Aquinas explains that the Holy Spirit's gifts are necessary to further perfect humans, even though they have theological virtues. He states that although the theological virtues are greater than the natural powers, nonetheless the natural powers are possessed more perfectly. Because the theological virtues are possessed less perfectly, they need to be further perfected so that humans can be guided more efficaciously by the Holy Spirit.[2] A good analogy is the difference between knowing simple arithmetic and knowing calculus. Although knowledge of calculus is greater than knowledge of simple arithmetic, most people possess the ability to do simple arithmetic more perfectly. They can easily do simple arithmetic but can only do calculus with great difficulty. Hence, to use calculus well, most people would need the aid of a teacher to help them when their own knowledge of calculus is insufficient. With the help of a teacher, these people would possess the ability to do calculus as perfectly as they possess the ability to do simple arithmetic. The same applies to the necessary aid of the Holy Spirit. Humans possess the ability to act by their natural powers more perfectly. They can do good natural actions easily, but they can only do divine actions with great difficulty. Hence, the Holy Spirit, the divine teacher, must give them special gifts so that they are properly disposed to perform the divine actions that flow from faith, hope, and charity. With these gifts, humans can do divine actions just as perfectly as natural actions. Because these gifts are necessary for salvation, upon receiving sanctifying grace, humans receive both the theological virtues and the gifts of the Holy Spirit.[3]

The traditional list of these gifts is from Isaiah 11:2–3. The Holy Spirit's seven gifts are *understanding, knowledge, wisdom, counsel, piety, fortitude,* and *fear of the Lord.*[4] The first four gifts further perfect the supernatural inclination of faith. Fear of the Lord perfects the supernatural inclination of hope. Wisdom perfects the supernatural inclination of charity (in addition to faith). Piety further perfects the ability of the will to seek the means of attaining the good actions that are intended by charity. Fortitude perfects the irascible emotions to work with the theological virtues, and fear of the Lord also perfects the concupiscible emotions to work with the theological virtues. Although there is some repetition, since wisdom and fear of the Lord perfect more than one power, the key point is that all the powers of the soul are supernaturally perfected even beyond the theological virtues.

The theological virtue of faith perfects the natural inclination of the intellect to know the truth. Recall that the speculative intellect has four steps: simple apprehension, understanding, discursive reasoning, and judging by higher principles. The last three of these steps are perfected by the virtues of understanding, knowledge (*scientia*), and wisdom. As would be expected, the Holy Spirit's gifts with the same names as the virtues (understanding, knowledge, and wisdom) also perfect these steps of the intellect. However, they perfect the intellect to act by means of the supernatural inclination of faith, which gives new concepts and a greater ability to understand. Thus, the gift of understanding perfects the ability of the intellect to join and separate concepts flowing from faith. In other words, this gift helps humans to understand the principles of the faith, such as the principle that there are three persons in one God or the principle that Jesus is fully God and fully man. The gift of knowledge perfects the ability of humans to reason from these principles of the faith. In other words, people with knowledge are good at the science of theology. For example, humans with knowledge might reason to the conclusion that Jesus must have a human intellect and will because he has a human nature. Finally, the gift of wisdom perfects the ability of humans to judge all other knowledge by the principles of faith. For example, the fact that humans have an immortal soul (a truth known through faith) means that they must also have a natural dignity.

Three gifts also perfect the practical intellect. The third step of the human action—understanding the end—is also perfected by the gift of understanding. The Holy Spirit perfects the ability of the intellect to set proper goals and understand divine laws. Knowledge can also perfect this step if reasoning is necessary to know the goal or law. The fifth step of the human action is counsel, which is the step where the practical intellect applies an intended end to a particular situation by researching and reasoning. The gift of counsel perfects the ability of the intellect to research and reason. The Holy

Spirit already knows the situation perfectly and which action corresponds most perfectly to the situation. For example, the Holy Spirit already knows which vocation will allow a person to most perfectly follow God's calling and cause the greatest amount of happiness. The seventh step of the human action is judgment. In this step, the practical intellect judges by higher principles held through faith. In addition to perfecting the speculative intellect, wisdom also perfects the practical intellect's ability to judge by principles held by faith. For example, someone with the gift of wisdom would judge that fornication is wrong because it contradicts the principle derived from the faith that sex should only take place in marriage. Table 9.1 shows the acts of the intellect and the virtues and gifts that perfect them.

Table 9.1. Virtues and Gifts in the Intellect

Steps of the Speculative Intellect	Virtues Perfecting Each Step*	Gifts of the Holy Spirit Perfecting Each Step
Simple Apprehension	Faith	
Understanding	Faith and Understanding	Understanding
Reasoning	Faith and Knowledge	Knowledge
Judging by the highest truths	Faith and Wisdom	Wisdom

Steps of the Practical Intellect	Virtues Perfecting Each Step*	Gifts of the Holy Spirit Perfecting Each Step
Simple Apprehension	Faith	
Understanding the end/goal	Faith and Practical Understanding	Understanding and Knowledge
Counsel	Faith and Prudence	Counsel
Judgment	Faith and Prudence	Wisdom
Command	Faith and Prudence	

* Faith perfects all the steps since it is a supernatural inclination. In other words, faith gives the intellect the ability to perform any supernatural steps. The virtues of understanding, knowledge, and wisdom are natural virtues and do not require faith.

An example that shows the role of the various the gifts of the Holy Spirit within the intellect is how a person uses scripture within the moral life. Paul notes that all Christians are part of the one body of Christ (1 Cor 12:12). The gift of understanding helps the reader to understand that Paul is talking about how the Holy Spirit unites humans to Christ, making them members of his Church. Paul then reasons that just as there are many parts of a body with many essential functions, members of the Church have many different essential functions. The gift of knowledge helps the reader to follow Paul's reasoning. Paul then notes that if Christians are part of this one body, they should all act as if they are part of this body: all doing their proper actions and sharing in the joy and suffering of the rest (12:27–31). Counsel helps the reader reason to her proper actions given her particular gifts and calling from God. Wisdom helps the reader to judge whether or not these actions conform with the truth that all Christians are part of the body of Christ.

The gifts that perfect the will are fear of the Lord, wisdom, and piety. Fear of the Lord perfects the supernatural inclination to hope (giving the ability to love oneself and to trust in the divine assistance). This gift causes people to seek eternal happiness because of fear of separation from God. Wisdom perfects the sixth step of the human action, consent. In consent, the will loves the potential actions presented to it by the intellect. With wisdom, the will loves one of the possible options more than the others. In other words, the Holy Spirit moves the will to love one of the options based on the rationale in the divine mind rather than the human mind. For example, when I was searching for my vocation, the intellect took counsel and presented the options of being a priest or getting married. My will then loved one of these options (getting married) more than the other one. Wisdom gives the will a disposition to be moved by divine reason to love the right action. The last gift in the will is piety. Piety is the gift of giving due honor to God. Piety perfects the will to act in such a way that God is honored in every action.

The gifts that perfect the emotions are fear of the Lord and fortitude. Fear of the Lord perfects the concupiscible appetite to fear God's just punishments (e.g., hell) and to desire heaven. Fortitude perfects the emotions to seek the difficult good of eternal life. Humans with the gift of fortitude stand firm through the many trials and sufferings of this life in order to attain eternal happiness.

In order to ultimately attain eternal happiness, God gives humans multiple perfections. He perfects them with grace, the infused virtues, and the gifts of the Holy Spirit. By means of these dispositions, the Holy Spirit can move humans to actions that bring supernatural happiness on earth and eternal happiness in heaven. The gifts of the Holy Spirit perfect the intellect, will, and emotions so that humans can be moved and guided more perfectly. Specifically, the intellect is perfected so that the Holy Spirit can guide the intellect to know divine truths and know the actions most in accord with the eternal law. The will is perfected so that the Holy Spirit can move the will to intend and choose the best actions. The emotions are perfected so that the Holy Spirit can move them to aid the intellect and the will in choosing good actions.

DIVINE AND HUMAN CAUSALITY WITHIN HUMAN ACTIONS

The gifts of the Holy Spirit make humans amenable to the guidance and movement of the Holy Spirit. Yet, if the Holy Spirit moves the intellect and will, how are these actions freely chosen by humans? In other words, as we saw in chapter 5, an action is not a human action if someone is forced to perform the action. Yet, God clearly influences human actions through the giving of laws (both the guidance of the Holy Spirit and other laws), through grace that gives them the ability to participate in divine nature, and through infused virtues and gifts. If God commands humans to perform certain types of actions and transforms them so that they are able to complete these actions, are humans truly free when they follow this law? And if divine power is the cause of actions ordered to eternal happiness, are humans truly free when they perform these types of actions? If humans are not free when they perform these types of actions, then these actions would not directly affect their journey to God. If, as I said in chapters 2 and 3, actions stemming from grace are essential to attain eternal happiness, then God's causality within an action must not remove freedom.

This section will examine the relation between divine and human causality within human actions to analyze how God causes humans to act freely.

God's knowledge and love are not like human knowledge and love. Human knowledge is caused by knowing something that exists in reality, and humans only love things that are good in some way. In contrast, God's knowledge of something causes it to exist. Likewise, God's love of something causes it to be good. For example, for all eternity God has known that each of us would exist here and now. Since he knows that each of us will exist, we do exist. Likewise, because he loves us, we are good. And because we exist and are good, others can know and love us. In a nutshell, God's knowledge and love cause things to be, and these things cause human knowledge and love.

Because God knows every human act that ever was or will be performed, God is also the cause of all human actions. However, God does not cause human actions without the involvement of humans. Rather, he causes human actions by moving and guiding humans to their proper act. In fact, God allows all of creation to share in his plan of bringing the universe to perfection. God created the universe in a perfect state of imperfection. All things are perfect in terms of their nature, yet they must still be perfected in terms of their action. I have already noted that God created the universe in this way so that humans and all other things can be more like God. One of the ways that humans can be more like God is by sharing in the divine plan of bringing the universe to its proper goal. Humans share in this divine plan when God moves and guides them to perform their proper actions. The fact that God moves and guides humans to their proper actions does not diminish the dignity of humans. On the contrary, it enhances their dignity by allowing them to share in the eternal act of God.[5]

God Is the First Cause of All Actions, and Humans Are the Second Cause

The relation between humans and God in actions is that God is the first (or primary) cause of all actions, and humans are the second (or secondary) cause of all actions.[6] This notion of primary and secondary causality was already explored in chapter 1 in the section on the relation between the body and soul. The primary cause moves and guides the secondary cause to perform its proper action. For example, the piano player (the first cause) moves the piano (the second cause) to make piano music. Both the player and the piano are true causes of the music, and both act in accord with their form. In other words, both the agent and the instrument perform their proper action. The piano player is limited by human nature and talent in moving the piano; likewise, the piano can only produce piano music. Analogously, God is like the piano player. Humans are like the piano. God moves humans to perform their proper actions: human actions. However, unlike the limited human piano player, God perfectly moves humans to their proper actions.

If God is the cause of all human actions, how can humans be free? After all, the piano is not free to determine the notes that it plays. The answer is that since the secondary cause is moved in accord with its nature, humans are moved to perform human actions. Human actions are free actions because they proceed from the intellect and the will. More specifically, the way that God causes humans to act is by causing the actions of the intellect and will.

In reference to the intellect, in order to understand something, the intellect requires both the power to understand and a concept (intellectual form) that can be understood. For example, in the act of understanding the nature of an elephant, the intellect requires both the power to understand what an elephant is and the concept of an elephant. God is the cause of both of these in the human mind. First, God is the cause of the power to understand. He creates humans with the power to understand and is constantly sustaining this power within the intellect. Second, God is the cause of all the concepts in the human mind. However, God does not cause these concepts immediately in the mind; rather, God causes these concepts by creating things that are known by humans. For example, God knows everything by knowing the divine nature, which is truth itself. Hence, in knowing himself, he knows that elephants exist in this day and age. Since God knows this, elephants do exist. In other words, the divine idea of the elephant in God's mind causes elephants to exist. When humans know what an elephant is, they have the concept of an elephant in their mind. Although the concept of an elephant within the human mind is limited by the weakness of the human intellect, it nonetheless participates in the divine idea of an elephant that is within the mind of God. Consequently, God causes all human thoughts by both giving the mind the power to understand and by causing the concepts that are understood.[7]

In reference to the will, in order to love something, two things are required: the power to love and a good object to love. Like in the intellect, God causes both the power and the object. First, God causes the power to love by creating the will with an attraction to the good and by constantly moving the will to love. Second, God causes the good object because he is the universal good that is the source of all goodness. Just as God's knowledge causes all things to exist, God's love causes all things to be good. Each has an appropriate amount of goodness based on how much it is like God. For example, humans are more like God than sea horses and are a greater good. Consequently, the goodness of all things comes from God. Therefore, when the will loves an object because of its goodness, the goodness ultimately comes from God. Even when someone loves pizza, the goodness of the pizza ultimately comes from God. Thus, God is the cause of all acts of the will by moving it to love and by being the source of the goodness of its objects.[8]

God causes all human actions by moving the intellect and the will to know and to love. Since acts that proceed from the intellect and will are free human actions, divine causality of human actions does not remove human freedom; rather, it causes human freedom. In other words, God causes human actions by causing humans to act freely. For example, suppose Joe performs the act of giving money to the poor. God causes his intellect to understand that giving to the poor is good and that this person is poor. God causes the goodness of the poor person. He also inclines Joe's will to love the person and to choose to help the person. In the same way, God causes all humans to freely act.

However, there is still another question. If God is the cause of all human actions, why are humans able to perform evil? How can God, who is pure goodness, cause an evil action? A return to the piano analogy is helpful. In cases of primary and secondary causality, both causes act in accord with their form. Therefore, even if the best piano player in the world is playing a beautiful piece of music perfectly, a broken and out-of-tune piano will cause the music to sound awful. Furthermore, although the sole cause of the badness in the music is the piano, the piano player still causes the bad music to the extent that it is music at all. In other words, the piano player is the cause of the bad *music* but not the cause of the *badness* in the music. In the relation between humans and God, both God and humans act in accord with their form. God, as pure goodness, moves humans to perform good actions in accord with the divine plan. However, humans, as we explained in chapter 2, have the ability to not perform their proper action and consequently can cause a defect in the action to which they are divinely moved. Although God is the cause of the defective action, he is not the cause of the defect.[9]

Evil is defined as "a lack of goodness when it should exist." In other words, evil is not a positively existing thing, but rather a privation of something. Like evil, darkness is also a privation. Darkness is a lack of light rather than an actually existing thing. An evil human action contains some defect so that the action is not as good as it should be. The defect can come from the intellect not knowing the truth, the will not loving the good, or the emotions seeking an improper good.[10] Because God is pure goodness and does not lack anything, he cannot be the cause of evil. Consequently, God is only the cause of an evil action to the extent that the action exists and has some goodness.[11] Humans are the cause of the evil action both by causing any goodness in the action and by causing any evil in the action. For example, suppose God was moving Joe to go to Mass on Sunday morning (because it was Joe's only chance to go to Mass). Instead, Joe freely chooses to sleep until noon. Because the body needs sleep, there is some goodness in sleeping. However, the goodness in the act of sleeping until noon is far less than the goodness in the act of going to Mass on Sunday. Technically speaking, the act of going to Mass on Sunday participates more perfectly in God's knowledge and love than the act of sleeping in on Sunday morning. The goodness of the act of sleeping until noon comes from both God and Joe. The evil, or lack of goodness, of missing Mass comes from Joe alone.[12]

A human action is an action that is freely chosen. God is the cause of all human actions, including evil actions. Divine causality does not restrict human freedom but is the very cause of human freedom by giving humans the ability to know and to love. An important point to draw from this section is the intimacy between God and humans in acting (even if the human is not aware of God's role). Both God and humans are true and intimate causes of human actions. Another point is that God gives humans (and other created beings) an important role in the implementation of his divine plan. God can do everything without the aid of created beings, yet in order for humans to become more like him, God works through them in bringing creation to its perfection.[13] In other words, God does not need the aid of humans to fulfill his plan, rather, he allows them to enter into his plan solely for their benefit. Furthermore, God gives humans grace, virtues, laws, and gifts to help them more perfectly participate in his act of bringing creation to perfection. Because humans become more like God when he works through them, they are able to participate more fully in his happiness.

INTERPRETING AND FOLLOWING THE MOVEMENT
OF THE HOLY SPIRIT

God moves humans to their actions even if they are not aware of it. However, because God wants humans be more like him, he wants them to actively, intellectually participate in his divine wisdom (the eternal law). In other words, God does not just want humans to fulfill his plan, he wants them to freely choose to participate in his plan, and to freely participate they must have some understanding of what they are doing. As declared in the Gospel of John, Jesus no longer calls us slaves but friends, for a slave does not know the overarching goals of the master (Jn 15:15). As God's friends, Christians are given the opportunity to discover their individual role within God's divine plan, the eternal law. They are called to use their intellect and will to discern the goals that God has for them. The way that they discern these goals is by being open to the guidance and movement of the Holy Spirit. Thomas explains this truth in the following way. Friends are of one mind and one heart with each other. Hence, "this is the proper mark of friendship: that one reveal his secrets to his friend. . . . Therefore, since by the Holy Spirit we are established as friends of God, fittingly enough it is by the Holy Spirit that men are said to receive the revelation of the divine mysteries."[14] Just as friends reveal their secret aspirations to each other so they can share in each other's goals, the Father reveals his goals to us through the Holy Spirit, who dwells in our hearts.

Recall from chapter 1 that because humans are made in the image and likeness of God, they discover their true personal identity through a sincere gift of self. Because God created humans to be fulfilled through loving relationships, any truly loving relationship results in a discovery of their own personal identity. However, to most perfectly understand their unique role in God's plan (and hence the true meaning of their lives), humans need to be in a loving relationship with God. They need to allow the Holy Spirit to move their intellect to discover God's goal for them and allow the Holy Spirit to move their will to make this goal their own. When they do this, they are truly the persons God created them to be, and when they contemplate their relationship with God, they are supernaturally happy on earth. When humans understand their role in God's plan, they become saints by being their true selves. Since the way to discover and implement this role is by discerning the inspirations of the Holy Spirit, learning to discern the movement of the Holy Spirit is an essential part of the moral life.[15]

The Guidance of the Holy Spirit Is *Not* Esoteric

Something is esoteric if it is hidden and not known by many people. Many people think that the guidance of the Holy Spirit is only known by a few people who are privileged by God. However, God wants all people to be happy. He wants everyone to discern his unique plan for them. However, just like in any relationship, communication with one's friend is necessary for knowing the needs and goals of one's friend. So although the Holy Spirit's divine guidance is open to everyone, like in human relationships, it does take some effort to discern it. Nonetheless, the goal of all people should be that they are guided by the Holy Spirit in every action, no matter how insignificant. Humans can be consistently guided by the Holy Spirit because God moves humans to be instrumental causes of actions.

Whenever an agent works through an instrument, both produce an effect in accord with their form. Likewise, when God moves humans, both God and humans cause actions in accord with their form. Since God is perfect, he perfectly moves humans to act in accord with the eternal law. Humans are also moved in accord with their form: human nature perfected by grace to participate in divine nature. Consequently, since humans participate in divine nature, the Holy Spirit can move humans to perform divine actions. Because grace perfects nature, these actions flow from the intellect, will, and emotions. Hence, when the Holy Spirit moves humans to divine actions, he moves them by supernaturally moving the intellect, will, and emotions. Therefore, to interpret the movement of the Holy Spirit, we must examine the operation of these powers.

The Holy Spirit moves the intellect to know the truth. Through faith and the gifts of understanding, counsel, and wisdom, the intellect is given the ability to know with supernatural clarity what to do in a particular situation. Since humans are created to act in accord with their reason, and since grace does not destroy human reason but perfects it, when discerning what to do, humans must first and foremost follow their intellect. Because grace perfects nature, in order to follow their intellect humans must go through the steps of the human action. They should first pray for guidance from the Holy Spirit and form goals that are ordered to union with God (step 3). Next, they should take counsel by doing the research and reasoning required to make a good decision (step 5). Finally, they should judge whether or not their action is in accord with their intended goal and also judge whether it is in accord with the higher goals/ principles (step 7). An essential element of this step is judging whether or not the action is in accord with the written element of the new law that God has given to all humans. God's plan for humans as individuals will not contradict God's plan for all humans.

If we pray for the guidance of the Holy Spirit, are guided by faith, thoroughly take counsel on a particular situation, and make sure that our judgment does not violate God's law, then we may assume that the Holy Spirit has moved us to this decision. If we are fervently attempting to follow the guidance of the Holy Spirit, we must trust that God will give us the gifts necessary to perfect the intellect to properly discern his plan. Examination of past actions can help show how the Holy Spirit guides the intellect. Because God moves humans in accord with their nature, the movement of the Holy Spirit is not esoteric. When humans by the power of grace make good goals, take proper counsel, and judge wisely, they are being guided by the Holy Spirit (even if they are unaware of this guidance). Because God's knowledge is the source of all moral truth, when humans identify actions ordered toward God, they participate in God's eternal law.

The Holy Spirit also moves the will to love the true good. Once the Holy Spirit moves the intellect to know the proper action in a particular circumstance, the will must love both the end and the means to attain the end, or else the action will not be performed. Perfected by hope, charity, wisdom, and piety, the will is moved by the Holy Spirit to desire the right end and to choose the right action. Normally, the intellect (aided by the gifts of counsel and wisdom) determines the proper action to be chosen. In these cases the Holy Spirit simply moves the will to love the good action that is determined by the intellect.

However, sometimes the Holy Spirit moves the will to love a particular action even when the intellect does not know why this is the best action. In other words, through the gift of wisdom, the Holy Spirit sometimes moves the will to love a particular action simply because God knows that the action is best. The Holy Spirit can move the will to actions beyond the power of the intellect because, on earth, love of God can be more perfect than knowledge of God. In other words, through faith, humans do not know God as he is but only know God through divinely revealed effects. Although faith comes before charity, through charity, humans can love God as he is, not just an effect of God.[16] Charity unites humans to God, and their will can be directly moved by the divine intellect to love a particular action.[17] For example, why do certain men desire to be priests while others want to get married? If asked about the cause of these desires, they will eventually get to the point where they say, "I just love this more. I cannot explain why." In these cases, the Holy Spirit, through the gift of wisdom, is moving these men to consent to one action over another.

Often humans must make complicated decisions that require knowledge of many contingent and unknowable variables. For example, when Joe decides to get married to Kate, he does not know many of the future consequences of this decision. Even if he takes good counsel by learning a great deal about Kate, he still does not know if she will be in an accident, get a disease, or what all. Joe does not know the future consequences of the decision, but the Holy Spirit does know. The Holy Spirit can move Joe's will to love a particular action even if Joe does not know why he loves it. Hence, when discerning the movement of the Holy Spirit, if humans are unable to intellectually determine the proper decision, they should then ask, "What course of action do I love the most?" An analysis of their proper love can help them identify the movement of the Holy Spirit.

Even though a particular action is loved more than another, it must still be judged to be in accord with reason and the written element of the divine law.[18] The Holy Spirit may move the will to love actions that are beyond the power of the intellect to understand, but he does not move humans to actions that are contrary to human reason. Nor will the Holy Spirit move humans to actions that are contrary to the written element of the divine law. For example, after determining that I loved getting married more than I loved becoming a priest, I still had to judge whether the reasons why I loved getting married were truly ordered to God. If I only loved getting married because I thought I would make more money in the secular world, then the Holy Spirit was not moving my will to this decision.

If humans fervently seek God, pray for guidance from the Holy Spirit, and love an action that is judged to be good by the intellect, then they should assume that the Holy Spirit is moving their will to love this action. The judgment of the intellect is essential; for although the Holy Spirit can move the will to actions beyond the power of the intellect to understand, he never moves the will blindly or moves it to go against reason.

Finally, the Holy Spirit also moves humans to emotionally desire the proper things. Just as the apostles were filled with zeal for the Lord after receiving the Holy Spirit (Acts 2), so also the Holy Spirit moves the emotions to act in accord with whatever the intellect and the will are moved to do. However, because the natural inclinations of the emotions are generally less perfected by grace than are the natural inclinations of the intellect and will, humans should be particularly wary of attributing the movement of the emotions to the Holy Spirit. Consequently, the emotions should never be followed if they contradict the judgment of the intellect. In fact, generally an action determined to be good by the intellect should still be done even if the emotions desire to do something different. Nonetheless, because the emotions are also perfected by the gifts of the Holy Spirit, it is proper to examine their reaction when making important decisions. For example, I have a friend who was engaged to a woman for five years. He never felt emotionally at peace with the idea of marriage and would not commit to a particular wedding date. Eventually they broke up, but my friend fell in love again. He actually bought another engagement ring, but again he did not feel at peace with the decision to get married. Today he is an outstanding Catholic priest, and his emotions are at peace. Thus, although emotions should only be followed with great caution, if the emotions are not at peace with a major decision, then people might want to check and make sure that they have taken proper counsel and have judged properly. Although the Holy Spirit moves the emotions, an emotional desire is not from the Holy Spirit if it violates the judgment of reason or the choice of the will.

In the original state, humans were created so that the intellect directed the will, which directed the emotions. Because grace perfects nature, the Holy Spirit moves these three powers in the same order: first the intellect, then the will, then the emotions. Since all actions that flow from grace must be in accord with divine wisdom, the Holy Spirit moves humans to every action that is done out of love of God, not just the difficult or important ones. In other words, the movement of the Holy Spirit is not esoteric, and humans should *constantly* seek the guidance of the Holy Spirit.

Because knowledge causes love, which causes unity, friends seek to know the goals of their friends. Because they love their friend, they then make their friend's goals their own. They then become united and share in each other's actions. In relation to God, Jesus became human so that we could become friends with God. Through the guidance and movement of the Holy Spirit, we can make God's goals our own. We can then participate in God's infinite action and fulfill our unique role in this action. Because a secondary cause acts in accord with its form, the virtues and gifts of the Holy Spirit perfect humans so that they can be guided more efficaciously by the power of the Holy Spirit. However, just as there are different degrees of participation in the eternal law, there are different degrees of participation in the movement of the Holy Spirit. Although God offers the guidance, humans can choose not to cooperate with it and will then only participate in the guidance at a very low level. Nonetheless, when humans are guided by the Holy Spirit to divine actions of great intensity, they perfect the infused virtues and grow in supernatural happiness.

10

SIN, TEMPTATION, AND VICE

The Road to Unhappiness

Nearly all people at some point in their lives have felt the allure of some type of sinful action. Some are tempted by greed, others are tempted by lust, anger, sloth, or pride. These sinful actions can be alluring because they can cause false happiness (especially if someone is not formed in the virtues). As we saw in chapter 3, this false happiness can ensnare a person and keep him or her from attaining the true happiness found in loving relationships with God and others. Furthermore, sinful actions generally make others unhappy also. If these actions become vices, they can especially hinder humans in attaining happiness because they corrupt the natural inclinations of the soul and make evil actions easy, prompt, and joyful. Since every human action either starts, increases, or decreases a habit, it is essential to study evil actions (sins) in order to better understand what actions to avoid and why to avoid them. In addition to looking at these evil actions, we should also examine their causes. In chapter 2, on the history of human nature, we looked at one of the internal causes of these evil actions: the corruption of the natural inclinations caused by our fallen nature. Other causes of sin include temptation and vice. First, we will cover the concept of sin in general, then we'll discuss temptation briefly, next the notion of vice, and, finally, a powerful remedy against sin and vice, the sacrament of reconciliation (confession).

SIN

Humans are created to be in loving union with God. Any action that violates this loving union is going to be a sin because it prevents humans from doing what they were made to do. Because the eternal law guides all humans to this loving union, sin is defined as "any human action that is contrary to the eternal law."[1] To properly understand sin, this definition needs to be examined. If the sin is a *human action*, it must be voluntary. Sin is a free turning away from God's love. As we saw in chapter 4, *acts of a human* may bring great evil into the world, but they are not sins. Furthermore, a human action can consist of a word, deed, thought, or even chosen desire. Someone can commit interior sins of pride, lust, or anger that also go against love of God. Finally, humans know the eternal law through the participation of their intellect in it. The well-formed human conscience speaks with authority because the intellect participates in divine knowledge. Consequently, sin can also be defined as "a word, deed, thought, or desire that is contrary to human reason." Or, because the eternal law orders humans to their proper ends, sin can also be defined as "any human action that is not ultimately ordered toward the end of unity with God."

Because humans sin when they fall short of performing their proper actions, sin is a lack of goodness in an act. It is the choosing of a false good over a true good. In other words, it is a type of evil action, since sin is a lack of goodness in the moral realm, when such goodness should exist. Evil is a deprivation. It is not a positively existing thing but a lack of something that should exist: the lack of goodness in a human action.[2] Consequently, God, as goodness by nature, cannot and does not cause sin. Nonetheless, as we saw in chapter 9, God is the first cause of a sinful *act* inasmuch as the act exists and has goodness.[3] However, God is not the cause of the defect in the action. The defect is caused by the intentional choice of a human. Thomas Aquinas uses the analogy of a broken leg that causes a limp. The first cause of the *walk* with the limp is the soul. The second cause of the *walk* with the limp is the leg. However, only the leg is the cause of the *defect* in the walk, the limp.[4] So also both God and humans are the cause of the *acts* of sin, but only humans are the *cause* of the *sin*.

Because the role of original sin is so important in the moral life, when people think of sin, they often think of two types: original and personal. However, although original sin was a sin in the full sense of the term for Adam and Eve, for all of their descendants, original sin is only a sin in the analogical sense. In other words, the effects of original sin are *contracted* by all other humans; original sin is not *committed*. For an act to be a sin in the full sense of the term, it must be freely chosen. Thus, for humans today, original sin consists of the effects of this first sin that have been passed on to us. These effects include the destruction of the following harmonious relationships: (1) between humans and God (the loss of sanctifying grace), (2) between humans, (3) within the soul itself, and (4) between the body and the soul. However, as we saw in chapter 2, these harmonies are restored in various degrees through the gift of grace.

A personal sin is a human action that is contrary to the eternal law. It refers to all those sins that have been freely committed by people. In chapter 5, an action was determined to be good if it had a good end and a good object. Furthermore, the degree of goodness was determined by the circumstances. A personal sin occurs when a person freely chooses an action that has either an evil end (the action is ordered to something other than God) or an evil object.[5] For example, suppose someone steals money in order to build a religious monument (good end, evil object). Since the object of stealing is evil, the action is evil. If the person understands what she is doing, then the action is a personal sin. Likewise, if someone donates money to a good cause for purely prideful reasons (where the ultimate end is personal glory, not God), then the action is also evil because it has an evil end. The object of some actions can never be ordered to God, and freely performing these actions is always a sin. Examples of these intrinsically evil actions are murder, blasphemy, apostasy, pride, and adultery.

Just as the degree of goodness varies from action to action according to the circumstances, so also does the degree of evil vary. Recall, that a circumstance is anything related to an action that does not change the species (object) of the action, such as who, where, when, and how the action is performed. For example, both the act of giving money to the poor from one's excess and of giving from one's necessities have the same object. However, the act of giving from one's necessities is a greater good. The circumstance of where the money came from increases the goodness of the act. Because of circumstances, the degree of goodness in the same type of action can vary immensely. Likewise, the degree of evil can vary from one sin to another. For example, a lie that completely destroys the reputation of a person is far worse than the lie that a child tells in order to get another cookie. Both are lies (and sins if freely chosen), but the gravity of evil is far worse in the first case. In some cases, the degree of evil is so great that the sin completely destroys the relationship between the sinner and God. If a sin *completely destroys* this relationship, then the sin is called a *mortal* (deadly) sin. If the sin only *injures* the relationship between the sinner and God, then the sin is called a *venial* sin.

MORTAL SIN

A mortal sin is a human action that completely destroys friendship with God.[6] Mortal sins contradict the charity that unites us to God, breaking the unity with God. The First Letter of John makes this distinction when he states, "All wrongdoing is sin, but there is sin that is not deadly (mortal)" (1 Jn 5:17). An analogy drawn from relationships between humans helps to explain the concept of mortal sin. A true relationship is caused by the love of friendship between two humans. Since humans show their love through their body, actions are necessary to manifest this love. Likewise, freely chosen actions that violate the spiritual or physical welfare of another person show a lack of love. Some actions by their very nature so seriously harm other people that they are incompatible with love for a person (assuming that the person performing the action knows what he is doing and freely chooses it). Other actions harm the relationship, but they do not completely destroy it. For example, if a husband intentionally and severely beats his wife, he may say that he loves her, but his actions show otherwise. On the other hand, if a husband says a mean thing to his wife, his love for her will be diminished but not destroyed.

Just as evil actions can be so serious that they destroy a human relationship, sins can be so serious that they destroy the relationship between humans and God. In other words, the evil action shows that the sinner does not have love of friendship for God. Without love of friendship, the unity with God that is essential for salvation is destroyed. Not that God stops loving the sinner, but the sinner has stopped loving God. In other words, God loves everyone and desires that all are united to him in a loving relationship. However, humans must freely perform their proper actions and love God in order to be united to him for all eternity in heaven. If humans do not love God, God will honor their choice and allow them to go to hell. As Paul asks, "Do you not know that the unjust will not inherit the kingdom of God?" (1 Cor 6:9). For Paul, to be just is to be faithful to the covenant. To be faithful, Christians must have faith and love of God. Paul then gives a list of sins that destroy the loving relationship with God. He notes that people such as fornicators, idolaters, adulterers, practicing homosexuals, thieves, greedy people, drunkards, and others will not inherit the kingdom of God (6:10).

Aquinas further explains how to determine whether or not a particular sin destroys charity (love of friendship of God). He notes that all acts are to be ordered by charity to God, and that sin violates this order. If the violation goes against God as the ultimate end, it is a mortal sin. However, if the violation is only against something referable to the ultimate end, it is a venial sin.[7] When humans perform actions, there are often many intermediate ends between the action and God. For example, Joe does his best work on his homework. Joe does his homework to learn. Joe learns to help others. Joe helps others because he loves God. God is the ultimate end, but the proximate end is doing his best on his homework. If Joe commits a mortal sin, the action is so serious that it necessarily contradicts the ultimate end of loving God. However, if Joe commits a venial sin, it only violates an intermediate end. For example, if Joe intentionally spends hours playing on the computer, causing him to not do his homework, Joe violates the end of learning. This would be the venial sin of sloth. On the other hand, if Joe intentionally and seriously harms another human, Joe commits a mortal sin because his action directly contradicts the ultimate end of love of God.

As can be seen by the example, if Joe is going to commit a mortal sin, the action must be seriously wrong, since only a seriously wrong action necessarily contradicts love of God. Also, Joe must freely choose it, since only freely chosen actions manifest a person's love. Finally, Joe must know that the action is wrong, since humans are only culpable for what they know (or should know). An analogy from personal relationships helps to show why a sin is only mortal if the above conditions are met. For humans to show that they no longer love another person, their actions must be serious, they must know what they are doing, and they must freely choose the action. For example, I remember a time when a distraught young man came to me for advice. I will call him Bob. Bob's fiancée had been passionately kissing another man. He wanted to know if he should call off the engagement. For a fiancée to passionately kiss another man is an action that directly contradicts the end of being engaged; hence, the action is serious enough to show that she does not love Bob as a future husband. He then told me the rest of the story. His fiancée lived in another country thousands of miles away. It was her twenty-first birthday, and she had never consumed alcohol before in her life. Since it was her twenty-first birthday, Bob encouraged her to go out and experience a night of drinking. By the end of the night, she was passionately kissing another man. Although the action seriously contradicts an engaged relationship, she was drunk and had no prior knowledge as to how alcohol would affect her.[8] Consequently, she did not freely choose to perform this action, which was contrary to their relationship. Since love is only manifested through free actions, there was no reason to believe that she did not still love Bob as her future husband.

Just as only a serious action done with full knowledge and consent can destroy a human relationship, so also three conditions are necessary for an action to be a complete rejection of God (a mortal sin): (1) the action must be *grave matter*; (2) the person must *know it is seriously wrong*; and (3) the person must *freely choose* the action.

A sin is grave matter if it is a serious violation of the eternal law. Since the eternal law orders humans to follow their natural and supernatural inclinations, mortal sins violate these inclinations in a serious way. For example, a mortal sin can directly contradict the inclination to know and love God (sins such as blasphemy, hatred of God, intentional denial of divine revelation), the inclination to love others and live in community (sins such as murder, adultery, theft, seriously endangering the lives of others, violating the dignity of workers), or the inclination to attain one's own spiritual and physical welfare (sins such as missing Mass on Sunday without a serious reason, getting drunk, using harmful drugs).[9]

The next necessary condition for a sin to be mortal is that a person must have full knowledge that the action is seriously wrong. For example, today people can grow up in a culture where fornication is seen to be a normal means of recreation. Some people may be so influenced by the culture that they may not even question whether fornication is truly a good action. Hence, although committing fornication is a grave matter, it would not be a mortal sin for them. They would have invincible ignorance in thinking that fornication is good. Now, if at some point they begin to reflect upon the harmful effects of fornication on either individuals or the community, then it might become a mortal sin for them. In other words, people can have an erroneous conscience (false judgment in the intellect). Because peoples' consciences participate in the eternal law, they are required to follow them. However, since humans participate in the eternal law by knowing divine, natural, and human laws, they must always form their conscience before acting. Intentional ignorance (when humans choose not to seek the truth) increases the severity of the sin. The severity is increased because these humans intentionally refuse to do what love of God requires: learn God's goals to make these goals their own.

The last necessary condition for a sin to be mortal is that it must be freely chosen. In other words, it must be a human action. As we saw in chapter 5, ignorance, disordered emotions, bad habits, coercion, and other things can all diminish and even remove voluntariness within an action. However, if humans know that they have a bad habit or disordered emotion that leads them to sin, they must also attempt to avoid all occasions where these causes of sin exist. If they do not attempt to avoid these occasions, then they are still culpable for the sin. For example, if a man is in the habit of getting drunk, and he knows that he cannot withstand the temptations of a bar, then he must avoid bars in order to avoid sin. Because he knows of his weakness, placing himself in a position of grave temptation is a failure to love God.

Because all three of the above conditions must be present for a sin to be mortal, it is difficult for humans who are seriously trying to follow God to commit a mortal sin. These humans are in the habit of doing all things out of love of God and making God their ultimate end. Hence, even if they do an action that is seriously wrong, they often lack complete freedom when they perform the action. Nonetheless, if people do not consistently seek to cultivate good habits, they will probably sooner or later fall into mortal sin.

Because mortal sin destroys charity, it causes a self-imposed separation between the sinner and God. Eternally sharing in God's happiness comes from union with God, and without love this union is impossible. Hence, if humans commit a mortal sin and die unrepentant, they will be eternally estranged from God (because they chose not to love him). This eternal punishment is called "hell" and is a place of ultimate unhappiness because humans there are not in loving relationships with God and others. Just as the happiness of doing an action out of love of God is a foretaste of the happiness in heaven, the unhappiness resulting from intentionally breaking relationships with God and others is a foretaste of the unhappiness in hell.

Although sin results in great unhappiness because it destroys love of God, God is always willing to forgive those who commit mortal sins. In other words, charity is a gift from God, and God wants to mercifully infuse charity into the soul of the sinner. However, since grace perfects nature, humans must cooperate with God and repent so that their love of God can be reestablished. The normal means for repairing the breach caused by mortal sin is the sacrament of confession, which we will examine below.

VENIAL SIN

A venial sin is any human action that is contrary to the eternal law but does not meet the three necessary requirements for a sin to be mortal. In other words, the sin is not seriously wrong, or only some knowledge of its seriousness is known, or only limited voluntariness exists. Just as some actions injure but do not destroy human relationships, venial sins do not destroy the relationship with God, but they do injure it. Although venial sins do not destroy charity, those who truly love God will seek perfection and will strive to avoid even venial sins. In other words, some people have the attitude that because venial sins do not keep them from heaven, they are not a big deal. This attitude shows a lack of love of God. Imagine if I went home to my wife and said, "Honey, we have a good life here. We have a house, nine kids, a twelve-passenger van. What's the minimum I can do and still stay in this relationship? I'm not going to do any actions that completely destroy the relationship; I just want to know the minimum." I can assure you that her response would not be positive. Nor should it be, because seeking the minimum in a relationship is not love. Love drives a person to attempt to remove all impediments to the relationship and to constantly seek to deepen the relationship. So also in reference to God, avoiding mortal sins is not enough. Love requires that one seeks to remove all venial sins and attempts to continually grow in union with God.

Venial sins are also harmful because they can be the start of vicious habits that can lead to a mortal sin. Take, for example, people who hurt others by stealing large amounts of money. They would usually first form a vice by stealing smaller amounts money before they would commit this serious sin.

Sins are human actions that are contrary to the eternal law. The eternal law guides humans to their proper actions, causing people to be naturally or supernaturally happy on earth and eternally happy in heaven. Since a sin contradicts the guidance of eternal law, it will ultimately result in unhappiness, even if it temporarily causes false happiness. Mortal sin is particularly harmful because it can result in eternal *un*happiness. This unhappiness caused by mortal sin begins here on earth, where people are made unhappy because they are not knowing and loving God and others. Venial sins also restrict our ability to be happy, only to a lesser degree.

TEMPTATION

Humans are naturally inclined to good actions. However, in order for good human actions to be performed (before humans have a particular virtue), they need the aid of others to guide them and move them to these actions. This guidance and motivation takes the form of laws (in the general sense of the term). These laws are necessary for moral development for two reasons: first, because the natural inclinations are corrupted by original sin; second, because God created humans with an extraordinarily high end that is unattainable without the aid of others. God made humans this way so that parents, grandparents, teachers, mentors, saints (and angels), and friends can be more like God by helping others grow in virtue. Humans are created in the image of the Trinity, and many different members of society must work together to form good people. Analogous to the way that many different members of society guide and motivate others to actions in accord with their natural inclinations, many different members can also guide and motivate humans to bad actions flowing from the corrupted inclinations. The inordinate desires that come from these tarnished inclinations and the guidance and motivation of others are two different forms of temptation.

Temptation can have interior causes or exterior causes. The interior causes come from the corrupted inclinations and vicious habits. As we discussed in chapter 2, because of original sin the intellect's ability to understand and reason is impaired, the will's love of the true good is diminished, and the emotions are unruly. Furthermore, the proper ordering of these powers is somewhat inverted. Because the intellect and the will are the highest powers of a human, these rational powers should direct the emotions. However, with the corruption of the inclinations, often the emotions blind or cloud the intellect, causing it to justify evil actions. The emotions can also influence the will to choose these evil actions. Instead of the intellect and the will leading the emotions, the emotions begin to lead the intellect and the will. Because of the corruption of the inclinations, temptation takes place when the emotions desire a false good known through sense knowledge. The emotions desire this false good and then influence the intellect, causing it to determine ways to attain this false good. The emotions also influence the will, causing the person to love the false good and (if the unruly emotions are strong enough) to choose the sinful action.[10] For example, George might be tempted to look at pornography either when he senses something outside of him that evokes the lustful desire or when his imagination forms an image that evokes the desire. The emotions then impair the proper function of the intellect, causing George to consider different ways to view pornography. George's will might then love the improper bodily pleasure more than the true good found in a proper understanding of friendship with women. Because of his corrupted inclinations, the emotions, following sense knowledge, can tempt George to perform evil actions.

The exterior cause of temptation is the misleading guidance and movement received from others. Just as others are necessary to guide and move humans to good actions, others can also guide and move humans to evil actions. This distorted guidance and motivation is another form of temptation. When authority figures enact unjust laws, they are sources of temptation. When peers attempt to counsel or motivate their "friends" to do evil, they act as sources of temptation. When members of the media promote improper actions and lifestyles, they can act as sources of temptation. The fallen angels (demons) can also be exterior causes of temptation by causing humans to imagine false goods or inciting the passions to desire false goods.[11] In all of these cases the proper role of humans (or angels) is distorted, for instead of helping to make other humans more like God, they make other humans less like God.

VICE

Just as repeated good actions form virtues, repeated evil actions form vices. And, just as virtues can cause even better human actions, vices can cause actions that are even more evil. These evil actions lead to great unhappiness. The unhappiest people are generally those who are trapped in terrible vices that destroy their loving relationships. For example, the vice of drunkenness destroys families and isolates friends. The vice of pornography destroys marriages and the ability to have the love of friendship with members of the opposite sex. (Pornography turns people into objects to be loved with love of use.) The vice of greed separates people and social classes because things are loved more than people.

Like all habits, vices make sins easy, prompt, and emotionally joyful. They also determine the soul to perform a particular type of action by destroying the proper acts of the intellect, will, and emotions. Because these powers are further corrupted by vices, humans with vices can lose freedom. For example, alcoholics and drug addicts often lose their freedom to act rationally. Without freedom, they will need the guidance and motivation of others to quit their vicious habits. The help of others is essential because a vice further corrupts the natural inclination of a power of the soul to perform good actions. If humans without vices need the help of others to perform good actions, how much more will people with vices need this aid? They will normally need the guidance and motivation of friends, family, or professionals to hold them accountable for their actions (laying down the law), or this help can come from the grace of God. Since God normally works through secondary causes, usually both the help of others and grace are necessary. For example, God works through a priest to hold people accountable for their vices when they come to the sacrament of confession. The priest gives them a penance in order to turn the vice into a virtue, and God gives them grace. Consequently, if people find that a sin is easy, prompt, and emotionally joyful, they need to get the help of God and others to overcome their vice.

Just as there are virtues in the intellect, will, and emotions, there can also be vices in these three powers of the soul. In the intellect, vices such rashness and inconstancy corrupt the ability of the intellect to take good counsel and to command properly. Also, intentional doubt corrupts faith. In the will and emotions, any habitual excess or defect of desire is a vice. For example, in the will, dishonesty, disobedience, and impiety are vices that corrupt the ability of the will to love properly. The concupiscible emotions are corrupted by vices of excessive desire (lust, drunkenness, gluttony, etc.) or lack of desire (insensibility, lack of desire for food, etc.). The irascible emotions are likewise corrupted by vices that go to an extreme, such as cowardliness (too much fear) or foolhardiness (too much daring). Since the perfection of all of these powers is necessary to perform good actions, vices in any of these powers can hinder the ability to perform good human actions.

Just as similar good actions performed with a particular intensity cause virtues, similar evil actions performed with a particular intensity cause vices. Vices, along with the effects of fallen nature, become an interior principle of evil actions. However, unlike virtues that increase freedom by perfecting the powers of the soul, vices remove freedom by further corrupting the natural inclinations to free actions. They also ultimately result in the unhappiness of the person and others. Table 10.1 parallels the map to happiness.

Table 10.1.   Map to Unhappiness

Fallen Nature→	Corrupted Natural Inclinations→	Temptations from Others (including unjust laws)→	Evil Human Actions (sins)→	Vices →	Worse Human Actions→	Unhappiness

When looking at this table, it is important to realize that fallen nature does not automatically cause humans to form vices and become unhappy. The natural inclinations to the true good are corrupted; they are not destroyed. Humans are not necessarily entrapped by their fallen nature, and, furthermore, God offers grace to everyone. In all likelihood, most Christians probably vacillate between performing actions flowing from grace and performing actions flowing from the corrupted inclinations. Although the chart has its limitations, it can be helpful in showing how temptation, sin, and vices fit into a teleological system and how they ultimately lead to unhappiness.

THE SACRAMENT OF RECONCILIATION

Having analyzed mortal sin and its effects, we may now analyze the normal way that God removes mortal sin within the Catholic Church. The sacrament of baptism removes all sin, but for those already baptized, reconciliation (more commonly called "confession") is the normal means of having a sin forgiven. Jesus forgave the sins of many while he was here on earth, but when he went to heaven, he sent the Holy Spirit to continue his mission of forgiving sins. However, because the Holy Spirit must be sensed through physical signs (like the Son was sensed through the body of Jesus), the Holy Spirit continues the mission of forgiving sins through the Church, specifically, through the bishops and those appointed by them. Hence, Jesus says in John 20:21, "As the Father has sent me, so I send you." Jesus then breathes on the apostles (a sign of the Holy Spirit) and says, "Receive the Holy Spirit, whose sins you forgive are forgiven them, and whose sins you retain are retained." Christ continues his mission of forgiving sins through the apostles and their successors—bishops and priests.[12]

Often in the past, the sacrament of confession was confined to a very legalistic framework. The priest was like a judge representing God. He listened to the sins and doled out the appropriate penance as a temporal punishment for the sins. In fact, over the centuries an entire genre of books called "penitential manuals" were developed to aid priests in determining the proper penance for a particular sin. Although there can be positive aspects of understanding confession this way, in general this is a very deontological way of looking at confession. The moral life becomes focused on the relation between sins and punishment. *In a teleological system, confession is primarily a sacrament manifesting the loving relationship between a Christian and God.*

To deepen personal relationships, humans should seek to avoid offending each other. They should constantly assess whether or not they have hurt others. Furthermore, when they discover that they have offended others, they should immediately apologize and seek to do something to repair the damage done to the relationship. Their love for each other drives them to attempt to remove and repair all impediments to their relationship. Love of God also inspires Christians to do the same things in relation to God. They should constantly assess whether or not they have offended God. If they have offended God, they should apologize and attempt to make up for their sin. Confession provides a venue for Christians to express their love for God. It requires that they constantly examine their consciences to identify any sins they have committed. They then orally confess their sins and tell God that they are sorry for offending him. Finally, they show their love for God by performing their prescribed penance. Confession is not for God's benefit; it is for the benefit of Christians. Because of God's mercy, he always offers his forgiveness to sinners and wants them to rekindle their love of him. Confession allows them to physically express their love, and because humans express their love through their bodies, they greatly benefit from this sacrament.

Confession also specifically helps humans to grow in love for God in the following ways. First of all, it restores the grace lost by sin. If the sin is mortal, then it restores the grace that was lost by the sin and reconciles humans to God. Since the infused virtues flow from grace, these virtues are also restored and elevated, giving the penitent greater power to overcome vices and temptation. Although venial sins do not remove grace, confessing them likewise strengthens grace and gives the penitent greater power to overcome vices and temptation. Second, confession holds sinners accountable for their actions. Because of the corruption of the inclinations by sin, humans with vices normally need the aid of others to overcome these vices. In confession, divine aid is given through a physical person who can be seen and heard. The priest is able to give practical, spiritual advice to help penitents avoid sin. Furthermore, the priest gives the penitent a penance. To conquer a vice, a person must usually replace it with a virtue. The act of prescribing a penance gives the priest an opportunity to prescribe acts of virtue to destroy the vice. Finally, confession causes humans to consistently evaluate their relationship with God. In human relationships, love requires that all impediments to the relationship be removed. Hence, those with great love will constantly communicate with their beloved in order to find all the ways that they have offended their beloved. Once they recognize these offences, they can work to remove them. So also, frequent confession requires humans to constantly examine their consciences so that even the slightest of venial sins can be removed. The great saints recognized this valuable aspect of confession. For example, St. Benedict required all of his monks to confess all of their sins to the abbot.[13] Both St. Teresa of Calcutta and St. John Paul II are reported to have gone to confession more than once a week. Christ instituted confession so that his followers could perfect their loving relationship with him.

Although the Catholic Church requires her members to go to confession only once a year if they have a mortal sin, if people truly want to grow in their relationship with Christ they should go much more frequently.[14] All mortal sins must always be confessed with true sorrow in order to be forgiven. If the penitent is truly sorry, venial sins are forgiven even without confessing them. However, those who strive for a perfect, loving relationship with God will also want to confess their venial sins (within reason).[15]

Since good actions flowing from grace are the way that humans progress on their journey to eternal happiness, sin causes them to regress on their journey. All sin not only hinders the pursuit of eternal happiness but also inhibits happiness on earth. Mortal sin is particularly horrible, as it destroys the loving relationship that humans have with God. Because humans are happy when they are in loving relationships with others, when one person is unhappy generally others are also going to be unhappy. Thankfully, God gives his followers the gift of confession to help overcome the effects of sin and vice.

11

COMPLETING THE MAP
TO HAPPINESS

Throughout the previous chapters, we have examined various elements of the moral life, such as nature, grace, law, virtue, and happiness. In order to understand how these different elements function, I also noted how they are related to each other. For example, an important theme throughout this book has been how virtues perfect the natural inclinations so that humans are able to perform the actions of knowing and loving that cause happiness. This chapter will take all the moral elements covered in this book and show how they relate to each other. First, I'll show in general how all the elements work together for those who are striving to attain eternal happiness, then show how they work together within the performance of a human action perfected by grace and accompanying virtues, and, finally, how they work together for those who are attempting to form virtues in others. After showing how these various elements work together, in a brief section we'll look at how this complete methodology relates to other moral systems. Last of all, we will analyze the topic of human freedom, since the relation between all the moral elements gives the necessary background for a proper understanding of freedom.

PUTTING ALL THE PARTS TOGETHER

Recall the coffeemaker analogy in chapter 1. In the analogy, the family needed to look at the form (nature) of the coffeemaker to determine what it was made to do. They would then be able to determine that it was made to brew some sort of liquid. With the help of the owner's manual, they could easily figure out how to make coffee. Now that they know how to make coffee, the coffeemaker can be used perform its proper actions. Although humans are far more complicated than coffeemakers, this book has followed the same format. First, we covered human nature, and then we studied its end (happiness). Next we examined the Bible (the owner's manual) to determine the proper methodology. Also found within the Bible were the written precepts of the divine law. However, unlike coffeemakers, humans also need grace, virtues, and the gifts of the Holy Spirit. With all of these different perfections, humans are able to perform their proper actions.

Now that we have covered all of these different elements of the moral life, we can present the complete map for the journey back to God. The beginning point is human nature. Humans are made to know and love God and others and to be united with God and others in a community. This human nature is fallen, yet open to redemption. From human nature flows the natural inclinations that give humans the ability to perform human actions of knowing and loving others. However, the natural inclinations are not sufficiently powerful to cause humans to immediately perform the actions necessary to enter into loving relationships with others.[1] Humans were created to be perfected within a community, and the help of others is essential to guide and motivate them to their proper actions. Parents, teachers, and other authorities must formulate human laws (based on natural law) to guide humans to their proper actions. With this guidance, humans are able to perform good human actions.

Humans freely choose these good actions, nonetheless the primary cause of these actions is the virtue of the parents and authorities who guide and motivate them. These wise mentors continuously guide and motivate humans until humans are able to develop virtues through the repetition of good actions. These virtues allow humans to fully perfect their natural inclinations. With these virtues, humans can perform good actions by their own power.[2] Virtues perfect the intellect, will, and emotions so that humans can perform the acts of knowing and loving that are necessary for establishing loving relationships with God and others. Since happiness comes from knowing and loving God and others, these actions result in natural happiness. Furthermore, since humans are happy when they perform loving actions for others, when they are happy, others are also generally happy. For example, Joe was constantly formed by parents and teachers so that he would acquire the virtue of justice. Justice allows him to become good friends with Kate. Now his acts of love of Kate flow from his knowledge and love. With this perfected knowledge and love, Joe can contemplate the good of being united to Kate. Joe is happy and so is Kate.

However, natural happiness is not the ultimate end. Humans have an infinite desire for the good, and they seek eternal happiness. Thankfully, human nature is redeemed, and grace perfects it.[3] Grace causes humans to participate in divine nature. By the power of divine nature, humans have the supernatural inclinations of faith, hope, and charity. These theological virtues incline humans to divine actions that are accomplished through the movement and guidance of the Holy Spirit and the written element of the divine law. Since God works through secondary causes, often the Holy Spirit works through parents and other spiritual mentors to guide and motivate humans to perform divine actions.[4] However, in order to be more perfectly guided by the Holy Spirit, humans also need the gifts of the Holy Spirit that dispose them to his movement.

Although humans first receive the infused cardinal virtues when they are given sanctifying grace, these virtues are perfected by like actions flowing from grace. The divine law guides humans to human actions that are divine by participation, which, when done repetitively, perfect the infused cardinal virtues. These virtues, along with the theological virtues and gifts, perfect the intellect and will so that humans are now able to supernaturally participate in God's knowledge and love. By means of God's knowledge and love, humans can perform better divine actions and have supernatural happiness on earth. Like natural happiness, this supernatural happiness is shared with others. Finally, when humans die, they will have eternal happiness. Because grace perfects nature, for every step on the level of nature, there is a corresponding supernatural step (see table 11.1).

Table 11.1 is a chart of the journey to God showing how important the aid of other humans and God are for the attainment of eternal happiness. Even on the supernatural level, God works through the Church to give supernatural grace, and the Holy Spirit guides and motivates humans through parents and other teachers. With the aid of others, virtues are perfected and humans are able to have a taste of eternal happiness by performing divine actions on earth.

Table 11.1.   The "Big Picture" of Moral Life (The Happiness Chart)*

Participation in divine nature: Grace →	Theological virtues and Gifts of the Holy Spirit →	Divine law →	Participated divine actions →	Infused cardinal virtues →	More perfect divine actions →	Eternal happiness
Nature →	Natural inclinations →	Natural and human law →	Good human actions →	Natural virtues →	More perfect actions →	Natural happiness

* From what we learned in chapter 10, a further section detailing fallen nature could also be added to the bottom of the chart to show how fallen nature causes corrupt inclinations, which are moved toward evil human actions by the devil and the bad influences of others. These bad external laws cause sin, which causes vices and ultimately results in unhappiness. Since Christians are redeemed, yet still have the effects of original sin, they are capable of performing both actions that flow from grace and actions that flow from fallen nature.

The chart shows that in order for humans to attain the ends to which they are naturally and supernaturally inclined, they need the help of laws and virtues. In chapter 7, on law, table 7.1 showed how the particular natural inclinations result in various laws. In chapter 9, on the gifts of the Holy Spirit, table 9.1 showed which virtues and gifts perfected the various natural inclinations. Since this chapter shows how all the different elements fit together, these two charts can now be merged and expanded. The following chart in table 11.2 links natural and supernatural inclinations to their particular laws, virtues, and actions. The chart is not meant to be exhaustive but only to give some more specific examples of the teleological nature of morality. Part II of the book will cover the virtues found on the chart in table 11.2 (and others) in detail.

Table 11.2.   Specific Laws and Virtues Perfecting Various Natural and Supernatural Inclinations

Natural and Supernatural Inclinations	Some Relevant Laws	Some Relevant Virtues	Proper Actions
To God	Duty to love God above all things: *first commandment*	Faith, hope, charity, humility	Loving union with God on earth and for eternity
To live in community	Duty to love others as God loves them: *fourth through tenth commandments*	Charity, justice, mercy	True friendship with others
The inclination of the intellect to know the truth	Duty to learn about God, others, and the world	Faith, understanding, and wisdom	Knowing God, others, and the rest of creation
The inclination of the will to love the good	Duty to do good, to love God, others, and oneself	Charity, hope, justice, humility	Loving all things the proper amount
The inclination of the emotions to seek the true bodily good	Duty to emotionally desire proper amount and type of pleasure	Temperance, fortitude	Proper actions are filled with joy
To procreate and raise children	Duty not to lust: *sixth and ninth commandments*; duty to raise holy children	Charity, justice, temperance, chastity	A happy family life based on loving union
For the body to be alive and healthy	Duty to live a healthy lifestyle	Temperance, fortitude	Actions conducive to health
Material goods necessary for performing proper actions	Duty to use material goods to help others: *seventh commandment*	Justice, temperance, liberality	Consuming in moderation and using material goods to help others

MORE PERFECT DIVINE ACTIONS

On the "Big Picture" chart (table 11.1) showing the progression from human nature to eternal happiness, the last box before eternal happiness is "more perfect divine actions." These are the most perfect of all human actions, and they also show how all the different elements of the moral life collaborate to cause an action. Every one of these actions is ordered to *eternal happiness* and is an application of a *law* (goal). *Virtues* and *gifts* that flow from *grace* are required to perfect the *powers of the soul* to understand the law and to apply it. By going through the twelve steps of the human action, we can see the role of all these moral elements (see chapter 5, section titled "The Twelve Steps of the Human Action").

Before the action begins, the supernatural inclinations of faith, hope, and charity must perfect the intellect and the will to apprehend things and desire them (steps 1 and 2). Just as the natural inclinations to know and love are the foundation of all natural human actions, these supernatural inclinations are the foundation of all divine actions. The concepts of these things are then combined or separated to form an end or goal (step 3). Although the ultimate goal is happiness, most moral actions begin with intermediary ends that are ordered to a particular ultimate end. These ends take the form of laws. In order to properly understand these laws, the intellectual virtues of understanding, knowledge, and faith, and the Holy Spirit's gifts of wisdom, understanding, and knowledge are needed to perfect the intellect. Once the end (universal premise) is determined, the will must intend this premise (step 4). The virtues of justice, hope, charity, and the Holy Spirit gifts of piety and fear of the Lord perfect the will to properly intend this.

For example, Joe needs to decide what he is going to do the summer before he marries Kate. He has always wanted to do missionary work, but he also knows he will need money to pay for the wedding. To make this decision, Joe needs many concepts that could come from natural simple apprehension, such as the concepts of money, job, summer, and so on. However, he will also need concepts that come from his faith, such as missionary work, the Christian view of God, and a proper understanding of a wedding ordered to Christian marriage (step 1). Joe desires the concept of missionary work through the virtues of hope and charity (step 2). He then sets a goal, which becomes a law for him: "I will do missionary work this summer" (step 3). In order for Joe to know the relation between missionary work and his quest for eternal happiness, he needs the virtues of understanding, knowledge, and faith, along with the appropriate gifts of the Holy Spirit. Finally, Joe intends this goal/law (step 4) because of his love of God (charity), hope for attaining heaven, and love of others (justice).

Having intended the goal/law, the intellect then determines how to apply this goal/ law in a particular situation. The virtue of prudence and the Holy Spirit's gift of counsel are needed to research the situation and properly reason to the best possible action (step 5). The gift of wisdom is needed to move the will to love the best option (step 6), and along with prudence it also helps the intellect judge the best action (step 7). Prudence is further needed to command the action (step 9). The virtues of justice, hope, and charity perfect the will to consent to, choose, and execute the proper action (steps 6, 8, 10). Finally, understanding, wisdom, and faith (and the corresponding gifts) are needed to contemplate the good of the action. Charity, hope, justice, and piety perfect the will to joyfully rest in the good attained.

Joe takes counsel and determines how he could do missionary work (step 5). Prudence and the Holy Spirit's gift of counsel aid his intellect to research and reason well. Because he loves God and others, he consents to the possibility of doing missionary work (step 6). However, when he judges by higher principles, he realizes that God has called him to the vocation of marriage (step 7). Joe must go back and take counsel again to see if missionary work will contradict the responsibilities that come with getting married. Whatever Joe decides, he will need prudence and the Holy Spirit's gifts to come to the best decision and to command it (steps 5, 7, 9). He will choose (step 8) and perform (step 10) this action out of love for God (charity) and love for others (justice). His faith, coupled with the virtues and gifts of understanding and wisdom, perfect the intellect so that he is happy (step 11). Charity, justice, and piety perfect the will so that he is also filled with joy at having performed the right action (step 12). The chart in table 11.3 shows how it all fits together.

Table 11.3.   The Perfections of Each Step of the Human Action

Steps in the Intellect	Virtues Perfecting Intellect	Gifts Perfecting Intellect	Steps in the Will	Virtues Perfecting Will	Gifts Perfecting Will
1. Simple Apprehension	Faith		2. Desire the Good	Hope Charity	
3. Understanding the End (Law)	Practical Understanding Knowledge Faith	Understanding Knowledge	4. Intention	Justice Hope Charity	Piety Fear of the Lord
5. Counsel	Prudence Faith	Counsel	6. Consent	Justice Hope Charity	Wisdom Piety Fear of the Lord
7. Judgment	Prudence Faith	Wisdom	8. Choice	Justice Hope Charity	Piety Fear of the Lord
9. Command	Prudence Faith		10. Execution	Justice Hope Charity	Piety Fear of the Lord
11. Contemplation of the Good	Understanding Wisdom Faith	Understanding Wisdom	12. Joy	Justice Hope Charity	Piety Fear of the Lord

The emotions, following sense knowledge, are also involved in every human action. Since intellectual concepts are linked to sense knowledge, and knowledge of individual situations must come from sense knowledge, there are always various sensual goods that attract or repel the emotions within a human action. The virtues of temperance and fortitude and the Holy Spirit's gifts of fear of the Lord and fortitude are needed to keep the passions in accord with reason. For example, Joe will need temperance and fear of the Lord to control his desire for material goods that can be obtained through money. Without temperance, the intellect and will could be swayed by the emotions to choose a job because of an inordinate desire for material goods. He will also need fortitude to persevere and to avoid laziness.

Chapter 5 noted the importance of learning the twelve steps of the human action so that defects in the action could be identified and virtues could be prescribed to fix the defects. Now we have just seen the virtues and gifts that perfect the various steps of the human action. Consequently, if humans are failing to perform good human actions, they can go through the steps of the human action to isolate the problem. Once the problem is found, they can work on a particular virtue or ask someone to help them complete the particular step of the action. They can also pray to the Holy Spirit and ask for an increase of the appropriate gifts.

GIVING DIRECTIONS FOR THE JOURNEY

An important theme throughout this book is that for children to develop virtues, wise and virtuous mentors are necessary to guide and motivate them to perform good actions. God created the world to participate in his plan of bringing the universe to perfection so that created beings could be more like God by causing goodness in others. Hence, when mentors guide others to good actions, not only do they help others, but they are especially like God. Another way of explaining this point is that God wants everyone to be happy by entering into loving relationships with him and others. However, in order for them to be happy, they need mentors to train them in virtues. Out of love for God, virtuous humans likewise desire that others are happy and seek to train the next generation. When they train the next generation, humans are like God in participating in his knowledge, love, and happiness. Hence, once humans become virtuous, it is their job to train the next generation by guiding and motivating others through the forming of laws, exhortations, and a proper culture. Two points can be drawn from this truth that humans are made to guide and motivate others to virtue. First, humans must seek to grow in virtue in order to train others. Second, a lack of virtue in parents, teachers, lawmakers, and other mentors can have disastrous effects on the next generation.

In regard to the first point, mentors must already have virtues because in order to properly form laws to guide and motivate others, virtues are needed to perfect the intellect to determine the proper law for the situation. The virtues of faith and practical understanding, and the gift of understanding, are necessary to form laws that will guide children and others to actions that will form virtues. The person with understanding can determine the natural law by studying the natural inclinations, and precepts of the divine law can be found by looking at the supernatural inclinations (especially faith). The virtue of prudence is essential to perfect the intellect to determine the best way to enforce these laws. The will must also be perfected by charity and justice to intend and enforce these good laws. Finally, the emotions must be perfected to help the lawgiver persevere and properly use anger.

For example, parents might understand that it is important that their children learn to be attentive during Mass. The virtues and the gift of understanding help parents determine this law, and charity and justice help them intend it. However, the way that young children are attentive is different than the way older children are attentive. Hence, prudence will be needed to help parents determine how to enforce this law in a particular situation. Justice and charity are needed to perfect the will to enforce the law. Generally, it takes months or even years for children to be in the habit of being attentive in Mass. Hence, fortitude is essential to consistently apply this law at every Mass and to regulate anger when the children are bad. Therefore, parents, grandparents, teachers, lawmakers, and other moral guides must develop virtues in order to guide children and others to form good habits.

Every generation must guide and motivate the generation that comes after it. Normally, this training in virtue begins in the family.[5] Prospective parents and others should work on developing the virtues needed to train children. Even those not directly raising children can influence the next generation by helping to form a proper culture. The Vatican II fathers noted that because of the social nature of humanity, culture aids humans in developing their bodily and spiritual qualities.[6] However, there can be authentic elements of culture that help humans properly develop and false elements of culture that can keep humans from performing their proper actions. All humans should work to transform culture into a proper culture where the good news of Christianity permeates and guides all social ideas and institutions. In order to properly transform culture, humans must not only grow in all the virtues but also incorporate these virtues into law, education, art, media, science, and other social institutions.[7]

The second point is that because each generation trains the next generation, a lack of virtue among parents and others will have long-term effects. Consequently, strong families composed of parents that love each other and their children and good schools that form students in all the virtues are extremely important to the moral formation of humans. Society should work to ensure that all who form the next generation, especially families, have the spiritual, moral, and material resources to raise good children.

OTHER MORAL SYSTEMS ARE INCOMPLETE

Moral theology can be very complicated. There is no single rule to follow in every situation. Rather, there are multiple elements of the moral life, such as nature, grace, law, virtue, and happiness. In addition, there are multiple steps to an action, with multiple virtues and gifts perfecting each of these steps. An analogy with health can be helpful to understand why moral theology is so complicated. The primary way to attain a healthy life is to eat properly and exercise. However, to specify what this means, one must learn about vitamins, minerals, calories, fats, carbohydrates, proper exercises to strengthen muscles, and so on. In other words, remaining healthy can be very complicated. The same is true with moral theology. All of moral theology can be summarized by the statement that *humans should know and love God and others*. Yet, to specify what this means one must learn about virtues, laws, grace, actions, happiness, and so on. The problem with most other philosophical and theological moral systems is that they are too simplistic. They miss certain important elements of the moral life. Just as a health plan that did not take into consideration vitamins would be incomplete, so also a moral methodology that does not take into consideration the role of law or virtue is incomplete.

The point of this section is not to systematically compare the moral system developed in this book with any other moral system but simply to note that although most other moral systems have some truth, they are generally incomplete. If they did not have some truth, then no one would follow them. However, they usually miss some important elements. I will give two brief examples.

There are various deontological moral systems (rule- or duty-based moral systems). The deontological tendencies of the Old Testament have already been covered. Another example of a deontological system is found in the moral philosophy of Immanuel Kant, an influential Enlightenment philosopher. Kant argued that the morality of an action is determined by whether or not a person always commands himself to act in such a way that he would want all others to command themselves to act in the same way in the same situation.[8] This law that Kant wants all people to follow is called the *categorical imperative*. Because Kant's moral system is focused on following duty, it is a deontological moral system. Following the law is a necessary element of the moral life since the natural inclinations need the guidance and motivation of others in order to form virtues. However, it is only one element of the moral life, and deontological systems tend to neglect the role of grace, natural inclinations to an end, virtue, and happiness.

Another moral system is utilitarianism. Although there are various forms of utilitarianism, the basic idea is that humans should always act in such a way as to bring the most good to the most people. Again there is some truth in this moral system; humans should in general use prudence to bring as much good as possible into the world. However, utilitarianism neglects the role of law and the necessity of virtues, such as wisdom, that perfect the person to determine the true good in a given situation. Furthermore, grace and the guidance of the Holy Spirit (who always knows the greatest good) are also neglected. Finally, this system neglects the truth that some actions are always evil and cannot be done to bring a greater good.

The key point we want to make here is that although there are many simpler methods of morality, which contain some truth, all of these systems neglect essential elements of moral development.[9] If attaining health is complicated, why should we expect the moral life to be any less complicated? However, even though it seems complicated, this moral system should be familiar to most people because it simply articulates the traditional way of raising children and other traditional moral practices. For centuries, good parents in various different cultures have sought the happiness of their children. For the sake of their children's happiness, parents have disciplined their children and trained them to perform good actions. This training resulted in their children forming good habits. Furthermore, within the Catholic Church, parents have brought their children to the sacraments to receive grace and have taught them the truths of faith. They have guided their children by the precepts of divine law and have helped them to perfect the infused virtues. Ultimately, these parents want their children to be eternally happy.

Humans are destined for the highest of ends (God's happiness), yet they do not have the ability to attain this end by their own power. Humans need help to share in God's happiness, and Jesus Christ offers them this help. Because the gift of God's grace is so extraordinary, the consequences of rejecting or accepting it are also extreme. To reject God's gift is to reject the loving union with God that fulfills the longings of the human heart. To accept this gift is to share in divine nature, which gives humans the abilities to enter into the loving friendships that the heart desires. Yet, as we noted in chapter 4, St. Paul states that grace is only one very important part of the journey—humans also need faith, hope, and charity, divine guidance in the form of the law, and virtues. Furthermore, since God works through humans to form others, humans must act upon these gifts from God and aid others in attaining true happiness.

FREEDOM

A complete moral methodology gives the proper background information for understanding freedom. Actions are free if they result from the intellect and will working together to determine and choose a particular action. Actions are free when the intellect knows both the end of the action and at least one way to attain the end and the will chooses the action based on its love of the end.[10] In other words, humans are free when the intellect properly understands the end, takes good counsel (if necessary), and judges. Likewise, the will must intend the end, consent, and choose the action. Since the emotions can hinder or overpower the acts of the intellect and will, they must be trained to follow the intellect and will. The more perfect the acts of the intellect, will, and emotions, the greater the freedom of a person. If humans do not understand what they are doing (a defect in understanding) or improperly apply an act to a situation (a defect in counsel and judgment), they lack freedom. For example, the person who

is not able to think because he is overcome by anger or the person who does not realize the consequences of his actions lacks freedom. Likewise, if someone is forced to do
something against his will, he is not free.

Because moral freedom is dependent upon both the intellect determining which
actions can be ordered to happiness and the will loving properly, the greater the perfection of the intellect and will, the greater the freedom.[11] Modern theories of freedom
often miss this point. John Paul II speaks of two understandings of freedom: artificial
freedom and authentic freedom.[12] An examination of these two understandings of
freedom gives insight into the true nature of freedom.

Artificial freedom is the more modern understanding of freedom. It can be defined as "an arbitrary choice between contraries." In this view, freedom lies solely in
the will. The role of the intellect is not to guide the will to good choices, but simply to
provide the will with possible options. The choice is arbitrary, because an evil choice
is just as free as a good choice. Humans with artificial freedom are most free when they
can do anything they want—even if the action leads to the unhappiness of themselves
and others. In other words, this freedom is most perfect when there is no force outside
of the will influencing humans in any way. Hence, any law, argument, natural inclination, or virtue would be seen as imposing upon their freedom. Even divine guidance
removes this freedom, since humans must be free to do whatever they will.[13]

A good analogy showing the relation of artificial freedom and law is that of tug of
war. A woman is on one side of the rope, and the law is on the other side. The more the
woman pulls away from the law, the freer she becomes. The more she is under the influence of the law, the less freedom she has. The goal is to be completely free from the
influence of any laws or any other things that will determine her to a particular type
of action. This is the freedom found in Adam and Eve when they created their own
moral norms. It is also the freedom found in the rebellious adolescent who believes
that the good laws of her parents have taken away her freedom.

Authentic freedom is "the freedom to do great things." In the moral life, it is the
freedom to fulfill our natural inclinations by being happy. Unlike artificial freedom,
which is the freedom to do whatever we want, authentic freedom is the freedom to do
what all humans ultimately want (even if we do not understand it): acts resulting in
great happiness. To be able to perform these good actions by their own power, humans
by nature must have virtues. In order to attain these virtues, they must first be guided
and motivated by others. For example, to be good at playing the piano, humans must
first follow the rules of music theory taught by their teacher. If they just bang randomly
on the piano, they will never become great piano players. By practicing under the guidance of their teacher, they eventually form the habit of being a good pianist. Now they
are free to play any type of music or even to compose music. Those who do not develop the habit of piano playing are free to either play poorly or not at all, but they are
not free to play well. Another example is the freedom to do math. Unless humans learn

the basic rules of arithmetic and practice adding, subtracting, multiplying, and dividing, they are not free to calculate the best deal at a grocery store. It is the same with the moral life. Unless humans are guided by others to form habits and are given the grace of God, their intellect, will, and emotions are not perfected. Without these perfections, they are not free to perform the actions that will make them happy. Humans who do not know the true good are not free to be truly happy. Likewise, defects in love and unruly emotions remove the freedom to be happy.

A good analogy for the relation between authentic freedom and the law is that of a guide leading a mountain climber with a guide rope. The law is the guide, and it guides humans to true happiness (the top of the mountain). The more readily a person follows the good law, the freer the person becomes. Unlike artificial freedom, authentic human freedom is not attained by independence from God (and human laws in accord with eternal law), but it is attained by sharing in God's power, wisdom, and love (called "participated theonomy"). Perfect freedom is increased by perfecting the intellect, will, and emotions through grace and the virtues. It is modeled after God's freedom, whose perfect will is identical to his perfect wisdom.[14]

An improper view of freedom causes people to invent false rights. It makes people believe they are completely self-ruling: free to kill others (abortion), free to die when they please (euthanasia), free to use property only for themselves (rigid capitalism). The view of authentic freedom causes people to recognize that they are most free when they know and love God and others. True freedom is contrasted with a slavery to sin. Those who sin have a defect in their ability to know, love, or seek the proper bodily good. Hence, those who sin lack freedom.[15]

Authentic freedom and true happiness always go together, and false freedom and false happiness also always go together. Authentic freedom results when humans participate in God's wisdom and love because they have grace, virtues, and are guided by the Holy Spirit. Likewise, when humans participate in the God's wisdom and love, they perform the actions that they were created to perform, and are able to share in God's happiness. When humans have false freedom and do what they "want" to do, they attain false happiness. Their happiness is often fleeting and always incomplete. Just as false happiness can trap humans and keep them from being truly fulfilled, so also false freedom can cause humans to believe that they are able to create their own moral norms.

HUMAN FREEDOM AND DIVINE CAUSALITY

With authentic freedom, freedom is increased the more humans participate in God's wisdom and love. However, to make sure that the proper relationship between God's causality and freedom is understood, I am going to cover three modern views of this topic. In these three views, the relation between humans and God is that of *heteronomy*, *autonomy*, and *participated theonomy*.[16] Participated theonomy is the proper way to understand the relation between human freedom and divine causality.

Heteronomy literally means "rule by another." The idea is that the ruler is extrinsic or foreign to the one being ruled. This view of the relation to God is found in a deontological system where God arbitrarily rules humans. He makes certain laws based solely on his will and enforces them through his power.[17] Humans must follow these laws or else God will kill them (or send them to hell). In other words, the reason for following these laws is because God says to follow them.

With this view, God's intervention in human actions (by means of his laws and punishments) always takes away freedom. God's laws force humans to perform actions that they do not want to do. Thus, humans are most free when they are not under any divine obligations. An example of this view can be found in much of the moral theology of the eighteenth through nineteenth centuries. Many moral theologians were involved in debates as to when a law was binding on a person and when a person was free from the confines of the law.[18] For example, a theologian might try to invent cases when the law of not murdering did not apply to a particular person (e.g., cases of duels, etc.). The goal of many of these theologians was to maximize human "freedom" and to minimize divine obligations. The problem with this view of heteronomy is that it fails to recognize that God moves and guides humans to freely perform their proper actions. The heteronomous view turns God into a tyrant who arbitrarily makes laws. It fails to understand how God can guide humans without removing human freedom.

Autonomy literally means "self-rule." Although technically humans are self-ruling when they are moved by God, the idea behind this view is that humans are the sole cause of their actions.[19] Even though this view may appear to be the exact opposite of heteronomy, in reality it is just the other side of the same coin. This view also holds that God is extrinsic to humans and that his guidance always results in the removal of human freedom. The only real difference between the two views is that the proponents of autonomy do not believe that they are bound by God's coercive power. Consequently, humans are most free when there is no influence from God and others on their actions. This belief that humans must "freely" determine their own standards of right and wrong is very common today. However, autonomy has the same problems as heteronomy. Proponents of autonomy also fail to understand how divine guidance results in free actions that fulfill human nature. Rather than sharing in divine wisdom to make the best decision, autonomous people reject divine wisdom and replace it with limited human wisdom. Those who hold the notion of autonomy can easily become entrapped in this form of false freedom and miss out on true happiness.

Participated theonomy is the proper view of our relation to God. Theonomy literally means "rule by God." The term "participated" shows that God's governance is not heteronomous but rather a rule where humans participate in divine wisdom and love.[20] This view recognizes that the human intellect functions most perfectly when it shares in divine wisdom, and that the human will functions most perfectly when it shares in divine love. Since freedom comes from the intellect and the will functioning properly, true freedom comes from participating in God's rule. Both God and humans intimately act as first and second causes when they cause good human actions. Unlike in heteronomy and autonomy, where separation from God's influence is the goal, with participated theonomy separation from God is always a defect that will ultimately lead to unhappiness.[21]

Only actions that are freely chosen (i.e., human actions) cause humans to move forward or to move backward on their journey to God. Actions are most free when they flow from a properly functioning intellect and will. In order for the intellect and will to be perfected, they need to be guided by laws and perfected by virtues. The most perfect happiness and freedom on earth takes place when humans are able to perform more perfect divine actions by participation. The greatest happiness and freedom will ultimately come in the full inheritance in heaven.

Part II

THE INDIVIDUAL VIRTUES
AND LAWS

P art I explains the moral life in general by showing how the different principles of the moral life relate to each other. For example, natural and divine laws cause
good human actions, which perfect the virtues. Whereas part I shows how to attain
happiness in general, part II treats particular laws and virtues so that the reader will
know specific actions to pursue and avoid.

Since the role of law is to guide and motivate humans to become virtuous, the different laws will be treated within the framework of the virtues. In other words, since
laws are ordered to virtues, the second part of this book is organized by the cardinal
and theological virtues. *Subvirtues*, which correspond to the cardinal and theological
virtues, will also be analyzed, along with the gifts of the Holy Spirit. For example, in
studying justice, we will also study the virtues of honesty and obedience and the Holy
Spirit's gift of piety. A study of the individual virtues shows which actions are necessary to perfect them. Once we know the necessary actions, then we can analyze the
particular laws that guide and motivate humans to perform these actions. Following
the tradition of the Church, we will place special emphasis on the Ten Commandments. However, the Ten Commandments will be expanded by the teachings of the
new law and natural law in order to give a more detailed account of how to become
virtuous. We'll also analyze the sins against these commandments, and the vices against
the individual virtues.

The order of the material in this second part will follow the order of development of virtues flowing from grace. Faith is first, since all other infused virtues build upon it. Hope and charity come next. Then we will see the infused cardinal virtues, which apply the theological virtues to particular situations. The order of the cardinal virtues will follow the order of the powers of the soul. Prudence, which perfects the intellect, is first, followed by justice (perfecting the will), temperance, and fortitude (perfecting the emotions).

12

FAITH

The First Virtue of the Moral Life

Faith is the theological virtue that perfects the natural inclination to know the truth. Just as the natural inclination to know comes before all natural human actions and virtues, faith comes before all divine actions and infused virtues. The natural inclination to know provides the concepts that are necessary for humans to understand goals and to reason to human actions. Without this natural inclination, humans cannot know anything and therefore have nothing to intend or choose. Since the will follows the intellect, all the virtues of the intellect and the will follow from this inclination. Faith, as a supernatural inclination, provides divine concepts that are the foundation of all knowledge that flows from grace. All supernatural actions, and all of the infused virtues, follow faith. Thus, faith is the first virtue to be examined. In the first part of the book the order of the presentation of the material often went from inclination, to act, to habit. However, this order is changed in this second part because the infused virtues are treated. Since they are infused with grace, they normally exist before (or are infused at the same time as) the actions they cause. Hence, we will first look at the virtue of faith and then the nature of an act of faith. Then, we will examine the gifts of the Holy Spirit that perfect faith, understanding, and knowledge. Finally, we'll study the law that corresponds to faith and the sins that violate faith.

THE VIRTUE OF FAITH

Unfortunately, because of past debates between some Catholics and some Protestants, faith has often been separated from works. Some Protestants have claimed that salvation is from faith alone; some Catholics have responded by emphasizing the necessity of works for salvation. Although this explanation of the debate is overly simplistic, the practical result of these disputes is that often in the past faith has been given a negligible role in moral theology.[1] In reality, nothing can be farther from the truth: *the virtue of faith transforms humans and empowers them to begin fulfilling their unique role in God's divine plan.* There is no separation between faith and works because faith is an essential component of the moral life.

As I explained in chapter 4, St. Paul states that faith is the first virtue of the moral life and that all other virtues follow it. Grace transforms nature and makes humans a new creation because they are able to participate in divine nature. Faith acts as a supernatural inclination following from this participation in divine nature. Just as the natural inclinations are interior drives to proper actions, the virtue of faith acts as an interior drive to all actions ordered toward knowing and loving God as he is. With faith, humans are capable of participating in God's knowledge and learning God's unique plan for them. They now know that God has become human and that he extends the offer of friendship to them. They can learn God's goals for them and, out of love, can make these goals their own. Consequently, faith transforms people's lives and makes them capable of doing things they could never do without it. They now have new goals, and they seek ways to fulfill these goals. People who truly believe in Christ begin to realize that everything they do should be done out of love for God and, therefore, they now live a different lifestyle than they would without faith. They are incorporated into the body of Christ, and the Holy Spirit works through them, causing them to build up the body of Christ and to help others grow in true happiness.

The habit of faith is infused when one receives sanctifying grace. The normal means of receiving this habit is through baptism. Once people have this habit, they have the power to believe as soon as their brain is developed enough to perform the action. Like any virtue, faith is strengthened by repeated acts of faith. Although some acts specifically show faith, such as prayer (especially the Creed and Eucharistic adoration), any action that is done out of love of God (known through faith) is an act of faith. Hence, to perfect faith, people should pray and consciously think about how their acts are ordered to God. People who truly have the virtue of faith easily and joyfully believe all of God's teaching and frequently implement this faith through faith-filled acts. Hence, if people are plagued with doubt, they should practice acts of faith to overcome this doubt.

Although faith is the beginning of salvation, it must be formed by charity to be the living faith that actually saves. Knowledge causes love, which causes unity. So also, faith causes charity, which causes union with God (salvation). Although faith is the beginning of salvation, without charity it will not save. The Letter of James explains how faith without works will not save. James notes: "For just as a body without a spirit is dead, so also faith without works is dead" (2:14–26). Since works are caused by charity, faith must be animated by charity to bring salvation. Charity is the form of faith in a way similar to how the soul is the form of the body.

The theological virtue of faith is the supernatural inclination to know God and his revelation. Therefore, faith is the foundation of all actions and virtues ordered to God. Faith perfects the intellect to apprehend supernatural concepts, to understand divinely revealed principles, and to reason to divine truths. With the help of the other infused virtues and gifts, faith gives humans the ability to determine and command divine actions. Faith, when animated by charity, results in great supernatural happiness on earth and eternal happiness in heaven.

THE ACT OF FAITH

Faith is the act of believing in God as the First Truth and believing in all those truths that God divinely reveals. Because an effect is always like its cause, humans by their natural ability can come to some knowledge of God (the cause) by looking at creation (the effect). However, because of the weakness of the human intellect and the influences of original sin, this knowledge will always be very limited. So that humans could perform their proper actions of knowing and loving him, beginning with Adam and Eve, God gradually revealed himself to the Israelite community. When the time was right, God sent his Son, "the eternal Word who enlightens all men, to dwell among men and to tell them about the inner life of God. Hence, Jesus Christ, sent as 'a man among men,' 'speaks the words of God.'"[2] In order that humans may experience supernatural happiness on earth and eternal happiness in heaven, God revealed his inner life through his Son. Faith is the act of believing the revelation of the eternal Word.

Although faith perfects natural knowledge, it is not the same as natural knowledge. A comparison of the different ways that intellectual statements (thoughts) exist within the human mind is helpful to explain faith. Some thoughts are held by *knowledge*, others are held by *faith* (either natural or supernatural), and still others are held by *opinion*. For something to be considered *knowledge* in the traditional sense of the term, it must be logically derived from principles known with certainty. These principles must be understood through one's own experiences. For example, mathematical truths, such as $2 + 2 = 4$, would be considered knowledge.

However, individual humans are only able to experience a limited number of things, so a lot of the information in their minds must come from the knowledge of other people. This trust in the knowledge of others is called "natural faith." Natural faith flows from the natural ability of humans and is not the same as the theological faith we are considering in this chapter. Natural faith is defined as "the act of choosing to hold something as true based on the authority of the teacher." Both the intellect and the will are involved in natural faith. The intellect understands the truth, and the will chooses to consider it to be true based on the authority of the teacher. For example, as a child, David chooses to believe that humans are made of cells based on the knowledge of the biology teacher. If David continues to study biology, he will eventually be able to prove for himself that humans are made of cells. At this point, his natural faith becomes knowledge.

A third way that intellectual statements exist within the mind is when the intellect holds something as an *opinion*. As with faith, the *will chooses* to accept this information.[3] However, unlike with faith, the certainty of an opinion comes from evidence and not from the authority of a teacher. This use of the term "opinion" is a little different from the modern use of the term, where someone can have an opinion with no evidence supporting it at all. However, the way the term "opinion" is used here, evidence is required, and the greater the evidence, the greater the certainty that the opinion is true. For example, if a student does very well on a test, the professor has the opinion that the student understands the material. However, the professor does not know this for certain since the student may have cheated or simply memorized the right things. The more comprehensive the test, the more evidence the professor has that the student understands the material.

Natural faith is like both knowledge and opinion. It is like knowledge because it is certain. It is based on the knowledge of someone else. In other words, as long as the source is trustworthy, there is no reason to doubt that it is true. Natural faith is also like opinion in that the will chooses to have the intellect assent to the truth.

Theological (supernatural) faith is like natural faith in that the believer also chooses to hold something as true based on the authority of a teacher who has knowledge of the truth.[4] However, with theological faith, the teacher is God. Because God is all-knowing and completely trustworthy, the principles of faith can be held with absolute certitude.[5] Theological faith is also like natural faith in that both types of faith lead to knowledge (*scientia*). When children first begin to learn a science, they do not necessarily understand the principles, but they must accept them as being true based on the authority of the teacher. In time, the children are able to understand the principles and reason to conclusions by their own power. Their natural faith leads to knowledge. So also with theological faith, belief in the divinely revealed principles is the first step toward knowing God as he is. In other words, because grace perfects nature, humans do not learn a science all at once but are taught the science little by little. So also, God, as the divine teacher, does not immediately give us divine *knowledge* but instructs us little by little.[6] Furthermore, since humans are guided by other humans to full knowledge of something, it is appropriate that God works through humans to spread the faith. The act of passing on the faith allows both the teacher and the student to be more like God. Consequently, humans have faith now and perfect knowledge in heaven. Believing this knowledge is the first step to salvation, the full inheritance when humans will see God as he truly is and share perfectly in his knowledge.[7]

Through theological faith, humans are able to understand truths that are beyond their natural ability to grasp. Natural faith requires a concept in the mind, the ability to understand that concept, and the will to cause the intellect to assent to the truth of the concept. For example, because of the knowledge of the teacher, David has the concept of a human cell in his mind. He understands what a human cell is, and he chooses to accept this knowledge as true. So also with theological faith, the divine teacher, God, gives humans concepts to understand, the ability to understand them, and moves the will to choose to assent to them. Since grace perfects nature, the principles of faith must begin with sense knowledge. Thus, God first gives humans additional physical signs and images that manifest him.[8] For example, the physical actions and words of Christ reveal God. However, even with these additional signs and images, the human intellect is not strong enough to apprehend and understand the principles of faith without additional grace. Hence, God also gives the intellect the power to supernaturally apprehend concepts from the signs and images, and he gives the intellect the ability to combine or separate these concepts into propositions that are understood.[9] Finally, God's grace moves the will to choose to accept these propositions as true. Consequently, the truths of the faith, the understanding of these truths, and the ability to hold them as true all come from a participation in divine nature.

Through faith, humans believe in God and the truths that are divinely revealed. The fullness of this revelation was through the Son, Jesus Christ, who became human. However, because Christ ascended into heaven, the mission of proclaiming and interpreting this divine revelation was bestowed on the Church with the guidance of the Holy Spirit.[10] Beginning in the New Testament and expanded over time, the Church formed a creed that contained the essential elements of the faith.[11] Consequently, believing in God also entails believing all the articles of the Creed and all the teaching necessary for salvation as proclaimed by the Church. These articles must be explicitly believed if a person has the opportunity to properly learn them.[12] However, if people do not have this opportunity, they must at least implicitly believe these truths. In other words, they are saved by believing as much about God as is possible given their situation.

Many things that God revealed for humans can also be known by natural knowledge. For example, the fact that God exists, and many of his attributes (such as that God is one), can be known by natural knowledge. God revealed truths that can be known naturally, since without this revelation many people would not have reasoned to these truths, or if they did, they would have a great deal of error mixed with the truth. For example, many ancient cultures reasoned to the existence of a divine cause, but they mistakenly thought that there were many (often competing) gods who caused the earth and governed it. Consequently, for the happiness of all people, God revealed many truths that can also be known naturally. These truths are called "preambles to the faith" since they come before the faith and help to show its intelligibility.

Because faith and natural knowledge (science) come from the same source, they cannot contradict. In other words, with both faith and natural knowledge, the intellect participates in divine knowledge. However, with faith, the participation is supernatu-ral; with natural knowledge (science), the participation is natural. If faith and science appear to contradict each other, then either the truth advocated by science is wrong or the believers misunderstand what belongs to the essence of the faith.

GIFTS THAT PERFECT FAITH

Because of the limitedness of the human intellect, humans require the teaching and guidance of other people to extend their knowledge to things that they would not be capable of knowing on their own. For example, scientists build on the knowledge of those who came before them. Imagine if scientists could only use the knowledge that they discovered. Humans would never have gotten out of the Stone Age. Hence, natural faith extends and perfects natural knowledge by opening the mind to the truths dis-covered by humanity over the centuries. If students continue to learn, they will even-tually get to the point where they know these truths by their own power. Their natural faith has turned into knowledge. There is a time period when they have natural faith in their teacher but do not yet have knowledge. During this time, the truths presented through natural faith are greater than the truths held by their knowledge, yet they are possessed less perfectly by the intellect since they are not yet knowledge. For example, when a chemistry student first learns the periodic table, she accepts it as true based on the authority of her teacher. Although these truths about chemistry expand her current knowledge, she possesses them less perfectly than the truths she holds by knowledge. Hence, to use the periodic table and to work toward knowledge of the different ele-ments, she will continue to need the guidance and help of her teacher.

Since grace perfects nature, natural faith teaches us about theological faith. Theo-logical faith extends what the natural intellect can know by enriching it with divine knowledge. This life on earth is like the transitory period between the time when a student first begins to learn a science through natural faith in the teacher and the time when the student actually has knowledge of the science. On earth humans have faith in God but do not yet have knowledge. Theological faith perfects knowledge, but like natural faith, it is possessed less perfectly than knowledge. Hence, additional aid from the Holy Spirit is needed to further perfect it. The Holy Spirit's gifts that further per-fect faith are understanding and knowledge. These gifts perfect the intellect so that it can be guided by the Holy Spirit more perfectly to divine truths.

Just as the virtue of understanding perfects the intellect to join or separate con-cepts that have been apprehended through the natural power of the intellect, the gift of understanding perfects the intellect to join and separate truths that have been ap-prehended by the supernatural power of the intellect. With this gift, humans can have a deep grasp of the principles of the faith. They are able to form true propositions that correspond to divine revelation. From these truths they are able to reason to other conclusions (the science of theology). For example, through the gift of understanding the early Church Fathers were able to form the statement that Jesus Christ is fully God and fully human. When we hear this statement today, the gift of understanding helps us to grasp how Jesus can be both fully God and fully human. Just as there are degrees of participation in God's knowledge, so also there are different degrees of understanding a truth. With the gift of understanding, humans can participate in God's knowledge at a significantly higher level. This greater understanding allows them to be more perfectly guided by the Holy Spirit.

Just as the virtue of knowledge perfects the intellect to reason to conclusions by the natural power of the intellect, so also the gift of knowledge perfects the intellect to reason to conclusions through the supernatural power of the intellect. For example, the gift of knowledge could perfect the intellect to reason to the conclusion that because Jesus is fully divine, he has the power to save all humans. Likewise, because he is fully human, he can suffer and die. In actuality, what we are doing in this entire book is reasoning to conclusions from the principles of the faith. For example, the conclusion that humans cannot cause actions ordered to eternal happiness by their natural power is derived from the principle that grace is essential for salvation. However, unlike natural knowledge, because the gift of knowledge is a participation in the divine knowledge, the Holy Spirit can guide humans to the conclusions of arguments without them having to go through the reasoning process. Consequently, if you ever suddenly came to a conclusion about the faith without going through the reasoning process, it may have been the Holy Spirit working through the gift of knowledge.

Just as natural understanding and knowledge are necessary for the human intellect to fulfill its inclination of knowing the truth, so also these gifts of the Holy Spirit aid the intellect in fulfilling its supernatural inclination of knowing divine truth. These gifts allow humans to know God more perfectly, resulting in better divine actions. They also perfect the ability of the intellect to contemplate God here on earth, resulting in greater happiness.

THE COMMANDMENT THAT PERTAINS TO FAITH

In performing divine actions, humans are guided by the divine law. Since faith is the foundation of all moral actions, all the commandments are required to guide humans to acts of faith. However, since other commandments correspond more properly to other virtues, only the first commandment will be analyzed in this chapter. The first commandment is "I am the Lord your God, you shall have no other God's before me." In its original context, this commandment called the Israelites to be faithful to God and God alone.[13] When interpreted in light of the New Testament, this commandment requires that one have living faith in God. Because faith is required for salvation, to freely reject the faith is a sin. In other words, because faith is necessary for humans to have true happiness, the New Testament speaks of the necessity of faith (Gal 3:26). Furthermore, since humans are transformed to do greater things through the virtue of faith, our faith also affects the happiness of those around us. So that sin may be avoided and the habit of faith increased, we will analyze the sins of unbelief (incredulity), refusal to learn revealed truth, and atheism.

Unbelief (incredulity) is the sin of refusing to assent to revealed truth or choosing to doubt it. If the entire faith is rejected, then one commits the sin of *apostasy*. If only part of the faith is rejected, one commits the sin of *heresy*. Apostasy is a total rejection of the Christian faith. This was the sin committed by those who denied the faith when faced with persecution in the early Church (assuming that their choice was free). Although today there are still many places on earth where Christians have been killed because of their faith, often the temptation to apostatize comes from peer pressure. Modern humans usually commit the sin of apostasy by denying the faith in either word or action in order to fit into a particular group of people.

Heresy is obstinate denial of one or more revealed truths. Since faith is considered true because of the authority of the teacher, to reject one of the essential truths of the Faith is to reject their source, God. Hence, if people properly understand the truths of the Faith and obstinately choose to disbelieve one of them, they no longer have theological faith but opinion. To actually commit the sin of heresy, people must understand that they are contradicting the faith and continue in their denial. For example, Arius continued to deny that Jesus was God by nature even after this view was condemned at the Council of Nicaea. If the denial is not obstinate or the people do not understand that their view is heretical, then they do not commit the sin of heresy, even though they are in error. The real danger of heresy is that it makes people have a false knowledge of God so that they cannot approach God, but only the false object of their opinion. In other words, the heretic has exchanged his faith for an opinion that will not cause actions ordered to eternal happiness.

Chosen doubt is the sin of freely choosing to doubt the truth of the faith. Chosen doubt is not the same as the temptation to doubt. Many great saints have been tempted to doubt the existence of God but have not committed this sin. For example, because of her great love for Christ, St. Thérèse of Lisieux sought to share his sufferings. Christ allowed Thérèse to suffer by allowing her to be constantly plagued with doubt towards the end of her short life. Since her entire life was devoted to service of Christ, the inner turmoil caused by these temptations was a great burden. However, even while her emotions tempted her to doubt the existence of God, her will firmly assented to the truth of her faith. She even wrote the Creed in her own blood and kept it close to her heart to show her sincere belief.[14] She was tempted, but she did not sin.

Although the temptation to doubt is not a sin, it can lead to the sin of *chosen doubt*. In order to show when doubt becomes sinful, let's analyze the three steps showing the evolution of temptation to sin. The first step of a temptation is when the emotions desire something sinful in response to sense knowledge from either something outside of the person or inside the person's imagination. Since this emotional response to something sinful precedes the operation of the intellect and will, this is not a human action and thus also not a sin. For example, the sight of an improperly dressed woman could cause the emotions of a man to desire the woman in a lustful way. However, this emotional response is not yet a sin.

In the second step, a person allows the emotions to move the intellect to put together an argument of how to attain this false good. In other words, the man takes counsel by researching the situation and reasoning to a possible sinful conclusion. For example, the man begins to think of ways to seduce the woman and begins to imagine the scenarios. If these thoughts precede the act of judgment in the intellect, then they are not yet sinful. However, if the man in the judgment stage decides to continue taking counsel when he knows the act is wrong or continues to think about this false end (even though he judges that he should not), then he is already committing a sin in this step.

In the third step, the person freely chooses the sinful action and then performs it. This is always a sin. Consequently, in reference to the sin of chosen doubt, if the emotions simply tempt humans to doubt, they are not yet committing a sin. However, if they choose to continue to dwell on the doubt in their intellect instead of thinking of why God must exist, they commit a sin. If they simply choose to doubt the faith, they also commit a sin.

Another sin against faith is *willful refusal to learn revealed truth*. Because knowledge causes love, which causes unity, those who truly love others will seek to know more about the one they love so they can share in the life of the other person. A refusal to learn more about the needs and goals of another is a refusal to deepen a relationship. Humans who love God constantly seek to know more about God in order to make his goals their own. Those who refuse to learn more about God sin by showing a lack of love.

The last sin to be analyzed is *atheism*. Atheism is "the sin of refusing to believe that God exists." Atheism is a serious sin because it violently contradicts the natural inclinations that humans have toward knowing God. However, just because one is an atheist, does not mean that he or she commits the sin of atheism. For example, some people learn about God through "Christians" who live a sinful lifestyle. Consequently, these people associate the concept of God with the particular sinful actions performed by the believers. This tarnished concept of God would contradict their natural inclinations to truth and goodness, causing them to choose not to believe in God. Others choose not to believe in God because they have never been taught about God in an intelligible way. Assuming that these people are not given the opportunity to learn the proper concept of God, they do not commit the sin of atheism because they do not understand what they are choosing to reject. Consequently, often the greatest cause of atheism is Christians who scandalously live lifestyles contrary to the nature of God or who explain the truths of Christianity in an irrational manner. In order to help others be happy through faith in God, Christians must live a holy lifestyle. They must also learn more about God so they are able to answer the objections of those who do not yet understand the basic truths of the faith.

FAITH AS THE FOUNDATION OF THE MORAL LIFE

In order to correct the Christians in Rome who were bragging about their natural or old covenant perfections, Paul insisted that salvation requires faith in Jesus Christ (Rom 3). By believing in Jesus Christ, the intellect is perfected so that humans can know something of the interior life of God. This divine knowledge leads to hope that God will grant them eternal happiness, and it leads to charity (love of God as a friend). When perfected by the Holy Spirit's gifts of understanding and knowledge, this divine knowledge allows the intellect to be guided by the Holy Spirit to discern which actions will lead to eternal happiness. Furthermore, because of faith, the mean of the infused virtues of justice, temperance, and fortitude is determined by divine law rather than natural law.[15] Consequently, the entire Christian life is built on the virtue of faith.[16]

The foundational role of faith is also seen by looking specifically at how it transforms the actions of the believer. Since faith perfects the natural inclination of the intellect to know and since this inclination is the cause of all the various steps of the intellect, faith perfects all the acts of the intellect.[17] Faith perfects simple apprehension, so that the intellect is able to apprehend supernatural concepts from divinely revealed images. It also perfects the step of understanding, so that through these divine concepts, humans are able to form goals and laws that are in accord with the divine law, rather than just natural law. Since faith changes the goals and laws of humans, it also changes the actions that are ordered to these ends. It perfects the step of taking counsel by first giving the intellect the ability to be guided by the Holy Spirit to understand the situation more perfectly and then by giving the intellect the ability to reason to a conclusion with supernatural power. It also perfects judgment, so that the actions are judged by the principles of faith (the divine law). Consequently, humans with faith should act differently than those without faith. They have supernatural concepts from which they form higher goals and find different ways to attain them.

Since faith is so important, sins against faith must be avoided. These sins can substantially hinder the ability to humans to attain supernatural happiness, since faith is the first virtue of the Christian moral life. Faith gives humans the ability to believe in the Trinity and all that the Father reveals through the Son by the power of the Holy Spirit. This revelation contains the divine plan for humanity revealed in the Bible. By looking at this plan, humans can know the beginning and the end of their ultimate journey. With the guidance of the Holy Spirit, they can also discern the way they must "walk" in order to attain this end. Whereas faith illuminates the map for the journey to happiness, sins against faith darken and corrupt the map and, hence, deter people from attaining their proper end of friendship with God.

13

HOPE

Trust in God's Mercy

Benedict XVI, in his encyclical *Spe Salvi*, notes that the gospel message causes a close relationship between faith and hope. Benedict contrasts the message of Christianity with that of the pagan religions of the first century AD: "Here too we see as a distinguishing mark of Christians the fact that they have a future: it is not that they know the details of what awaits them, but they know in general terms that their life will not end in emptiness."[1] In other words, the very fact that God has revealed that he is a loving God who desires that humans spend eternity sharing in his happiness gives humans hope. The very act of believing in the gospel results in hope, which brings meaning to the lives of Christians. Through this hope, they already begin to share in the happiness of God. Whereas faith is the first virtue of the Christian moral life, hope is the second, because hope is the proper response to the message of Christianity.

As we've seen throughout this book, the natural inclinations of humans drive them to their proper actions. Both faith and hope function as supernatural inclinations driving humans to perform actions ordered toward eternal union with God. Faith causes humans to assent to the good news of Christianity, and hope transforms the lives of Christians, who now have a future in God. Consequently, like faith, hope is foundational to the moral life. In this chapter, I will examine the nature of hope, the Holy Spirit's gift that perfects hope (fear of the Lord), and the sins against hope.

THE NATURE OF HOPE

Whereas faith perfects the natural inclination of the intellect, hope perfects a natural inclination of the will. In the will, two natural inclinations have been identified: an inclination to love oneself and an inclination to love others. The natural inclination to love oneself results in *love of use*, defined as "love of something else for a benefit that will be received." The inclination to love others results in *love of friendship*, "loving others for their own sake." Hope perfects the natural inclination to love oneself, causing humans to love God for the benefit of eternal happiness.[2] On the natural level, a virtue is normally not needed to perfect the will's inclination to love oneself. Generally, this inclination is powerful enough that people are able to love themselves just fine without the need for a virtue. However, because a natural inclination can never cause divine actions ordered to eternal happiness, a theological virtue *is* needed to perfect love of self so that humans are able to supernaturally love God for the benefit of eternal happiness. Hope is a supernatural inclination that gives the will the ability to love good actions for the sake of obtaining eternal happiness and avoiding separation from God.

Although hope perfects the natural inclination to love oneself, it is not a selfish love of use. *The theological virtue of hope primarily causes humans to trust in God's mercy in their lives.* On a natural level, if someone expects a benefit from another human, they must trust that the other person is able to provide the benefit. If the other person does not have the ability to provide the benefit, then the love of use is in vain. For example, if Joe loves his boss because she has the power to promote him, he has love of use of his boss. However, if his boss does not have this power, then the love of use is in vain. Because humans love God, with the theological virtue of hope, humans trust that God will give them the help that they need to be with him for all eternity.[3] Hope can be defined as *the virtue perfecting the will to seek the good of eternal life by trusting in God's mercy.*

Based on this definition, there are two elements in hope. The material element is love of use of God. The formal element is trust in God's divine assistance.[4] In created things, the form orders the matter and determines its nature. For example, as we saw in chapter 1, the soul (the form) orders the matter of the body and causes this matter to be the body of a human. Therefore, since hope perfects the will and the will performs acts of love, the matter of hope must be an act of love. In this case, it is an act of love of use. The form is trust in God's aid. The love of use is ordered in such a way that in seeking the good of eternal happiness, it trusts in the divine assistance. The trust in divine assistance makes the love an act of hope. In other words, in loving God as the source of eternal happiness, the will trusts in God's divine aid, which makes the possession of eternal happiness possible. Consequently, the object of hope, that which we hope to obtain, is God, who is both the cause of hope (divine assistance) and the end that we hope to obtain (for the sake of eternal happiness).[5] Since many acts and gifts are necessary to attain this end, we also hope for all those things that are essential for attaining eternal happiness. For example, we ask God to help us love others so that we may obtain heaven. Ultimately, hope is trust in God's divine mercy that is offered to humans. Out of his mercy, God offers friendship to us and forgives our sins. Since God is our friend, we trust that he will help us perform actions ordered toward divine happiness.

Although hope perfects the will, an examination of the emotion of hope can also help explain the theological virtue of hope. Emotional hope is the desire to obtain a difficult or distant good. For example, students hope to get a good grade. To obtain this goal, they must work hard, and the emotion of hope drives them to do the work. The theological virtue of hope drives humans to work to attain the difficult good of eternal happiness. Because it drives humans to perform good actions, it is foundational to the moral life.

Hope is important because it causes good actions, but it is not perfect love. Love of use is always less perfect than love of friendship. So also hope is less perfect than charity. Nonetheless, since grace perfects nature, it is essential that humans have the virtue of hope. Often in human relationships, knowledge causes love of use, which causes love of friendship. Human relationships often begin with a person first loving another for a benefit to be attained. Then, after getting to know the other person, this love of use turns into love of friendship. For example, perhaps Joe first dated Kate because he saw her as a prospective spouse (love of use). However, over time Joe begins to love Kate for who she is, whether she becomes his spouse or not (love of friendship). It is the same with the theological virtues: faith causes hope, which causes charity. Humans first believe in God and, therefore, believe that in his mercy he will give them eternal happiness. Through hope, they desire this happiness and trust that God will give it to them. Finally, they begin to love God for his own sake (charity). Once they love God for his own sake, hope is increased because they desire to spend eternity with their friend. Thus, they have an even greater desire for eternal happiness and a greater trust in God's power. Since humans move from love of self to love of others when forming friendships, the theological virtue of hope is essential for attaining friendship with God.

This friendship with God is not an exclusive friendship between individuals and God. As we've already seen throughout this book, salvation is not individualistic. Love of God requires love of others. So also, hope is not individualistic. Because humans love God and others, they desire that others also have eternal happiness, and they hope that God will aid others in attaining this happiness.[6] Benedict XVI explains that hope is not an individualistic hope for oneself alone. Just as Christ gives his life for all, Christians should also live for all. Benedict states: "Being in communion with Jesus Christ draws us into his 'being for all'; it makes it our own way of being. He commits us to live for others, but only through communion with him does it become possible truly to be there for others, for the whole."[7] Our hope in Christ drives us to enter into loving unions with others by giving of ourselves. We hope for the complete harmony found in the full inheritance where we share in God's happiness. In other words, we hope not only that the unity between God and humans is restored and elevated, but also that the unity between all humans is restored and elevated. As a community united in Christ, we hope together and hope for each other.

Hope not only leads to eternal happiness, it is also important for supernatural happiness on earth. Because humans must cooperate with God's grace and choose to know and love God, humans on earth cannot be absolutely certain that they will receive eternal life. Humans cannot directly know the depths of their own soul (for they only know themselves by their actions), so they cannot know for certain that they will always cooperate with God's grace and know and love God. Paul speaks of this uncertainty when, after exhorting the Philippians to be united in mind and heart to others in imitation of Christ, he states, "Work out your salvation with fear and trembling" (Phil 2:12). Paul shows that if Christians do not follow the will of God, they can lose their salvation. This lack of security could cause great unhappiness if attaining salvation was strictly up to humans. However, humans have hope that God in his mercy will help them to obtain eternal happiness, and a great deal of certainty can be found in trusting in God. God loves humans more than they love themselves, and he will offer them the necessary graces to persevere to the end. Thus, hope keeps humans from discouragement and allows them to begin contemplating the distant good of eternal life.

As a virtue, hope is increased whenever an act is done that manifests trust in God's mercy. For example, if Joe goes to Mass because he trusts that God will help him get to heaven, he is performing an act of hope, or if he prays for divine assistance to overcome temptation, he is performing an act of hope. Constantly seeking eternal happiness and asking for God's assistance perfect the virtue of hope.[8] Since hope perfects the natural inclination to love oneself, the perfection of the virtue results in a greater love of God for the benefit of eternal happiness and a greater trust in God's assistance. Despite the importance of the virtue of hope, it is still an imperfect form of love compared to charity. Consequently, in the full inheritance, hope is replaced by charity, since humans are able to love God as he is.

THE GIFT OF FEAR OF THE LORD

The gift of the Holy Spirit that perfects hope is *fear of the Lord*. Fear of the Lord can be easily misunderstood. Humans should not fear God as if he were an evil tyrant arbitrarily making laws; rather, they should fear the just punishment that God will inflict upon sinners in order to motivate people to do the good actions that will make them happy. In other words, God is like a good father who enforces his good laws with punishments to move his children to do the actions that will make them happy. In reference to both God and humans, fear of a perceived evil can cause people to turn to a proper good. For example, my children clean their rooms out of fear of being given the punishment of more chores. So also, because humans can be strongly tempted to do evil, even good Christians will occasionally need the fear of going to hell as a motivation to do good and avoid evil. Fear of the Lord perfects the virtue of hope so that humans can then be moved by the Holy Spirit to perform good actions.

To better understand fear of the Lord, a traditional distinction has been made between three types of fear: worldly fear, servile fear, and filial fear.[9] Worldly fear is fear of things that harm the body but not the soul.[10] A fear of snakes and spiders is a worldly fear. Worldly fears are always bad if they cause someone to act irrationally.[11] The opposite of worldly fear is the virtue of courage, which transforms the emotions so that fear does not overcome the intellect. Many of the saints faced martyrdom without fear because they knew that God would ultimately take care of them, even if they died. For example, the Mohawk Indians often marveled at the bravery of St. Isaac Jogues, even while they tortured him by chewing and burning off the ends of his fingers. Isaac did not have worldly fear of suffering and death because he had hope in God. Fear of the Lord is not a worldly fear.

Servile fear is the fear that servants have of their masters. It is a fear of God's just punishments. This is the understanding of fear of the Lord in a deontological moral system. Before the time of Christ, servile fear referred to the fear of the material punishments that would be inflicted upon the Israelites for breaking the covenant.[12] In the New Testament, servile fear is the fear of hell.[13] This is a good type of fear of the Lord, since it drives humans to perform good actions. However, it is an imperfect fear, since humans are not necessarily doing the good out of love of God.

Filial fear is the fear of a mature child toward a loving father. This is the type of fear found in a teleological moral system based on love (cf. 1 Jn 4:18). It is the fear of being separated from God because of sin. Because love unites humans to God and sin diminishes or destroys love, humans with filial fear avoid sin because they do not want to harm their relationship with God. In human relationships, this is the fear that a child has of disappointing or making a parent unhappy because the child does a bad action. Filial fear is the proper fear of the Lord, and it exists when hope is perfected by charity. Since gifts of the Holy Spirit are dispositions that perfect humans so that they can be more perfectly moved by the Holy Spirit, the gift of filial fear gives humans the ability to be efficaciously moved by the Holy Spirit to avoid sin in order to avoid separation from God.

THE COMMANDMENT THAT PERTAINS TO HOPE

Like faith, the commandment that pertains to hope is the first commandment, *I am the Lord your God; you shall have no other gods before me.* Recall that the first commandment requires humans to be completely faithful to God. In the New Testament, faithfulness to God requires that Christians have hope in God, who calls them to be united to him for all eternity. Consequently, actions that destroy or damage the virtue of hope are sins. In other words, hope is essential to salvation, and actions contrary to it are sins because they hinder the ability of humans to be united to God.

There are two sins against hope: despair and presumption. Despair is the sin of not trusting in God's divine assistance. People with despair believe that God will not give them the grace necessary for salvation or that he will not forgive their sins. For example, I know of a girl who, after committing a sin of lust, did not believe that God would ever forgive such a horrible sin. Consequently, she despaired of attaining heaven and would not repent and go to confession. Despair is a very serious sin for two reasons. First, the person with despair acts as if God is a tyrant and not a merciful father. Second, people with despair do not repent and reestablish their relationship with God. God is always offering forgiveness for sins, but humans must accept this forgiveness by repenting. Consequently, despair is sometimes called "the sin against the Holy Spirit that cannot be forgiven" (Mt 12:31–32). The inability for it to be forgiven is not because God does not have the power to forgive but because the sinner will not accept the forgiveness.

The second sin against hope is presumption. Like despair, presumption contradicts trust in God's assistance. However, presumption goes to the opposite extreme. It is the sin of believing that humans can be saved by their own power, or that they do not need the institutions and practices established by Christ in order to be saved. For example, if Catholics think that their mortal sins will be forgiven without going to confession, they commit the sin of presumption. This sin is also very serious because it keeps people from seeking God's grace, since they do not believe that they need it.

Hope perfects the will to seek the difficult (but possible to attain) good of eternal life by trusting in God's divine assistance. Since God is the infinite good desired by the will, the attainment of God himself will bring the greatest happiness to humans.[14] The theological virtue of hope disposes humans to God as their end and determines the will to perform actions in accord with this end. The virtue of hope perfects the will to seek eternal happiness in all its steps within the human action. For example, if Joe performs the act of going to Mass, hope causes him to desire the good of Mass and to intend the goal of going to Mass because of his desire to attain eternal happiness. Hope then causes him to consent and choose the best way to get to Mass. Finally, hope drives Joe to execute the action of going to Mass because of his desire for eternal happiness.

Although hope causes people to perform good actions, because it is a love of use, it requires charity in order to be completed. When God is loved as a friend through charity, humans have an even greater desire to be united with God and even greater confidence in God's assistance. Hence, hope especially causes good actions when it is perfected by charity.

14

CHARITY
Friendship with God

Charity, love of friendship of God, is the most excellent of the virtues.[1] First, it is a theological virtue. The theological virtues are greater than the cardinal virtues because their object is God, but the cardinal virtues are ordered to things ordered to God. For example, the object of the theological virtue of faith (what we believe) is God and all things that he reveals; the object of the cardinal virtue of prudence is human reason, which determines actions ordered to God. Second, charity is the greatest of the theological virtues because it attains God himself. Through faith, humans do not know God as he is, but they know God only through his revelation. Through hope, humans also do not seek God himself, but the eternal happiness that comes from trust in his divine assistance. Charity causes love of God as he is and attains God himself. Furthermore, in the full inheritance, faith will be replaced by knowledge of God. Since in the full inheritance humans will no longer need to trust in God's assistance to attain eternal happiness, hope will also be replaced.[2] However, charity is not replaced. It is only perfected, since it already causes humans to love God as he is. Consequently, charity is the greatest of the virtues, and it orders all things to God.

Charity is related to eternal happiness in the same way that the natural inclination to love others is related to natural happiness. The natural inclination to love gives humans the ability to choose good actions and is essential to happiness. Without love, nothing will ever make a human happy. So also, charity gives humans the ability to perform actions ordered to eternal happiness and is essential for supernatural and perfect happiness. Like faith and hope, charity is at the foundation of the entire moral life. In this chapter we will first examine the nature of charity, then we'll analyze the subvirtues under charity, followed by the beatitudes, which are necessary for charity, then the Holy Spirit's gift of wisdom, and, finally, the commandment that accompanies charity, and the sins against this commandment.

THE NATURE OF CHARITY

Charity perfects the natural inclination of the will to love others. The proper action of this natural inclination is love of friendship, where others are loved for their own sake. Hence, charity is love of friendship of God.[3] The virtue of charity perfects the will to love God as he is. To properly understand charity, we'll do a more detailed analysis of love and the six types of love mentioned so far in this book.

Love in its most basic form is an attraction to a good. It is the attraction that the will has to the good known by the intellect, or the attraction that the emotions have to the good that is known through sense knowledge. For example, the intellect knows that friends are good in and of themselves, and the will is attracted to them. Likewise, because other humans are necessary for the survival of the body, when friends are sensed (or imagined), the emotions are attracted to them.

Because of this attraction to the good, humans seek to be united to the good. In the case of love of friendship, the attraction to the good of friends causes the will to seek to be united to them by making their needs and goals its own. For example, Joe's love of Kate causes Joe to make Kate's goal of doing well in college his own. He now works to make sure that Kate does well in college. Thus, the attraction to the good that comes from love causes people to sacrifice (give of themselves) for others. In the case of love of use, the attraction to the good caused by love drives humans to attain the good for their own self. For example, love of use causes Joe to love his shoes because they keep his feet warm. Thus, he wants to own shoes. In the case of emotional love, love drives humans to seek to attain the good that is sensed. For example, emotional love of pizza drives humans to eat pizza. Emotional love of friends drives people to seek and to enjoy each other's company. Consequently, because love is an attraction to a good, it moves people to seek union with the things that are loved.

Love can be divided into six types: two types in the emotions and four types in the will. For these six types, every type of natural love has a supernatural counterpart, since grace perfects nature. The six types of love and the corresponding natural inclinations are listed on table 14.1.[4]

The first type of love is *natural emotional love* (love of the passions). Emotional love is the emotional attraction to something that is sensed as good. This is the feeling of love that people get when they seek or obtain a good that is known through sense knowledge. For example, people have the emotional reaction of love when imagining

Table 14.1 The Different Types of Love

	Natural Inclination	Natural Act of Love	Supernatural Act of Love
Love in the Will	Love of Others	Love of Friendship	Charity
	Love of Self	Love of Use	Hope
Love in the Emotions	Desire for the Bodily Good	Natural Emotional Love	Supernatural Emotional Love

their friends, their favorite foods, their warm bed on a cold day, and so on. When love is discussed in the media, generally people are talking about emotional love. Popular magazines or movies often portray people who search their feelings in order to determine whether or not they are truly in love. Because humans are naturally inclined to have emotional love, it is a wonderful thing to have in a relationship. It motivates people to passionately do good for others. However, unless the emotions are trained through virtues, they are not rational. People can have emotional love for both good and bad things (such as drugs). Emotional love can also come and go, as when people speak of "falling into" or "falling out of" love. A relationship based solely on this type of love is doomed to failure because emotional attraction does not provide the stability needed for a permanent relationship. Nonetheless, if a relationship is built upon the proper foundation of love of friendship, emotional love is a wonderful good, and the emotions can be trained to always ardently seek the good of the other.

The second type of emotional love is *supernatural emotional love*. When the emotions are perfected by the infused virtue of temperance and the gifts of the Holy Spirit, the Holy Spirit can move the emotions to love God and others supernaturally. For example, often at the beginning of the spiritual life, God will grant the gift of emotional love to Christians. This love drives Christians to pray and serve God with great passion. They are filled with the emotional joy of the Holy Spirit. This supernatural love makes it very pleasurable for them to pursue a loving relationship with God and also to serve others.[5]

The other four types of love on table 14.1 are in the will. Love of the will is the attraction that the will has to the good known by the intellect. Everything has some goodness in it, and when the intellect knows this good, the will can be attracted to it. The will can either be attracted to persons who are good in and of themselves (love of friendship), or it can be attracted to something because of a good that benefits the person loving (love of use/concupiscence). Both love of friendship and love of use have supernatural counterparts. Charity is supernatural love of friendship, and hope is supernatural love of use. Hope and love of use were already examined in the last chapter, so this chapter will only focus on love of friendship and charity.

Love of friendship is the traditional term indicating the most perfect form of love of others.[6] In authentic friendship, the will is attracted to the goodness that friends have in and of themselves, apart from any benefit that the lover might attain. This attraction compels humans to know each other to the very depths of their souls as the will loves the inner goodness found within humans. Once the goals, needs, sufferings, joys, and so on within the soul of the other person are discovered, the will spiritually unites to the other person by making these goals, needs, sufferings, and joys its own.[7] The mutual love between friends causes them to have the goal of mutual happiness, which is all the greater because it is shared. Hence, friends seek to delight in the presence of each other by being together, speaking together, and being united in all things. Through knowledge and love of friendship, they become of one mind and one heart.[8] They share a single action in imitation of the Father, Son, and Holy Spirit, who are one infinite act. For example, spouses who are true friends are united in performing the action of helping their children and each other get to heaven. Each spouse has a particular role in this single act. By means of these loving relationships, humans discover their true identity and find natural happiness.

Because love of friendship spiritually unites people through the sharing of goals, it causes people to perform actions ordered to the other person. The end of these actions becomes the happiness of their friends. The greater the love, the more they are driven to help their friends be truly happy. Because the action is ordered to their friends, the goodness of the action comes especially from its being performed for their friends. For example, if Joe washes Kate's car, he does not wash the car because he loves the car. He washes the car because he loves Kate. The primary goodness of this action comes from his love of Kate. If the love is great, Joe is able to perform even difficult actions easily, promptly, and joyfully. Because love of friendship most perfectly fulfills the natural inclinations of humans, it is the greatest type of natural love.

Charity is love of friendship of God. With charity, God is loved because of his own goodness, apart from any benefit received from him.[9] Since God is the infinite good, he fulfills the will's attraction to the infinite and universal good. As with natural love of friendship, charity drives humans to know the inner life of God as they seek his infinite goodness. Charity then causes humans to make God's goals, his universal plan, their own.[10] Through faith and charity, humans are united to God.[11] Just as a husband and wife share a single action, humans, through charity, participate in the eternal act of God. By participating in God's eternal plan, humans discover their role in the universe and have supernatural happiness on earth and eternal happiness in heaven.

Because charity causes humans to make God's goals their own, all actions caused by charity are done out of love of God. It is easy to see how great actions, such as enduring martyrdom or joining a convent, are done because of love of God, but even smaller actions, such as eating a healthy breakfast or cheering up a friend, can be done out of love of God. When people consciously recognize that they are doing their actions out of love of God, even difficult acts of loving, such as giving away all their possessions, overcoming their sinful desires, and dying for others become easy and joyful for those who truly love God.[12] Just as importantly, charity can cause the repetitive actions of daily life to be easy and joyful when they are done out of love for God. Most people are not called by God to do objectively great actions, but all people are called to do *all* of their actions, no matter how insignificant these actions seem, out of love of God.[13] Because these actions are done out of love for God, even seemingly insignificant actions can result in great happiness. In fact, because the actions are done out of love of God, greater love results in a greater potential for happiness.

In natural love of friendship, the unity of mind and heart causes people to love their friends' friends. For example, if Joe loves Kate, he makes Kate's goals his goal. Kate wants her friends to be happy. Out of love for Kate, Joe will also seek the happiness of Kate's friends. So also with charity, out of love for God, we must love all other people. Unlike human love, which is attracted to a good thing, God's love causes all things to be good. The more he loves a thing, the greater its goodness. Thus, God loves all things in proportion to their goodness. Through charity, humans share in God's love of all things and, therefore, love all things proportionately to their goodness out of love for God. Because humans have a greater goodness than material things or animals, humans must be loved more. Love of God requires that we love all humans, including ourselves and our enemies. By loving other people out of love for God, humans can love them unconditionally, even if the other people disappoint or injure them. The term "charity" is often used today to mean an altruistic love of others. Although there is some truth in this description, technically, charity is first and foremost a love of God. Others are loved because of this love of God.

As charity is increased in humans, their union with God also increases. In other words, growing in charity is salvation, for this fulfills our supernatural calling. On earth the more we love God, the more we seek to know God through faith and the more we share in God's power through prayer and self-rule. In heaven, the more we love God, the more we know God (and thus everything) and the more we share in his power.

Because charity orders all things to God, there cannot be any perfect virtues without charity.[14] For a virtue to be good in the full sense of the term, it must help humans attain God himself (the ultimate end). Since charity causes all actions to be done out of love of God, all virtues must be ordered to God by charity, or they are only partial virtues. These virtues (without charity) can cause natural happiness, but they are unable to unite humans to God and bring eternal happiness. Even virtues like faith and hope are unable to save without charity.[15] Because charity orders virtues to God, charity is called "the form of the virtues."[16] Charity orders virtues so that their actions ultimately lead to God because they are acts of love of God. For example, an act of martyrdom is materially an act of fortitude, but it is formally an act of love of God. Just as the virtues must be formed by charity to save, so also the old law and the natural law must be infused with charity to save. If humans do not follow the law out of their love for God as a friend, the law will not bring them to God. As St. Paul notes, love fulfills the law (Rom 13:8–10).

Charity is the most perfect of the six types of love and also the most important of the supernatural inclinations. Charity gives humans the ability to love God by the power of his love. By means of this divine love, humans are spiritually united to God. This union with God inclines humans to love all others out of their love for God. No virtue causes such a strong inclination to act as does charity, nor does any virtue cause as much joy in acting as charity causes.[17]

Like all virtues, charity increases by doing like actions of a greater intensity. Thus, humans must continue to perform further acts of charity with greater love of God. Any action done out of love for God is an act of charity. Some actions love God directly, such as contemplating and loving God in prayer. Other actions love God by loving other things that are ordered to God, such as loving all other people (including our enemies). The key to increasing charity is to perform both of these types of actions with ever-greater intensity. Humans should strive to think of the goodness of God whenever they perform an action.

As humans grow in the virtue of charity, their union with God increases. Thomas Aquinas speaks of three stages of charity on earth.[18] The first stage refers to those just beginning to grow in charity. In this stage, people work hard just to avoid committing sin. Their inclination to love God is not very strong yet, and it needs to be perfected by following the law. Because the virtues are weak in this stage, the Christian moral life is a constant struggle, and it is often not enjoyable. The second stage refers to those who are progressing in charity. These people are in the habit of avoiding sin and are not tempted as often. Therefore, they can focus their attention on increasing the virtue of charity through their good actions. The third stage refers to those whose habitual love is so perfect that their union with God causes every act to be done out of love for God. They easily, joyfully, and promptly love as God loves. Since they are already continuously performing good actions, they focus on increasing the intensity of their actions. The people in this third stage are filled with supernatural happiness because of their great love of God.

SUBVIRTUES UNDER CHARITY

All true virtues are ordered to God by charity, and all actions flowing from the infused virtues are also acts of charity. Nonetheless, there are some virtues that directly relate to charity. These are virtues that specifically perfect the will to love God beyond the love caused by justice. Both justice and charity perfect the will to love God and other people. However, justice perfects the will to give to other people and God what is naturally owed to them, while charity goes beyond this love to give them more than is naturally owed to them.[19] In reference to people, justice perfects the will to give others their natural needs, those determined by natural law. Charity perfects the will to go beyond the natural needs and to give other people more than their due.[20] For example, justice perfects the will to use all of one's excess material goods to help others. Charity further perfects the will to give from one's necessities. In point of fact, there is a great deal of overlap between the virtues under justice and the virtues under charity. Furthermore, with infused justice, the acts of justice are also acts of charity since they are ordered to God by charity. Nonetheless, the following nine virtues especially pertain to love of friendship of God. The virtues specific to charity are *humility, prayer, mercy, benefi- cence, friendliness, almsgiving, hospitality, evangelization,* and *fraternal correction.*

Humility

Charity drives humans to make God's goals into their own goals. In order to make God's goals their own, humans need the virtue of humility. They must recognize their own intellectual and moral weakness and seek to participate in the wisdom and love of God. By means of the virtue of humility, humans subordinate their own interests to those of God and others. St. Paul emphasizes that humility is necessary for humans to become of one mind and heart with others when he says, "Do nothing out of selfish- ness or out of vain glory; rather *humbly* regard others as more important than your- selves, each looking out not for his own interests, but everyone for those of others." Paul then calls people to imitate Christ, who "*humbled* himself, taking the form of a slave."[21] When people are only focused on their own interests, they are only thinking of themselves. They do not seek to learn and fulfill the needs of others. Humble people follow the example of Christ and give of their lives in order to be united to God and others in loving relationships.

Although the virtue of humility is primarily in the will, it also pertains to the in- tellect. Humility can be defined as an accurate understanding of one's own goodness in proportion to God and others and the proper love of self and others that follows from this understanding.[22] Humble people recognize that in regard to their human nature they are not greater than other people and especially not greater than God. Based on this recognition, they love themselves and others the proper amount. They do not love themselves so much that they are unable to enter into friendships with God and others. In other words, humble people recognize that they should not have only love of use for others (having others serve their interests); rather, they should have love of friendship. They also recognize that God is infinitely greater than they are, and that they should love God more than they love themselves. When humans are perfected by faith and charity, the greatness of God as both creator and savior is even more mani- fest. In relation to God, humans not only recognize their limited nature but also their sinfulness, and they worship God, who shows them the way to eternal happiness. They also willingly subject themselves to other people in imitation of Christ, who humbled himself to share in our humanity.[23]

Humility is the mean between the vice of pride and the vice of not recognizing one's own self-worth as created and redeemed by God (and, therefore, not having the appropriate love of self). Prideful people erroneously believe that they are greater than God or other humans. There is always an element of self-deception in the prideful person. Although the intellect is deceived, if the person is truly committing the sin of pride, the deception will stem from an improper love of self. (Normally the emotions are also involved in this self-deception.) In other words, prideful people *choose* to believe that they are more important than they really are. Because of this belief, they consider their own goals and interests to be more important than those of God or other people. For example, Adam and Eve committed the sin of pride by creating their own standards of morality in opposition to those of God. In doing this, they acted as if they were greater than God. Because prideful people focus only on their own needs, they cannot have love of friendship for God or others.

On the other extreme, those who do not know and love themselves properly also have a vice. God became man so that humans could participate in divine nature. By participating in divine nature, humans have an important role in bringing the universe to its perfection. Because humans share in the divine plan of God, God calls them "friends."[24] Ironically, those who do not see themselves as being worthy of God's friendship fail to recognize the true greatness of God. They fail to seek to fulfill God's plan because they do not believe that they are worthy or able. Humble people believe that they can do great things, not by their power, but by the power of God who works within them.[25] Because both the excess and the defect to humility keep people from making the goals of God their own, they are both sins contrary to charity.

Since humility is necessary for people to have love of friendship of both God and others, it is an extremely important virtue. Furthermore, without humility, any good action can be done for prideful purposes. For example, someone could give money to the poor for the end of human glory. Thus, St. Gregory the Great calls humility the mother of all virtues, because, without it, any good action can be done with a prideful intention, making the object of the act pride.[26] The beauty of humility is that in seeking to subject oneself to God and others, humans are actually elevated by participating in God's nature.[27]

Prayer

Prayer is the virtue of easily, joyfully, and continuously communicating with God.[28] In human friendships, in order for humans to know each other and to show their love to each other, they must continually communicate. The world is constantly changing, and the individual needs and sufferings of each human change with it. Without regular and in-depth communication, it is impossible for friends to know each other's goals and needs. Furthermore, humans are fulfilled by expressing their love. Love is shown through bodily signs, which are also forms of communication. Without communi-

cation, humans are unable to show their love to each other. In other words, communication causes knowledge, which causes love, which causes unity, and communication
is the means through which love is shown. In both cases communication is ordered
to unity.

Communication with God is also ordered to unity. Although God's divine plan
does not change, humans and the world around them do change. Hence, humans must
listen to God regularly in order to know how to best participate in his plan. Furthermore, humans are fulfilled by loving God and must communicate this love for God
through various bodily signs. Consequently, because communication with God primarily consists of knowledge coming in and love going out, the two most basic types
of prayer will consist of knowing God and loving God. All other forms of prayers are
elaborations of these.

The first basic type of prayer refers to all those acts by which humans learn more
about God and his plan for them. God has divinely revealed himself and his will to
humans since the time of Adam and Eve. The highpoint of this revelation was when
the Son revealed the interior life of God through the human nature of Jesus Christ.
The Holy Spirit continues this mission of the Son by inspiring his followers, the
Church, to transmit the fullness of this revelation to each generation.[29] This revelation
has been passed down by the Church to our generation through Sacred Scripture and
sacred tradition. Since humans learn through their senses, prayer must include learning about God by listening to and reading the words of scripture and by experiencing
the practices of tradition. Also, because the transmission of divine revelation was en-
trusted to the Church, Church teaching must also be studied. Furthermore, since humans learn from the wisdom of those who came before them, the writings of the saints
can be particularly helpful in learning about God and his plan. Finally, the Holy Spirit
continues to guide the intellect to greater understanding of divine revelation and God's
plan for each individual. Hence, all humans should spend time contemplating the
greatness of God and thinking about how to fulfill their divine calling. Practically
speaking, this type of prayer will include participating in liturgical celebrations, meditating upon scripture, tradition, and the lives and writings of the saints, and allowing
the Holy Spirit to guide the intellect. These last two forms of prayer, by necessity, require that some silent time be devoted to God on a regular (preferably daily) basis.[30]

The second basic type of prayer refers to all those acts whereby humans communicate their love to God.[31] Prayers are not for God's benefit; they are for our benefit.
Humans are fulfilled by performing acts of love that are based on their knowledge.
Because humans are body and soul, they must communicate their love through their
bodies. In order to better understand how humans can communicate their love to
God, a close look at how humans communicate their love to each other is helpful. The
obvious way that humans communicate their love is by telling others that they love
them. However, a large portion of communication is nonverbal, especially when it
comes to communicating love. Humans also communicate their love through spending

time together, giving gifts, performing acts of service, physically touching (such as hugging), and speaking kind words (in addition to "I love you").[32]

Humans must also show their love of God through bodily signs. Thus, throughout history humans have shown their love of God in these same five ways. They show love by *spending time* with God, such as when they spend time adoring God in the Eucharist or spend time contemplating his greatness. Humans also show love of God by *giving gifts*. Before the time of Christ, humans gave gifts to God by offering sacrifices of animals and grain to God. Since Christ is the one eternal sacrifice, Christians no longer sacrifice animals or grain; however, they can still give gifts to God by offering the Father his only Son at Mass and by giving gifts to other people out of their love for God. They are also able to show love of God by making their daily lives a sacrifice that is united to the one sacrifice of Christ. They make their lives a sacrifice by constantly performing *acts of service* for God and others. They are able to show love of God through *physical touch* when they receive Christ in the Holy Eucharist and by physically showing love to others out of love for God (such as in marriage). Finally, humans show love of God through *speaking words* of praise and adoration. These words can be spoken in either formal prayer (such as the Rosary) or informal prayer. Although all humans will have a particular way of showing love to God that they prefer, they should be able to show love of God in all of the above ways.

Because humans can allow the Holy Spirit to constantly guide their intellect and can offer every action as a sign of their love for God, humans can truly pray without ceasing, as Paul requests in 1 Thessalonians 5:17. Although humans can make their entire lives a prayer, these two basic forms of prayer come to their perfection in the Mass. The first part of Mass, the liturgy of the Word, focuses on teaching humans about God and his plan for them. Through the scripture readings and the homily, knowledge of God comes into the intellect. The second part of Mass, the liturgy of the Eucharist, focuses on humans showing their love to God. The infinite sacrifice of Jesus himself is offered as a *gift* to the Father. Humans participate in this sacrifice by offering to the Father all the *acts of service* they have performed. They are also able to *physically touch* Jesus by receiving his body and blood in Holy Communion. During this time, they are able to *spend time* with Jesus, and throughout the Mass they *speak and sing his praises*. The Mass is the most perfect form of communication with God, and the ensuing union with God is manifested by the physical sign of Holy Communion.

Because humans rely on others, an important element of communication between humans is asking for the help of others. For example, friendships are strengthened when one friend asks for help, and the other friend complies. So also, a large portion of spoken prayer consists of petitions to God, our heavenly friend. However, if God already knows our needs and already knows his response, why should humans bother to ask for God's help? The answer is twofold. First, when God answers our prayers, the person praying acts as a secondary cause of God's gifts to the world. Although God has planned on causing a particular gift for all eternity, he also has always planned on causing it through someone's prayer. For example, suppose my sister is sick, and God plans on healing my sister. However, God works through secondary causes because he wants the secondary causes to be more like him. Hence, he causes me to freely choose to pray for my sister, and through my prayer I am a secondary cause of her getting well. Consequently, prayers have true power to change the world. Because of the power of prayer, some of the most powerful people in the world are the monks, nuns, elderly people, and others who devote their lives to prayer. The second reason that humans should pray is that prayer causes humans to humble themselves before God and to become open to his will. By praying for something, humans recognize that God has a divine plan, and if he does not grant their request, it is ultimately for their own good.

Prayer is essential to the moral life because through it humans learn God's plan and express their love of God. However, it also helps people to grow in other virtues by giving them the ability to act with greater intensity. In human relationships, in order to increase the love between people, loving actions must be done with continually greater intensity. One way to increase this intensity is for humans to spend time contemplating (or observing) the good features of their beloved. By contemplating the good features of their beloved, they get into the habit of thinking about their beloved and loving the good within them. Furthermore, by focusing on the good, their emotions are trained to love with greater passion. Consequently, when they perform good actions for their beloved, their intellect consciously recognizes that the action is done out of love for the other; the will is motivated to love the action out of love for the person, and the emotions cause the action to be done passionately.[33] In other words, they do not just thoughtlessly go through the motions of loving each other. For example, after thinking about the goodness of Kate all day, Joe eagerly seeks to help Kate study, even if it means sacrificing by not watching his favorite football team.

Spending time contemplating the goodness of God and his gifts also causes humans to act with greater intensity. They become more conscious of the fact that they are doing each action because of their love of God, and their will and emotions are trained to act with greater passion. Because an increase in the intensity of actions is necessary to further increase virtues, a devout prayer life is an important step in perfecting charity and the other virtues. Many of the saints recognized this fact and spent hours every day in prayer.[34] Prayers focused on meditating upon the life of Christ, such as the Rosary, are particularly effective in helping humans grow in virtue.

Prayer is communication with God. When humans communicate with each other, they are able to express the thoughts and loves within the depths of their souls. Their intellect is able to communicate inner truths through words and actions. The will is able to express its love in the same way. Other people can understand these truths by means of their intellect and can share in these truths by means of their will. Thus, unity among humans primarily comes through the actions of the intellect and the will. In reference to God, unity must also be obtained through the communication made possible by acts of the intellect and the will. Humans communicate with God in any action where the intellect seeks to know God and his plan and any action where the will expresses love of God. The most perfect form of prayer is the Mass, where humans learn about God by listening to the Word and love God by offering the perfect gift of the Son to the Father.

MERCY

Mercy is the virtue of having a compassionate heart for another's troubles and then choosing to find a way to alleviate the unhappiness of the other person.[35] Merciful people share in the sufferings of others because their love of God causes them to make the sufferings of his children their own, and this love further causes them to seek to bring happiness to those in distress. The mercy that humans have for each other is a participation in the mercy of God and humans should seek to imitate God's merciful actions.

In a deontological understanding of morality, mercy is predominantly equated with God forgiving the sins of the people.[36] This aspect of God's mercy is important; however, in a teleological system, the primary aspect of God's mercy is that he acknowledges the unhappiness of humans and comes to humans as a friend so that they can participate in his perfect happiness.[37] Paul describes this divine mercy in Philippians 2. Paul exhorts the Philippians to imitate the attitude of Christ by making the interests of others more important than their own. For Christ, "though he was in the form of God, he did not regard equality with God something to be grasped. Rather he emptied himself . . . coming in human likeness . . . becoming obedient to death, even death on the cross" (Phil 2:6–8). Humans have an intense natural desire to be in the "form of God" (participate in divine nature and be perfectly happy). Yet, they are incapable of attaining this "equality with God" by their own ability (it cannot be "grasped"). Without divine aid, humans are incapable of attaining the true happiness that they naturally desire. Hence, God in his mercy "empties himself," comes in "human likeness," and suffers for us. In order to alleviate our unhappiness, the divine Son becomes human so that we can become children of God and participate in divine nature. Through this participation in divine nature, humans are able to know and love God and share in his happiness.

Furthermore, as our friend, God continues to guide and move humans so that they can ultimately be happy. He teaches us how to have love of friendship for others and gives us the grace to perform loving actions. In the current state of the down payment, love of friendship requires a sacrifice of self, as was shown by Christ on the cross. Hence, as our friend, God's mercy entails giving humans the grace to love others no matter how painful or difficult it is—because when these acts are done out of love for God, they result in the happiness God intended for us to have (even if it requires one to grow in virtue to recognize this). In other words, mercy does not mean that God excuses humans from a difficult situation, which he allows for their spiritual growth;

rather, mercy means that God gives them the grace that transforms them in order to prevail in the situation.[38] In his mercy, God empties himself so that we can become his friends and be truly happy.

In imitation of God's mercy, humans with the virtue of mercy should also seek to enter into permanent friendships with those outside their normal social sphere. Just as God extends the bonds of friendship to those who are separated from him, humans should do the same. They should make an effort to become true friends with people who are "separated" from them by social, cultural, or religious divisions. Mercy requires that humans help others to be happy. Yet, to help others be happy generally requires more than just giving them material aid or exhorting them to do good actions. Attaining happiness often requires a change of lifestyle. Hence, to help others to be happy humans, we must love them enough to patiently assist them to grow in virtue over the course of years. Merciful humans must do what God did for them: become true friends with others. Consequently, the merciful person seeks out people of different social, cultural, or religious backgrounds. She attempts to learn the deepest needs and goals of these other people. Her love then drives her to make their need for authentic happiness her own. Friendship of this type takes a great deal of time and effort.

Becoming friends with someone outside of one's normal social sphere is not an easy task to accomplish. It requires people from diverse backgrounds to come into contact with each other in a manner that is conducive to the fostering of friendship. Generally, in order for humans to form these types of friendships, they must become members of organizations that bring them into contact with people of different social, cultural, or religious backgrounds. Furthermore, the organization should cultivate true humility on the part of all involved and provide a venue for true friendships to develop.[39] Examples of these types of organizations could include work places committed to being a true community, small businesses ordered toward the common good, humanitarian organizations devoted to helping the poor, schools, health-care organizations, or groups within churches. These types of organizations allow people to accomplish acts of mercy that they could not accomplish on their own and, most importantly, provide a venue in which friendships can develop. Only by forming these friendships can unity among people be established and lifestyles conducive to authentic happiness be cultivated. Consequently, the merciful person seeks to join or form these types of organizations and then humbly begins to know and love others of diverse backgrounds.

I have worked with a wonderful organization that creates this type of venue. In this organization, volunteers take food, clothing, and other necessary items to the homeless. They load these items into vans and personally deliver them to the homeless communities. They then humbly and lovingly give these material items to the poor and homeless. Although these material items are important, the most important thing that they give to the homeless is friendship.[40] Over time, the regular volunteers get to know and love the homeless people. They begin to understand their specific needs and goals. They begin to perform the actions that help these people to become truly happy. Sometimes these actions are as simple as helping someone attain a job or helping them consistently take necessary medication. However, often these actions consist of giving them the guidance, motivation, and support to make lifestyle changes. These latter actions can require years of patient, loving support and exhortations. However, over time, unity forms between these people, and the lives of both the volunteers and the homeless are perfected. This is just one example of this type of organization. I have seen the same mutually beneficial friendships develop in prison ministry, in schools, in the workplace, in nursing homes, sports events, and other places. These organizations are successful because they provide a venue for humble and loving interaction to take place. They imitate the mercy of Christ, who humbled himself in order to become friends with us and offered his own life as a sign of his love.[41] Although humans only have the time and abilities to form a few of these friendships throughout one lifetime, in imitation of Christ they should attempt to prudently seek out these relationships.

The second aspect of God's mercy is that he forgives our sins. God loves us and wants us to share in his eternal happiness. Consequently, he always offers forgiveness, but it is our responsibility to accept it. Likewise, the virtue of mercy requires that humans forgive others. Humans are made to be in loving relationships, and the destruction of a relationship through hatred and anger causes great suffering. Because harming another person through word or deed diminishes or destroys relationships, mercy especially moves people to *forgive* others so that the relationship can be repaired. The Letter to the Ephesians sums up the virtue of mercy when Paul says, "Be kind and compassionate to one another, forgiving each other, just as in Christ God forgave you" (4:32).

BENEFICENCE

Beneficence is the virtue of doing good to others. Beneficent people make the bodily and spiritual needs of others their own because of their love for God. They are consciously seeking to know the needs of all others, beginning with those closest to them and expanding their love for others in progressively wider and wider circles.[42] In other words, they get into the habit of recognizing the needs of other people and of making these needs their own. They begin with their family and then expand this habit to include friends, neighbors, and so forth until the needs of the poorest villager in remote Africa become their own.[43] When looking at the needs of others, the needs of the poor should take precedence over the needs of all other people.[44] Of course, no human has the ability on earth to learn and fulfill the needs of all other humans; hence, humans must use prudence in doing good for others. The key is that humans get into the habit of constantly looking for the needs of others and doing whatever they can to fulfill them. At the very least, they can pray for them.

Friendliness

Friendliness is the virtue of communicating with others in a cheerful and loving manner. People with the virtue of friendliness are constantly seeking to bring joy to others through a kind word, a smile, or a hug (if appropriate). These people go out their way to form loving relationships with others. Their good actions extend beyond their close friends to complete strangers. For example, if people with this virtue see a new person at church or school, they will go and meet the person to bring them into the community. The virtue of friendliness helps spread the love of God to all others.

Almsgiving

The virtue of almsgiving is the disposition to give not only from a person's superfluous goods but also from one's necessities. As we will see in chapter 17, justice requires that material goods be consumed in moderation and that all other goods should be used for the benefit of others. The virtue of almsgiving perfects people so that, out of love for God, they even give from their necessities.[45] Jesus's comments about the poor widow sum up this virtue: "I tell you truly, this poor widow put in more than all the rest; for those others have all made an offering from their surplus wealth, but she, from her poverty, has offered her whole livelihood" (Lk 21:3–4).

Evangelization

Evangelization is the virtue of constantly seeking to spread the gospel of Jesus Christ by performing all actions out of charity and further seeking opportunities to spread the faith to others verbally. The word "evangelization" is derived from the Greek word meaning "good message." The gospel is the good message because it proclaims that the deepest desires for human happiness can be fulfilled. Pope Francis explains: "Sometimes we lose our enthusiasm for mission because we forget that the gospel responds to our deepest needs, since we were created for what the gospel offers us: friendship with Jesus and love of our brothers and sisters. If we succeed in expressing adequately and with beauty the essential content of the Gospel, surely this message will speak to the deepest yearnings of people's hearts."[46] Humans yearn for the happiness that comes from friendship with God and others, and God became a human and died on the cross so that humans could share in this friendship. This joyful message gives humans hope and an earthly participation in the eternal happiness of the full inheritance. Since charity drives humans to make God's goals their own, humans with charity seek to give others the knowledge of God that will make others happier.[47] Pope Francis describes the role of love of Jesus in evangelization: "What kind of love would not feel the need to speak of the beloved, to point him out, to make him known? If we do not feel an intense desire to share this love, we need to pray insistently that he [Jesus] will once more touch our hearts."[48]

Based on the example of Jesus, I want to emphasize four components to the virtue of evangelization. First, in order to evangelize others, Christians must truly love those they seek to evangelize and must clearly show this love through their actions. In a world full of the constant marketing of superfluous products and ideologies, Christians will only be taken seriously if they truly love others. Second, Christians must exemplify the love that they teach in their own lives. Humans are naturally inclined to happiness and joy; thus, when Christians radiate the love and joy of Jesus Christ, other humans will seek to find the cause of this joy. Third, along with this universal mandate to live the gospel in all aspects of one's life, Christians should prudently spread the gospel through their words whenever they have the opportunity. Although in evangelization the loving actions should come first, the words are necessary to ultimately convey the good news. Finally, Christians must invite those they evangelize to become a part of a welcoming community—ultimately the Church, but also smaller organizations where those learning about the Faith can receive the personal love and support they need. These components imitate Christ, who also showed his love for all and lived out this love in his own life. He further proclaimed the gospel message by his words and finally invited his followers into the Church. In the modern world of social media, the way the gospel is spread can vary, but the message should always accompany authentic love for others.[49]

Fraternal Correction

Fraternal correction is the virtue of correcting others who are sinning.[50] Those with charity desire that all humans are happy on earth and attain eternal happiness in heaven. Sin, especially serious sin, is an impediment to true happiness, both in this life and the next. Consequently, out of love of God, humans should attempt to help others avoid sin through both their words and their examples. For example, Joe might explain to his friend George that looking at pornography is wrong and that these acts seriously endanger his happiness. As we saw with mercy, Joe must also cultivate a friendship with George so that he can see the happiness that comes from healthy relationships with a woman and not from pornography. Although fraternal correction is a sign of great love, it must be carried out with extreme prudence and tact. People often believe that they are personally being attacked and hated when others try to correct their behavior. Sometimes correcting the actions of others will only make things worse by causing those who are sinning to not only continue to sin but also to separate themselves from what might be the only good example in their lives. Consequently it is always wrong to encourage others to sin, but sometimes it is better to cultivate a stronger relationship with other people rather than to correct them directly, with the goal of correcting them in the long run through good examples and words.

Hospitality

Although it could be argued that hospitality is a combination of mercy, beneficence, and friendliness, it will be covered as a special virtue because of its prominence within the Benedictine tradition. *The Rule of St. Benedict* reads: "All guests who present themselves are to be welcomed as Christ, for he himself will say: 'I was a stranger and you welcomed me.'"[51] St. Benedict goes on to state that guests should be greeted with humility and honored because Christ is welcomed in them: "Great care and concern are to be shown in receiving poor people and pilgrims, because in them more particularly Christ is received."[52] St. Benedict clearly shows how charity causes people to welcome others into their homes (and lives) and to honor them as if they were Christ. Traditionally, this virtue was especially important because travelers would need shelter and protection on their journeys. In modern times, this virtue can be extended to humbly serving and honoring visitors, the homeless, and other poor people.

Some scholars assert that the virtue of hospitality is the Christian counterpart of the secular "virtue" of tolerance.[53] Gertrude Conway notes that although the secular "virtue" of tolerance often leads to a relativism that is harmful, hospitality allows humans to truly love and honor others of all backgrounds. She notes that tolerance is based on indifference, but hospitality is based on love.[54] Because the secular "virtue" of tolerance causes a person to affirm all culturally accepted beliefs and ideologies in others, it contradicts important Christian virtues, such as evangelization and fraternal correction. With the virtue hospitality, others are loved and treated as friends, which means making their authentic needs one's own (but not their false or artificial needs and desires).

These subvirtues that flow from the virtue of charity further explain how charity helps perfect the will within human actions. Humility allows people to enter into loving relationships with God and others. Prayer perfects the will to seek greater knowledge of God and to seek to express love of him. Mercy, beneficence, friendliness, almsgiving, and hospitality all perfect the will to desire to identify the authentic needs of others and to fulfill them out of love for God. Evangelization and fraternal correction perfect the will to make the spiritual needs of others one's own and to work to fulfill these spiritual needs by teaching about Christ and how to attain him.

THE GIFT OF WISDOM

The Holy Spirit's gift that perfects charity is wisdom. It may seem odd that wisdom is the gift that perfects charity, since natural wisdom is a virtue that perfects the intellect, and charity is in the will. However, because charity perfects the will to attain God himself, the wisdom of God can move the will in a way beyond the power of the human intellect. Natural wisdom causes humans to judge by higher principles. The Holy Sprit's gift of wisdom likewise causes humans to judge by higher principles, except that, in the case of the gift of wisdom, the higher principles are within the divine mind. As we noted in chapter 9, friends share their goals (secrets) with each other. Through the gift of wisdom, the Holy Spirit shares his secrets (our unique role in God's plan) with us.[55]

Because of the union with God attained by charity, the Holy Spirit is able to move the will to love a possible action in accord with the eternal law. Generally, this movement of the will takes place in the step of consent (step 6). After a person takes counsel to determine the best options to attain an end, the will then consents to the activity of the intellect. Sometimes God moves the will to love one of the options more than another, even if the intellect does not know why the action is loved. Even after the will consents to an action, the intellect must still judge the action to make sure that the movement of the will was truly from the Holy Spirit. The Holy Spirit's gift of wisdom also perfects the intellect to judge whether or not the actions are truly ordered to God. Even if the intellect does not fully understand why the will is moved to love a particular option, it can still judge whether or not the action can be ordered to God.

For example, suppose that Joe is a sophomore in college, and he has to choose which classes to take. Joe intends to take classes that help perfect him as a person. For the intellect to determine the best way to attain this goal with practical certainty, it should reason from the highest end to an action that can be done here and now. The highest end is eternal happiness. The next highest end is the way of life that God calls someone to live (one's vocation—for example, being either a priest or a husband and father). Joe's vocation should be ordered to eternal happiness. The next highest end is the occupation that Joe is going to pursue (such as being a teacher or an engineer). Joe's job should be ordered to his vocation. In other words, Joe should not take a job that would not allow him to fulfill his role as either a priest or a husband and father. The next end would be the choice of Joe's major, which should be ordered to his occupation. If Joe wants to be an engineer, then Joe should major in engineering. Finally, the classes Joe takes should be ordered to attaining an engineering degree. However, suppose that Joe does not yet know what vocation, occupation, or even major that God is calling him to. All that Joe's intellect can do is think of some classes that in general should help him toward a number of likely occupations or majors. Although the intellect cannot determine the best classes with practical certainty, the Holy Spirit does know the classes that will help Joe the most throughout his life. The Holy Spirit through the gift of wisdom can move the will to love certain classes, even if Joe is not completely certain why he wants to take them. Then, the Holy Spirit perfects the intellect to judge whether or not these classes are truly reasonable ways of attaining his future goals. For example, if Joe wants to take a class just because it is an easy "A," then the love of the class is probably not from the Holy Spirit. Wisdom perfects charity because it helps humans determine which actions show love of God the most.

THE BEATITUDES

The beatitudes are internal dispositions that are necessary conditions for charity.[56] In Matthew 5, the beatitudes are at the beginning of the Sermon on the Mount. Matthew considers the Sermon on the Mount to be a fulfillment of the law given to Moses on Mount Sinai. The Mosaic law, which can be summarized by the Ten Commandments, was the obligation of the Mosaic covenant. If the Israelites kept the law, God would bless them with material blessings. If they broke the covenant, they would be killed like the bulls that were slain to seal the covenant (Ex 24:1–8). The Sermon on the Mount extends the old covenant, so that not only must the Ten Commandments be kept externally, but Christians must also be internally good, as is seen by the commands prohibiting anger, lust, and hate (Mt 5:21–43). To be internally good especially means that Christians must love God and all others so that they can be children of their heavenly Father.[57]

The beatitudes are written in the manner of a covenant, with an obligation and a blessing. Both the obligations and the blessings of the beatitudes perfect the old covenant's obligations and blessings. The obligations are perfected because they now include internal dispositions that are necessary to have the love that allows people to be happy in this life and the next.[58] The blessings are perfected because they now refer to the spiritual blessings found in eternal happiness. The beatitudes are blessings given to us from God so that humans can have charity and a foretaste of the happiness of eternal life. In fact, the word "blessed" (*makarios* in Greek) can also be translated as "happy."[59] The beatitudes tell humans how to be truly happy.

The first beatitude is "Blessed are the poor in spirit, for theirs is the kingdom of heaven." Those who are poor in spirit are humble. Humility is absolutely essential for any loving relationship, especially one's relationship with God. The opposite of humility is pride. Prideful people always consider their own needs and goals more important than those of anyone else, including God. Consequently, they cannot have love of friendship, which requires them to make the needs and goals of others their own. Without humility, charity is impossible. Because humility is essential for loving relationships, it is the first obligation of the new covenant. In contrast with the pride found in original sin, humility gives humans the interior disposition to share in the loving mission of Jesus. The blessing of this beatitude refers to God's promise to Abraham that his descendants would be a great kingdom (Gen 12:2). Those who are poor in spirit are members of more than just the earthly kingdom of Israel; they are members of God's kingdom.

The second beatitude is "Blessed are they who mourn, for they will be comforted." To love others is to share in their sufferings. Because of our fallen nature, suffering is inevitable in this life, and enduring suffering is an essential aspect of loving others while on earth.[60] Christ came not as a glorious political leader but as a suffering servant to teach us how to truly love others and share in authentic happiness. As friends with Christ, Christians seek to share in his mission as a suffering servant. By the power of the Holy Spirit, Christians attempt to continuously sacrifice for others and become a channel of God's merciful love. So although in general Christians should be joyful, when they love Christ and others, they will suffer and mourn with them at the appropriate times.

For centuries, Israel was waiting for the Messiah who would end their sufferings. The blessing of this beatitude shows that those who lovingly share in the sufferings of Christ will be comforted through supernatural happiness in this life and through eternal happiness in heaven.

The third beatitude is "Blessed are the meek, for they will inherit the land." Those who are meek can control their anger. When humans are inflicted with suffering, one of their first responses is to get angry with God and others. Unjust anger can destroy a loving relationship.[61] It causes people to retaliate and keeps people from forgiving each other. In reference to God, it keeps people from enduring suffering out of love for God and keeps them from seeking to understand the divine plan behind the suffering.[62] The blessing of this beatitude refers to the land promised to Abraham and his descendants. However, within the new covenant, the land takes on a spiritual meaning and refers to wherever God's saving grace is present.

The fourth beatitude is "Blessed are those who hunger and thirst for righteousness, for they will be satisfied." In the biblical context, to be righteous is to be faithful to the covenant. Under the old covenant, to be righteous was to keep the Ten Commandments. With the new covenant, righteousness refers to knowing and loving God through faith and charity. Hence, this beatitude guides people to seek union with God through knowing and loving him. If they seek union with God, their infinite desire for the good will be satisfied.

The fifth beatitude is "Blessed are the merciful, for mercy shall be theirs." Mercy is a subvirtue under charity, and it gives people the ability to have a compassionate heart for others. In Luke's version of the Sermon on the Mount, he ends the call to love others with this: "Be merciful just as your Father is merciful" (Lk 6:36). Mercy is an essential component of charity since love of God requires Christians to love all others. The blessing of this beatitude notes that God's gift of grace is more than humans deserve by nature. In other words, the very fact that God offers us the grace of salvation is because of his mercy.

The sixth beatitude is "Blessed are the clean of heart, for they shall see God." To be clean of heart is to be devoted to God above all other things. Charity exists when humans love God above all other things. It is unique among the virtues in that it attains God himself. Faith does not directly attain God himself, for God is known by knowing his created effects, such as nature and divine revelation. Charity is the opposite. God is loved in himself, so all other things are loved out of love of God.[63] By means of charity, humans will attain eternal happiness and fulfill the blessing of this beatitude by seeing God as he is. Once humans see God as he is, they will also know all other things through their knowledge of God.

The seventh beatitude is "Blessed are the peacemakers, for they will be called children of God." Peace should be seen as synonymous with the unity that comes forth from charity.[64] Those who love God seek unity with God and all others. Peace is attained by being united to all others through sharing in the one divine plan of God. To be peacemakers, humans must do more than just prevent wars and violence (although this is also included); they must also help others know and love God so that all can be united by sharing God's divine plan. Or in other words, as the blessing notes, all those united will share in God's nature as children of God. By union with Christ, Christians are children of God "and if children, then heirs of God and joint heirs with Christ" (Rom 8:16). Christians will share in the inheritance given to Christ for all eternity: the divine nature.

The eighth beatitude is "Blessed are they who are persecuted for the sake of righteousness, for theirs is the kingdom of heaven." Love requires that friends are faithful to each other, even if this means being persecuted by others. So also charity requires that humans participate in the mission of Christ, even if this means being persecuted by others. Throughout the history of Christianity, thousands of people throughout the world have been tortured or martyred because of their love of God. Since the kingdom of God exists wherever Christ's saving grace is present, enduring persecution out of love of God is a visible sign to all that God's kingdom is present on earth.

The beatitudes are internal dispositions that are necessary for charity. Humans cannot enter into a loving relationship with God unless they are first humble (poor in spirit). Love requires that they share in his sufferings and be willing to undergo persecution for his sake. Love also requires that humans do not get angry with God, who does all things for their benefit, and that they hunger and thirst to do his will. They must love God above all others and love others because of their love of God. Their love of others will cause them to have mercy on others and to create unity as peacemakers.

SINS AGAINST CHARITY

The commandment that goes along with charity is the first commandment: *I am the Lord your God, you shall have no other gods before me.* This commandment requires that humans love God above all other things. Since love of God results in love of others, all the other commandments also pertain to charity. In other words, since humans always choose to attain the end they love most, breaking any of the commandments is a violation of charity. If the commandments are broken in a serious way, then charity is destroyed. However, since the other commandments will be covered in greater detail in chapters 16 to 18, we will now look at the sins against the first commandment and the sins against the unity among humans that flows from charity. We will first analyze sins against love of God (*pride, lukewarmness, sloth,* and *hatred of God*), then sins directly against love of others (*envy, discord, schism,* and *scandal*).

PRIDE

As we saw with humility, the prideful person, because of an improper self-love, deceives himself by believing that he is greater than he really is in relation to others. Pride is most serious when a person believes that she is even greater than God. This person considers herself to be the ultimate good. A consequence of this self-elevation is that prideful people consider their own interests to be of greater importance than the needs and goals of others. In other words, all actions are done for an ultimate end. If humans consider themselves to be the ultimate end, then all actions will be done for their own benefit. In this case, all other humans, and even God, are only loved with love of use. Love of friendship and the authentic relationships that flow from this love are impossible for people who believe that they are the most important good. Consequently, it is impossible for those with this form of pride to have charity.

Like all sins, there are degrees of pride. The most serious sin of pride is when people consider themselves to be greater than God. However, people also commit the sin of pride in two other ways. First, they commit this sin when, out of improper self-love, they deceive themselves by believing that they are greater than other people. Second, pride exists when people believe that they are holier than they really are. These two forms of pride also have serious consequences, and they violate charity.

In reference to the first of these two forms of pride, people can improperly consider themselves greater than others for a variety of reasons, such as wealth, talents, power, race, ethnic background, or even holiness. If people simply recognize that they are more talented or virtuous than others, they do not commit the sin of pride (as long as this recognition is true).[65] However, if their disproportionate self-love causes them to consider themselves to be a greater good (end) than others, then they commit the sin of pride. Because of their self-love, they will order their actions toward their own good and never toward the good of the people who they believe are beneath them. Their pride prohibits them from having love of friendship with these other people. Since charity requires that we have love of friendship with all other humans, this form of pride also violates charity.

Those who believe that they are holier than they really are also commit the sin of pride. Their pride keeps them from discovering their sins and from turning from their wickedness. For example, Gregory the Great notes that because of pride people are deceived into thinking that their vices are actually virtues.[66] He says that cruelty is often considered justice, immoderate anger is considered righteous zeal, a lack of strictness is considered gentleness, hoarding goods is considered frugality, stubbornness is considered to be constancy, fear is considered to be humility, prideful speech is considered to be defense of the truth, sloth is keeping the peace, and slowness in doing good is termed judgment.[67] The key point is that because prideful people have inordinate self-love, their intellect can be deceived into thinking that their vices are actually virtues, and, thus, they do not try to overcome their vices.[68]

Pride can cause any good action to be ordered to the sinful end of self-elevation rather than to God. Even the holiest of people can be tempted to think, "Look how holy I am compared to those around me." Pride causes one to do a good action with a bad intention. Since the person with pride loves his own goals more than those of God and others, pride has traditionally been considered to be the root of all sins.[69]

LUKEWARMNESS

In Revelation 3:16 the divine Son states, "Because you are lukewarm, neither hot nor cold, I will spit you out of my mouth." In the Old Testament, people are spewed forth from the land when they break the covenant.[70] In other words, they lose the covenant promises because they break the covenant. Hence, the Son is saying that those who are lukewarm in the practice of their faith forfeit the new covenant promise of eternal happiness. Why is lukewarmness a violation of the new covenant? The new covenant requires that all people love God, and if people are lukewarm, they are not loving. Recall the earlier analogy about a husband asking his wife, "What is the minimum that I can do to stay in this relationship?" Even if the husband is not planning to seriously hurt his wife, he does not really love her. Love drives people to ask, "What is the most that I can do in this relationship?"

There are two primary ways that relationships are destroyed. One way is through a violent breakup where one or both members of the friendship wills an evil action toward the other. However, the much more common way for relationships to be destroyed is through neglecting to spend the time and effort necessary for maintaining the relationship. Those who are not vigilant about maintaining their relationship slowly grow apart over time and eventually no longer share needs and goals. Our relationship with God is the same. It can just as easily be destroyed by lukewarmness as by hatred of God.[71] Love requires that people ardently seek to do God's will. In the Revelation passage quoted in the last paragraph, God would rather have the people be cold than lukewarm, because lukewarm Christians are a scandal to all those outside the faith.

SLOTH

When most people think of sloth, they think of laziness. However, laziness is primarily a sin against fortitude, not a sin against charity. Slothful people can be very hard working, but they are not doing the proper actions. Sloth is the sin of choosing to avoid doing the actions that God is calling a person to perform. In other words, charity requires that humans make God's goals their goals and perform every action out of love for God. Instead of doing what they know God wants them to be doing, slothful people do other things. These other things may be good in themselves, but they are not what these people know God is calling them to do at that moment. For example, when done in moderation, spending time on Internet sites to learn about friends and family is a good thing. However, if students are spending time on these sites when they should instead be studying, they are committing the sin of sloth. They are not doing what their calling from God requires them to do. People with sloth may work very hard. For example, if a father spends nearly all day at the office and does not spend the proper amount of time raising his children, he is definitely not lazy, but he is committing the sin of sloth. Traditionally, sloth has been described as a sorrow toward a spiritual good. This sorrow keeps people from performing spiritually good actions.[72] In other words, it is a vice where humans see good acts as unpleasant and do something else instead.

Hatred of God

The greatest natural inclination in humans is to the universal good of God. Therefore, of all the sins, hatred of God is the most repugnant to human nature. Because it is so contrary to human nature, it is also very difficult to commit. Generally, humans who believe that they hate God are actually hating a completely incorrect image of God. Nonetheless, humans with a vicious will can hate God because he is the source of things like natural disasters, punishments for sin, and other things that may cause real or perceived suffering. If someone truly knew what they were doing and freely chose to hate God, then hatred of God would be the most serious of all sins. However, since ignorance in the intellect and unruly emotions decrease the voluntariness of actions, most people who hate God are probably only minimally culpable for their actions. In addition, because love of God requires that humans love all others, hatred of other humans is also a serious sin.[73]

Envy

Envy is a sin against love of others. Envy is the sin of sorrowing at another's good fortune or rejoicing at another's misfortune. For example, if George is happy when Joe loses his job, George commits the sin of envy. If two people are really of one mind and heart, then they rejoice in each other's good fortunes and sorrow in each other's misfortunes. One of the great things about friendship is that it allows humans to be happy when good things happen to other people. Because they can share in the happiness and joys of others, humans can experience much greater happiness than if they only focused on themselves. Envy is contrary to the love of friendship.

Discord

Whereas charity unites many hearts as one, discord destroys the unity between hearts. Discord is the sin of destroying unity between people either by fighting with others or by causing people to fight with each other. In both cases, the sin is caused by people not making the goals and needs of others their own. Discord is a sin against concord or peace. It is the opposite of being a peacemaker who seeks to unite minds and hearts. For example, suppose Jill shares a suite with a group of girls. If she gets into a fight with one of the girls, she causes discord to exist between them. If she begins to try to bring other girls into the fight, then she can cause discord among all the girls in the suite as they begin to pick sides. The sin of discord is particularly serious if it breaks the unity between people that stems from faith and love of Christ.[74] If discord is done by speech, then it is called contention.

SCHISM

Schism is the sin of separating oneself from the unity of the Catholic Church. Unlike heresy, where someone denies an essential element of the faith, those who commit the sin of schism still believe in the fullness of the faith. However, they intend to sever themselves from the Church. Aquinas states: "Now the unity of the Church consists in two things; namely, in the mutual connection or communion of the members of the Church, and again in the subordination of all the members of the Church to the one head . . . the Pope. Wherefore, schismatics are those who refuse to submit to the Pope, and to hold communion with those members of the Church who acknowledge his supremacy."[75] Like discord, schism is a sin against peace.

SCANDAL

Scandal is the sin of acting, speaking, or living is such a way that others are led to think that an evil act is permitted. Those who commit scandal lead the young or those who are morally weak into sin. For example, suppose Megan lives with her boyfriend before they are married in order to save money. She frequently invites her teenage sister to their house. Even if Megan and her boyfriend are not intending to participate in sexual activities, they still commit the sin of scandal. They commit this sin because they could cause Megan's sister to believe that sex before marriage (or placing oneself in a state of temptation to have sex before marriage) is acceptable.[76]

When the young or the morally weak are present, it is essential not only to avoid sin but also to avoid appearing to commit sin, lest others be led to believe that an evil action is good. Because others are led astray in scandal, it functions as a type of temptation and is the opposite of the guidance mentors are called to give. Those who lead others to sin cause vices, which result in unhappiness.[77]

Although every sin is against charity, by contradicting love of God, the above sins are directly against unity with God or others. Pride keeps people from having love of friendship with God and others. Lukewarmness keeps people from loving intensely and thus decreases their unity with God. Sloth violates unity because people with sloth do not make God's goals their own. Hatred of God completely destroys unity with God, and hatred of other people destroys unity with other people. Envy destroys unity with other people because those with envy do not share in each other's joys and sufferings. Discord and schism are sins where unity between humans is directly destroyed. Finally, scandal keeps people from being united to God and each other by leading the morally vulnerable to vice.

CHARITY IS THE greatest of all types of love. It is an attraction to God himself and causes people to seek to be united to God. Because of this desire for union, humans can perform all of their actions out of love for God. Thus, charity causes all actions and virtues to be ordered to God himself. Since every virtue is ordered to God by charity, technically the acquisition of any virtue helps humans to act with charity. However, there are some virtues that when cultivated especially cause humans to grow in charity. These virtues, such as prayer and mercy, help humans to grow in greater unity with God and with all others. The beatitudes are obligations of the new covenant to know and love God through faith and charity. By following the beatitudes, charity and the ensuing unity with God are increased. To help humans know what God wants them to do, the gift of wisdom perfects charity. Finally, the sins against charity destroy unity with God and other people.

The theological virtues of faith, hope, and charity act as supernatural inclinations to divine actions. They supernaturally perfect the natural inclinations. On the natural level, the natural inclinations are perfected by the acquired virtues so that they are powerful enough to cause humans to perform good actions by means of their own knowledge and love. Since grace perfects nature, just as the natural inclinations cause more perfect human actions through the acquired virtues, the theological virtues cause more perfect divine actions through the infused cardinal virtues of prudence, justice, temperance, and fortitude. Therefore, we will next study the infused cardinal virtues.

15

PRUDENCE

The Virtue of Making Good Decisions

Once humans have faith and charity, they are able to perform actions ordered to the goal of eternal happiness. They can now seek God in every good action that they perform. With the help of the gifts of understanding and knowledge, they are able to form many goals that are ordered to the ultimate end of eternal happiness. The virtue of charity gives them the ability to intend these goals. However, even if humans intend to love God in all their actions, they may not know the best way to love him. Finding the right action in every situation is often very difficult. Situations can be very complex, and many possible actions can appear to be the best. Following laws can help, but even laws must be applied to a particular situation. To find the actions that most conform with the eternal law, which is God's plan for each individual, humans need the virtue of prudence. Prudence is the virtue that perfects the intellect to determine and command the best way of attaining an end. In other words, prudence perfects the intellect to be good at applying goals and laws to particular situations. Since the intellect applies goals to a situation in the steps of counsel, judgment, and command, prudence perfects all of these steps. In this chapter we will first examine the steps of counsel, judgment, and command, along with the corresponding subvirtues under prudence, then we'll look at the Holy Spirit's gift of counsel, and, finally, we'll treat the vices against prudence.

THE NATURE OF PRUDENCE

In order to perform an action, the intellect must intend an end (a goal or law) and determine the way to apply this end to particular situation. Prudence is used to find the proper means to apply an intended end.[1] For example, humans with the virtue of understanding know that helping the poor is good. By means of the virtue of justice they then intend to help the poor. Prudence allows the reason to find the best way to help the poor and then commands the action. In determining and commanding the best action, the intellect goes through three steps: counsel, judgment, and command. All three of these steps must be perfected for someone to be considered prudent.

COUNSEL

Once a goal is intended, humans begin to take counsel. In this step, they begin an inquiry into how to reach the intended end. They start with the end, the most universal premise, and reason to more and more particular premises until they come to a conclusion that can be performed at that moment. For example, if Kate's end is to graduate, she then asks, "What do I need to do to graduate?" She determines that she needs to pass her classes. She then asks, "What do I need to do to pass my classes?" She eventually comes to an action she can do at that moment, such as study or get a good night's rest.

Each time humans reason to a new a conclusion that becomes a new premise, they complete a practical syllogism. A practical syllogism has a universal premise (the law or goal), a particular premise that reflects the situation, and a conclusion. For example, the premise that helping the poor is good is a universal premise. The premise that the best way to help the poor in this situation is to give money to a relief agency is the particular premise. The conclusion would then be that it is good to give money to a relief agency. In order for humans to apply a law or goal to a situation, they must do *research* to determine the particular premise and *reason* to a conclusion. For example, in determining how to pass her class, Kate needs to research all of the relevant aspects of the situation, such as how well is she prepared for an upcoming test, how well does she function on low sleep, and so on. She learns that she is not well prepared and therefore needs to study a great deal. She then reasons to the conclusion that in order to pass the class she must study that night.

The subvirtue under prudence that perfects counsel is *euboulia*. *Euboulia* is derived from the Greek words *eu* ("good") and *boule* ("counsel") and literally means "good counsel." *Euboulia* perfects the practical intellect to move from the universal propositions (the end) to a particular action by researching and reasoning. Aquinas explains that an ideal act of counsel includes the following five steps: "memory of the past, understanding of the present, shrewdness in considering the future outcome, reasoning which compares one thing to another, and docility in accepting the opinions of others."[2] Therefore, when researching, the intellect first considers relevant past experiences. Next, it understands the current situation and forms the particular premise. Then it determines whether or not the universal premise (the goal or law) can be applied in this situation.[3] If it can be applied, then the intellect uses reason to derive the proper conclusion from the syllogism.[4] Since prudence is concerned with particular matters, which are of an infinite variety, no human can consider them all sufficiently. Thus, the last step is to seek the advice of the wise. Humans with the virtue of *euboulia* are able to understand all the important aspects of a situation and determine whether or not a law or goal applies in this situation.

For example, suppose Kate needs to decide how much to study for a test. She first considers past experiences. Was the amount that she studied in the past sufficient for similar tests? She continues her research by looking at the present situation—how well prepared is she? How much material does the test cover? She then inquires, based on her current situation, whether she can fulfill her goal of studying enough to pass. If she can, she then reasons to a conclusion: she needs to study for five hours. Throughout the entire process, the advice of other humans can be helpful or even necessary. She might consult with other students who have had this professor before. She should especially seek the help of the Holy Spirit. Even though all of these steps do not need to be followed in every action, someone possessing *euboulia* easily and competently does what is necessary to make good decisions.

Although the primary function of prudence is not to determine goals, its methodology does teach humans how to set good goals.[5] In reasoning to an action, one begins with the highest or most universal goal and reasons to an action that can be done in the particular moment. The same is true with setting goals. Humans should begin with the most universal or highest goal and reason to more and more particular (or lower) goals. Since all actions should be ordered to love of God, the highest goal is the attainment of God for all eternity. The next highest goal can vary with different people, but it is generally the state of life (or vocation) that God calls someone to fulfill. After this goal, the next highest goal might be serving others through one's occupation and so forth. Goals are good if they are truly ordered to God and all relevant higher goals. Consequently, to make sure that a goal is good, it can be helpful to begin at the highest goal (attaining God) and work backwards until a goal fitting the current situation can be determined.

Although counsel is an indispensable step in many actions, it is not always necessary. With most actions that humans perform, they have already taken counsel. If Joe always goes to Mass every morning before work, he does not have to take counsel each time he wakes up—he has already done it. Sometimes people do not take counsel when they should, and they instead perform an action without thinking about the best way to attain it. For example, many people do not take good counsel in determining what vocation God is calling them to. The key is to make sure that counsel is (or was) taken on all important decisions, and if a situation should change, counsel should be taken again.

JUDGMENT

Once a possible action has been determined by counsel and the will consents to it, the action must be judged to determine whether it is in accord with the law or end. The action must be judged to be both in accord with the proximate end (the goal or law intended) and the higher ends, including the ultimate end.[6] If two or more possible actions emerge from counsel, then judgment determines which action is most in accord with the intended end and the higher ends. For example, imagine that Joe and Kate get married and have many children. Joe works hard during the week and *intends* the goal of getting some recreation on the weekend. He takes *counsel* and decides to go golfing every Saturday and Sunday. He then *judges* this decision. Golfing would indeed fulfill his intention of recreation. He then must judge by higher goals. Is the act of golfing ordered to the higher goal of being a good father and husband? If golfing on weekends causes him to neglect his obligation to help his wife and children attain eternal happiness, then golfing is not a good action. Since Joe loves God by loving his family, if the act contradicts his responsibilities toward his family, it also contradicts his ultimate end of doing all things out of love for God. If Joe's vocational responsibilities are compromised, then he would be committing the sin of sloth by golfing.

An example showing how an action would not attain the intended goal (rather than higher goals) might be fraternal correction. Joe could intend to correct his friend George by telling him that getting drunk is wrong. Joe must then judge whether or not this act would actually attain his goal of correcting George. He might judge that instead of immediately telling George that getting drunk is wrong, he might have to cultivate a stronger friendship before telling him that it is wrong.

Whereas counsel reasons from the more universal to the more particular, judgment determines whether or not a particular action is ordered to more universal ends. In other words, counsel derives lower principles from higher ones, while judgment determines whether lower principles are properly ordered to higher ones. Judgment ensures that humans are consistently acting in conformity with their highest ends. Furthermore, it is the act of judgment that ultimately determines whether or not an action is moral. Counsel finds the means of attaining any goal that is intended by the will, even if the goal is evil. Judgment not only verifies whether or not the action attains the goal; it also determines if the action is good, the goal is good, and if the action is ultimately ordered to God. Because it determines the morality of an action judgment is the act of following one's conscience.

Since the intellect judges by both the intended end and the higher ends, two virtues perfect the act of judgment. *Synesis* perfects the ability of the intellect to judge whether or not an action would attain the intended goal. Practical wisdom (in the Greek this virtue was called *gnome*) perfects the ability of the intellect to judge by higher goals.[7] Those with the virtue of *synesis* are good at determining whether or not an action will fulfill their intention. If there are multiple possibilities, they are good at determining the best action to attain their intention. Those with the virtue of practical wisdom judge all their actions by their higher ends. They are good at determining if the action is truly good and ordered to God. For example, if Kate is hungry, she might have the goal of satisfying her hunger. Through *synesis* she might judge that eating ten jelly donuts would fulfill her goal of satisfying hunger, but through practical wisdom she should would judge that it would violate her higher goal of health.

COMMAND

Command is the ability of the intellect to cause the will to implement whatever action the intellect has judged to be good and the will has chosen. For example, if Kate decides that she will study for eight hours, her intellect must constantly remain *focused* on studying for those eight hours (less needed breaks). It must constantly be commanding the will to study. It must also constantly be evaluating the situation to determine if the situation has substantially changed. If the situation has substantially changed, then the intellect must determine whether to continue doing the action or whether to determine a new goal. Command is the chief act of prudence since prudence is right reason applied to action.[8] A defect in counsel or judgment diminishes the voluntariness of an action, because the person does not fully understand what is being done. However, a defect in command does not diminish voluntariness since the person already knows what should be done. Thus, a defect in command is particularly sinful, and a virtue is especially needed to perfect it. Prudence itself is the virtue that perfects the intellect to command well. Although prudence perfects the ability to take counsel and judge, it especially makes humans good at commanding an action that has already been chosen.

PRUDENCE IN GENERAL

Not only does prudence perfect the intellect to determine the proper action, it also perfects the intellect to find the mean in the moral virtues. Prudence discovers the mean both by determining the proper intensity of the appetitive powers (the will and emotions) and by determining the proper object of these powers. An example of determining the proper intensity is found in the virtue of piety. Piety is the virtue perfecting the will to give honor to those who cannot be repaid. Traditionally, piety was owed to God, parents, and country. Prudence determines the proper amount of honor be given to these persons. Too little honor results in the vice of impiety. Too much honor (for those other than God) results in idolatry. (Of course, there is no limit to the amount of honor that can be given to God.) An example of determining the proper object is the virtue of chastity. Chastity orders the emotions to have the proper amount of sexual desire. Prudence determines what sexual actions should be desired (because they are good actions) and what sexual actions should not be desired (because they are evil actions).

Acquired prudence is very difficult to attain because many experiences are necessary to properly determine the right action in the numerous different situations people will encounter in their lives. In other words, acquired prudence cannot be in young persons, for they can never have lived through enough life experiences to have practical wisdom (but the advice of others can help). However, infused prudence, which is given by God, allows the Holy Spirit through the gifts of wisdom and counsel to make up for the young person's lack of experience so that even a child can be wise. For example, many young saints have acted with a wisdom beyond their years.

Like all virtues, infused prudence is perfected by performing like actions of greater intensity. Humans must practice making and commanding good decisions. They should practice all of the steps perfected by prudence. To practice taking good counsel, humans should attempt to form a habit of thinking and reading about various possible situations before they actually encounter them. They should think about what they would do in these situations and what others who have encountered these situations have done. When they are actually researching the situation, they must practice considering past experiences, and they should especially seek out the wisdom of others who have already made similar types of decisions. The Holy Spirit should always be consulted. After understanding the situation, they should practice reasoning to conclusions. Finally, they should reflect on past decisions to determine what they should have done differently.

To practice judgment, humans need to get into the habit of judging whether or not the proposed action will actually fulfill their intention. *Most importantly, they must get into the habit of always judging actions by higher principles.* Whenever they act, they need to ask themselves how the action will affect other people and whether the action is actually ordered to God. Once they get into this habit, they can consciously begin the task of devoting every moment of their life to serving God. Not only will this help them perform good actions, it will also significantly increase their happiness since they will be contemplating God in performing their actions.

Finally, humans must get into the habit of commanding good actions. They need to practice staying intellectually focused until the action is completed. Sometimes an action can take years to complete. Although it is impossible to think about an action every moment over the course of years, humans need to develop a habit of staying focused so that they command themselves to work on the action whenever the opportunity arises.

In addition to the virtues of *euboulia* (good counsel), *synesis*, and practical wisdom, there are a number of other virtues that go along with prudence. These virtues are docility, foresight, the ability to reason well, and caution. Docility is the virtue of being open to the wisdom of others. Since humans cannot experience every situation, they need the advice of wise people, the teachings of the Catholic Church, and the inspiration of God in order to know the proper action.

Foresight is the virtue of being able to "foresee" a future goal and figure out how to attain it. Those with the virtue of foresight have a vision of what they want to attain, and they do the proper actions now in order to fulfill their vision. For example, parents have a vision of their children as good adults, and they establish good habits in their children now so that their children will become good adults. All good leaders have the virtue of foresight.

The virtue of being good at practical reasoning is just what it sounds like and needs no further explanation. The virtue of caution perfects the intellect to be careful to avoid doing evil when performing an action. Often an action that appears good can have evil effects that are not foreseen. Caution causes people to try to think of the future consequence of their actions before they act.[9]

Although prudence is not as excellent as the theological virtues, the theological virtues must work through prudence to cause their proper actions. Faith and charity provide the supernatural inclinations to perform divine actions, but prudence determines the actions themselves. Without prudence, humans will not be able to implement faith and charity into their lives. Prudence perfects the intellect to determine and command the actions that lead to eternal happiness. The greater the prudence, the greater the participation in the eternal law and the more perfectly humans are able to share in God's divine plan.

THE HOLY SPIRIT'S GIFT OF COUNSEL

Since prudence perfects the intellect to take good counsel, it is fitting that the gift of the Holy Spirit that perfects prudence is counsel. This gift perfects the intellect so that God can guide the intellect to determine the best action to fulfill a particular law or goal. In many actions there are multiple variables that are nearly impossible to understand and that make it difficult to determine what to do. The gift of counsel helps the intellect determine what aspects of a situation are important to the action and helps the intellect understand these aspects. God already knows the best action, and the Holy Spirit can guide the intellect to a greater understanding of the situation. For example, political decisions, such as how the government of a country should interact with a violent foreign dictator or how to fix the health-care industry, are extremely complex and include many variables that are unknown or difficult to understand. Even actions such as helping a friend or determining the best way to help a student can have variables that are difficult to determine. The gift of counsel helps the intellect better understand the situation so that better actions can be determined. This gift works with the gift of wisdom, which perfects the ability of both the intellect and the will to judge by divine principles.

VICES AGAINST PRUDENCE

All the Ten Commandments are applied to a particular situation by prudence and could be treated under this virtue. However, since the commandments more directly pertain to other virtues, none of them will be treated here. There are four vices against prudence: rashness, foolishness, inconstancy, and negligence.

Rashness (precipitation)[10] is the opposite of *euboulia*; it is failure to take good counsel. Humans are rash when they fail to take the time to properly assess the situation and reason to a conclusion. For example, Joe is rash if he does not research a car before he buys it.

Foolishness is the opposite of *synesis* and practical wisdom. Foolish people fail to judge whether or not the action is in accord with either the intended end or the higher ends. These people may be very good at fulfilling their goals but still perform evil actions. For example, a young woman might have the good goal of making her parents happy but end up having an abortion to fulfill this goal. She would perform an evil action, because she fails to judge by the higher principle that humans have a right to life because they are naturally inclined to it.

Inconstancy is the vice of failing to command what has been chosen. A sin of inconstancy takes place when people have already determined and chosen a good action, but they instead choose a different, evil action (including not acting at all) because of the influence of the emotions on the reason. For example, Kate might choose to study and actually begin studying, but then she becomes distracted and instead watches a movie. Inconstancy is especially common in people with the vices of sloth, laziness, and lust.

Negligence is the vice of failing to perform the proper actions in the present in order to avoid possible future bad effects from an action. It is a failure to be attentive to what should be done in a particular situation. For example, it is negligent to leave a loaded gun where a child can get it. It is also negligent for parents not to discipline their children.

PRUDENCE PERFECTS the intellect so that humans are able to govern themselves and others. If prudence is acquired, it gives people the ability to perform "more perfect human actions" and attain greater happiness. If prudence is infused, it allows the intellect to be supernaturally guided by the Holy Spirit so that humans can perform "more perfect divine actions" that are ordered to eternal happiness. Since infused prudence causes specific acts of charity, actions flowing from it are done with supernatural knowledge and love. Consequently, they cause supernatural happiness on earth. Those with prudence are also able to make laws that guide and motivate others, especially children, to grow in virtue. These parents and wise mentors have the practical wisdom that is necessary to form the next generation.

Prudence and the subvirtues of *euboulia*, *synesis*, and practical wisdom also give further guidance on how to perfect particular steps within the twelve steps of the human action. If people have trouble taking counsel, the virtue of *euboulia* and the Holy Spirit's gift of counsel will help them. If people have trouble judging, they need the virtues of *synesis* and practical wisdom, along with the Holy Spirit's gift of wisdom. Finally, prudence itself perfects the ability of people to command good actions.

16

JUSTICE
Part One

Justice is the virtue of giving others what they deserve. However, there are different ways of understanding this definition. In today's world, when most people feel that they have been treated unfairly, they want justice. Generally, this means one of two things. They either want the persons or group that treated them unfairly to be punished, or they want to be compensated for their loss.[1] This incomplete sense of justice evolved from a more deontological understanding of the term. In a deontological system, morality is about following laws and receiving external rewards and punishments. Hence, in this type of system, justice is primarily focused on two things: the rewards and punishments for keeping or breaking the law and the proper compensation for the exchange of goods (in the broad sense of the term). For example, if a person steals a loaf of bread, he has violated justice by not paying for the bread (not giving proper compensation), and he deserves justice (a punishment) for breaking the law. Justice is the virtue of giving others what they deserve, where what they deserve is determined primarily by the law, which can be from God (as in heteronomy), the civil authority, or an autonomous subject (as when people claim to have false rights).

Although there is some truth in this more deontological understanding of justice, in a teleological system the focus is different: *the most important aspect of justice is that it perfects the ability of humans to love others.* Humans generally have no trouble loving themselves, but they need the virtue of justice to perfect the will to love God and others in order to give others what they truly deserve. The things that humans truly deserve (rather than just claim to deserve) derive from two sources: human nature and human actions.[2] In other words, some things are due to other humans by their very nature, while other things are due to other humans because of their actions. In relation to their nature, humans have an authentic need for all those things that are necessary to attain true natural happiness. These authentic needs can be known from natural law and correspond to the natural rights of humans. For example, humans have natural rights to things such as food, education, friendship, and religion because all of these things are necessary for natural happiness. Justice causes humans to love others by giving them those things necessary to attain true happiness. For example, because humans love others and make the needs of others their own, the just person gives food to the poor because food is essential for true happiness. In relation to human actions, if someone puts their own work and effort into something, they deserve either to have some ownership of the thing they worked on or to be compensated for their work. Humans are perfected by their actions, and their work becomes an extension of their personality. Consequently, justice requires proper compensation for human work. For example, if people work all day in a factory, they deserve a *just* wage. A wage that is both proportional to the amount and type of work that they did and that is sufficient for them to attain the goods that fulfill their natural rights.[3] Again, because justice perfects the ability to love others, the just employer loves the employees and pays them just wages.

Based on this teleological understanding of justice, *justice can be defined as the virtue perfecting the will to love God and others by giving them what is owed to them, either on account of their natural needs or on account of their actions.*[4] Justice both perfects the will to give others all those things that are necessary for them to attain natural happiness, and it perfects the will to give others just compensation for their actions. This compensation might be material, but it might also be such things as honor, gratitude, or praise.

Because humans *deserve* all their natural rights, the modern use of the term "justice" is not entirely wrong. People who have been deprived of their natural rights should be given justice: their natural rights should be reinstated. However, if people seek justice in cases where they are deprived of a *false* right, they completely miss the true meaning of justice. False rights do not lead to happiness, and those who love others only make the *legitimate* needs of others their own. They do not make the artificial or false needs of the other their own. For example, people claim to have the right to make and distribute pornography. This is a false right, and friends do not help others attain false needs that ultimately lead to false happiness.

Authentic rights are all those things that are necessary for humans to fulfill their nature by entering into loving relationships with God and others. Examples of these rights are the right to life (and all those things intrinsically related to this right, e.g., food, health care, security), education, religion, truthful communication, property, work, culture, to be part of a family, to properly raise children, and all other things that flow from natural law. Justice perfects the will to love others by constantly giving others their natural rights.

Many of these natural rights have a corresponding virtue that perfects the will to give this right to others. For example, honesty is a virtue that deals with the natural right to truthful communication. Also, since humans deserve just compensation for good actions, there are many virtues dealing with how to repay others. For example, piety is the virtue of giving due honor to those who can never be materially repaid. Because there are many natural rights and types of situations that require compensation, there are many subvirtues that correspond to justice. Since humans have an obligation to give others what they need to attain natural happiness, there are also many commandments that correspond to justice. In this chapter, I devote a short section to justice in general, then we will analyze the subvirtues that correspond to justice. Next there is a section on the first four commandments, which pertain to justice. (We will cover the fifth, seventh, eighth, and tenth commandments in chapter 17.) And, lastly, we will look at the vices and sins against justice, with their corresponding commandments.

JUSTICE

Justice perfects the will to love others and God by giving them what they naturally deserve. Because the will is an appetitive power, justice, like temperance and fortitude, seeks a mean between excess and defect.[5] However, whereas temperance and fortitude seek a mean in relation to the subject, the mean for justice is external and based upon the *relation* that the subject has to the person or thing that is loved. For example, in practicing temperance, the amount of food that one person should desire will be different than the amount of food that someone else desires, because of differences in metabolism, size, exercise, and so on. Hence, the mean is dependent upon the subject because it varies with every person. However, with justice the mean is external and based on the relation that a person has to others. For example, children must obey their parents. Too little love of parents, resulting in a lack of obedience, is the sin of disobedience. Too much love can result in children even obeying unjust laws, which would be contrary to love of God. The relation that the children have to their parents dictates the amount and the way that they should be loved.

There are different types of justice based on the different relations between humans. The types of justice are *commutative, distributive,* and *social.*[6] Commutative justice refers to the mutual dealings between humans. For example, in the economic sphere, just prices must be paid for property and just wages for labor. Distributive justice refers to the relation between a larger entity (such as the state or a corporation) and the individual. Generally, this type of justice refers to how the government must distribute goods justly by not favoring one group over another. It can also refer to how any larger institution, such as a corporation, distributes its goods to individuals. The distribution does not necessarily have to be equal, but any discrepancy in amounts between individuals must be for the good of the whole while respecting the needs of each individual. Social justice refers to the relation between each individual (or institution) and the common good. All humans must do all things for the sake of the common good.[7] For example, when investing money, people should not seek to make large profits at the expense of the common good.[8]

Justice is increased, like all other virtues, by doing like acts of a greater intensity. Since justice perfects love, it is increased whenever people make the natural needs of others their own and work to fulfill these needs. Just people are constantly observing others to determine what they need to be naturally fulfilled. Their love then drives them to give these people their natural needs. Since justice is based on relationships, in seeking to fulfill the needs of others, just people begin with those to whom they have the closest relationships and work out from there. For example, I would begin by honoring God. Then, I would seek to meet the natural needs of my wife and children, both material and spiritual. Then, I would seek to meet the natural needs of my students for education. Then, I would seek to meet the needs of my extended family and friends and so forth. Those with greater needs must also be given preference. Hence, I must especially seek to meet the material and spiritual needs of the poor.[9] No human has the time or resources to fulfill all the needs of all others, but just people seek to aid as many people as possible. Prudence is required for humans to determine how to best use their time, talent, and material goods in serving others. Just people further seek to love with as much intensity as possible in helping others.

SUBVIRTUES UNDER JUSTICE

Humans, who have both a body and a soul, require many different things in order to be naturally fulfilled. Because the soul works through the body, the body must be given proper care. Thus, humans have natural needs, such as food, shelter, and health care. Furthermore, the soul must be perfected through education and training so that it can perform its proper actions of knowing and loving. Hence, humans have additional needs, such as education, religion, and work. Although justice in general perfects the will to fulfill all of these needs, because there are so many, a variety of different virtues under justice must be attained so that humans are in the habit of giving others their basic rights. We now examine the virtues of *piety, religion, friendship, gratitude, obedience, honesty, liberality, industry*, and *stewardship*.

PIETY

Friends will do good things for others without expecting any repayment, but because of their love, those who receive these good things seek to repay their benefactors. Hence, justice requires that we repay others for things that they give us. Sometimes, however, people give us things that either should not be repaid (like certain gifts from a friend) or cannot be repaid. Piety is the habit of giving honor to those whom we can never repay, because the things they have done for us are too great. Piety is first and foremost directed to God, who has given us everything. Piety must also be given to our parents, our nation,[10] our teachers, and the saints. In other words, these persons have all done things for us that are beyond material worth. We can only repay them by giving them honor. In reference to created persons, piety is the mean between impiety and idolatry. Those who do not give the proper honor to their parents, nation, teachers, and saints commit the sin of impiety. Those who give too much honor commit the sin of idolatry, since they treat them like God. God can never be given too much honor.

Religion

Because honoring God is categorically different from honoring humans or saints, there is a specific virtue devoted to honoring God: religion. This virtue perfects the will to honor God as our creator and governor. Since God can be known by natural reason, all people can have the virtue of religion in various degrees. Although God does not need the honor of humans, religion is a virtue because humans honor God *not* for his sake, but for their sake, so that their ability to love him will be perfected.

God is honored through acts of worship. Through worship, humans express their praise of God and acknowledge his excellence. Specific acts of worship are acts of devotion, prayer, adoration, sacrifice, and making vows and promises to God.[11] Throughout human history, humans in nearly all cultures have practiced the virtue of religion in these ways.

An important aspect of the virtue of religion is reverence. Reverence refers to the way that religious activities are performed. Humans with the virtue of religion not only worship God through acts of devotion, they worship God in a *reverent* manner. Reverence arises from the distinction between the sacred and the profane. When humans are in the presence of God, they recognize that the way they act in worshipping God should transcend their mode of acting in the secular world. For example, Moses in the presence of God removes his sandals (Ex 3:5). Ezekiel falls on his face before the Lord (Ez 1:2), and the twenty-four elders in the book of Revelation fall down before the thrown and worship God (Rev 4). Reverent actions manifest the humility of humans in the presence of the infinite God.

Another aspect of religion is tithing. Traditionally, "to tithe" meant to give one-tenth of one's income. However, I am using the term to mean any money that is given to the Church. Almost universally throughout human history, worship has taken place within a community.[12] Within the Christian tradition, true worship takes place within the Church where the praises and sacrifices of the people are united to the one sacrifice of Christ. Hence, the Church is essential to worship, which is essential to human happiness. Consequently, humans have a natural law obligation to materially support the Church. Prudence is necessary to determine how much money should be given based on the needs of the Church and the wealth of the individual.

Friendship

When a person performs many acts of love of friendship toward another, the virtue of friendship is perfected.[13] True friends are in the habit of constantly loving each other by making the needs, goals, and sufferings of the other their own. The habit of friendship results in a unity of mind and heart between humans.

Since humans are required to love all others out of love for God (charity), it might seem odd to have the subsection of friendship in the section on justice. The relationship between charity and the virtue of friendship is similar to the relationship between charity and the virtue of religion. Love of friendship of God (charity) requires that due honor be given to God (religion). Nonetheless, humans have a natural inclination to honor God, from whom all things come, and thus even apart from charity humans are required to give honor to God. Because justice perfects the will to love others by giving them their natural rights, religion is an act of justice. Charity then perfects the virtue of religion so that when honoring God, he is not only loved naturally but also supernaturally.

The same relationship applies to the virtue of friendship. Charity also requires that humans love all other humans. However, in order for humans to be naturally happy, they must enter into permanent loving relationships with other humans. Friends are essential to happiness because they help move and guide humans to good acts, they give humans someone to know and love, and they allow humans to share in the joys and happiness of their friend, with whom they are of one mind and heart.[14] Because friends are essential for natural happiness, humans have a natural right to have friends. Consequently, friendship is a virtue under justice, which perfects the will to give others their natural rights. Although it is impossible to be good friends with everyone because of our limited nature, humans should prudently seek to be friends with those who have few or no friends. Charity then perfects this love of friendship, so that other humans are not only loved for their own sake but also out of love for God. Even when humans love others out of love of God, they must still practice acts of friendship towards others to grow in greater unity of mind and heart.[15]

Gratitude

When people do something good for someone, that person's will loves the good that was done and responds with an act of love. Hence, people seek to repay others. Sometimes good actions are given as gifts, and the giver does not wish to be repaid, or the gifts are too great to repay. Those with love of others respond with gratitude. Gratitude is the virtue of being thankful for gifts that are received. Gratitude can be either directed toward God, who has given us everything, or toward other humans. An important part of worship is giving thanks to God. In fact, the word "eucharist" comes from the Greek word *eucharisteo* meaning "to give thanks." Gratitude is also closely linked to happiness, because when one performs an act of gratitude, she is contemplating the goods she has received.

Obedience

Obedience is the virtue of obeying authority figures immediately and joyfully. Obedience extends first and foremost to God, who rules by his eternal law. However, since God rules by means of secondary governors, humans must also be obedient to those in authority over them. For example, civil leaders and parents establish human laws based on the eternal law as known through the divine and natural laws. The magisterium of the Catholic Church guides humans with divine laws and human laws derived from these divine laws. Humans must be guided and moved by laws in order to grow in virtue and attain happiness. Because human laws perfect the powers of the soul, they increase authentic freedom. Since obedience is essential for humans to freely attain happiness, justice requires that if a law is just, it must be obeyed.

Obedience is the mean between disobedience and obeying those laws that are unjust or do not apply in a particular situation. Unjust laws should not be obeyed since they guide humans to evil actions that cause unhappiness for themselves and others. Those who obey unjust laws, due to a lack of justice, have too much love for the lawgivers in that they will obey humans over and against God. In cases where the law does not apply to a situation, the virtue of obedience might mean disregarding a lower law for the sake of a higher law. Even the best of human laws are not comprehensive enough to cover every situation, as seen in chapter 15 with the virtue of practical wisdom, which determines when a law does not apply to a particular situation. The virtue of equity (*epikea*) perfects the will to choose and execute what practical wisdom determines. In other words, because good humans are in the habit of obeying laws that apply in normal situations, it can be difficult to disobey in an extraordinary situation when the law does not apply. The virtue of equity perfects the will to love the right action in these situations. For example, if humans are in the habit of following the speed limit, it can be difficult for them to prudently exceed it in a situation where they must speed to save someone's life (the higher end).

Honesty

Honesty is the virtue of always communicating the truth. As seen in chapter 14 in the section on prayer, communication is ordered to unity. Humans cannot share each other's needs and goals unless their knowledge of each other is true. Communication of the truth is essential for true unity. Lies and falsehoods destroy relationships—and society. All segments of society, from the economic sphere to the medical sphere, require honest communication for them to perform their proper functions of aiding society. The virtue of honesty is the mean between lying and divulging more truth than one should. Just as lies can destroy unity, gossiping and telling other truths that should not be spoken can also destroy unity.

Because honesty is the virtue concerning the communication of truth, it also pertains to how truth is conveyed. Although intermediary instruments (such as written letters) have always been used to communicate with others, face-to-face communication, where both people are able to observe the verbal and nonverbal language of others, is extremely important to loving relationships. In modern times, because of the increase in technology, digital forms of communication often replace face-to-face communication. It is not uncommon to go to a public place and see an entire group of people focused solely on their handheld devices. They may be in the physical presence of each other, but they are not communicating love to each other in a meaningful sense. Certainly, these devices can be very important and helpful in society, but they can also diminish and harm personal relationships. Love of friendship requires that humans at certain times focus their complete and undivided attention on those whom they love. Piety and the respect of others also require that in certain situations humans should be completely attentive to others. For example, it is disrespectful to text, surf the Internet, or play games in a classroom setting (unless there is an emergency situation requiring texting).

Because improper use of technological devices in communication is a violation of justice, the prudent person would find the mean between the defect of never using technology in communication and the excess where technological devices diminish or destroy the truly meaningful communication that is necessary for maintaining love of friendship.[16] The prudent person will intentionally seek to spend time in face-to-face communication with their family, friends, and others. This person will recognize that it can be rude to use one's handheld devices when sharing a meal with others. At the same time, they will also properly use technology to build unity within society, such as using technology to communicate with others in foreign countries.

LIBERALITY

Liberality is the virtue of spending and acquiring money (or other material goods) in the right ways and in the right amounts. All humans need material goods in order to fulfill their natural inclination to bodily health. Consequently, all humans have a natural right to the material goods that are necessary for human fulfillment. Liberality perfects the will so that humans obtain and use their material goods in a way that sustains the natural rights of others. Liberality is the mean between miserliness and prodigality. The miser does not spend enough; the prodigal person spends too much.

To specifically show how liberality perfects the will to help others, it is helpful to see how liberality is the mean in three different aspects of attaining and spending material goods: spending on oneself, spending on others, and acquiring money/material goods.

In reference to spending on oneself, Christians with liberality only spend what is necessary to meet their bodily and spiritual needs. Their extra money is used to help others. In contrast, misers do not spend enough money on themselves to live a life with dignity. For example, a miser might refuse essential medical care even though he has the money to pay for it, or he might refuse to heat his house even when he is sick. Prodigal people spend too much money on themselves. They buy and accumulate many things that they do not truly need. In the United States, the consumeristic culture causes people to have a tendency toward the vice of prodigality.[17] Most people have far more than they need, but others are lacking even the essentials of human dignity. Because the just person loves others, the essential needs of others become her own. Hence, humans fail to love others when they overconsume material goods when others lack essential goods.

In reference to spending on others, liberality again consists of spending the proper amount. Misers fail to spend enough money to meet the natural needs of others, even if they have more than enough for themselves. Prodigal people spend more than they can afford on others or spend money that is essential for their own physical and spiritual well-being. Whereas American culture tends to push people toward prodigality when it comes to spending on themselves, it causes people to be miserly when it comes to spending on others. Guided by natural law, people with liberality will use their excess income to help others. One way to help others is by giving money directly to the poor; however, people can also help others by giving them jobs or by investing in businesses that provide jobs for others.[18] The divine law moves the mean of liberality even closer to prodigality, as it calls humans to give even from their necessities.[19] Prudence must be used to determine how much should be spent on oneself and how much should be spent on others. When deciding whether or not to buy something for oneself, one can judge by higher principles by asking the following question: "Is this really necessary for my physical or spiritual well-being?" Even if humans answer yes to this question, they must still be careful because disordered emotions can cause them to invent false or artificial needs.[20] For example, many Americans wrongly believe that they "need" a luxurious house, when in fact a more modest house would satisfy their natural inclination to shelter. Consequently, in addition to the question of whether or not one truly needs a particular material good, one should also ask a further question to determine if the need is authentic. Perhaps they could ask, "Would a poor person in an underdeveloped country agree that this is necessary for physical or spiritual well-being?" If they realize that they do not truly need a particular material good, then, because of their love for others, people with liberality will not buy the item. Instead, they will use the money to help others.

In reference to acquiring money, people with liberality will acquire the proper amount of money in the proper way. In other words, because goods are distributed through the exchange of currency, some money is essential for people to meet the necessities of life. For example, if I have the opportunity to make enough money to support my family, I should attempt to do so, as long as I am not harming others or neglecting my family by doing this. In fact, Catholic social teaching says that people should make enough money to raise their families with dignity and to eventually acquire some property.[21] It is not wrong for people to make more money than they need, provided that they do not violate the natural rights of others when making the money and that they use the extra money for the good of all. The terms "miserly" and "prodigal" do not quite convey the meaning of the excess and defect for liberality used in this way. The defect is when people choose not to make enough money, even though they have the opportunity and a moral obligation to make money. The excess is when people harm others in order to make money, either by taking advantage of the hardships of others or by participating in immoral activities. People take advantage of the hardships of others when they overcharge the poor for an essential good (such as food or health care) or when they do not pay just wages to their employees.[22] Examples of making money in immoral ways include working in the pornography industry, participating in human trafficking, and selling illegal drugs.

Industry

Industry is the virtue of performing the proper type and amount of work.[23] Work is a natural right and is very important for human fulfillment. Humans serve others through their work, are personally perfected by their work, and are united by working with others.[24] Consequently, industry perfects the will to desire to help society by working. Work is defined as any activity that aids society and perfects humans. The defect is not working enough or performing immoral work. The excess is working too much at the expense of one's spiritual welfare. This virtue is distinct from liberality in acquiring money, because people can, and often do, work without getting paid. For example, parents work very hard raising children but usually are not materially compensated for their work.

Stewardship

Stewardship is the virtue of taking care of the created world. In the secular world, it is sometimes called "environmentalism" or "conservation." As Pope Benedict XVI states, "The environment is God's gift to everyone, and in our use of it we have a responsibility towards the poor, towards future generations, and towards humanity as a whole."[25] Stewardship perfects the will to love God and others by taking care of the environment. Benedict continues, "In nature, the believer recognizes the wonderful result of God's creative activity, which we may use responsibly to satisfy our legitimate needs, material or otherwise, while respecting the intrinsic balance of creation."[26] In other words, the environment is God's gift to humans to be used to help humans attain happiness, and it must be preserved and protected for current and future generations. The defect is neglecting the environment or abusing the environment.[27] The excess is treating the environment as more important than the human person.[28] Although the environment must be cared for, the welfare of individual humans cannot be sacrificed for its sake.

Pope Francis echoes these words of Pope Benedict by emphasizing that justice toward future generations requires that all humans work to safeguard the environment.[29] He also demonstrates the link between taking care of the environment and taking care of the poor. Often the destruction of the environment especially hurts the poor, who do not have the resources to protect themselves.[30] He exhorts "every person living on this planet" to practice an "integral ecology."[31] Ecology is the study of "relationships between living organisms and the environment in which they develop."[32] Francis extends this primarily biological term to include the relationships that humans have with the environment, each other, and, most importantly, God. Someone with an integral ecology recognizes that stewardship is an essential component of loving relationships with God and others. Francis notes: "We are faced not with two separate crises, one environmental and the other social, but rather with one complex crisis which is both social and environmental. Strategies for a solution demand an integrated approach to combating poverty, restoring dignity to the excluded, and at the same time protecting nature."[33]

THE HOLY SPIRIT'S GIFT OF PIETY

The gift of the Holy Spirit that perfects justice is piety. As we've seen a couple times already, piety is the virtue of giving reverence to those who have given us benefits we cannot repay. This reverence is first given to God, who has given us everything, and second to our parents, country, and others. Both God and people are honored through actions. For example, great people can be honored for their excellence through a public ceremony. Parents can be honored by children obeying and respecting them. God can be honored through worship, but also by any action that is done to show his glory on earth. Consequently, humans can be motivated by piety to do any good action. Through the gift of piety, the Holy Spirit perfects the will to show the glory of God in all of a person's actions.

COMMANDMENTS PERTAINING TO JUSTICE

Although God revealed the Ten Commandments so that the Israelites could be a happy and flourishing community, they can also be known by natural reason. Hence, they illustrate different ways that humans should act in order to strengthen loving relationships within society. Consequently, let's look at all of the commandments, except for the ones specific to temperance (the sixth and ninth), in this section. We'll analyze the first four commandments in this chapter, and the fifth, seventh, eighth and tenth in chapter 17. We will study the sins and vices that contradict justice in the context of their corresponding commandment(s).

FIRST COMMANDMENT

The first commandment is "I am the Lord your God, there shall be no other gods beside me." This is the general commandment to be faithful to God. Justice requires that God be honored and worshipped. The sin against this commandment is idolatry, where something else is loved more than God. In its original context, this commandment prohibited the worship of rival ancient Egyptian and Canaanite deities, but modern idols are generally things like power, pleasure, money, or oneself. In other words, they are any ultimate end of one's actions other than God. Even in the time of Christ, money and material goods were already considered a common false god. In warning against greed, Jesus states, "No one can serve two masters . . . You cannot serve both God and wealth."[34]

To specify how the ancient Israelites are to be faithful to God alone, a second part of the commandment is added: "You shall not carve idols . . . you shall not bow before them or worship them."[35] Although this passage prohibits the normal ways the Israelites would have worshipped other ancient gods, it has been misinterpreted in the past. Some, such as the Byzantine Iconoclasts in the eighth century, believed that this passage prohibited the use of icons (images of God and the saints) in worship.[36] However, veneration of images that represent God is not worship of a graven image. Humans know and love by means of their body. Their knowledge of other people comes from sense knowledge. Thus by looking at pictures of others, or reading letters written by others, their knowledge of other people grows. Furthermore, sensual images and words accompany concepts in their mind, giving them the ability to string together concepts in thought.[37] Because sensual images and words are essential to thought, when humans look at pictures of other people or read words written by other people, they think about them. If these are people they love, these images can make them happy. So also with God, pictures, stained glass windows, statues, the written and spoken word, and other images of God teach humans about God and cause humans to think about him.[38] For example, the Son appeared as a human because knowledge begins with sense knowledge, and love is expressed through the body. By venerating the image of God or venerating a saint (who is an image of God), humans worship God, whom these images represent.[39] In fact, God required the ancient Israelites to venerate material things that represented him, such as the ark of the covenant, the tabernacle, and the temple.[40]

Anything that represents God must be treated with reverence. This includes churches, pictures and statues of God and the saints, and other sacramentals, such as rosaries and holy water. The saints must also be treated with reverence since their very life communicates the goodness of God. Desecration of a holy object is the sin of *sacrilege*.

Second Commandment

The second commandment is "You shall not take the name of the Lord in vain." Since other images of God must be treated with reverence, it should be no surprise that God's name must be treated with reverence. Peoples' names are "images" of who they are; their names represent them. Because God's name represents him, justice requires that it be treated with respect. People should only use God's name when speaking of God in a reverent way. They should avoid using God's name in common expressions and especially avoid cursing or speaking badly about God. *Blasphemy* is the sin of treating God's name in a disrespectful manner.

Third Commandment

The third commandment is "Keep holy the Lord's Day." The virtue of religion requires that a certain amount of time be devoted to God. However, as with all aspects of religion, the command is for our sake, not because God needs our worship. By natural reason alone humans can know that if some time is not periodically set aside to devote to a particular cause or club, then the cause or club will quickly dissolve. However, it is difficult for humans to determine what frequency of their meetings ensures the greatest involvement in their cause of club. Hence, through divine revelation, God declared that every seventh day should be devoted to him. In other words, God required that every Sabbath be celebrated, lest the Jewish faith be lost. Yet, God not only wanted the Jewish faith to continue; he wanted each person in the community to keep the Sabbath so that the Jewish faith would flourish in them making them happy. The same reasoning applies to the Church today. God wants all humans to be happy, and he wants the Christian faith to flourish in them. Furthermore, because happiness is the act of contemplating the good that is known and loved, humans must set aside time to contemplate the greatness of God and his gifts in their lives.

When creating the earth, God "rested" on the seventh day (the Sabbath). He then commanded the Jewish people to do the same. Hence, the Jewish people devoted the seventh day of the week, which is Saturday, to God. However, when Christ rose from the dead, his human nature was transformed. This transformation was the beginning of the new creation. Since Christ rose on Sunday, for Christians, Sunday became the "Lord's Day."[41] It fulfills the Jewish Sabbath as a participation in the eternal "rest" of God. In other words, Sunday worship expresses the belief that Christians are a new creation in Jesus Christ, and through him, we already begin to participate in the "rest" of eternal happiness. The apostles first began this tradition of meeting on Sunday to break bread (reenact the Last Supper, or say Mass).[42] Consequently, since the time of the apostles, the Church has interpreted the third commandment as referring to Sunday, the Lord's Day.

There are two primary aspects of participating in God's eternal "rest" on Sundays. First, people should attempt to avoid their ordinary daily labor.[43] Second, Catholics must attend Mass. In reference to avoiding work, Sunday should be "set apart." Sunday should be seen as a participation in the full inheritance, a foretaste of the life to come. It should be a day devoted to enriching and enjoying the loving relationships between humans and between humans and God. Because it is a sign of the life to come, mundane labor should be avoided if possible.[44] Furthermore, humans have an obligation of letting others rest on Sundays. However, any labor that prefigures the actions of the next life is allowable. Hence, recreational, familial, cultural, or entertaining work can be done. For example, community festivals are excellent Sunday activities because they contribute to the unity of a community, even though people must work at the festivals if they are to run smoothly. Charitable work and spiritual work are always allowed because they prefigure the actions of the full inheritance.[45] Finally, necessary work, such as that of a doctor or nurse, can also be done. Prudence is essential to determine what work should be done, and what work should be avoided. When people spend their Sundays doing work, other time should be set aside for leisure. In other words, if humans are unable to "rest" on Sunday, then another day should be set aside.[46]

Catholics must also attend Mass on Sunday. The Eucharist (Mass) is a visible, public sign of worship of God. It most perfectly fulfills the Sabbath, since at Mass humans share in the divine "rest" by being united to Jesus, who unites them to the Father. In other words, the full inheritance consists of an eternal union with the Father by being united to the Son through the Holy Spirit. At Mass, humans are united to the Son by the power of the Holy Spirit. The Son unites us to the Father, allowing humans to participate in the full inheritance here on earth.[47] Therefore, just as it was obligatory for the Jewish people to keep the Sabbath, it is *gravely* obligatory for Catholics to go to Mass on Sunday.[48] Catholics must also go to Mass on holy days of obligation.[49] If people have a serious reason (such as sickness, lack of a priest, inability to get to Mass, etc.), then they are excused from Mass, but they should still spend extra time in prayer. Although attending Mass is a requirement, this law guides and motivates people to form the virtue of religion. Once humans have the virtue of religion, they no longer go to Mass because they have to, they go to Mass because they want to.

FOURTH COMMANDMENT

The fourth commandment is "Honor your father and mother." It is within the family that virtue is first taught. Without the moral training given by their parents, children would lack the freedom to perform good acts, and their happiness would be greatly restricted. Since their parents brought them into the world and raised them, piety requires that they honor their parents in return. Not only do children have an obligation to honor their parents, parents have an obligation to raise and educate their children. Finally, society has an obligation to help parents in fulfilling this duty. In covering this commandment, we will analyze the duties of children, parents, and society.

Regarding their duties, children have an obligation to honor their parents. The way that children honor their parents changes as their relation to their parents changes. When they are dependent upon their parents, children must obey their parents. If children are to acquire virtue, they must be guided and motivated by their parents to do good actions. Obedience is essential if children are going to grow in virtue and happiness. As children get older and go out on their own, they develop their own prudence and no longer have the obligation to obey their parents. Nonetheless, they still must honor them by respecting them and any advice that their parents give. Finally, as their parents begin to lose the ability to care for themselves, justice requires that children take care of their parents. Honoring their parents requires that children be involved in the care that is given to them. They should not simply abandon their parents in nursing homes or other care facilities. Their parents should be allowed to live out the rest of their lives with dignity, preferably either with or in close proximity to their children. With the virtue of justice, children honor their parents because they love them and not because they are required to.

Justice also requires that obedience and respect be given to civil authorities. Civil authorities are necessary to order society toward the common good.[50] Consequently, the just laws of a nation must be obeyed. Out of piety, citizens also honor their country by working for the betterment of their country, voting, and paying taxes.

Just as justice allows children to properly love their parents, justice also causes parents to desire the happiness of their children. Because of their relationship to their children, parents have the primary responsibility of educating and training their children in the virtues necessary for attaining happiness. In the case of infused justice, the primary goal of parents is to help their children attain eternal happiness. Chapter 11 told of the role of parents and mentors within the complete moral system. Parents have an important role in helping children attain the virtues necessary to be happy. Parents must first help their children receive sanctifying grace by taking their children to the sacraments. Grace gives children the supernatural inclinations (the theological virtues) to perform divine actions, but like the natural inclinations, these inclinations are not strong enough in themselves to cause good actions without the help of other people. Parents must then help their children develop the theological virtues by teaching them the faith and encouraging hope and charity.[51] Next, they guide and motivate their children to perform good actions that are in accord with the natural and divine law. By continuously guiding and encouraging their children, eventually the infused cardinal virtues become more perfect, and their children become more and more capable of knowing and loving good actions without the help of other humans. These perfected virtues give their children the ability to be supernaturally happy. By regularly bringing their children to the sacraments and constantly training them, parents help their children to have the freedom to choose to love Christ and others.

In helping their children acquire virtues, there are three important steps. First, parents must provide proper and age-appropriate experiences for their children. Second, they must teach their children how to properly interpret these experiences. Third, there should be repetition in these activities in order to form habits. For example, suppose a child already knows his letters and the parents are going to teach him how to read. First, they will have the child look at actual words, such as "cat" or "go" (the experience), then they will teach the child how the letters come together to form the words (interpreting the experience), and next they will require the child to practice sounding out the letters in words over and over again (the repetition). They will then increase the intensity of the experiences by having the child string various words together to further build the virtue. The same three steps can be seen in the development of other virtues. For example, to teach justice, parents might take their child with them to work in a soup kitchen or read the child a book about helping the poor (the experience). Second, they will talk to their child about why they worked in the soup kitchen or about the meaning of the book. Third, they will continue to increase the intensity of these types of activities until the virtue of justice begins to form in the child. Most of the experiences needed to form the virtues in children can be found within the environment of a family. However, as children grow in virtues, parents will often need to provide new experiences to their children that extend into the larger and even global community (such as working with others to raise money for the victims of an earthquake in Nepal). They will also need the help of others in the community, such as grandparents, teachers, coaches, and religious mentors.

Since all of the powers of the soul must be perfected in order for children to be virtuous, parents should consciously focus on inculcating *all* the intellectual and moral virtues. They should attempt to establish virtues within the *intellect* by developing their children's learning and reasoning skills. Parents should also teach their children the truths of the faith and other moral teachings so that their children can wisely order their lives in accord with these truths. To instill prudence within their children, they must slowly increase the responsibilities (experiences) of their children so that their children can practice making good decisions. They should talk to their children about their decisions and help them see what was good about the decision or how to make better ones (the interpretation of the experiences). In doing this, parents must on the one hand avoid giving their children too much responsibility too quickly, and on the other hand they must avoid completely sheltering their children from moral decisions (make sure the experiences are age- and person-appropriate). The key is to not place children in positions of responsibility until they are ready. For example, when my children are very young, they are not allowed to leave the yard on their own.

As they get older, they can perhaps cross the street if someone is watching them, but they can go no farther. Finally, they get to the point where they are allowed to go farther away. To make sure that their children realize that the laws established by their parents help them to be free to be happy, parents should frequently explain the rationale behind the law.

Parents should work to establish virtues in the *will* by aiding the natural inclination of the will to love the good. They must guide their children to love truly good things (especially God). The first thing they must do is be a good example. To be a good example, they must love their children and make sure that the love is evident. They also must *joyfully* love each other. It is extremely important that parents maintain a strong loving relationship with each other as an example for their children. This loving environment is the first and most important experience for a child. In addition, parents should *joyfully* love all other people, and especially God. The happiness that comes from loving should be evident to the children to entice the natural desire of their children's will. Parents should also present truly good things as being worthwhile activities. For example, they could make going to daily Mass a family a priority or have their children work with them in helping the poor, either financially or through good actions. Regularly reading stories to their children that teach the value of doing good things and loving God can be especially helpful in enticing the will. In all of these cases, the children should be taught why the parents do these things in age-appropriate ways.

In addition to these actions that aid the will in loving the true good, parents must make sure that their children are constantly doing good actions, even if their children do not love these actions yet. By getting their children into the habit of always acting in a loving manner, the habit will be easily established once the will begins to love the true good. Finally, parents should promote and participate in activities that strengthen the family bond. In other words, the family should do lots of good activities together. They should preferably eat at least one meal together as a family and do a lengthy family activity every Sunday. All in the family should participate in daily family prayer. By getting the children to develop a proper bond with their parents and siblings, their children will be more likely to choose good actions taught by their parents than to follow temptations stemming from others.

Parents must also transform the *emotions* of their children to always desire the right actions by helping their children attain temperance and fortitude. The emotions are not rational in children, so the only way that they can be trained is by appealing to another emotion through punishment and rewards. Good actions must be consistently rewarded and encouraged, while evil actions must be consistently punished. The virtues will only be developed if children are consistently doing the same type of actions. Training children to become virtuous takes *constant supervision*. Either a parent or another trusted person should always be monitoring young children. As with the virtue of prudence, as the children grow in virtue, they can gradually be given more and more responsibility (increasing the intensity of the experiences). For example, to acquire fortitude, children need regular chores and family duties. Parenting is hard and long work, for a child can only learn to be virtuous by being constantly trained in real-life situations. It is not sufficient for parents to seek just a little quality time with their children, for the people that spend the most time with their children will often have the most influence on them. Prospective parents should attempt to grow in virtue now, for a good parent needs all the virtues to train their children accordingly.

Because strong families are essential to the proper functioning of society, justice also causes members of society to aid parents in raising virtuous children. Parents have the primary responsibility of educating and raising their children. If they have this responsibility, they also have this natural right. Thus, justice requires that society must recognize the legitimate right of parents to raise and educate their children. Society must also create an environment conducive to parents achieving their goals of raising virtuous children. If parents need aid from society to meet these goals, then those within society must help them.[52]

The family is the original cell of all social life. In other words, because humans are made in the image of the Trinity, they are made to live in a community. The most basic unit of society is the community of the family. It mirrors the image of the Trinity and is the place where moral virtue begins in children. Since the future of society is found in the children, when families are strong, society is strong. Parents who devote their lives to raising virtuous children directly contribute to the good of society in a nearly unparalleled way. Because moral formation of children is so important, the Church has stated that mothers (or fathers in certain situations) have a right to stay home and raise their children.[53] Society should make sure that mothers (or fathers) of young children are not forced to work outside the home because of economic hardship.

Because of the importance of the family to the good of society, the members of society should work to make sure that parents have all the economic and educational resources that they need to properly raise their children. Ideally, the economic resources should come from the wages of the parent or parents who are working, but if the employer is unable or unwilling to pay sufficient wages to raise a family, then friends, family, the Church, and even the government may be required to help them.[54] Although there are usually many educational resources available to families (both public and private), families should be careful to discern whether these resources will truly help their children grow in virtue before taking advantage of them. All individuals can help strengthen families by offering to help a family through tutoring their children or through other acts of service.

17

JUSTICE

Part Two

Justice perfects the will to love others by giving to them their natural rights. The natural rights of humans flow from the natural law. Consequently, in order to understand the proper acts of justice, we must study particular natural laws. Although the Ten Commandments are divinely revealed, they are a good summary of the natural law. God knew that because of the effects of fallen human nature, the ancient Israelites would have trouble determining the precepts of the natural law that were essential for their community to flourish. Thus, God revealed these essential precepts (the Ten Commandments) to them so that they could be happy. By reviewing the commandments that specifically pertain to justice, a more complete notion of the virtue of justice emerges. Chapter 16 analyzed the first four commandments. This chapter will analyze the fifth, seventh, eighth, and tenth commandments.

FIFTH COMMANDMENT

The fifth commandment is "You shall not kill." In the original context of the Old Testament, perhaps a better expression of the commandment is "You shall not murder." Humans have a natural right to life, and justice perfects the will to respect and protect the lives of others. In its original context, the commandment primarily prohibited murder and other physical violence. In the Sermon on the Mount, Jesus extends this commandment to also prohibit anger, hatred, and vengeance against others (Mt

5:22–48). Any harm to others is prohibited, including emotional and spiritual harm. The just person avoids not only physically hurting others but also hurting the feelings of others through meanness or biting sarcasm. Furthermore, infused justice perfects the will to turn the other cheek and to love all others, including our enemies (Mt 5:48).

The fifth commandment as interpreted through the teachings of Jesus requires humans to love all others, and we have already covered this aspect of the commandment in earlier chapters. However, numerous moral questions surround the material act of killing, and the remainder of this section will analyze these moral questions by showing how actions like self-defense and just war have a different moral object than the act of murder.

All intentional homicide (murder) is forbidden by this commandment. Direct and intentional killing of anyone from the moment of conception until natural death is gravely sinful. Also forbidden are any actions that put others in grave danger, such as driving with excessive speed or drunk driving.

Self-defense

Although the act of murder is wrong, killing can be done in self-defense or to save the life of an innocent person.[1] The object of the act of self-defense is different from the object of murder. Chapter 5 explained how the object of an action is determined. The object is the same as the intention if (and only if) that which is chosen is in conformity with what is intended (where "in conformity" means that the reasoning is valid, the premises accurately reflect the situation, and the action is judged to be in accord with higher ends). In other words, the object is the same as the intention if the intellect acts correctly in the counsel and judgment stages. Otherwise, the object is different from the intention. In the case of self-defense, the intention is to save one's life. When taking counsel, the person finds that there is no other way to save one's life than to kill the aggressor. The person then reasons that given this situation, he should attempt to kill the aggressor. When judging, the person first judges that the action is ordered to the end of saving one's own life. Then the person judges that it is ordered to the ultimate end of God because the good of one's own life is just as great as the good of the aggressor, and humans are required to love and take care of themselves. To further ensure that their judgment is correct, the person judges by the written divine law, about which we read in the *Catechism of the Catholic Church*: "Love toward oneself remains a fundamental principle of morality. Therefore it is legitimate to insist on respect for one's own right to life. Someone who defends his life is not guilty of murder even if he is forced to deal his aggressor a lethal blow" (§2264). Because the person researched, reasoned, and judged correctly, the object of the action is the same as the intention: saving one's life in self-defense.

However, there are two situations where the object of the act would be murder and not self-defense. First, suppose a person hated his neighbor and was just waiting for the situation to arise when he could kill his neighbor in "self-defense." In this case, even if the situation was such that the object would be self-defense if the person had a good intention, because the person's intention is bad, the object would be murder. In cases where there is an evil end, the object is always the same as the evil end. Since the person was seeking to kill his neighbor, the best moral description of the action is murder and not self-defense. Second, the person might have a good intention, but because of faulty research, reasoning, or judging, he might actually be murdering the other person. For example, suppose someone has a good intention of saving his property but then chooses to kill a harmless intruder to fulfill this intention. This act of killing someone is not in conformity with the intention of saving property, because the life of a person is a greater good than that of property. The failure in the action took place in the judgment step, where the murderer failed to judge properly by the higher principle of the sacredness of life. Hence, even if the intention is to save property, the object of the act is murder. Because it can be difficult to determine the proper action in cases of self-defense, prudence must be perfected to make sure that people properly evaluate the situation, reason logically, and judge correctly.[2]

ABORTION

The morality of abortion is one of the most debated issues in contemporary politics, but the Catholic Church has consistently considered direct abortion to be sinful since the time of the apostles.[3] A person must be considered a human from the first moment of conception, and to kill this young human is prohibited by the fifth commandment. The story of the pregnant Mary visiting the pregnant Elizabeth illustrates the Church's understanding that human life begins at conception (Lk 1:39–45). Shortly after Mary conceives Jesus by the power of the Holy Spirit, she goes to see her cousin Elizabeth. Upon Mary's arrival, John the Baptist, the baby in Elizabeth's womb, leaps for joy. Even though Jesus would have been no bigger than a dust particle, the primary theme of the story is the interaction between him and John the Baptist. Even before they are born, John the Baptist "prepares the way for the Lord." Both Jesus and John the Baptist are not only human persons before they are born, but they are also already fulfilling their divinely appointed missions. Consistent with the gospel story, the Church has always considered direct abortion to be a serious sin.

Although direct abortion is wrong, a distinction can be made between a direct abortion, which is murder, and an indirect abortion, which is morally allowable. An indirect abortion takes place when the baby is killed as an unintended effect of saving the life of the mother. The object of a direct abortion is different than the object of an indirect abortion. The object of a direct abortion is abortion (murder)—since the abortion is either intended or the action of killing the baby is not in moral conformity with a different good intention. For example, if a young woman believes that having a baby would ruin her career, she might intend the good of saving her career. In order to save her career, she then chooses to abort her baby. The object of this act would be abortion, since the act of killing her baby is not in moral conformity with her intention of saving her career. She failed to take proper counsel by not looking into all of her options. She also failed to judge by the higher principles of natural and divine law. She failed to judge by the natural law stemming from the natural inclination to procreate and raise children. If she violates her natural inclinations to raise her children, she not only seriously harms another person, but she also impedes her ability to attain true happiness. She further fails to judge by the divine law in that the consistent teaching of the Church from the time of Christ is that direct abortion is gravely sinful.[4]

However, the object of the act of an indirect abortion is saving the life of the mother. In this case, the intention is to save the mother's life (and the baby's life, if possible). In taking counsel, the woman determines that there is no other way to save her life than to perform a medical procedure that results in the death of the baby. For example, suppose a woman has an ectopic pregnancy. An ectopic pregnancy is when the newly conceived baby implants somewhere other than in the uterus (usually the Fallopian tube). If the baby continues to grow in the Fallopian tube, then the Fallopian tube can burst, causing potentially deadly internal bleeding. The woman then reasons that there is no other way to save her life than to remove the section of the tube containing the baby (unintentionally causing the baby's death) in order to save her life.[5] She judges that this action is both in accord with her goal of saving her life and with higher goals, since she also has a natural inclination to love herself and stay alive. The American Catholic bishops also give guidance by noting, "Operations, treatments, and medications that have as their direct purpose the cure of a proportionately serious pathological condition of a pregnant woman are permitted when they cannot be safely postponed until the unborn child is viable, even if they will result in the death of the unborn child."[6] Thus, because she researches, reasons, and judges correctly, the object of the act is saving the life of the mother.

In the case of an ectopic pregnancy, the baby will die either way. What about cases where the baby could possibly live? Following the reasoning given above, the mother is still allowed to take actions to save her life even if the baby dies in the process. However, since the goodness of her life and the goodness of the life of the baby are roughly equal, the woman can also choose to sacrifice her life for the sake of her baby. The Catholic Church showed the heroic nature of this type of sacrifice by declaring a woman who gave up her life in this matter to be a saint: Gianna Beretta Molla.

Since a baby is considered to be a human from the moment of conception, embryonic research that kills or harms embryos is also forbidden. For example, embryonic stem cell research, which destroys embryos in order to harvest stem cells, is considered to be a serious sin. (However, adult stem cell research, which does not kill a baby, is highly encouraged.)

Because a baby is such a great good, the only intended good great enough to allow for an indirect abortion is the good of the life of a mother. In all other cases, such as an intention to avoid the emotional trauma from a rape or the intention to save the baby from a painful life in the case of a deformity, the good of the baby's life is still greater. If the baby is killed, the object of the act would be abortion. In other words, although these are truly good intentions, the choice of ending the life of the baby is not in conformity with them (because of a failure to judge properly by higher principles), and to kill the baby would be a direct abortion.

WAR

War is a horrendous evil that not only results in the death of many people but often completely destroys societies. All nations have the duty of working and praying for peace. If a nation uses military force against another nation for any reason other than to defend innocent people, then the war is considered to be an unjust war. Those who participate in an unjust war commit the sin of murder (if they know the war is unjust). Nonetheless, just as individuals have the right to defend themselves against an unjust aggressor, a nation also has this right. Consequently, a distinction can be made between an unjust war, which violates the fifth commandment, and a just war, which is morally allowable. Because war has such horrible effects, over the centuries rigorous principles were created in order to make sure that nations do not unjustly attack other nations. In other words, the principles were created in an attempt to identify when a war is just and to prevent all unjust use of military force. These principles are called *just war principles*, and for a war to be considered just, it must meet *all* of these principles. Although the principles have developed over time, the following are meant to represent the tradition in general:[7]

1. The intention must always be to defend life and never for revenge, increasing power, and so on. Both the governing authority and the soldiers involved must have this good intention.
2. Military force can only be used if a country is protecting innocent people from lasting, grave, and certain damage.
3. Military force must be a last resort. There must be no other way of defending these innocent lives. All other forms of diplomacy with some chance of success must be exhausted.
4. The actions must be called by a legitimate authority.
5. There must be some chance of success. Humans must love their enemies, and they can only fight to save others. If saving others is not possible, then fighting is not allowable.
6. The evils created must not be graver than the evil eliminated, and the fewest possible soldiers (on both sides) should be killed.
7. Innocent citizens may never be intentionally killed.

The first four principles must be met before a country can enter into a war. (Sometimes the fifth and sixth are also in this category.) The last three principles determine the morality of actions within a war. If all of the first six conditions are not met, then a country should not go to war with another country. Or, if a country has already declared war, then a person who knows that the war is unjust should not participate in the war. In the midst of the political turmoil at the time of war, it can sometimes be very difficult to determine whether or not a war is just (especially for the individual). Sometimes various good people will disagree over whether or not a war is just. For example, in 2003, the United States attacked Iraq. It was very difficult at the time to determine whether or not innocent people were being protected from lasting, grave, and practically certain damage or whether the United States was the unjust aggressor. It was also difficult to determine whether or not the United States was the proper authority to declare the war or whether they were violating international law by attacking without the approval of the United Nations. Prudence is especially necessary for people to determine whether or not a war is just and whether they should participate in it. Even if the war is just, certain actions within the war might not be just, such as the targeting of civilian populations with either conventional or nuclear weapons. These actions must also be avoided.

CAPITAL PUNISHMENT

Just as humans have a right to defend themselves, the state also has a right to defend its citizens. In order to defend itself, a state can even execute a criminal for the sake of the common good. The *Catechism* states that the death penalty is allowable if "this is the only possible way of effectively defending human lives against an unjust aggressor. If, however, non-lethal means are sufficient to defend and protect people's safety from the aggressor, the authority will limit itself to such means."[8] In other words, if society can be safeguarded by placing the aggressor in jail or something similar, then the aggressor should not be killed. Hence, although the Church is not essentially opposed to the death penalty, it believes that it is almost never allowable in developed countries. If the intention is the safety of the citizens of a state, and there are other means that are less destructive than capital punishment, then practical reason requires that these other means be chosen.

SUICIDE

Suicide is the act of intentionally killing oneself and is always gravely wrong. It contradicts the natural inclination that humans have to conserve their lives. It further violates justice by being contrary to love of God and love of others. God created everyone to fulfill a particular role in his divine plan, and every moment that humans are on earth is included in this plan. Those who love and honor God seek to fulfill his plan and will not end their lives prematurely.[9] In order to help humans understand why people who are suffering still participate in God's plan, Jesus died on the cross to show us the value of suffering out of love of God. Suicide also violates love of others. Love requires that humans live every moment of their lives loving their fellow humans. Sometimes the most important way that humans love others is by allowing others to have the opportunity to sacrifice for them. Even those who believe that they are burdens on their family are very important for the salvation and happiness of their family, since humans are perfected when they help others.[10] The action of committing suicide shows a rejection of oneself, friends, family, and ultimately God (even though this message is often not intended).

Although suicide is gravely wrong, those who commit it are often hampered by extreme depression, grave fear, substance abuse, or other suffering. These conditions can hinder or in some cases even remove the voluntariness of the action. Those contemplating suicide should be treated with extreme compassion and need the love of others along with proper medical help. Aaron Kheriaty, associate professor of psychiatry at the UC Irvine School of Medicine and author of *The Catholic Guide to Depression*, notes that severe depression is a "potentially fatal illness" that can be every bit as deadly as a heart attack or cancer.[11] Furthermore, he notes that the scientific evidence shows that the most predictive factor of suicide is not how much a person is suffering or how many symptoms a person has, but it is rather a feeling of complete hopelessness. He continues by stating that there is no medical prescription that can fix hopelessness, but hopelessness can be fixed through loving relationships with others and God. (This is not a denigration of the importance of medication, psychotherapy, and other behavioral practices, which Kheriaty states are also often essential in treating depression).[12] The point that I am making is that the route to true happiness is never attained through suicide, but it can be found in loving God and others. However, often those suffering a mental illness require enduring and patient love from others in order to form these types of relationships. Furthermore, because God is merciful, humans should not despair of the eternal salvation of people who have taken their own lives.[13]

Euthanasia

Although all suicide stems from some type of suffering, society often makes a distinction between suicide in general and euthanasia, a type of suicide where someone seeks to avoid a more chronic suffering often experienced towards the end of their life. Since suicide in general violates justice, euthanasia also violates justice. The word "euthanasia" comes from two Greek words meaning "good death." It can refer to the act of killing oneself in order to avoid suffering or to the act of helping people kill themselves. In addition to the active killing of people, euthanasia also includes the omission of normal life essentials before natural death.[14] For example, humans can actively kill others by giving a drug overdose, or they can kill by omitting normal life essentials when they remove food and water so that the person dies of dehydration. Euthanasia contradicts the natural inclination that all people have to life. In cases where people receive assistance in killing themselves, euthanasia violates justice by being contrary to love of God and others in the same way as suicide.

Although euthanasia is wrong, it is not euthanasia by omission for dying humans to reject overly burdensome medical treatment. Dying humans do not have to try every conceivable form of medical treatment. For example, suppose a woman is dying of cancer and has tried all the normal means of fighting the disease. Does she morally have to try every experimental drug with the hope that she might extend her life another year? *A distinction can be made between euthanasia and overzealous treatment.* To continue to resort to medical treatment when all realistic hope for a cure is lost is overzealous treatment. Just as euthanasia is not rational because it fails to recognize the importance of human life, overzealous treatment is also irrational because it fails to accept the human condition. Humans must eventually die in order to attain eternal life.

In order to help guide patients, or their proxies, to prudentially determine the difference between morally essential treatment and overzealous treatment, John Paul II stated, "In such situations, when death is clearly imminent and inevitable, one can in conscience 'refuse forms of treatment that would only secure a precarious and burdensome prolongation of life, so long as the normal care due to the sick person in similar cases is not interrupted.'"[15] In other words, the treatment is overly zealous if the following three conditions are met: (1) death is imminent and inevitable, and (2) the medical procedures are burdensome or disproportionate to the expected outcome, and (3) the treatment is not normal care.[16] Death is imminent and inevitable when someone is truly dying and not just plagued with a sickness or injury that can be reasonably treated given the medical care available.[17] Medical procedures are disproportionate to expected outcomes if the burdens they cause outweigh their potential benefits. Finally, normal care, such as food, water, comfort, hygiene, and so on, should not be viewed as a type of medical treatment, but simply as the basic care owed to all humans beings on account of their dignity.

Life-sustaining treatment cannot be rejected if the person has a reasonable chance of recovering from a sickness or injury, because to reject available treatment in this case would amount to euthanasia by omission. However, if the person is truly dying, then treatment that causes more burdens than benefits can be rejected. For example, suppose a woman has cancer, and she was not cured by the normal means of treating cancer. She fulfills the first criterion that death must be imminent and inevitable. She can then seek to determine whether additional treatment (that might extend her life but will likely not save her) is more burdensome than beneficial. In determining whether to continue treatment, she can consider the effects of pain (both on herself and her family), her financial situation, the possible good she could accomplish by living longer, and other factors. In other words, she must use her prudence to look at all aspects of a situation that could be considered a true burden or benefit. For example, having young children might cause her to attempt to live longer than if she did not have young children.

Artificial nutrition (food) and hydration (water) are generally not considered medical treatment but are instead basic health care. Consequently, normally speaking, providing food and water, even artificially, is obligatory.[18] Food and water can be withheld if the patient is truly dying, and the food and water do not meet their proper ends of nourishment and alleviation of suffering.[19]

The fifth commandment prohibits all harm to others, including physical, emotional, spiritual, or verbal abuse. Jesus calls all people to love their enemies. Since justice perfects an appetitive power, prudence is necessary to find the mean in all of the above cases. In cases of loving the lives of others, the defect of love results in murder, abortion, unjust war, suicide, or euthanasia. The excess happens when the good of the lives of others are considered to be the ultimate good itself. For example, the excess would result in people never defending the lives of other innocent people because killing would violate the highest good of life.[20] This excess love of life contradicts self-defense, just war, and the legitimate right of the state to defend itself. In the case of prolonging one's life, the excess would result in the choosing of overzealous treatments.

SEVENTH COMMANDMENT

The seventh commandment is "You shall not steal." Because the body requires material goods to properly function, humans have a natural inclination to necessary material goods. Furthermore, by working, humans participate in God's plan of perfecting the created world. When humans work, created goods are transformed in a way that reflects the personal being of the workers. The greater and more perfect the work put into the transformation, the more it reflects the workers. Since these products or services become an extension of the workers, the workers have either a right to these products or a right to be justly compensated for their work.[21] For example, the way nurses take care of patients manifests their very selves. A building manifests the personality of its architect and builders. Consequently, because humans require property in order for the body to function, and property is an extension of one's being, all humans have a natural right to property.[22]

Because material goods are so important in the spiritual and physical development of humans, justice requires both that humans do not steal another's property and that they use their material goods to ensure that all humans have the necessities of life, including property. To make sure that humans use their property correctly, two principles must be considered when judging how to use material goods. These principles are the *universal destination of goods* and the *right to private property*.[23]

The *universal destination of goods* states that material goods are for the benefit of all humans. God is the first cause of all material goods. He both gives us the created world and moves humans to produce more goods from the created world. Thus, even though humans produce material goods, the first cause is God. God creates material goods to meet the needs of all people. Hence, material goods are "universally destined" and fulfill their function when they meet the needs of *everyone*. Because God created the world to meet the needs of all people, justice requires that humans use their material goods to fulfill the legitimate needs of others.

Whereas God is the first cause of material goods, humans are normally the secondary cause of material goods. Humans put their own sweat, blood, and very being into the formation of material goods. Because these goods are an extension of each person, humans have a *right to private property*. In other words, humans can *freely* choose how to use their material goods. Since humans share in the work of producing material wealth, they have a right to share in the wealth that is produced.

Justice perfects the will to give others what is owed to them either on account of their nature or on account of their actions. The universal destination of goods requires that humans give others the material goods necessary to fulfill their natural inclinations. The right to private property requires that humans have the opportunity to freely use their material goods as just compensation for their actions. At first glance it might seem that these principles contradict each other. If material goods are ordered to the needs of all humans, then how can humans have a right to freely use them? However, recall that true freedom does not mean the ability to choose anything at all (either good or evil). True freedom comes from participating in God's knowledge and love. God desires that material goods be used to help all others. God gives material goods to humans so that they can be spiritually perfected when they use these goods to help others. In other words, humans have the right to use property, but they are most free when they choose to use their property for the benefit of all people.[24] A good analogy to the use of private property is the use of one's talents. God gives humans talents so that they can help others. Humans are free to choose how to use their talents, but truly free humans use their talents for the benefit of others, since this is what fulfills them and brings true happiness. So also with property, humans are more like God when they use their property to help others.

But how is property used for the benefit of others? Must it all be given away like it was in the very early Church?[25] To determine how to prudently use property, a distinction must be made between two different types of property: goods of production and goods of consumption. Goods of production are all the material goods that are used to produce more material goods. Examples of these types of goods are land, factories, and raw materials. Goods of consumption are all the material goods that are consumed, such as food, clothing, housing, recreational goods, and energy used to heat or cool a house. Many material goods can be either goods of production or goods of consumption depending upon how they are used. For example, if a vehicle is used solely for recreational purposes, it is a good of consumption. However, if it is used for work related purposes, then it is a good of production. The same is true with land, energy, computers, and many other things.

Goods of production must be used to benefit others as determined by the needs of the common good. As always, the poor must especially be considered. For example, a factory that produces cars benefits society since transportation aids the common good. However, goods of production are not benefiting others if they are used to produce something that violates the common good, such as pornographic materials. Another way that goods of production are misused is when in the production process activities are performed that denigrate human dignity, such as not paying just wages to employees, providing unsafe working conditions, or taking advantage of the hardships of the poor.[26] Although people who own goods of production will ideally make a profit,[27] they must first and foremost use their property to help others. Thus, it is not wrong to own large amounts of goods of production, provided that these goods are used to truly help others live a dignified life. Since God created the world to meet the needs of all people, to not use these goods for the benefit of others is a sin against the seventh commandment.

Because of the universal destination of goods, goods of consumption must also be used for the benefit of others. However, if goods of consumption are consumed, then how can they be used to benefit others? If humans stop eating, drinking, wearing clothes, and so on, they will not be able to survive to help others. Hence, even these goods can be ordered to the common good since the common good requires that all have access to the necessities of life in order to flourish. However, these goods only benefit others if they are consumed in *moderation*.[28] Unlike goods of production, owning or using too many goods of consumption is sinful, since these goods are not being used as God intended them to be used. For example, although it is necessary to spend time and resources on recreation, it is wrong to spend an excessive amount on recreation when others are dying of starvation. Those who overconsume when others are not able to live a life of dignity are not loving others because they fail to make the true needs of others their own. As seen in the section on liberality in chapter 16, people with the virtue of justice do not consume more than they need, and they use the excess to help the poor. To determine whether or not humans are consuming in moderation, they should ask, "Do I really need this to be physically and spiritually fulfilled?" Then because of the great temptation to create artificial needs, they may also need to judge whether or not this particular need is authentic.[29] This temptation to create artificial needs is especially strong in developed countries, where people become accustomed to superfluous goods and believe that they truly need them. It is important for people in developed countries to truly interact with those in extreme poverty to help them determine what they actually need to consume and what they use to aid others.

Most people in the United States have more material goods or income than they truly need. How can they morally use this extra wealth? They can always give their extra wealth to the poor, either directly or through an agency that works with the poor.

They can also turn their wealth into goods of production and use it help others.[30] For example, they could start their own business to provide a service that is truly good for society and that gives people jobs. They could invest their money in a company that truly helps society.[31] The key is that people first and foremost use their money to help others and only secondly to make a profit. Another way to look at this truth is from the perspective of love of others. Justice is based on love of friendship of others. As seen in chapter 14 on charity, love of use of others is allowable, as long as it is subordinate to love of friendship. So also in the economic realm, humans are able to have love of use of others, as long as it is accompanied by love of friendship. For example, when humans enter the market seeking to make a profit, they have love of use of others since they enter into relationships in order to benefit financially. This act of seeking financial gain is fine provided that it is accompanied by a true love of friendship, where those seeking financial gain are first and foremost seeking to fulfill the needs of those they interact with. Investing money in economically depressed areas in order to help others can be an excellent way to love others. Whether those with superfluous income give their money to the poor or use it to start a business, prudence is needed to determine the best way to use one's extra wealth at any particular time.

There is a common misconception among Christians that if they give a certain percentage of their income (perhaps 10 percent) to the Church and the poor then they fulfill their moral requirements. However, love requires that *all of one's property must be used to help others.* The key is to prudently determine whether the best way to help others is by consuming a necessary good, by giving money to the poor or the Church, or by investing in a business that helps the poor. Because religion is a necessary need, there is a moral obligation to prudently help the Church. Furthermore, the poor will always need some direct aid and must always be considered first when determining how to use resources.

Since there is a right to private property, theft is forbidden. However, if a person is violating the universal destination of goods by hoarding more than he needs, taking property in times of extreme necessity is not theft.[32] For example, in a case where there is no other practical way to get food, and a father takes just enough to feed his family from someone who has more than he needs, the object of the action is not stealing but helping his family survive. The reason the object of the act is not stealing is because the principle of the universal destination of goods is a higher principle than the right to private property. In fact, the one hoarding the goods is stealing from the poor to whom these goods are destined.[33]

All forms of theft are forbidden, such as business fraud and materially taking advantage of the hardships of others (e.g., charging excessive amounts for a necessity of life when the poor have no other options). If employers do not pay just wages, they steal from their employees.[34] On the other hand, workers must do their best work for an employer. Furthermore, justice requires that promises and contracts are kept, provided that they are morally just.[35] The honoring of contracts is essential to economic and social life.[36]

Although humans have a natural right to possess material goods in order to physically and spiritually flourish, they do not have a natural right to an excessive amount of material goods. In fact, consuming too many goods or misusing goods is an impediment to love of God and others.[37] When justice is infused by charity, the needs of the poor become our needs because we love God. People with the virtue of justice seek to help the poor within the economic realm by consuming in moderation, using their goods to fulfill the legitimate needs of others, and working for the benefit of others.[38] Wealthier nations also have a grave responsibility to help poor nations become economically stable.[39] The seventh commandment is fulfilled by loving our neighbors and making sure that they have all the material necessities for physical and spiritual growth. As Jesus points out in Matthew 25, we must help fulfill the bodily needs of others, because "whatever you do for the least of my brothers, you do for me."

EIGHTH COMMANDMENT

On both a personal and societal level, human relationships require that people tell the truth. Personal relationships must be based on honest communication in order to grow and flourish. Likewise, a society cannot function unless its members tell the truth. For example, within the economic realm, if humans cannot trust each other, their ability to complete business transactions is significantly hindered. On a political level, if humans cannot trust politicians or the media, their ability to participate in government is destroyed. Because divulging the truth is essential for human flourishing, humans have a natural inclination to tell the truth and a natural right to receive it. The eighth commandment, "You shall not bear false witness against your neighbor," pertains to the necessity of humans to tell the truth in order to be happy.

The original context of this commandment dealt with falsely testifying against others. In Jewish law, if two people accused someone of violating the law, then the person they testified against could be punished. The eighth commandment kept people from abusing this law and falsely accusing others. For example, in Daniel 13, Susanna is falsely accused of committing adultery. Her two accusers "bore false witness" against her. Jesus extends this commandment to require that all people always tell the truth (Mt 5:37).

Because truth is ordered to the unity of humans, they must build the unity of society by spreading and proclaiming those truths necessary for natural and supernatural happiness. They proclaim these truths through their words, lifestyles, social communications, media, and art. Honesty is the virtue of properly communicating truths that lead to unity between people. The honest person seeks the mean of properly loving others by revealing truth that causes unity. The defect occurs when either essential truths are not revealed or when other people are intentionally deceived. The excess occurs whenever truths that destroy unity are revealed. In other words, in a fallen world, it is sometimes prudent to keep certain truths secret. The excess occurs when too much truth is revealed. Sins of excess include revealing information that destroys another's reputation (for example, by gossiping),[40] revealing information that will hurt others (without a serious reason to reveal it),[41] revealing information that will cause fighting (contention), revealing confidential information given under the seal of secrecy, and boasting or bragging (even if the boast is true).

Most sins against honesty stem from a defect in the proper love of others. Perjury is the sin of intentionally misleading others while under oath—especially in a judicial proceeding. Another sin is not revealing truths that are essential to the unity of friends, family, or society. For example, if there is a misunderstanding between family members that Dan can resolve by revealing some information, Dan has an obligation to reveal this truth. Lying is the sin of hindering unity among humans by intentionally deceiving others. The *Catechism* notes, "To lie is to speak or act against the truth in order to lead someone in error."[42] A type of lying is cheating on tests and homework. By cheating, humans lie about what they truly know, harming both themselves and others. A particularly grievous sin of lying occurs when people intentionally deceive others by misrepresenting the truths of the faith. If a lie brings grave spiritual or physical injury to others, it can be a mortal sin. Finally, it is also a defect in revealing the truth to encourage another to do an evil act.

Humans are naturally inclined to know the truth. Without the fulfillment of this natural inclination, they are unable to enter into loving relationships within society and with God. Consequently, humans have a natural right to be told all truths that are conducive to their spiritual and physical well-being. Prudence is required to determine what to say and what to keep hidden.

TENTH COMMANDMENT

The tenth commandment is "You shall not covet your neighbor's goods." Justice requires humans to respect the property of others, and charity requires humans to rejoice in the blessings of others. (Envy is a sin against charity.) When humans seek the material goods of others to the extent that they wish evil upon them, they break this commandment. In other words, it is not wrong for humans to desire the goods of others in moderation. However, this desire should not contradict the love of friendship, which causes humans to rejoice in the good things that others have. If this desire violates this love, then it is the sin of covetousness. For example, if a child wants a neighbor's bicycle so much that he begins to dislike the neighbor, then he violates the tenth commandment.

The vice of greed also violates this commandment. Greed refers to an inordinate desire for material goods. Material goods are necessary because they are ordered to the health and functioning of the body, which is ordered to the proper operation of the soul: knowing and loving God and others.[43] Humans with the virtue of poverty of heart have the proper amount of desire for material goods. They realize that these goods are necessary in moderation for humans to be fulfilled physically and spiritually. Too little desire for material goods is a vice. People who have too little desire for material goods neglect the necessities of the body. On the other hand, people with greed have too much desire for material goods and love material goods more than they love God and others. Greed is a particularly dangerous vice today because the overabundance of material goods can bring a great deal of false happiness while destroying true happiness.[44] An inordinate desire for material goods causes people to spend their time and energy attempting to attain more goods rather than loving God and others. The Bible shows the extreme danger of greed by comparing it to idolatry.[45]

The virtue of proper desire for material goods can be called either a "spirit of poverty" or a "poverty of heart."[46] In imitation of the lifestyle of Jesus, humans are called to recognize that material goods must always be subordinate to spiritual goods. Humans with the virtue of poverty of heart love others and God so much that they consider the needs of others more important than their own material goods. They are willing to prudently give their material goods to others anytime that someone needs these goods more than they need them.[47]

THE LAW GUIDES and motivates people to perform good actions that perfect the virtues. The different laws that relate to justice cause the subvirtues that correspond to justice. The first through third commandments guide people to actions of giving God the honor he deserves. These commandments increase the virtues of religion and piety. The fourth commandment causes children to honor their parents, increasing the virtue of piety. It also guides parents to give children their proper needs and guides society to give families what they need to raise virtuous children. These actions increase the virtue of justice in general. The fifth commandment guides humans to respect the lives of others. These actions also increase the virtue of justice in general. The seventh commandment guides humans to meet the material needs of others and to give others a comparable payment for goods, labor, or services. It perfects the virtues of liberality, industry, and stewardship. The eighth commandment guides humans to the virtue of honesty. Finally, the tenth commandment prohibits the coveting of the goods of others and helps people acquire the virtue of poverty of heart.

18

TEMPERANCE

The Virtue of Enjoying Truly Good Things

Now that we have analyzed the virtues perfecting the intellect and the will, it is time to analyze the virtues that perfect the emotions. The emotions have a key role in human actions because of their influence on the intellect and the will. By means of this influence, the emotions can drive humans to either good or evil actions. If the emotions are properly ordered, they can make the performance of good actions easy and very pleasurable. However, if they are unruly, they can make the performance of good actions very difficult and unpleasant. In fact, unruly emotions can sometimes completely overrun the intellect and the will, making good actions impossible. For example, when placed in a situation where there is a temptation to get drunk, humans with the virtue of temperance can easily and joyfully avoid drunkenness. On the other hand, those without temperance will struggle to avoid drunkenness (if they are able to avoid it at all). Even if they do avoid drunkenness through sheer will power, they may be filled with the emotion of sorrow.

As seen in this example, the virtues that perfect the emotions help people perform good actions. The perfected emotions can cause the intellect and will to act with great intensity. It is much easier for humans to have love of friendship for others when they are emotionally in love with them. For example, it is much easier to serve those who have a personality we find pleasant than those who really annoy us. It is difficult to perform good actions if someone has to overcome the emotions of hatred, anger, or sorrow.

Not only will properly disposed emotions aid the intellect and the will in performing good actions, but they also make the actions pleasurable. When a good action is performed, the intellect is happy, and the will is filled with joy. If the emotions are perfected by virtue, they will also be joyful at the performance of a good action. The truly virtuous person has great emotional joy upon completing a good action, even if the good action requires a large sacrifice. For example, suppose a wealthy man gives up all of his wealth in order to join a monastery. If he is truly virtuous, upon completing the action the intellect performs the act of happiness by contemplating the good of the action. The will is filled with joy as it rests in the good of loving God, and the emotions are filled with emotional joy because they love serving God and others more than material goods.

A significant portion of society seeks emotional pleasure in actions contrary to love of God, such as sex outside of marriage or overconsumption of drugs or alcohol. Because of the relation between the body and the soul, these actions often result in an emotional high. However, even though they result in an emotional high, because they contradict the way God created humans to act, they will ultimately cause unhappiness. When the emotions are perfected by the virtue of temperance, humans can have great emotional joy (even a great emotional high) when they do good actions. They can be filled with joy when they avoid immoral sex and when they drink in moderation. Consequently, the virtues that perfect the emotions are important because they aid the intellect and the will in causing good actions and in avoiding evil actions. They make bad actions unpleasant, and they make good actions easy and pleasurable.

Because natural inclinations are corrupted by unruly emotions, the early stages of the Christian moral life might not be considered to be fun. Things are only "fun" when the emotions receive pleasure from the activity. When the emotions are unruly and desire a false or apparent good, humans are only able to perform the good action when either someone else compels them to perform the action or their intellect and will forcibly overcome the contrary emotions. In both cases, the person acts against their emotional desires, and the action is not emotionally pleasurable (at least not initially). However, as the emotions are perfected by virtues, the emotions begin to desire good actions and the completion of the action becomes quite pleasurable. As virtues perfecting the emotions are attained, the Christian moral life becomes "fun" and enjoyable. Since it can take a lifetime to perfect the emotions, it might appear that most Christians are doomed to a joyless and unexciting life of faith. Although some Christians unfortunately appear to live this way,[1] Christians can and should be joyful by thinking about the aspects of the life of faith that are emotionally desirable. Moreover, the Holy Spirit's gifts can perfect the emotions so that even a beginner who is open to the Holy Spirit can experience the great joy and pleasure of Christianity.[2]

The two virtues that perfect the emotions are temperance and fortitude. This chapter will analyze the virtue of temperance. It will first study temperance in general and the subvirtues that correspond to it. Because the emotions have such an enormous influence on the intellect and the will, normally laws are needed to motivate humans to do actions that build these virtues within the emotions. In other words, humans need the help of those outside of them to overcome unruly emotions. Hence, the last major section of this chapter will study the commandments that guide and motivate humans to perform the actions that perfect the virtue of temperance.

TEMPERANCE

So that the body stays alive, the emotions are naturally inclined to seek pleasurable activities. However, because someone can desire the pleasure itself, but hate the hard work required to attain the pleasure, two inclinations can be identified within the emotions. The concupiscible appetite desires pleasure in itself (and hates pain). The irascible appetite seeks the difficult means of attaining the bodily good (or hates the difficult means). Temperance is the virtue that perfects the concupiscible appetite and fortitude is the virtue that perfects the irascible appetite. For example, whereas temperance perfects the emotions to desire the proper amount of pleasure from food, fortitude perfects the emotions to seek the difficult good of working in order to attain the food.

Temperance transforms the passions (emotions) of the concupiscible appetite to seek the proper pleasures (derived from bodily goods) as determined by the intellect.[3] The intellect determines both the proper amount of pleasure that should be sought and the proper type of pleasure. Since temperance perfects the emotions to follow the intellect, it causes the emotions to have the proper amount of desire (not too much and not too little) and to desire the proper pleasurable objects. For example, the temperate person desires exactly the right amount of food (not too much and not too little) and the right type of food, as dictated by the intellect.

In order for the body to survive, humans (and other animals) derive emotional pleasure from actions that are in general good for the body. Hence, for the most part, emotional pleasure is a good thing and should be enjoyed. God created humans as bodily beings, and it is proper that humans take pleasure in acts necessary for the functioning of the body, such as eating good food, sleeping, and relaxing through interaction with family and friends. To not take pleasure in good actions is the vice of insensibility (a defect in the proper amount of emotional joy). If someone avoids an essential good action specifically because it is pleasurable, they commit a sin of insensibility. For example, puritans might avoid the sexual act within marriage specifically because it was pleasurable. However, because the emotions are not rational, unless they are trained to participate in reason, they will seek pleasure even when it is harmful. For example, because reproduction is necessary for human survival, the emotions will generally seek the pleasure of sex. They do not understand that acts like adultery actually destroy human happiness. Thus, although pleasure is good in itself, it is often necessary to abstain from pleasurable acts for the sake of a greater end.[4] In other words, pleasure must be limited in certain areas in order to perform actions that are truly ordered to happiness. By avoiding immoral actions that cause short-term pleasure, even greater pleasure can be obtained in the long term through the perfection of the emotions. Prudence is necessary to determine when pleasure should be sought and enjoyed and when it should be avoided.

Once the emotions are perfected by the virtue of temperance, they participate in reason, and they only desire the bodily pleasure that comes from good actions. In other words, the natural inclination to seek the bodily good as determined by reason is perfected, and the emotions connaturally desire only bodily goods that truly lead to happiness. For example, temperate people enjoy eating in moderation and emotionally despise the act of overeating. They are filled with sorrow when they overeat. In fact, temperate humans not only despise performing bad actions, but they have an aversion to seeing others perform bad actions. This aversion to the bad actions of oneself and others is called *shame*. The temperate person feels shame at seeing immoral actions. For example, Joe might feel shame if he sees his friends drinking in excess.

Because the emotions are so unruly as a result of the effects of fallen nature, it is difficult to obtain the virtues that perfect them. Often, in order to perform good actions, humans must, through sheer willpower, override the emotions and go to the opposite end of the spectrum (either toward an excess or defect). This act of willing the good in opposition to contrary emotions is called *continence*.[5] (The term "continence" can also mean abstaining from sex, but this is not the way the word is being used here.) In cases where humans are strongly attracted to an excess, in order to hit the mean (the middle), they must aim toward the defect, and vice versa if attracted to the defect. For example, suppose George has a tendency toward gluttony (excessive desire for food). In order to attain the virtue of eating in moderation, he must force himself to only eat what he needs. Furthermore, he will need to fast (aim toward the defect) in order to perfect the emotions to desire the mean.[6] An analogy that helps explain continent actions is the bending of an iron bar. If a bar is bent and you want to straighten it, you must bend it beyond straight in order for it to be straight when it snaps back. In order to change vices into virtues, humans must also go to the opposite extreme in order to hit the mean.

Although continence is essential for developing virtue, it is not a virtue. Continence requires the overriding of contrary emotions. In the virtuous person, the emotions are properly ordered, which causes her actions to be easy, prompt, and joyful. Continent acts are still difficult, and not always joyful.

Historically, there are three main areas that the virtue of temperance moderates: desire for food, drink (alcohol), and sex. However, I am also going to show the need for temperance in moderating the desire for recreation and in moderating emotional love of others.

Proper Desire for Food

Temperance perfects humans to desire the proper amount and type of food. The intellect, perfected by prudence, determines the proper amount and type of food to be eaten in order to attain health. If the person has temperance, her emotions will follow her intellect and only desire the proper amount and type of food. If she still desires too much or too little, she might have enough willpower to eat the proper amount, but she does not yet have the virtue of temperance. The virtue of temperance allows her to not only have healthy eating habits but to enjoy eating healthy.

The excess of desire for food is the vice of *gluttony*; the defect is a lack of desire for food such as seen in cases of *anorexia* (see note 37 in chapter 8). In order to perfect the virtue of temperance, she will need to practice eating healthy food and eating in moderation. If she has a tendency toward gluttony, she will need to practice continence and intentionally eat too little food in order to train the emotions to eat the proper amount over time. If she has too little desire for food, she might have to force herself to eat more food than would normally be prudent.

Sobriety

Sobriety is the virtue that moderates the proper desire for alcohol and drugs. The excessive desire for alcohol is the vice of drunkenness. The defect would be feeling that all use of alcohol is wrong. In virtues that perfect the emotions, the mean is in accord with the subject. In other words, the mean will vary with the dispositions of different people. For example, some people can drink more than others and still be drinking in moderation. For those people with a genetic disposition toward drunkenness or who have (or have had) the vice of drunkenness, the mean for them is to desire no alcohol at all. The same mean can also apply to people in situations where it is illegal or immoral for them to consume alcohol.

The sins against sobriety are serious because they cause humans to lose their freedom. As we saw in chapter 1, the ability to know and love and the corresponding freedom that flows from this ability is what distinguishes humans from the rest of the created world. When humans are morally drunk, they lose their ability to reason properly and thus lose their freedom.[7] Drunkenness causes humans to lose that which is distinct to them: the ability to freely perform good human actions.[8] Drunkenness becomes a serious matter (and if known to be wrong and freely chosen it becomes a mortal sin) when the intellect's ability to judge becomes impaired.[9] Judgment is the step of the human action where one determines whether the action corresponds to higher ends. In other words, it is the step where one determines if the action is good or bad. Without the ability to judge, a human is not free. The action of getting drunk can especially cause false happiness that can substantially hinder the acquisition of true happiness.

Sobriety not only applies to the moderate use of alcohol but also to the proper use of all drugs. For those drugs that can remove freedom (either through impairing reason or causing an addiction that hinders humans from knowing and loving), the virtue of sobriety causes humans to have no desire for the drug unless it is needed for legitimate medical reasons. In other words, the mean for these morally harmful drugs is no desire at all. In cases where a harmful addiction can easily develop, using even a small amount can be mortally sinful.

As we also saw in chapter 1, the soul (the first cause) and the body (the instrumental cause) work together to cause actions. Because emotions are in the body and in the soul, the movement of an emotion within the soul causes a corresponding chemical change in the body. For example, when someone has the emotion of love, chemicals such as adrenaline (which can increase your heart rate and cause you to sweat), dopamine (causing the feeling of great pleasure or ecstasy), and oxytocin (giving feelings of attachment) are released by the body.[10] In fact, according to Helen Fisher, the dopamine-induced pleasurable feeling that people have when they are in love is the same feeling that people have when they take cocaine, nicotine, or morphine.[11] Thus, not only do the emotions cause a chemical change in the body, but a chemical change in the body can cause an "artificial" emotional feeling. I say "artificial," because these emotions are not responses to sense knowledge but are caused artificially by the use of drugs.[12] For example, if someone uses nicotine, the dopamine levels are elevated, and the person feels the same pleasure that would normally come from truly experiencing a bodily good, such as an intimate conversation with a friend. This artificial pleasure can take the place of authentic pleasure that humans should experience for the good of the body and soul.[13] Artificial pleasure allows people to have emotional pleasure without actually exerting the effort to do pleasurable activities that are truly good for the person. These artificial pleasures result in false happiness since they deter humans from doing the activities that lead to the true happiness found in loving relationships.

Some types of drugs, such as cocaine and methamphetamines, produce an extreme emotional high within the soul. Normally, it takes many actions to form either a virtue or a vice within the emotions. However, if the emotional reaction is intense enough, the emotions can be disposed to a particular end by a single action. In other words, a single action can cause a habit. Normally this in not possible by natural means alone.[14] However, certain drugs can create an artificial high that is so intense that they can cause a vice (an addiction) in a single action for some people. (On the other extreme, the Holy Spirit can move humans to experience such emotional pleasure that an infused virtue is greatly perfected in a single action.) Consequently, it is always a serious sin to use any drug that has the potential to seriously hinder freedom (except for legitimate medical reasons).

CHASTITY

Chastity is the virtue that perfects the emotions to properly desire sexual pleasure. The pleasure resulting from the sexual act is a good thing because it motivates people to procreate children and helps unite people in permanent, loving relationships. However, because both children and permanent relationships are such important goods, the possibility of misusing the sexual act is immense. The misuse of the sexual act can destroy families, harm children, emotionally and spiritually injure other people, and in the end damage society. In fact, the virtue of chastity is essential for humans to truly love others.[15] Both within marriage and outside of marriage, chastity is required for humans to treat others as persons to be loved for their own sake and not as sexual objects. Consequently, the virtue of chastity is very important, and the sins against chastity are generally serious. Chastity perfects the emotions to desire only sexual actions that take place within the proper context of marriage. Only within this context, where the enduring love of God unites a couple, can the sexual act be ordered to true love and happiness.[16] The excess of improper sexual desire is the vice of lust, and the lack of proper sexual desire is a form of insensibility.

Lust is a disordered desire for sexual pleasure or a disordered exercise of sexual pleasure. For example, lustful people may desire to have sex with someone they are not married to. Even in marriage spouses can have lust by desiring their spouse primarily as a sexual object of pleasure rather than as a person to be loved as a friend. In other words, they lust by having emotional love (or love of use) of their spouse (or someone else) without love of friendship. Lust is often associated with sexual desire in general. However, proper sexual desire is a good thing that contributes to the unity of a marital relationship. The distinction between lust and proper sexual desire is that lust reduces all feminine (or masculine) values to that of a sexual object. In other words, the problem is not that one human sexually desires another person; the problem is that the lustful person does not desire the whole person but only the body for sensual gratification. The other person is not loved for his or her own sake, but only for the sensual and emotional pleasure that comes from the sexual act. Since love of friendship is essential for true unity to develop, lust contradicts the natural and supernatural inclinations to be united with others.[17]

A common sin that exemplifies lust in our society is pornography. Pornography violates chastity because it turns humans into sexual objects. It contradicts love of friendship by causing humans to be loved solely for sensual gratification. It harnesses the strong desire that humans have to the sexual act but separates this desire from the love of friendship that results in true unity. People with the vice of viewing pornography begin to view members of the other sex as sexual objects rather than as people made in the image of God. Because this vice corrupts the emotions by causing them to work against love of friendship, it can devastate families and keep people from forming loving relationships with members of the opposite sex. Jesus shows the seriousness of pornography when he states that those who look lustfully at other people commit adultery with them in their heart (Mt 5:27–28).

The defect of proper sexual desire is a form of insensibility. This vice can be a problem within marriages if it hinders the ability of spouses to express their everlasting love or hinders their ability to procreate. The sexual pleasure that results from truly good actions within marriage is a blessing from God that helps strengthen the unity between a husband and a wife. Paul, in 1 Corinthians 7:1–5, proclaims the importance of the sexual act within marriage by encouraging married couples to have sex, unless they have a serious reason to abstain.

A subvirtue under chastity is the virtue of purity. Purity is a virtue that moderates the proper use of physical actions, which show affection but can tempt one to lust (for example, kissing, hugging, etc.). In other words, humans show their love through their bodies, and it is appropriate for people to show physical affection to others. However, the wrong type of physical affection, physical affection in inappropriate situations, or too much physical affection can contradict the love that these actions are meant to symbolize. For example, it would be inappropriate for young a woman to passionately kiss a priest. So also, it is inappropriate for unmarried couples to perform any actions that are by their nature ordered to the sexual act or any actions that cause them to lust. Because different actions will tempt different people, the mean in physical actions (between lust and not showing love through physical touch) will vary with each couple. However, for all people there are certain actions that are only allowed in marriage. This will be further discussed in the sections on the sixth and ninth commandments.

OTHER SUBVIRTUES UNDER TEMPERANCE

Similar to material goods and talents, every moment of one's time must also be devoted to loving God and others. However, because humans must grow and remain healthy both physically and spiritually in order to properly love God and others, a certain amount of time must be devoted to one's own perfection. For example, education and sleep both take a lot of time, but both are necessary if humans are going to fulfill their divine calling. Time must also be spent on recreation and relaxation. Humans require leisure time in order to recuperate both physically and spiritually.[18] Recreation and relaxation are pleasurable because they are necessary for the functioning of the body and soul. Thus, there is a virtue of desiring the proper amount of leisure and the proper type of leisure. In today's world, many people go to the extremes. Some people work all the time and fail to take leisure (the defect). However, in developed countries, the vast majority of people spend far too much time on recreational activities. For example, many people spend an excessive amount of time playing on the computer, playing video games, listening to music, following sports teams, or watching television. Although some recreation is necessary, too much becomes the sin of sloth because these humans are not using their time to love God and others. Prudence is required to determine how much recreation time is necessary for humans to maximize their physical and spiritual potential.

Recreation is not only important for human functioning but is also a necessary part of human culture.[19] For centuries communities have joined together in recreational activities that both unite them as a true human community and express their cultural identity. For example, sports activities (such as the Olympics in ancient Greece) and festivals (such as Oktoberfest) both unite the individuals within a community and reinforce the community's cultural identity.[20] On the level of family and friends, games are a very important way to grow in virtue and love of others.

An additional aspect of the virtue of proper recreation is the ability to use humor both for personal growth and to strengthen relationships with others.[21] The ability to laugh at the unexpected, whether in jokes, stories, or life, is very important to the recreation of the body and soul. A sense of humor helps humans contextualize the miseries of life and the temptation to despair. Furthermore, humor can be an excellent way to reach out to others and to make time spent with others enjoyable. However, humor can also be improperly used, such as in sarcastic comments that hurt the feelings of others and damage loving relationships.

Another important subvirtue under temperance is the habit of having the proper amount of emotional love of other humans. It is good to emotionally love one's friends and family. The person with this virtue even emotionally loves strangers and enemies. This love motivates them to perform acts of love for strangers and even enemies with great intensity. Too much emotional love of others (that is not in accord with reason) can cause people to idolize others or to seek to fulfill the harmful wishes of others. For example, sometimes people in a romantic relationship will be blinded by their emotional love for their partner. They will not be able to think rationally and will often do imprudent things.[22]

Too little emotional love makes it difficult for people to perform acts of love of friendship for others and to enter into loving relationships with them. For some people, even proper emotional love of family and friends can be difficult. These people will not have the wonderful emotional joy that comes from interpersonal relationships. To increase this virtue, people must constantly do good actions for others and contemplate the good in others, even when they have no emotional love for the other person.

THE VIRTUE of temperance is very important because improper emotional desire can damage relationships and result in the unhappiness of both the one without temperance and those he interacts with. To increase temperance and the subvirtues corresponding to temperance, humans must practice eating, drinking, showing physical affection, recreating, and even emotionally loving in prudent ways. In many cases continence must be practiced because of the human tendency to seek the excess or defect. For example, if people desire recreation too much, they must go to the defect and spend less time recreating. In the cases of emotional love of others, if people do not have emotional love for a person, they must go to the extreme and shower the person with kindness.[23] If they have too much emotional love so that their reason is impaired, they should spend some time apart (if possible). When temperance is infused with charity, all temperate activities and even acts of continence are done out of love of God. These acts of continence help humans to grow in self-discipline and allow them to share in the sufferings of Christ.

GIFTS OF THE HOLY SPIRIT

Since the gift of fear of the Lord, which is often paired with temperance, has already been covered in chapter 13, a specific gift of the Holy Spirit will not be paired with temperance. Instead, we'll examine the way that the Holy Spirit perfects the emotions in general. The Holy Spirit supernaturally perfects the emotions to desire the proper pleasure that results from good actions and from good loving relationships with God and others. A result of this supernatural desire is extreme passion in acting and an intense emotional joy upon completing the actions. For example, upon receiving the Holy Spirit, the apostles were so exuberant in their preaching that they were accused of being drunk. Peter even had to deny the accusations by stating, "These people are not drunk, for it is only nine o'clock in the morning."[24] Like with the apostles, often the Holy Spirit will give people great emotional desire and joy when they spend time in prayer or spend time helping others. By giving people this emotional desire and joy, the spiritual life is much easier and much more pleasant. When the Holy Spirit perfects the emotions, humans become more amiable to his guidance and movement. The Holy Spirit can move them to joyfully perform the loving actions that result in their happiness and the happiness of those around them.

COMMANDMENTS CORRESPONDING TO TEMPERANCE

The sixth and ninth commandments correspond to temperance. These two commandments regulate sexual behavior by prohibiting adultery and the coveting of another's wife. Because sexual morality is so very important to the strength of the community, God revealed these two commandments in order for the Israelites to be happy in ancient times and in order for modern humans to be happy today. Following these commandments leads to an increase in the virtue of chastity.

Sixth Commandment

The sixth commandment is "You shall not commit adultery." Although the ancient Israelites sometimes failed to understand this commandment and allowed divorce and remarriage, along with polygamy, Jesus shows its proper interpretation: the unity within marriage comes from God and cannot be broken by humans.[25] He further extends this commandment by saying that you shall not have lust for a woman (or man).[26] Thus, chastity consists of complete purity in both mind and actions. The chaste person does not seek the minimum allowed in sexual matters but seeks what makes a person the holiest.

The sexual act is ordered by natural and divine law to the higher end of *procreation as a human* (which by necessity includes the end of *unity*).[27] In other words, both nature and divine revelation teach that the sexual act exists for procreation and unity. On the natural level, humans, like all animals, are naturally inclined to propagate the species by means of the sexual act. More specifically, humans are naturally inclined to procreate and raise their offspring so that their offspring are able to perform their proper actions. In other words, the natural inclination is not just to have children but to have children that are able to ultimately perform good human actions. Because the proper actions of the different species of animals vary, the mode of procreation and care of offspring also varies. For example, some animals merely procreate and leave their offspring to fend for themselves. Others spend months, even years, raising their offspring so that they can perform their proper actions. The point is that since humans have a higher end than other animals, their mode of procreation and care of offspring will be different from that of all other animals.

Because humans are ordered to actions of knowing and loving God and others within a community, they must not only be taught how to physically survive, but they must also be formed in virtue so that they can enter into loving relationships with God and others. Since humans, compared to other animals, have few activities that can be done solely by instinct (habits are needed to do nearly everything), even physical survival requires the learning of trades and the ability to work with other people. On top of this, because of the complexity of humans, acquiring the virtues to enter into loving relationships requires years of guidance and motivation. Furthermore, fathers and mothers possess complementary perfections that contribute to the raising of virtuous children. The point is that the best way for humans to develop so that they can perform their proper actions is for them to be born into a stable environment where they can observe and receive the unconditional and permanent love of their mother and their father. In other words, *humans are naturally inclined to procreate in a human manner*, which is not the same manner as animals. Humans are naturally inclined to procreate within a permanent, loving union that provides the proper environment for children to truly learn how to know and love God and others. Although some animals are naturally inclined to have sex outside of monogamous relationships, humans are naturally inclined to have sex only within a monogamous relationship that is built upon lifelong love between the spouses.[28]

Because the natural inclination to procreation requires a permanent loving relationship, by nature the sexual act between humans communicates a permanent love between partners. Humans know each other through their actions, and all actions convey a particular message. For example, a hug generally conveys the meaning of love and acceptance. Some actions receive their meaning from society. For example, a high five in American society means "good job," but the action could just as easily show aggression. Other actions receive their meaning from nature because their very essence signifies a particular meaning.[29] For example, babies do not have to learn that a smile is a sign for joy, for as early as one month old, they automatically smile when they have emotional joy. Because the sexual act is ordered toward the procreation of children, and both the father and mother must unconditionally and permanently love each other in order to create the proper environment for these children, the sexual act by nature says, "I love you completely for the rest of my life."

This ability to communicate permanent love through the sexual act is a wonderful thing. As created in the image of God, who is everlasting love, humans are made to enter into lifelong, loving relationships. Furthermore, because humans express their love through their bodies, they are naturally inclined to communicate this everlasting love to each other. The sexual act becomes a means of expressing this everlasting love. It becomes a way that spouses can continually reveal their interior love for each other throughout their lives. If humans use the sexual act outside of marriage or for "purely recreational purposes," they change the meaning of the action from expressing permanent and unconditional love to at best expressing temporary love of friendship and at worst expressing pure lust. Since they have changed the meaning of the action, they have lost the normal way of conveying what every human naturally desires to honestly tell another human: "I love you completely and unconditionally for the rest of my life."[30] Unless they are able to restore this meaning to the sexual act, their ability to love completely will be hindered, and their happiness will be diminished (especially within marriage). Consequently, by nature the sexual act is ordered to both procreation and unity.[31]

Since grace perfects nature, it is no surprise that divine revelation confirms and gives even greater meaning to the natural meaning of sex. In Genesis 1:27–28, the procreative meaning is revealed. Immediately following the passage where humans are created in God's image, God blesses humans and says, "Be fertile and multiply." As created in the image of God, humans cooperate with God in the ability to procreate. Unlike animals, when humans procreate, God creates a new soul that is made to live forever in union with him. Consequently, the sexual organs take on a particular sacredness as the means through which God causes new human life.[32] Thus, the sexual act must be treated with reverence, and it must only be done within the proper environment of marriage. Marriage provides the stable environment necessary for these children to grow in loving relationships with God. When children see the divine love that unites husband and wife, they are first introduced to the love of God.

Genesis 2:23–24 reveals the unitive meaning of the sexual act. When Adam and Eve come to together as man and wife, they become one flesh. The New Testament further explains that the unity within marriage comes from the love within God and is a sign of the love between Christ and the Church.[33] The love between spouses flows from and signifies the love between and among the Father, Son, and Holy Spirit. It must reflect the unconditional and eternal love of the three persons. Since the Father gives all that he is to the Son (the divine nature), and the Son receives all that the Father is, spouses must imitate the divine persons by giving their entire selves to each other: their body, soul, and possessions for their entire lives.

Since the sexual act communicates the love between the spouses, when God's grace unites a couple in marriage, the sexual act conveys the unconditional and eternal love of God. It communicates a complete gift of oneself: body, soul, and possessions. In other words, divine revelation teaches that the sexual act means "I give of myself completely: body, soul, and possessions." The spouses now share each other and are spiritually united in a profound union (the two are made one flesh). Hence, the sexual act must only be done when the proper conditions for complete giving exist: within marriage where spouses have publicly declared their intention of complete and unconditional unity.

Because the sexual act is naturally and supernaturally ordered to the end of procreation in a human manner (which includes complete unity), all sexual acts must be judged by this higher end. In other words, in a teleological moral system to determine whether an act is morally allowable, the intellect must judge it by higher principles (step 7 of the human action). For example, as seen in the earlier section on the seventh commandment in chapter 17, the use of property should be judged by the higher principles of the universal destination of goods and the right to private property. If someone takes something that belongs to someone else (extraordinary situations aside), then they violate the right to private property, and the object of the action is stealing. *The higher principle by which all sexual acts must be judged is that all sexual acts must be ordered to procreation in a human manner.* The meaning of the term "procreation" in a human manner includes educating and raising children together with a permanent unity based on the love of the Trinity. If the action is not ordered to procreation and unity, then it is wrong because it violates the natural and supernatural inclinations. By judging acts by this principle, we can see that the following sexual acts are sins against chastity.

Fornication

Fornication, or extramarital sex, refers to sexual actions outside of marriage. Fornication violates the procreative end of sex because the sexual act does not take place within the stable environment necessary for the proper formation and education of children. It also violates the unitive end. No humans fully know the depths of their wills, and the human will can be very fickle. In other words, humans by their own power often change their minds and fall in and out of relationships. However, the unity in marriage is not founded on the weak love of the human will but on the infinite love of God. Consequently, the grace of God in marriage is necessary for someone to promise fidelity to a spouse until death.[34] Only by participation in the unchanging love of

God through the sacrament of marriage can humans honestly declare through the sexual act that they have unchanging love. Furthermore, marriage is a public institution, so the other members of the Church can aid the couple in fulfilling their call to a permanent union. In order to perform good actions, the guidance and motivation of others is often necessary. Consequently, just being in "love" is not enough. Humans must be married in order for the sexual act to truly be ordered toward unity in the full sense of the term. If people truly have love of friendship for members of the opposite sex, they will not pressure each other to have sex until they are married.

Free unions or living together before marriage also violates chastity. Even if the couple does not intend to fornicate, they place themselves in a position where they are tempted to fornicate. Furthermore, they commit the sin of scandal by publicly desecrating the proper concept of marriage and family.

Homosexual Actions

Homosexual actions also violate both the procreative and unitive ends of sex. The procreative end is violated because these actions cannot result in the procreation of life. The unitive end is violated because these actions cannot take place within a divinely established marriage, since God only unites men and women within marriage.[35] Although homosexual actions are sins, having homosexual tendencies is not a sin. Only human actions are sins. Hence, a sin is only committed if someone acts upon a homosexual tendency. Like all people who have tendencies toward sinful actions, those with homosexual tendencies are called to overcome their temptations and to live a life of loving union with God. All members of the Church should lovingly and prudently help them to form truly virtuous relationships.

With a spirit of humility, members of society should help people with homosexual tendencies live a chaste lifestyle. Homosexual "marriage" should be discouraged. To prohibit homosexual "marriage" is not discrimination. An action is only discrimination if a natural right of someone is being violated. For example, to prohibit a particular group of people from getting a proper education is discrimination, since a proper education is a natural right. However, homosexual "marriage" is not an authentic right; rather, it is a false right. Allowing homosexual "marriage" does not help people live a truly chaste lifestyle. However, it is discrimination to prohibit anything that those living a homosexual lifestyle have an authentic right to obtain. Among other things, those living a homosexual lifestyle have a natural and divine right to be loved by other humans, and virtuous people will love them by helping them be truly happy.

Artificial Birth Control

Artificial birth control (contraception or sterilization) also violates both the procreative and unitive ends of sex.[36] The procreative end is violated because couples using contraception are no longer participating with God in creating other humans. The unitive end is violated because the message of the sexual action is contradicted. The message that should communicate a complete gift of self is contradicted by an action (contraception), which by its nature is the rejection of an essential part of the spouse: one's prospective motherhood or fatherhood. In other words, because God works through humans in procreating and raising children, the ability to be a mother or a father is an important element of one's identity.[37] To reject someone's prospective motherhood or fatherhood is to reject an important part of that person. This rejection can be seen in the difference between the following two statements: "I want to have sex with you," and, "I want to have and raise a baby with you." The first statement may or may not convey love, but the second statement, if said seriously, manifests the love of a long-term commitment. Consequently, contraceptive sex prevents spouses from giving themselves completely to each other.

However, if contraception is not allowed, what can people do who have a legitimate reason not to have a child? In other words, procreation in a human manner also means not having children when there is a legitimate reason not to have them. Since procreation also means raising virtuous children, if humans know that the necessary conditions for raising virtuous children do not exist, then they should not have children. So, how are married couples to avoid pregnancy? For most of the history of the Christian Church, the answer to this question was that they must abstain. Paul, in 1 Corinthians 7:1–5, tells married couples that they should not deprive each other of the sexual act unless they mutually agree to abstain for a good reason. For Paul, the good reason is prayer.[38] Following the advice of Paul, married couples within the Church were always allowed to abstain if they had a serious reason.

In the middle of the nineteenth century, scientists began to understand the woman's reproductive cycle. They determined that women are not fertile all the time but only for a small portion of their menstrual cycle. Although it would take scientists a great deal longer to actually accurately determine which part of a cycle is fertile, as early as 1853 the Vatican was asked whether or not abstaining for a segment of the cycle to avoid pregnancy was allowed.[39] The Vatican replied that abstaining was allowed, provided that nothing was done to impede conception. This teaching continued the traditional teaching of the Church. Couples have always been allowed to abstain if they have a serious reason.

Periodic abstinence (more commonly called "natural family planning") is the practice of abstaining, for serious reasons, during the days within a cycle that a woman is fertile.[40] This practice is allowable because it does not violate the higher end of the sexual act in the way contraception does. In other words, periodic abstinence is in accord with the higher end of procreating in a human manner. Thus, although someone using contraception and someone practicing periodic abstinence may have the same intention, the object of periodic abstinence is different from the object of the act of contraception.

Recall that the object of the action refers to the moral species. It is the same as the intention if and only if the action is in moral conformity with the intention. In order for an act to be in moral conformity, the steps of counsel and judgment must be properly performed. Suppose Joe and Kate are married and have a legitimate reason for avoiding pregnancy (e.g., physical health, poverty, education, sake of the common good of a society). Based on this reason, they then form the good intention of avoiding pregnancy. Following this intention, they take counsel. They could determine three possible means of avoiding pregnancy: contraception, complete abstinence, or periodic abstinence. They would then judge by higher principles. Contraception violates the unitive and procreative ends of the sexual act. Contraception is not in moral conformity with the good intention of avoiding pregnancy. Hence, the object of the action would be contraception and not avoiding pregnancy.

On the other hand, abstaining from sex is in moral conformity with the good intention of avoiding pregnancy. Because humans are naturally inclined to procreate in a manner that includes raising holy children, there are times when couples should abstain because they realize they could not properly raise (more) children. In other words, if you are having sex, the act should be ordered to procreation as a human. However, if you cannot properly raise children now, then you should not be having sex. In both cases you are judging by the higher end of procreation in a human manner. Thus, as long as there is a prudent reason for avoiding pregnancy, periodic abstinence is allowed. Because it does not violate the higher end, it is in conformity with the intention, and the object of the act is avoiding pregnancy.

The following statements clearly show how contraception and periodic abstinence relate differently to the higher ends of the sexual act: (1) If a couple believes that the proper end of the sexual act is procreation and unity and they want to avoid pregnancy, then they will abstain. The act of abstaining emphasizes that the proper ends of the sexual act are procreation and unity; (2) If a couple does *not* believe that sex is ordered to procreation and unity, then they will use contraception in order to avoid pregnancy. In other words, periodic abstinence is in accord with procreation as a human because humans should only have children when the proper situation exists. Yet, humans should also be open to procreation and unity when they do have sex because of the spiritual nature of the sexual act for humans. Although the acts of contraception and abstinence may have the same intention, they are not the same action.

Although *complete* abstinence would be allowable, it would not be the best action because the sexual act allows Joe and Kate to express their marital love. However, if Joe and Kate practice periodic abstinence for a good reason, they will be having sex when they believe that they are infertile. Does having sex when they believe they are infertile violate the higher end of procreation? It does not. The sexual act is still open to procreation, since it is something *outside* of the sexual act that impedes procreation. God created females so that they are only fertile for part of their menstrual cycles. In other words, Joe and Kate would still be acting in a way that if the proper conditions existed she would get pregnant. Thus, this act is still a complete gift of self.

A good analogy to help show how the object of contraception is different than the object of periodic abstinence is the use of steroids to get stronger. Suppose an athlete wants to get stronger. This is a good intention. He then takes counsel and determines that he can either use natural means of weight training alone or he can do so while using steroids (an artificial means) to become stronger. He then must judge. Exercise is ultimately ordered to the good of health. Natural means of weight training (if done prudently) is ordered to the higher end of health. Steroids are generally harmful to the body and are not ordered to the higher end of health. (If the athlete is competing in a sport, the act would also violate the higher end of acting justly.) Consequently, the object of the act of using steroids is not an act of getting stronger but an act of using harmful drugs. Like the case of distinguishing between contraception and periodic abstinence, the intention for both the one using steroids and the one using natural weight training is the same, but the object is different.

Masturbation

Masturbation is clearly against both the procreative and unitive ends of the sexual act. Furthermore, it employs lust and does not treat the sexual organs with the dignity given to them by God.

Artificial Reproduction

Artificial reproduction includes actions such as artificial insemination and in vitro fertilization. If someone outside of the married couple is brought in to donate an egg or sperm, then the actions are called *heterologous* insemination and fertilization. If the techniques only involve the married couple, then the act is called *homologous* insemination and fertilization. Heterologous artificial reproduction clearly violates both the unitive and the procreative ends of the sexual act. It violates the unitive end because people other than the married couple are involved in the procreation of the child. Although these actions do end in procreation, they do not end in procreation as appropriate for humans. Recall that humans are naturally inclined to procreate and raise their children in such a way that their children are able to perform their proper actions. These children are not brought into the world by a mother and a father who are bound to each other. Homologous artificial reproduction violates the unitive end because the act by which the child is brought into existence is not a sexual act where the couple completely gives themselves to each other. In other words, the sexual act has been replaced by some technical process. Although artificial reproduction may be suitable for the procreation of other animals, because humans are made to procreate within permanent loving relationships, it is not the appropriate way for humans to procreate.[41]

Although artificial reproduction is wrong, it is allowable for couples to use technology to help the woman become pregnant, provided that a technical process is not substituted for the sexual act. In other words, technical procedures can assist the sexual act in attaining its proper end, but they cannot replace it. For example, fertility drugs are allowable, but in vitro fertilization is not.

Adultery

Adultery is marital infidelity. Marriage shares in the unity of the Trinity and cannot be dissolved.[42] Consequently, getting divorced and having sexual relations with another person is adultery. It is a form of fornication and is wrong for the same reasons that fornication is wrong. Adultery can have particularly devastating effects on families and children.

In serious situations, such as when one spouse is abusing the other spouse or abusing the children, the spouses may separate with the permission of the Church. Acquiring a legal divorce is allowable if it is the only way to secure the care of children.[43] However, if the marriage was valid, the spouses are still spiritually united by the love of God and are still considered to be married by both God and the Church. If one of these spouses has sex with a different person (either within or outside of a civil marriage), he or she commits adultery.

Because of the deontological tendencies found in moral theology, the sinfulness of marital infidelity and divorce and remarriage has often been emphasized. Although these are certainly sinful actions, what is often underemphasized is the truth that maintaining the unconditional unity between spouses is exceedingly important for the happiness of both the spouses and the children.

Sometimes spouses think that because they love each other they will always choose to stay together for the rest of their lives. There is certainly some truth in this belief, since love of friendship by its nature causes humans to seek permanent unity. However, over the course of a lifetime, because of the corrupted inclinations within humans, it is often the stability in marriage that ensures and protects the love. An unconditional commitment to stay together that is sworn before God and supported by the community is an absolutely essential aspect of long-term marital happiness. The reason this commitment is so important is that no human is perfect and tensions will inevitably arise in every close relationship. Because every marriage has some tension, one of the most important elements of any happy marriage is the ability of the spouses to forgive each other repeatedly.[44] This ability to forgive is highly supported by the permanent stability of marriage. This stability is essential to love, because when humans are angry with each other, the easy action to take is to avoid each other. Yet, as long as they avoid each other, spouses are unable to truly love each other. However, if they are forced to live together, then for the sake of their own contentment, they must take the initiative and apologize and forgive each other. The stability provides the spouses with the opportunity to overcome their selfishness and reconcile with each other. This act of reconciliation is at the very heart of true love and can result in an even stronger marriage. Hence, the unconditional stability of the relationship is extremely important to the happiness of parents and children, and actions that break this stability (without a serious reason) are completely contrary to the love God created humans to have.[45]

The importance of reconciliation to loving relationships is particularly demonstrated in a scene in the play *The Jeweler's Shop* by Karol Wojtyla (John Paul II). In the play, Anna's marriage with Stefan is in shambles. Their love has grown cold, and both of them are miserable and hate being with each other. Anna meets Adam, a prophetic figure in the play, who announces to Anna that the bridegroom is coming and that he will show Anna the way to true love.[46] Anna, filled with hope, eagerly goes to meet the bridegroom. However, when she finally sees the bridegroom, he has Stefan's face. Anna is perturbed and asks Adam why she saw the face of the man she hates but ought to love. Adam answers, "In the bridegroom's face each of us finds a similarity to the faces of those with whom love has entangled us."[47] Anna slowly begins to understand the significance of seeing Stefan's face on the bridegroom: when seeking the face of Love Incarnate, humans will always find the faces of those whom they are called to love, and this is especially true in reference to one's spouse. This interaction with the bridegroom changes Anna, and slowly her heart begins to change, causing her life with Stefan to become less burdensome.[48]

Although the perpetual unity of valid marriages should not be destroyed, the Church makes a distinction between valid and invalid marriages. Just as a complete rejection of another requires that one have full knowledge of the seriousness of the action and full consent in performing the action, so also choosing to be permanently united to another person requires that someone has full knowledge of the seriousness of the action and full consent. If one or both of the people getting married do not understand what they are undertaking or are not free in their decision, then the marriage is not valid. In other words, because they do not freely consent to the marriage, they are not united into one body. In this case, an annulment might be granted by the Church. An annulment is not a divorce but a statement by the Church confirming that the marriage never existed in the first place. People with an annulment are free to get a legal divorce and to remarry in the Church.

NINTH COMMANDMENT

The ninth commandment is "You shall not covet your neighbor's wife." Like the sixth commandment, the ninth also guides people to avoid lustful actions. In addition, like the tenth commandment, it prohibits coveting in general—even if another's wife (or husband) is desired as a complete person and not as a sexual object. Because marriage is the foundation of the family, it is especially important that humans not covet the spouses of others.

A subvirtue under chastity that pertains to the ninth commandment is the virtue of modesty. Modesty is the virtue of refusing to unveil what society and nature consider to be a sexual value. This virtue particularly relates to the ninth commandment because it keeps people from leading others into the sins of lust and covetousness. A sexual value can refer to anything connected to the sexual act that should be kept private by either societal or natural standards. Although modesty especially refers to the way that people dress, it can also refer to sexual values exposed in actions, movies, books, the Internet, or conversations. The key point is that because of the sacredness of marriage and the intense desire that many humans have toward the sexual act, sexual values should be kept private both to safeguard the dignity of marriage and to avoid leading others into the sin of lust.[49]

The standards for modesty are both societal and natural. Recall that an action can have both a natural meaning and a meaning given to it by society. Some actions by their very nature are ordered to the sexual act and must be kept private. Other actions do not necessarily express sexual connotations by nature but are given these connotations by the culture of a particular society. For example, what might be considered as sexually provocative dress in one society or setting might be completely appropriate in another. Prudence is necessary to determine what actions are modest and what actions could potentially tempt someone to lust.

BECAUSE TEMPERANCE requires that pleasurable goods are desired in moderation, people might be led to believe that advocates of temperance are against emotional pleasure. However, they could not be farther from the truth. Temperance perfects the emotions so that pleasure is experienced in actions that bring true happiness. The temperate person desires and enjoys actions where emotional love either increases the physical and spiritual health of a person or causes true loving relationships with God and others. The temperate person emotionally enjoys the proper amount of food, drink, recreation, and company of others. In fact, when people do not take pleasure in actions that are truly good for them, they have the vice of insensibility.

However, because of fallen nature, the emotions are unruly, and perfecting them is often a long and sometimes painful process. Continence will be required, and pleasurable activities that are not good will have to be avoided.[50] Since humans must often go to the other extreme to attain the mean, sometimes even painful activities must be performed. For example, it can be very painful for the alcoholic to abstain from alcohol, but this is the only way for him to develop the virtue of temperance. Generally, because of the corruption of the natural inclinations of the emotions, the assistance of others through laws and exhortations will be necessary for humans to train their emotions. For example, both the alcoholic and the anorexic will generally require the aid of others to attain temperance.

Because exterior assistance is necessary to perfect the virtue of temperance, laws moving people to temperate actions are essential. Since only the sixth and ninth commandments pertain directly to temperance, these were the only commandments covered in this chapter. However, many other laws could be treated that help guide people to the other subvirtues under temperance. For example, one law could be, "You should not spend an excessive amount of time on recreation and relaxation." Another law might be, "You should not get drunk or high." These laws and any other laws that lead people to form the virtue of temperance are also very important. Without the virtue of temperance, people are hindered in their ability to perform good actions, and they do not enjoy the actions when they do perform them.

19

FORTITUDE

The Virtue of Striving for Truly Good Things

Because humans are made in the image of the Trinity, they are fulfilled by a sincere gift of self. They are fulfilled by generously using their time, talents, and material goods to meet the needs of other humans. Thus, for their own happiness, the eternal law guides humans to perform difficult actions that involve extreme self-sacrifice. Although the particular way that each human fulfills God's plan will vary, all are called to devote all of their time and energy to fulfilling this plan. Some will be called to spread the Faith, both here and abroad. Others will be called to devote their lives to helping those in poverty (either material or spiritual poverty). Some may even lose their lives because of their divine calling. Still others will be called to be good mothers and fathers. Most are also called to activities that appear less glamorous in the eyes of the world but are extremely important in fulfilling God's plan. But no matter what role humans have in the divine plan, they are called to act with great intensity—to devote all their time, talents, and energy toward fulfilling their divine call.

Whether someone is dying for the Faith, raising good children, or being a good student out of love for God, completely devoting oneself to God can be very difficult. Unruly emotions will rebel in the face of difficulty. These emotions will fear and hate the sacrifice involved in hard work. They might despair of attaining the divinely appointed goals because these goals appear to be too difficult. They might then influence the intellect and will, causing humans to avoid the difficult tasks that will truly make them happy. On the other hand, if the emotions are trained by fortitude, they will drive the intellect and will to seek the difficult good. They will not despair at the magnitude of the task but will help the person strive on with hope. Fortitude is the virtue that has allowed Christians throughout the centuries to risk their lives and even face death with great passion. Fortitude continues to aid humans today in striving to perform the difficult tasks that every human is called to perform. This chapter will first examine the virtue of fortitude in general, then the subvirtues relating to fortitude, along with the corresponding vices, and, finally, the Holy Spirit's gift of fortitude.

FORTITUDE

Fortitude is the virtue that perfects the irascible emotions to aid humans in overcoming difficult obstacles in the performance of good actions. The irascible emotions of hope, daring, and anger motivate the person to seek the distant good, while the irascible emotions of despair and fear move the person to avoid the distant evil. In contrast to the concupiscible emotions, which seek pleasure in general, the irascible emotions seek the difficult means of attaining this distant pleasure. For example, temperance perfects the emotions to properly desire the emotional pleasure stemming from friendship, and fortitude perfects the emotions to drive a person to overcome any obstacles to performing acts of friendship. Friendship requires humans to share in their friend's goals and needs. Sometimes, if the emotions are not perfected by fortitude, performing loving acts that take lots of time and effort can be a real struggle. Fortitude drives people to easily and promptly overcome any difficulties when entering into the loving relationships that result in proper emotional pleasure. Another example of fortitude can be seen in the student who can easily, promptly, and joyfully study to attain the difficult good of passing the test.

There are two components to the virtue of fortitude: prudently fighting evil and enduring evil.[1] Traditionally, the first component concerned the fighting of evil on the battlefield. However, in general it refers to any action where humans actively strive to overcome a difficulty ("evil"). Many people will never fight evil on a physical battlefield. However, they will have to overcome many perceived evils in their lives. For example, they might have to fight the "evil" of cancer or another disease through aggressive treatments and lifestyle changes. They might have to persevere at their job to overcome various difficulties, such as distractions or underperforming co-workers. Athletes might have to practice hard and lift weights in order to perform at their full capacity. People might have to actively work for the civil rights of certain members of society. The key point is that under the first component of fortitude people actively persevere in order to attain a good end. If the intellect determines that it is wise to seek the good end, they will consistently and perpetually work to overcome anything that hinders the attainment of this end.

The second, and chief, component of fortitude is enduring evil. In this component, humans recognize that fighting the evil is no longer prudent, and they patiently

endure the evil (difficulty). For example, cancer patients who have exhausted all practical medical options must patiently endure the effects of the disease. Also, teachers
first actively seek to form virtues in their students, but realizing that the acquisition of
virtues takes time, they patently endure the poor work and attitudes of their students.
In addition, humans must often patiently await major events in their lives, such as the
birth of a baby or a marriage. Because patient endurance is the chief act of fortitude,
the ultimate act of fortitude is dying for God. Martyrs endure the evil of death, and
they overcome their fear of death through fortitude.[2]

In order to increase the virtue of fortitude, humans must persistently perform
whatever actions are necessary to attain their proper goals. Often these actions will be
very arduous or exhausting. However, if the intellect determines that a goal can be
prudently attained, fortitude is increased whenever these difficult actions are performed. If the intellect determines that a goal cannot be prudently attained, then fortitude is increased whenever humans joyfully and patiently endure the evils or difficulties that they cannot overcome.

VIRTUES UNDER FORTITUDE

Because fortitude perfects an appetitive power, the virtues that correspond to it are in
the middle, between an excess and defect. Prudence is necessary to determine when
to actively work to attain an end and when to endure. For example, too much daring
can result in foolish actions. Likewise, too little daring results in people not seeking to
overcome difficulties that can be conquered. The virtues under fortitude perfect the
emotions to seek to actively overcome difficulties when reason determines that it is
appropriate and when it is not appropriate to seek to endure them. We will next look
at the subvirtues of courage, magnanimity, perseverance, patience, and meekness in
this section.

COURAGE

Courage, or bravery, is the virtue that perfects the emotions to motivate the person to
act rationally in the face of great danger. Courageous people are able to overcome their
fear, and they desire to perform good actions even when they are in grave danger. Once
this virtue is perfected, the emotions follow the intellect so closely that courageous
people do not even have fear if the intellect determines that there is no danger. For example, suppose Joe is afraid of the dark. With continence, Joe can overcome his emotions and still function in the dark, but he does not have the virtue of courage until he
no longer has any irrational fears. Courage is the mean between the vices of cowardliness and foolishness. The coward has too much fear and too little of the emotion of
daring. Cowards are unable to act rationally in the face of danger. Fools have too much
daring and too little fear. They seek to perform dangerous actions in opposition to

right reason. For example, if George refused to go into shallow water to save a young child because he was afraid of water, he would be a coward. On the other hand, if George cannot swim, and he jumps into the middle of a deep, roaring river to get a $100 bill, then George is a fool.

MAGNANIMITY

One of the most important virtues under fortitude is magnanimity. The word "magnanimity" comes from the Latin words for "great" (*magnus*) and "soul" (*anima*). The emotions of magnanimous people drive their intellect to set high goals and drive their wills to intend them. In other words, magnanimous people want to accomplish great things in life.[3] Through faith and understanding, these people know that they are capable of doing great things with God's help. Their emotions then motivate them to discern the great actions that God is calling them to do. Once the intellect determines their divine calling, magnanimity compels them to seek this mission. Whether their mission is to be missionaries, loving spouses and parents, or teachers, magnanimity causes them to desire it. And, above all, magnanimous people desire to attain the goal of eternal happiness.

Magnanimity is the mean between pusillanimity (small-mindedness, or small-soulness) and seeking goals that are impossible to attain (such as goals that go against the way God has ordered the world). Pusillanimous people emotionally strive for goals that are too low—goals that are not in accord with their divine calling. These people fail to attain happiness because they do not seek to give their lives in loving service of God and others. On the other extreme, some people can set their goals too high. Although God works through us, our actions are still limited, because on earth we only have the down payment of the full inheritance. For example, given my height (or lack of), talents (again lack of), and vocational calling, it would be presumptuous to believe that I could become an NBA basketball star. Consequently, the virtues of understanding and wisdom are required to perfect the intellect to determine the proper goals in one's life.

PERSEVERANCE

Whereas magnanimity perfects the emotions to desire lofty goals, perseverance perfects the emotions to drive a person to attain these goals. Perseverance is the virtue that perfects the emotions to continue struggling to achieve the difficult good in the face of many obstacles. People with perseverance persistently work to attain a good goal. They continue to persevere even if the actions are difficult or monotonous, and if they fail, they try again and again. For example, parents must persevere in raising good children. They must guide and motivate their children to do good actions over and over again for many years—no matter how difficult the task becomes. Students must persevere by constantly attending class and studying.

Perseverance perfects the irascible emotions to have the proper intensity in seeking a good and also to have the proper amount of hope and despair. In relation to the first way that perseverance perfects the emotions, perseverance is the mean between laziness and overzealousness. The lazy person does not have the emotional desire to perform the difficult actions that are necessary to attain a goal. The overzealous person has too much desire to attain a difficult worldly goal. They are willing to pursue a goal even when prudence requires that they rest or do other activities. For example, the overzealous mom might neglect her spiritual life because her emotions are too focused on working hard to have a perfectly clean house. In relation to perseverance moderating hope and despair, the defect is despair (the vice and not the emotion) and the excess is presumption (similar to the sin against hope, only in this case it is in the emotions and not the will). When people have the vice of despair, the emotion of despair causes them to irrationally feel that they will not be able to perform the difficult action. Even simple actions can seem like a huge ordeal, and they fail to try to perform them. On the other extreme, those with the vice of presumption seek to perform tasks that are determined by the intellect to be impossible.

PATIENCE

Although many people equate fortitude with courage, patience is the chief subvirtue under fortitude because it perfects the chief component of fortitude: enduring evils. Patience is the virtue that perfects humans to endure evils when they are unable to actively combat them. Patient people endure evils either because they must endure these evils for the sake of a greater good or because they are unable to overcome the evil. For example, people might patiently wait thirty minutes in line at the supermarket because of the greater good of justice shown to neighbors. They could physically force themselves to the front of the line, but this would not be an act of loving their neighbor. An example of a case where people must be patient because they are unable to overcome an evil is when they must wait for political or cultural changes to take place. For example, while people are working to change the cultural and legal acceptance of abortion, they must be patient, since it will take time for their work to bear fruit. Patience can also help us share in the sufferings of others. Patience is the mean between having no emotional drive to overcome evil and impatience. People must first seek to fight evil before enduring it. However, if prudence determines that the evil either cannot or should not be overcome, then people must be patient.

MEEKNESS

Meekness is the virtue of being able to control one's anger. Anger is an emotional reaction to a perceived injustice. Anger can be used justly or unjustly. Just anger motivates people to rationally overcome injustice within society.[4] For example, in the twentieth century, just anger motivated many people to use peaceful methods to work for civil rights. Whereas just anger is harnessed by the intellect to perform good actions, unjust anger is not rational.

Anger can be unjust in three different ways. First, unjust anger occurs when someone is angry but has not suffered a true injustice. Because anger is an emotion, it follows sense knowledge. It can erupt against any perceived injustice, even if the injustice is not real. For example, suppose George is driving recklessly and crashes into the car of another person. George might be angry at the other person, even though the accident is primarily George's fault. No true injustice was done to George, and he should not be angry. Second, anger is unjust when it is too intense. There might be a very good reason to be angry, but the intensity of the anger is too great for the situation. For example, when children disobey their parents, just anger can be helpful in motivating parents to rationally discipline their children. However, if the anger is too intense and causes the parents to lash out irrationally, then they will commit a sin of unjust anger. Finally, anger is unjust when it is held for too long. Humans should only be angry until they have either worked to remedy the injustice or have realized that they are helpless to fight the evil. (At this point they should have patience.) For example, if Joe is still angry with his childhood friend who stole his homework in third grade, Joe would have unjust anger.

Meekness is the mean between the defect of apathy and the excess of unjust anger. Just as unjust anger is wrong, apathy is also wrong. Humans should use their anger in order to rationally fight injustice. Just anger helps motivate people to perform just actions. However, unjust anger can cause far more evil than the original injustice. It is particularly damaging to loving relationships. If people have the vice of unjust anger, they will probably have to practice continence in order to destroy this vice. They will have to force themselves to not be angry, even in situations where just anger is allowable.

THE HOLY SPIRIT'S GIFT OF FORTITUDE

As would be expected, the Holy Spirit's gift that perfects fortitude is the gift of fortitude. This gift is identical to the infused virtue of fortitude except that it allows the emotions to be even more perfectly moved and guided by the Holy Spirit. This gift aids people to bravely seek God's will, even if it will cost them their lives. It helps them to desire to be saints and to perform all the actions necessary to attain eternal happiness. It helps them to be patient and to control their anger because of their love of God and others. Even costly and difficult actions are enthusiastically sought when humans have the gift of fortitude. Abundant examples of the gift of fortitude can be found by studying the lives of the saints. Some endured great torture and suffered death because of their love of God. Others persevered by overcoming the daily difficulties found in everyone's lives. For example, St. Andre Bessette showed extreme magnanimity and perseverance. Andre was an uneducated porter (doorkeeper) who had a great devotion to St. Joseph. Because of his devotion, Andre began a campaign to erect a chapel in St. Joseph's honor. Despite having little money or building experience, Andre's work eventually yielded the Oratory of St. Joseph in Montreal. This church has the third largest dome of its kind in the world. Most would think Andre was crazy for desiring such a lofty goal; however, the Holy Spirit knew 2 million pilgrims a year would eventually visit the church.

Fortitude is a necessary virtue because untrained emotions can keep humans from doing the difficult actions that are necessary for them to enter into loving relationships with God and others. In this fallen world, people will suffer, and fortitude is necessary for us to share in their sufferings and to work to remove these sufferings (if possible). Not only is fortitude necessary to drive the intellect and the will to perform difficult actions, it also makes these actions much easier and more joyful. Well-trained passions make the moral life much more enjoyable. For example, it is subjectively easier and more joyful to walk ten miles to Mass when you are emotionally motivated than to walk a single block when your passions despise the walk. Fortitude makes it joyful to perform the difficult sacrifices and to have the patience that is necessary to sustain any loving relationship.

CONCLUSION

Following my explanation of how happiness is the act of contemplating the good that we know and love, one student responded, "But that's so simple." Because happiness for most people is fleeting, they believe that the recipe to happiness is very complex and esoteric. I responded by telling her that the concept is easy enough to understand, but acquiring the virtues necessary to actually know and love the highest goods requires a lifetime of hard work. It also requires the aid of God and many other people.

Humans have a natural inclination to happiness. However, this inclination is not strong enough to cause humans to immediately perform their proper actions of knowing and loving God and others. Humans need wiser humans to guide and move them to perform good actions. With the repetition of good actions, eventually humans develop the acquired virtues. However, it takes a lifetime to continue to perfect the acquired virtues by acting with always greater intensity. The intellectual virtues (especially wisdom) give humans the ability to truly know the higher goods of God and others. Justice gives humans the ability to love God and others. Through this knowledge and love, humans are able to enter into loving relationships with God and others. Prudence and justice further perfect the intellect and the will to continue to do good acts, which in turn perfect these relationships. Lastly, temperance and fortitude train the emotions so that the intellect and the will are aided in performing loving actions. Now that we humans have acquired the ability to know and love and have significant goods to love through our relationships, we can finally truly be happy. Furthermore, because humans are social beings, our natural happiness (or unhappiness) always affects others around us. However, the happiness flowing from these natural virtues is just temporary natural happiness, and not the permanent eternal happiness that we humans long to attain.

To attain the eternal happiness that humans truly desire, human nature must be perfected by God's grace. Humans must be transformed to participate in divine nature so that humans are able to perform divine actions. Since grace perfects nature, the theological and infused cardinal virtues are given to humans when they receive grace. The theological virtues perfect the natural inclinations, and the infused cardinal virtues perfect the acquired virtues. The theological virtues of faith, hope, and charity act as supernatural inclinations flowing from this participation in divine nature. The virtue of faith perfects the intellect to supernaturally share in God's knowledge. Faith gives humans new concepts and the power to understand and believe them. The principles of the faith become the basis of all further actions, as humans seek a supernatural goal and have the divine law to guide them. Hope and charity perfect the will to love this new goal, and they give humans the ability to perform divine actions determined by faith. The gifts of the Holy Spirit further perfect the inclinations of the intellect, will, and emotions so that humans are more perfectly guided by the grace of the Holy Spirit.

Although these supernatural inclinations give humans the ability to perform divine actions, like the natural inclinations humans must still be guided by others. In this case, humans are especially guided by the Holy Spirit, who guides the intellect and moves the will and emotions. However, because the movement of the Holy Spirit can be difficult to discern, humans are also guided by the written element of the divine law. Parents and other teachers help the young to understand the written element of the divine law and move them to perform actions in accord with this law. Through the repetition of these actions, the infused virtues are perfected. Traditionally, a significant portion of the written element of the divine law has been organized around the Ten Commandments, and thus we covered them in great detail throughout the last eight chapters of this book. These commandments teach people how to love God and others. They allow people to form the genuine loving relationships necessary for happiness.

When humans follow the divine law, they perform divine actions that perfect both the theological and infused cardinal virtues. Charity is applied through the infused cardinal virtues, which make people good at loving God through prudent, just, temperate, and fortitudinous actions. They are also good at loving others because of their love for God. With these perfected virtues, humans now have the ability to enter into supernatural loving relationships with God and others. They are now able to obtain supernatural happiness on earth and eventually eternal happiness in the next life.

In one sense, the concept of happiness is easy enough to understand; one just needs to know and love God and others. In another sense, because of the complexity of human nature, there are many steps involved in getting to the point where humans are truly free to know and love God and others. There are nearly an infinite number of possible actions that a human can do, some good and some bad. Because humans are not naturally determined to only perform the best actions of knowing and loving God, they will need grace, laws, and virtues. Many laws must be followed and virtues obtained to determine and choose the proper actions.

Likewise, because humans are naturally inclined to happiness, and the grace of the Holy Spirit drives humans to know and love God, in one sense happiness is easy to attain. However, forming and remaining in loving relationships takes hard work. A great deal of effort is needed to perfect the virtues necessary to truly love God and others. Christ's example of how to be happy shows us that obtaining true happiness is anything but easy. Christ shows us what true love entails when he dies on the cross and teaches us the meaning of a sincere gift of self. Because the loving sacrifice required for true happiness is so contrary to the corrupted inclinations of fallen nature, it was fitting that Christ suffered and died a public death in order to teach us the way to true happiness.

People should have a realistic view of the essence of happiness. It is difficult to obtain, and it takes the assistance of God and others. This book seeks to provide directions that will guide people to perform the type of actions necessary for true happiness. It further seeks to show people what they need to do to help others attain true happiness. Despite the difficulty of attaining the goal, humans should not be discouraged. God will help us on our journey to him. He will give us the strength to endure any difficulties and hardships along the way, and he works through others to help us on journey to him. Most of all, he gives us the virtues that make objectively difficult actions easy, joyful, and prompt for us. In speaking of the difficulty of following him, Christ says, "My yoke is easy and my burden is light."[1] Spending one's entire life serving God and others, even dying for Christ, is subjectively easy if one has strong enough charity and the gifts of the Holy Spirit.

NOTES

INTRODUCTION

1. I am using the term "moral theology" as synonymous with the term "theological ethics."

2. The pilgrim analogy can be found in the New Testament (cf. 1 Pt 2:11–12; Phil 3:20; Heb 11:13–16) and is frequently found in the works of the early Church Fathers, especially Gregory the Great (cf. *Morals on the Book of Job*, 18.47; 22.5; 23.46). Cf. *Catechism of the Catholic Church*, §302.

ONE. In the Image of God

1. This analogy is imperfect, but it does help show how the two disciplines can approach morality. The philosopher must first investigate what it means to be a human, and the theologian can begin with divine revelation.

2. A letter written the year following the Council of Constantinople (382) by a synod in Constantinople in response to Pope Damasus's invitation to attend a council in Rome sums up the Council of Constantinople's declaration of faith by stating, "According to this faith there is one Godhead, power and nature of the Father and of the Son and of the Holy Spirit; the dignity equal, and the majesty being equal in three perfect *hypostases*, i.e., three perfect persons."

3. Thomas argues that God must be pure act by stating that the first being must of necessity be completely in act and in no way in potentiality. The reason God must be pure act is that although in any perfectible thing potency comes before act, "absolutely speaking, act is prior to potency; for whatever is in potency can be reduced into act only by some being in act" (*ST* I.3.1). In other words, all things in potency must be moved to act by

something that is already in act. However, there must be a first mover who is pure act by nature. This first mover is what we refer to as God.

4. This principle is true in all areas of reality. For example, if I carve a statue out of granite, the statue is like its causes. It is materially like the granite from which it is carved (it is granite), and it is formally like the blueprint that preexists in my mind. So although it is not materially like me, it is like the plan I have in my mind. Likewise with God, all created things are like the ideas that preexist in God's mind. Another example can be found in the realm of physics, where for every action there is an equal and opposite reaction.

5. Among created things, a distinction can be made between their substantial act of being and accidental acts of being. The substantial act of being refers to all the perfections that a creature has to the extent they have a particular nature, while accidental acts of being refer to all other perfections that they have acquired by means of additional acts. In other words, all members of a species have the perfections that come with having a particular nature (the substantial act of being), but the further actions that a member of species does varies with each individual (accidental acts of being). For example, all oak trees have certain perfections inasmuch as they are oak trees, but only certain trees grow tall or produce acorns. Likewise, all humans have some goodness to the extent they are human, but only certain humans attain the further perfections of wisdom and virtue. Both the substantial and the accidental acts refer to something's being in general. Thus, Teresa of Calcutta's being refers not only to the perfections she had as a human but also refers to her perfections of being a holy person who loved others. Although this distinction between modes of being is made in creatures, since God is pure action, God is all perfections by nature. See Rziha, *Perfecting Human Actions*, 43–56, for a description of this distinction in the thought of Aquinas.

6. *Catechism of the Catholic Church*, §234, states, "The mystery of the Most Holy Trinity is the central mystery of Christian faith and life. It is the mystery of God in himself. It is therefore the source of all the other mysteries of faith, the light that enlightens them. It is the most fundamental and essential teaching in the 'hierarchy of the truths of faith.'"

7. Thomas notes that everything in God is one, except where there is an opposition of relation (*ST* I.36.4).

8. The term "spirit" comes from the Latin word for "breath."

9. Augustine sought to find a spiritual analogy for the Trinity in his book *De Trinitate*. He found several analogies of the Trinity within the soul. For example, he compared the Father, Son, and Holy Spirit to the memory of God, the knowledge of God, and the love of God.

10. Technically, sense knowledge that comes from the common sense is much more than just an image.

11. Thomas states that humans can have intellectual knowledge of a singular if the thing known is immaterial. For example, he states, "If there be an immaterial singular such as the intellect, there is no reason why it should not be intelligible" (*ST* I.86.1.3). I am grateful to Therese Cory for pointing out this passage.

12. This movement from knowledge to love is true for both sense knowledge and intellectual knowledge. For example, if chocolate cake is determined to be good by the

senses, then an emotional love for chocolate cake will follow. However, the same person who emotionally desires chocolate cake may have intellectual knowledge that cake is not healthy and, hence, will not love it intellectually. Or, a person may have intellectual knowledge that wisdom is good and, hence, love wisdom (intellectual love of the will) but still dislike studying to obtain it (emotional dislike).

13. Thomas states that love is the cause of union (*ST* I-II.28.1). He continues by noting, "So thus, to the extent that the things which belong to a friend the lover judges to be his own, the lover seems to be in the beloved as made the same as the lover. But conversely to the extent that he wills and acts for his friend as for himself, as regarding his friend as the same as himself, in this manner, the beloved is in the lover" (*ST* I-II.28.2).

14. See *ST* I-II.28.2, where Thomas states that in the love of friendship, the lover takes as his own whatever good or evil affects his beloved and makes his beloved's will his own. In this way, the lover feels the good or suffers the evil in the person of his friend.

15. This notion that knowledge causes love, which causes unity, is expressed by Benedict XVI in his explanation of the relationship between truth and love. One must have true knowledge of humans and God in order to be able to truly love (see *Caritas in Veritate*, §§1–6). This way of expressing knowledge of others as truth can be traced back to the writings of Romano Guardini, who highly influenced Benedict XVI and Pope Francis. See, for example, Guardini's "Truth and the Eucharist," 179–84, where Guardini explains how one must know the truth of the nature of the Eucharist to be able to truly love God present in the Eucharist.

16. See Philippians 2, where Paul exhorts all to make the interests of others more important than their own and to be of one mind and heart. He then goes on to give Christ as an example of someone who made our needs his own, for "though he was in the form of God . . ."

17. Furthermore, because of our bodies and the weakness of our intellects there are limits to how well we can know even ourselves, not to mention others.

18. See *ST* I.28.2 and 3; and I.29.4. Thomas states in I.28.2, "There is no accident in God; since all in Him is His essence. . . . Thus it is manifest that relation really existing in God is really the same as His essence."

19. The word is particularly suitable to express the relation between the Father and the Son since children are always of the same nature as their parents. Thus, to say that the Son is the only begotten Son of the Father is to say that he is divine.

20. See *ST* I.28.3, where Thomas states, "The very notion of relative opposition includes distinction. Hence, there must be real distinction in God, not indeed, according to that which is absolute—namely, essence, wherein there is supreme unity and simplicity— but according to that which is relative."

21. *Gaudium et Spes*, §24.

22. Things only have being by sharing in God's being. No created thing has being by nature, but only by participation in God. If something did have being by nature, then it would always have to exist. Since created things are brought into being by God, their being must share in God's being.

23. See Benedict XVI, *Caritas in Veritate*, §53: "As a spiritual being, the human creature is defined through interpersonal relations. The more authentically he or she lives these relations, the more his or her own personal identity matures. It is not by isolation that man establishes his worth, but by placing himself in relation with others and with God."

24. Because I am not God, I cannot say that my relations fully determine my individual personhood. Unlike in God, where relation is an essential attribute, in humans all the attributes that make us distinct are accidents flowing from our nature. Humans are distinct as having a separate matter, as having different thoughts, loves, and habits, and also through their relations. However, since the goal of knowledge and love is proper relations (unity with God and others), the most meaningful aspects of human individuality are manifested by relations with God and others.

25. Gn 2:24. Primary New Testament examples of how humans are created to be one are marriage (cf. Mk 10:1–15) and the Church (cf. 1 Cor 12).

26. This is also the view of religions that believe in reincarnation.

27. See *Catechism of the Catholic Church*, §365. Aquinas, following Aristotle, notes that the soul is the substantial act or form of the body: "And since every form has the matter proper to it, the soul must actualize just this special sort of body" (*Commentary on Aristotle's De Anima*, II.1.223).

28. Other powers include the vegetative, locomotive, and sensory powers. The vegetative is inclined to the actions of keeping the body alive, the locomotive to movement, and the sensory to acquiring sense knowledge. The sensory powers are essential to the emotions because they are the cause of the sense knowledge that is desired by the emotions. Because the emotions desire sense knowledge, they are traditionally referred to as the sense appetites or passions. The sensory power is also essential to the intellect and will as giving the phantasm from which intellectual concepts are abstracted; see *ST* I.77–83.

29. Thomas notes that all existing things are perfected by acting in accord with their form by means of their natural inclinations (*ST* I.42.1.1; *SCG* III.97). Thomas further explains that whenever there is a form, there is a corresponding inclination (*ST* I.5.5). Since every power of the soul is a type of form, there is a natural inclination for every power (*ST* I.80.1.3). For example, Thomas notes that the intellect is naturally ordered to know the true, the will to love the universal good, the irascible appetite to the arduous good, and the concupiscible appetite to the moderation of the delectable (*ST* I-II.85.3; cf. *ST* I.81.2).

30. In the case of spiritual beings, there can be intellectual knowledge of particular beings. For example, we have intellectual knowledge of God.

31. Nicholas Lombardo gives a good basic explanation of sense knowledge. He notes that the raw sense data obtained by the five external senses along with any raw images produced by the imagination from memories of past sense perception are synthesized by the common sense into a coherent whole; see Lombardo, *The Logic of Desire*, 23.

32. Although sense knowledge is not traditionally included as one of the three pertinent powers of the soul when it comes to causing free actions (i.e., intellect, will, and emotions), the power of sense knowledge is also extremely important to the causation of human actions, since the emotions follow it, and sense knowledge is always required to perform a concrete action in order to know the situation.

33. Thomas notes that whereas the intellect and will are properly said to be powers of the soul, the emotions are in the soul inasmuch as a person is a composite of soul and body (*ST* I-II.22.1). Lombardo, *The Logic of Desire*, 45, explains that although the emotions are primarily in the soul, they are only there through the medium of the body.

34. See DeYoung, McClusky, and Van Dyke, *Aquinas's Ethics*, 14–24, for more on Thomas's argument of how humans have the capacities of both the material and spiritual realm because they are "the borderline case" between the two realms.

35. A detailed explanation of the body is not the subject of the theologian but of the expert in anatomy and physiology.

36. If the body did not have this natural inclination, then doctors would be unable to help people get well. Doctors cannot make the body get well but must aid the body in performing its proper action.

37. Thomas explains that the body is not an exterior instrument of the soul, but an instrument that is united to it and its very own (*SCG* IV.41.10–11; see also *ST* I-II.79.2, and *De Potentia* 3.6.20). In heaven, the soul by the power of God's grace is able to act without the body. However, after the resurrection of the body, the soul will once more work through the body.

38. Likewise, physical gifts, such as a physical disposition to high intelligence, can greatly enhance the functioning of the person.

39. There are at least two possible epistemological explanations that can be given for how the intellect uses the brain in this life. One explanation is simply that whenever any intellectual understanding at all takes place, it is done through the functioning of the brain. Another possible explanation relies on the fact that humans must use sense knowledge as signs of intellectual concepts in order to think. In other words, people think in words (either written or spoken) or pictures. Words and pictures are sense images that represent intellectual concepts. Without these sense images, humans cannot string concepts together and make premises in order to reason to conclusions. Neural activity within the brain is the instrumental cause of these sense images. Either way, in theory science could evolve to the point where interior thoughts can be read by scanning physical brain waves.

40. See DeYoung, McClusky, and Van Dyke, *Aquinas's Ethics*, 22–24 and 34–35, for a good explanation of why the body is necessary for the functioning of the intellect. McClusky states, "According to Aquinas, human beings have the very lowest level of intellect possible. . . . we require so many examples and so much repetition—we possess intellective capacities to such a low degree—that God joins human intellects to sense-perceptive bodies so that they can gather the numerous experiences we need just to grasp abstract concepts like 'justice' and 'triangle'" (23).

41. The complementarity of the male and female bodies are signs of the eternal call to communion.

42. Fisher, "The Drive to Love," 90–92. Although I find the neurobiological results of the studies done by Fisher and her colleagues to be very helpful in explaining the relation between the body and soul, I do not endorse any of the conclusions that she draws from her studies.

43. Ibid., 101. See also an interview done with her on the *CBS Early Show*, July 19, 2010. In reference to brain scans of people experiencing romantic love, Fisher states, "We

found activity in a brain pathway that is exactly the same brain pathway that becomes affected when you're profoundly addicted to cocaine and nicotine."

44. With the term "sense images," I am referring to anything that can be sensed that is used by the mind to represent an intellectual concept allowing humans to string together concepts. Generally, humans think in words, which, because of their abstractness, allow complex reasoning to take place. However, humans can also think in pictures and, in fact, can think in both, as when a word in the mind is accompanied by a picture. Generally, sense images that are less abstract result in greater emotional responses.

45. All humans at times will not be able to think of the word that represents the concept they are looking for, but they are still able to think because humans ultimately think in concepts. However, if they do not have any words to think with, then they are unable to string together the concepts, and they cannot form sentences and reason to conclusions.

46. Since the body participates in the image of God through the soul, it should be no surprise that another important element of how humans are in God's image is through their masculinity and femininity. In the very statement where humans are said to be created in the image of God, the Genesis passages note that humans are created male and female (Gn 1:27; 2:21–25). *Catechism of the Catholic Church* notes that the "respective 'perfections' of man and woman reflect something of the infinite perfection of God: those of mother and those of father and husband" (§370).

TWO.   The History of Human Nature

1. Because the intellect can know that God exists and the will is ordered to the infinite good of God, all humans have a natural desire for God (see *Catechism of the Catholic Church*, §§294, 375). Because humans have an innate desire to enter into an eternal loving relationship with God through participation in the divine nature, humans are said to be universally called to holiness (*Lumen Gentium*, §5).

2. Because an effect is like its cause, by knowing the perfections of the effect (creation), Adam and Eve would have immediately known some perfections of the cause (God). This knowledge of God would have been imperfect since creation only manifests some of the attributes of God. Aquinas states that the knowledge would have been immediate because of the strength of the human intellect aided by God's grace. The more powerful an intellect is, the more it can understand immediately without the use of reasoning (see *ST* I.94). Because of the proper functioning of the intellect, these first humans would have been able to know God *through creation* more perfectly than we do today. However, they still would not have known that God is a Trinity or other truths revealed by Christ that are not manifested by creation. Divine revelation is needed to know these truths.

3. Augustine notes that the lower powers (emotions) were subject to the intellect, and the body was subject to the soul. The subjection of the intellect was the cause of the subjection of the lower powers, which was the cause of the subjection of the body; see *City of God*, 13.13. See also *ST* I.95.1 and 97.1.

4. Aquinas, "Sermon on the Lord's Prayer," 133.

5. Even today, Tibetan monks have learned to have greater control over their bodies, such as raising and lowering their body temperature at will. Furthermore, researchers have found that just imagining oneself lifting weights for a period of time each week caused people to increase bodily strength to nearly the degree of those who actually lifted weights for the same amount of time; see V. K. Rangathan, V. Siemionow, J. Z. Lui, V. Sahgal, and G. H. Yue, "From Mental Power to Muscle Power—Gaining Strength by Using the Mind," *Neuropsychologia* 42, no. 7 (2004): 944–56. In this study, those who actually lifted increased their finger abduction strength by 53%. Those who just imagined themselves lifting increased their strength by 35%, and those who did neither did not increase in strength at all.

6. For example, God's providence would need to ensure that the matter of their body was not radically destroyed by natural disasters and other calamities. Cf. *ST* I.97.2.

7. See *Laborem Exercens*, §§3–4, where John Paul II states that work is a fundamental dimension of human existence on earth. One way that man is in the image of God is that his creator has mandated that humans are to subdue the earth: "In carrying out this mandate, man, every human being, reflects the very action of the Creator of the universe." Man becomes more and more the master of the earth through his work. Through work, humans share in divine governance and creation.

8. See *ST* I.95.1, where Thomas notes that each power is subject to the power above it and ultimately to God.

9. This analogy is attributed to Peter Kreeft.

10. See *Catechism of the Catholic Church*, §§375, and 390: "The account of the fall in Genesis 3 uses figurative language, but affirms a primeval event, a deed that took place at the beginning of the history of man." My interpretation of this event, which follows that of John Paul II, *Veritatis Splendor*, §35, assumes a New Testament understanding of original sin.

11. The tree of life would be included in this group of trees, since the focus of the soul on God ensured the everlasting life of the body.

12. Whenever people make something for a purpose, they understand that only when the thing is able to properly function does it attain this purpose. For example, if manufacturers make a car with a gasoline-powered engine in order to fulfill the purpose of transportation, they know that the car will only function properly when given gasoline (or something closely related to it). If you put milk in the gas tank, the car will not go at all. The "creator" of the car understands what the car needs to fulfill its purpose. Likewise with God—he created us and knows what actions we need to perform in order to be happy.

13. The temptation of the serpent is that Adam and Eve will be "like gods who know what is good and bad" if they eat the fruit.

14. See *Catechism of the Catholic Church*, §§302–14. The *Catechism* notes that although creation has its own goodness and proper perfection, it was created in a "state of journeying" to an ultimate perfection yet to be attained.

15. Thomas makes a distinction between the goodness something has by its substantial form and the goodness that something has by its operation. The universe is already perfect in terms of its substantial forms as possessing the proper diversity of creatures to manifest God. However, the universe must still be moved by divine government to its

proper end, in particular, to the happiness of the saints, to be good unqualifiedly (*ST* I.73.1).

16. See *ST* I.103.6, where Thomas notes that it is a greater thing for something to be both good in itself and also to be the cause of goodness in others, than only to be good in itself.

17. *Catechism of the Catholic Church*, §§306–8. The *Catechism* further explains that God is the primary cause and humans are secondary causes of all actions. This distinction will be treated in chapter 9 in the section on how the Holy Spirit moves and guides humans.

18. Augustine stated that the most serious punishment for original sin is the ability to sin itself, for attachment to sin hinders our ability to be happy (*City of God*, 14.13).

19. Gn 2:24–25. See also John Paul II, *Man and Woman He Created Them*, sermons from December 1979 and January 1980, for more on the relation between man and woman in the original state.

20. The communion expressed by nakedness without shame is replaced by lust and domination of the other. The man for the first time can make his own interests more important than hers and is able to fulfill his own desires at her expense. For more on this issue, see John Paul II, *Theology of the Body*, sermons from May 28, 1980, to July 30, 1980.

21. Aquinas, "Sermon on the Lord's Prayer," 133, states: "But from the moment that the spirit and soul that stood between God and the flesh rebelled against God by sin, there and then the body rebelled against the soul. It began to be aware of death and infirmity, as well as the ceaseless rebellion of sensuality against the spirit."

22. Pope Francis explains that because of original sin, the harmony between humans and creation was disrupted and the "originally harmonious relationship between human beings and nature became conflictual" (*Laudato Si'*, §66).

23. See Augustine, *City of God*, 14.12. Augustine notes that the sin of disobedience, stemming from pride, was so severe that human nature became corrupted.

24. A good example might be seen in the mutation of genes. If the genes in one of the cells involved in sexual reproduction mutate, then this mutation is passed from generation to generation (assuming the mutation is not so serious that it kills the person).

25. The perfection of these harmonious relationships will take place in the new heavens and new earth after the resurrection of the body. However, even on earth humans have received spiritual gifts that are beyond those given to Adam and Eve. The greatest of these gifts is the Incarnation and the many special gifts that flow from it.

26. Although God is the primary cause of the grace of the inheritance, because God works through secondary causes, the normal means by which humans attain this grace on earth is through the sacraments of initiation (baptism, confirmation, and Eucharist). If humans do not have access to these sacraments or are never properly taught the importance of these sacraments, they can still accept the gift of the inheritance by seeking to know the truth and to love the good (both of which come from God) to the best of their ability. Within the Christian tradition, this is often referred to as the "baptism of desire."

27. See 2 Pt 1:4: "His divine power has bestowed on us everything that makes for life and devotion, through the knowledge of him who called us by his own glory and power. Through these he has bestowed on us the precious and very great promises, so that through

them you may come to *share in the divine nature*, after escaping from the corruption that is in the world because of evil desire" (emphasis added).

28. 1 Cor 13:12. It was only in the late seventeenth century that clear glass was invented, so to see in a mirror was to see a hazy or cloudy figure. The idea is that today we see God only imperfectly through faith, but then we will see God clearly as God sees us even now.

29. See, for example, Eph 1:13–14: "In him you also . . . were sealed by the promised Holy Spirit which is the first installment of our inheritance toward redemption." I am using the term "down payment" as another way of translating first installment. See also 2 Cor 1:22 and 5:5; Eph 1:14. The term "first fruits" also expresses the same idea (Rom 8:23).

30. There is an old story about a conversation between a doctor and a nun who both work in a hospital. It is after midnight, and the doctor is going home after having been called in for an emergency. The doctor notices that the nun looks tired and asks about her daily schedule. The nun notes that she is up every day at 5:00 a.m., and she prays and takes care of people until everybody is helped. Often she gets to sleep after midnight. The doctor responds that he would not work those hours for all the money in the world. The nun replies, "Neither would I."

31. When Thomas describes eternal glory (the full inheritance) he speaks of seven gifts (three in the soul and four in the body). These gifts are (1) the vision (knowledge) of God in his essence, (2) comprehension or understanding of God, (3) perfect enjoyment of God (the completion of our love for God), (4) impassability of the body (it will not suffer and die), (5) brilliancy of the body, (6) agility of the body (the body can be instantly present wherever one desires), and (7) subtlety of the body (being capable of being anywhere, just as Christ was able to appear in locked rooms, etc.); see "Sermon on the Sacraments," 269–70.

32. The normal means by which humans attain this grace on earth is through the sacraments of initiation (baptism, confirmation, and Eucharist). If someone does not have access to these sacraments or is never properly taught the importance of these sacraments, they can still accept the gift of the inheritance by seeking to know the truth and to love the good (both of which come from God) to the best of their ability.

33. Josemaría Escrivá states, "A Christian is a man who knows how to love with deeds and prove his love in the touchstone of suffering." A touchstone is a stone used to determine the purity of gold. Hence, suffering shows the purity of love (Escrivá, *Christ Is Passing By*, 90).

34. St. Francis taught that suffering done out of love of Christ resulted in happiness; see, for example, his description on how to attain perfect joy in "True and Perfect Joy," in *Francis and Clare*, 165–68. See also Thérèse of Lisieux, *Story of a Soul*, 156–57, 178, 218, and 238–40.

THREE.   Happiness

1. This book is in contrast with *Happiness: Happiness or Unhappiness Determined by Your State of Mind and Expectations, Positive Thinking, Happy Life, Better Life.*

2. See *ST* I-II.5.8, where Thomas notes that all humans desire happiness in general; however, not all desire what will make them specifically happy, since they do not know in what thing the general notion of happiness is found. See also *ST* I.83.1.5 and I-II.62.3.

3. For example, humans are naturally inclined to bodily health. Human health is a good thing that allows us to be happy, yet if humans are only healthy and do not have loving relationships with friends, etc., they will still not be happy.

4. Because humans have an intellect, they can always know there is something more, even if they do not specifically know what this good is. Because their will seeks the universal good of God himself, the will always desires this greater good and continues to push the intellect to know more. Even the emotions in humans, because they participate in reason (as trained and guided by the intellect), can constantly desire more and can be unfulfilled by finite goods; see *SCG* III.19 and 20.

5. Augustine, at the very beginning of the *Confessions*, states, "You have made us for yourself, O Lord, and our heart is restless until it rests in you" (1.3).

6. See *ST* I-II.1.1 and 6 for Thomas's explanation on how every act is done in order to attain an ultimate end.

7. In animals, which do not have the ability to know and love like humans do, happiness and emotional joy can often be equated. Because the emotions exist to drive animals to their proper actions of living and maintaining the species, they often have emotional joy when they do their proper actions and are happy.

8. Because happiness is an act of the intellect, and the intellect can be mistaken, even things that are not truly good can bring some happiness if humans think they are good (e.g., sex outside of marriage). However, like all evil things, these false goods will ultimately cause turmoil in people's lives, and upon discovering that they were pursuing a false good, they may become very unhappy.

9. *ST* I-II.3.2 and 3.5.

10. Thomas states that the very essence of happiness is an act of the intellect, but the proper accident of happiness is the act of the will (*ST* I-II.3.4). Both the acts of the will desiring the end and resting in the end further perfect happiness, just as humans are further perfected by their proper accident: performing their proper actions.

11. Cf. *ST* I-II.4.3.

12. Mass is structured to help ensure contemplation of God. In the first part of Mass, the Word of God is proclaimed, helping the person to think about God. In the second part of the Mass, the Eucharistic Liturgy reveals the love of God through the sacrifice of his Son.

13. *Nicomachean Ethics*, I.8, 1099b. Aristotle notes, "It [happiness] needs the external goods as well; for it is impossible, or not easy, to do noble acts without the proper equipment. In many actions we use friends and riches and political power as instruments; and there are some things the lack of which takes the luster from happiness, as good birth, goodly children, beauty; for the man who is very ugly in appearance or ill-born or solitary and childless is not very likely to be happy"; see also VII.13, 1153b.

14. In fact, the Gospels proclaim that the poor and misfortunate are even more likely to be happy than the wealthy, since wealth and fortune can be a distraction to the true happiness that comes from God (e.g., Mt 6:21 and 19:16–30). Even though union with God is

offered to all humans, some, through no fault of their own, know little about God. Hence, evangelization is necessary to help people to be happy.

15. Benedict XVI, *Caritas in Veritate*, §34, notes that because of the ideologies of individualism and consumerism, people fail to recognize that they are ultimately made happy by a sincere gift of self.

16. See Rom 1:18–32, where Paul notes that God allows sinful activities to come to their proper end of even greater sins. God allows this so that those committing sin eventually recognize that these activities do not lead to happiness and so they seek happiness in other ways.

17. Technically, once someone has grace, all of these actions become cases of supernatural happiness because these acts are ordered to love of God. Because the act of natural happiness involves the will, the actions are ordered to God by charity and, hence, become occasions of supernatural happiness, even though the person might not specifically be contemplating God.

18. The highest power in humans is the intellect, for it is through the intellect that the end is first attained. However, even though the end is attained through the intellect, the will is necessary both to desire the end and to rest in the end once it is known by the intellect; see *ST* I-II.3.4.

19. See *ST* I-II.3.8, where Thomas notes that the intellect attains its perfection when it knows the very essence of the First Cause, God.

20. To better understand how the degree of participation in God is only accidentally different when speaking of the degree of participation through grace on earth and grace in heaven, while the degree of participation is substantially different when comparing participation in God by nature versus that by grace, see Rziha, *Perfecting Human Actions*, 81–82. Cf. *ST* I.75.7.

21. See Vatican II, *Dogmatic Constitution on Divine Revelation* (*Dei Verbum*), §§2–8.

22. Teresa of Calcutta, at the National Prayer Breakfast in Washington, DC, February 1994, stated, "He [Jesus] gave up everything to do the Father's will—to show us that we too must be willing to give up everything to do God's will—to love one another as he loves each of us. That is why we too must give to each other *until it hurts*."

23. If humans make another human person their ultimate end, their expectations will eventually crush the relationship. Humans have an infinite desire for the good, and no other human is infinitely good. Consequently, in this type of relationship one of two things may eventually happen: either the lovers will recognize that their beloved is not perfect and will become bitter, or they will seek the missing goodness they desire in other sources. However, if humans are loved out of love of God, they can be loved properly and permanently.

24. Thomas notes in the prologue to question 6 (*ST* I-II) that happiness is to be gained by means of certain acts. Hence, after treating happiness, he analyzes human actions.

FOUR.   Moral Methodology in the Bible

1. Pinckaers, *Sources of Christian Ethics*. This theme runs throughout the book, but a good introduction to it can be found in the first two chapters.

2. Ibid., 254–79. For an example of one of these textbooks, (not in Pinckaers) see Joseph Schade, *Catholic Morality: A Manual* (Patterson, NJ: St. Anthony Guild Press, 1943). This book was written well after Leo XIII's call to use Thomistic principles in moral theology, so it speaks more of the virtues than many earlier manuals did. Nonetheless, the tone of book can already be deciphered from the dedication in the preface: "To Mary, the lawgiver's mother."

3. Pinckaers, *Sources of Christian Ethics*, chapters 6 and 7.

4. See Hillers, *Covenant*, 25–45.

5. The word "covenant" comes from the Hebrew "to cut."

6. See, for example, Gn 17:14; Ex 12:19; Ex 31:14; Lv 7:20–27; Lv 23:29; Nm 15:30–31; Is 53:8; Ez. 21:8; Ps 37:9, 22; Pr 2:22; Zec 13:8.

7. Gn 15:9–21. To seal the covenant, God asks Abram to cut in half a heifer, a female goat, and a ram (and to kill a turtledove and pigeon). God then passes between these dead animals and shows Abram that if God breaks the covenant the same thing will happen to God that happened to these dead animals. To the modern reader, this ceremony can appear a little unusual, but to Abram this ceremony would have given him great comfort as the normal way of making a contract.

8. Ex 23:24–33; Lv 18:5; Lv 26; Dt 26:16–19; Dt 28:1–14; Dt 30:15–20.

9. Hillers, *Covenant*, 48–54.

10. See also Ex 23:32 for the general commandment where God states that the Israelites are not to make a covenant with any other god. See Ex 20:1–17 and Dt 5:6–21 for the rest of the commandments.

11. The blood of the bulls is sprinkled on the altar (representing God) and the people. By having the blood sprinkled on them, the people consent to the terms of the covenant. The blood prefigures the blood of the covenant at the Last Supper (Mt 26:28; Lk 22:20). The Last Supper is memorialized at every Mass. However, at Mass the participants consent to the covenant not by being splashed with the blood of a bull but by drinking the blood of Christ, which unites humans to him.

12. Other examples include Kant's categorical imperative, legal positivism, emotivism, and existentialism.

13. However, the reward here is becoming more interior and less exterior to prepare for the new covenant.

14. The words "kindness," "salvation," "deliverance," and "comfort" are often used in a technical manner in the Old Testament. God's covenantal kindness refers to God bestowing the covenant benefits upon the people—a synonym for "kindness" in this context would be "faithfulness to the covenant." God has promised these benefits, and he will remain faithful. Salvation, deliverance, and comfort all refer to a reception of the covenant promises. See also Ps 7 for an example of God's salvation resulting from his covenantal justice.

15. See, for example, Dt 28; Ez. 18; Is 58–60; Jer 11; Jer 22:1–8; and Jer 31 (but note the prediction of the new covenant at the end of Jer 31).

16. See also Jer 31:31–34 about how the new law will be written on the hearts of the people. See Ps 51, where the sacrifice to God is a humble and contrite heart.

17. There are also other types of teleological moral systems that my book here does not endorse, such as consequentialism, utilitarianism, and proportionalism.

18. See Hos 1–3 and Ez 16 on how God is a faithful husband to Israel.

19. A good example of the two systems can be found in the suffering servant passage of Is 52:13 to 53:12. Recall that God allows the Israelites to offer sacrifices to have their transgressions of the covenant forgiven. This notion of sacrifice allows the moral system to become more and more interior over time. In Exodus and Leviticus, the requirements and regulations for sacrifices are simply stated. For example, the priest must splash the blood of the animal on the altar of the Lord, and in return the Israelites will be cleansed of all their sins before the Lord (Lv 16:18–19, 30–31; Lv 17:5–7). However, over time it becomes clear that God will not accept the sacrifices unless they are accompanied by a sincere contrition. For example, in Isaiah 1, God rejects their sacrifices and instead requests that they cease doing evil, that they seek to be faithful to the covenant, and "redress the wrong, hear the orphan's plea, defend the widow" (Is 1:16–18; see also Am 5:21–27; Mal 1:6–14; Jer 6:20; Prv 15:8 and 21:3). A sacrifice becomes a sign of interior love and devotion. This love can be expressed through the offering of valuable goods (such as animals). Isaiah 53 goes a step further and notes that the person can make his entire life a sacrifice to God. By outward appearance, it looks like the person has broken the covenant and is being punished by God as he is "cut off" from the land of the living (Is 53:8–9). However, in reality he has done no wrong and is instead an offering to God for the sins of the many (vv. 4, 10–12). Because he offers his life on behalf of the people, he shall see his descendants in a long life (vv. 10–12). The deontological system is being partially replaced by a teleological system in this passage. Under a deontological system, the people that sinned should be "cut off" like the animals that sealed the covenant. However, a sacrifice can be offered for the forgiveness of the sins. The teleological element can be found in the fact that a person freely offers his life for the forgiveness of sins. The free offering is an act of love and not just a mandatory fulfillment of the laws. Yet, the reward is still primarily material (for they do not yet know about eternal life).

20. See, for example, Pss 1; 4; 18:1; 40; 75; and 119 for examples where happiness is found in a relationship with God. However, despite the teleological elements of these psalms, there are still many deontological elements within them.

21. In contrast to the other gospels, Matthew primarily uses the term "kingdom of heaven" and only rarely the term "kingdom of God." He uses the term "kingdom of heaven" to keep the audience from mistaking the kingdom of God for an earthly political kingdom. The use of the term "kingdom of heaven" emphasizes the primarily spiritual characteristics of the kingdom of God.

22. 15:11. The word translated as "joy" (*chara*) is the same word used to speak of the happiness that comes from hearing the good news of Christianity. For example, the angels bring tidings of great joy when Jesus is born (Lk 2:10); Mary Magdalene is filled with great joy upon learning that Jesus has risen from the dead (Mt 28:8; cf. Lk 24:52); upon accepting the gospel in Samaria, the city is filled with great joy (Acts 8:8); the Thessalonians are filled with joy in the Holy Spirit upon receiving the Word (1 Thes 1:6).

23. The different understanding of the moral system is especially highlighted by looking at the terms used to refer to God in the two testaments. In the Old Testament, the primary metaphor applied to God is that of king emphasizing that the Israelites are primarily subjects. The term "father" is only applied to God a little more than twenty times; see O'Collins, *The TriPersonal God*, 12–14. However, in the New Testament, Jesus always refers to God as "Father" (unless he is quoting scripture). Jesus emphasizes that through him Christians can be in a loving friendship with God.

24. Mt 5:29. Jesus also notes that those who do not bear fruit will be cut down and thrown into the fire (Mt 7:19).

25. I am highly indebted to Pinckaers, *Sources of Christian Ethics*, chap. 5, for several of the main points of this chapter. Pinckaers does an exegesis of Romans 1–3 to show that salvation does not come through following the Jewish law or Greek wisdom. Rather, salvation comes through faith in the person of Jesus and through the charity that flows from faith. However, once humans have faith and charity, the Greek virtues are essential in applying faith and charity to their lives. Thus, although the Greek virtues are not sufficient to save someone, they are nonetheless essential to salvation.

26. See Rom 5:5 and 13:8–10; and 1 Cor 13:4–7. Note, especially, Gal 5:6: "For in Christ Jesus, neither circumcision nor uncircumcision counts for anything, but only *faith working though love*" (emphasis added).

27. 1 Cor 13:2. Paul continues by noting that "faith, hope, and love remain, but the greatest of these is love" (13:13). See also Rom 12; Col 3:14.

28. See Rom 8:38–39: "For I am convinced that neither death, nor life, nor angels, nor principalities, nor present things, nor future things, nor powers, nor height, nor depth, nor any other creature will be able to separate us from the love of God in Christ Jesus our Lord."

29. Cf. Phil 4:8; 1 Cor 6:9–10; 1 Thes 5:21.

30. With the transition from the old covenant to the new covenant, the function of law has now changed from primarily condemning to primarily guiding proper relationships. This change of function can be seen when Paul says, "Everything is lawful for me, but not everything is beneficial (*sumphero*)." The word *sumphero* can be translated as "profitable" or "good for." The idea is that some actions contradict membership in the body of Christ and should not be done, for they are not *good for* a person in that they keep the person from attaining true happiness.

31. Phil 4:8. I have used the translation from Pinckaers, *Sources of Christian Ethics*, 126.

32. Ibid.

33. See, for example, 1 Cor 13:4–7 and Gal 5:22–23. See also 1 Cor 2–4, which condemns natural (Greek) wisdom as foolish but praises Christian wisdom (wisdom transformed by faith).

34. Although I have not yet explained the role of hope in detail, hope is also an important element in Paul's theology (see, e.g., Rom 5 and 1 Cor 13:13). The role of hope will be explained later.

FIVE.   The Individual Steps on the Journey

1. See *ST* I-II.1.1, where Thomas notes that only those actions that are proper to man as man are properly called "human." Man differs from the irrational animals in that man is master of his actions through the powers of the intellect and will.

2. Ibid.

3. Technically speaking, unruly emotions can also hinder the functionality of the intellect, but this will be covered in the next paragraph.

4. See Cyprian of Carthage, *On the Lapsed*, 438–41. The local Council of Carthage in 251 followed the recommendations of Cyprian in stating how those who committed apostasy were to be reconciled to the Church.

5. For more on the relation between psychology and moral theology, see Ashley and O'Rourke, *Health Care Ethics*, 355–92.

6. For the steps of an action, see *ST* I-II.11–17. Other passages showing how the steps relate to each other are I-II.90.1.2; II-II.153.5; I-II.68.4 and I-II.17.3.1. See also Westberg, *Right Practical Reason*, chaps. 8 to 12, who gives a detailed analysis of the process of the moral act. He explains the structure of *ST* I-II.11–17 by stating that there are three basic parts to an act: intention (including the intellect's act of apprehension: I-II.12), choice (including judgment: I-II.13), and execution (including command: I-II.16–17). Because many actions can be determined without deliberation, deliberation and consent are treated after judgment and choice (I-II.14–15), even though in the moral act they precede them. Sherwin, *By Knowledge and by Love*, expands upon the work of Westberg to include *apprehensio* and *simplex voluntas* as the first steps of the intellect and will (84–85). Other earlier scholars posited twelve steps to a complete human act. For example, Oesterle, *Ethics*, 85, and Gilson, *The Philosophy of St. Thomas*, chap. 15. Interestingly, Karol Wojtyla, though approaching the human action from an entirely different perspective and using different terminology, also comes up with a similar list of steps in Wojtyla, "The Problem of the Will in the Analysis of the Ethical Act," 12.

7. For example, Mark Gola and John Monteleone, *The Louisville Slugger Complete Book of Hitting Faults and Fixes: How to Detect and Correct the 50 Most Common Mistakes at the Plate* (Chicago: McGraw-Hill, 2001), break hitting down into four mechanical stages in order "to determine where the mechanical breakdown occurs" (2).

8. See Rziha, *Perfecting Human Actions*, 190–214. In this work I use the writings of Thomas Aquinas to give a detailed explanation and comparison of the acts of the speculative and practical intellect and how the practical intellect relates to the will. Although all of the twelve steps of the human action are mentioned by Thomas, he never explicitly says that these are the twelve steps of the human action. Later commentators on Thomas, such as Charles-René Billuart (1685–1757), systematize the various passages that Thomas has on the different steps of the human action to form twelve steps (for some passages in Thomas, see *ST* I-II.11–17; 68.4; 90.1.2; II-II.153.5). Over the centuries, different variations of the twelve steps have emerged. The key point is not that these particular twelve steps are followed slavishly, but that people realize that there many different important

components to the human action. Many students over the years have found the twelve steps, as I list them, to be particularly helpful in solving difficult moral dilemmas and in identifying moral flaws. What Thomas does do in his writings is use many of the twelve steps as the foundation for understanding the virtues and the gifts of the Holy Spirit (see *ST* I-II.57.6; 58.4; 68.4; 94.1.2; II-II.45; 47.6–8; 51).

9. To help clarify the twelve steps of the human action, we will cover the acts of the intellect in general. The first act of the intellect corresponds to the first step of the human action. (In this case they are both called "simple apprehension.") The second act of the intellect corresponds to the third step of the human action. (Understanding corresponds to understanding the goal or end.) The third act of the intellect corresponds to the fifth step of the human action. (Discursive reasoning corresponds to counsel.)

10. The intellect understands things by turning to sense knowledge from which the nature or essence of a thing is abstracted. Things are composed of form and matter. The matter is sensed. The intellect is able to abstract the form from the matter, causing the form of the thing to be within the intellect in an intelligible mode. Hence, concepts are referred to as intellectual forms. Since the form is universal and the matter is particular, intellectual knowledge is of universals, but sense knowledge is of singulars; see *ST* I.84 and 85. See also Schmidt, *The Domain of Logic according to Saint Thomas Aquinas*, 177–201.

11. The necessity of properly understanding the concepts can be seen in Church documents dealing with the bioethical issues. Before going into particular issues, the documents always first define a person as "someone having great dignity from conception to natural death." See for example, Congregation for the Doctrine of the Faith, *Dignitas Personae*, §§1–10.

12. Although this is the third step of the human action, it is only the second act of the intellect.

13. The term "understanding" can also be used to refer to the concepts apprehended. Often the result of the first act is called "simple understanding." However, to avoid confusion I am calling the first act "apprehension" and the second "understanding" (it is also often called "judgment"). Although the first act of apprehension gives knowledge of something, this knowledge is imperfect and confused. It is imperfect because that which is in reality singular, diversified, and distinct is apprehended as universal and common, a result of the weakness of the human mind. Hence, the intellect must combine and separate the intellectual forms derived from simple apprehension in order to determine what forms are in reality together and what forms are not. See *ST* I.14.6; 58.4; 85; and *SCG* I.58. See also Schmidt, *The Domain of Logic*, 202–12.

14. A good example of the act of dividing concepts takes place when infants learn the difference between peeled apples and peeled potatoes. All of my children like to eat apples. At about eighteen months old, all of them have asked for a peeled potato, believing that the potatoes were apples. As a parent who encourages learning, I have always given them a piece of potato, which they promptly spit out. They then understand: a potato is not an apple.

15. In morals there are degrees of universality. These goals are already somewhat particular inasmuch as they apply to a single person, yet they are universal in the sense that

they apply to the person's life in general. The following laws are examples of more universal laws that apply to all people: humans should pursue their vocation, students should graduate, humans should drive safely, and humans should not steal or lie.

16. This premise assumes an earlier premise stating that in this situation the clothes must be inexpensive and must fit.

17. Because not everything that can be attributed to something can be known by immediate understanding alone (the second act of the intellect), the mind must reason to conclusions by means of a middle term. This use of a middle term to join or separate particular things is discursive reasoning; see Schmidt, *The Domain of Logic*, 242. In Thomas, see *ST* I.58.3 and 4; 79.8; 85.5; II-II.49.5.2; *SCG* I.57; *Expositio Libri Peryermenias* I.1.

18. A recent discourse between my father and my four-year-old niece gives a good example of joining concepts through discursive reasoning. My niece did not like the new puppy (Rusty) that my father (her grandfather) had recently received. (She did not like the puppy because the puppy nipped at her.) She then asked her grandfather to confirm a premise that she understood: bad people go to hell. She then reasoned to the conclusion, "Rusty is going to hell." The assumed premise is that Rusty is a bad person. The argument is of course not sound because Rusty is not a person. However, it is valid reasoning.

19. The retreat master was Fr. Michael Jackels. He is now a bishop.

20. Earlier in the chapter I noted that if a human judged an action, then it was a human action even if the freedom was diminished.

21. I am speaking here of intellectual joy (joy of the will). There is another type of joy in the emotions (see chapter 1) that may or may not always accompany happiness; in fact, one can have emotional joy and be unhappy, and vice versa.

22. See *ST* II-II.153.5, where Thomas shows how lust affects several of the different steps of the human action.

23. This is a morally good action, assuming that the painkillers are taken to control the pain and not specifically to cause death. See *Catechism of the Catholic Church*, §2279.

24. The Thomistic principle is that all that is received is in the receiver according to the mode of the recipient (e.g., see *ST* I.84.1). For example, although humans receive knowledge through sense knowledge, it exists in the intellect in an immaterial way because the intellect is spiritual. In relation to form and matter, this principle shows that matter cannot receive a form that is unsuitable to it. For example, the body of a dog can only contain the substantial form of a dog, it cannot be formed by a human soul and be a human (despite stories and movies like *The Shaggy Dog*). The matter would not be proportionate to the form. For more on this principle, see Wippel, "Thomas Aquinas and the Axiom 'What Is Received Is Received according to the Mode of the Receiver.'"

25. The use of the end, object, and circumstances to determine the moral goodness of an action has been part of moral theology since the time of Thomas (see *ST* I-II.18.4). However, how these terms have been used has varied. For example, in a teleological moral system, an action is good if it leads to the ultimate end. Hence, the order to the ultimate end must be taken into consideration. When morality is treated in more deontological terms, the ultimate end is less important, so the intended or proximate end is often referred to as the end to which the action is ordered. To be more specific, sometimes moral-

ists will say that the three determinants of an action are the intention (rather than end), the object, and the circumstances. The substitution of "intention" for "end" is caused by a more deontological understanding of the action (but the moralist may not be aware of this).

26. If someone does not have correct or explicit knowledge of God, then the act must at least be ordered to the good to the best ability of the agent.

27. Technically, when the higher end is evil, and the means to the end is good in itself (e.g., going to work to embezzle money), the higher end determines the object (species) of the action. The best moral description of the act is no longer going to work but embezzlement.

28. Thomas explains: "The object is not the matter of which (a thing is made), but the matter about which (something is done); and stands in relation to the act as its form, as it were through giving it its species" (*ST* I-II.18.2.2). In other words, the object refers to the manner that someone acts, not the effect of the action.

29. The determination of the species of an action can be compared to the determination of the species of a substance. For a substance, the proximate genus plus the specific difference determines the species. For example, the species of dog is differentiated from other members of the genus *canis* because of a dog's unique physiological features and ability to be domesticated (the specific difference). However, why is the species considered to be a dog and not a basset hound or a beagle? Because traditionally a basset hound and a beagle are not considered to be substantially different in terms of their physiology or essential function. In other words, the description that most properly describes the essence of Rover is dog—whether or not he is a beagle is accidental. So also in morals, the best description of the essence of the action is its object. Long, *The Teleological Grammar of the Moral Act*, states that the object is the "most containing, formal, and defining moral species" (25, 28, 73). See also Pilsner, *The Specification of Human Actions in St. Thomas*, 30–37, for more on the comparison between finding the species of substances and the species of actions.

30. The end and the object can be very closely related. Generally, the intended end determines the object, but in some cases even a higher end can determine the object. Hence, *why* someone is doing something is often a description of *what* one is doing. For example, the answer of why you are driving will usually give the object of the action: to go to work, to embezzle money, etc.

31. Long, *The Teleological Grammar of the Moral Act*, explains this point in a similar manner. He states, "For if and only if the object is naturally (*per se*) ordered to the end, will the moral species derived from the end be most formal and most containing and defining" (25–26). Long goes on to give an excellent description of how it is essential to know whether or not a particular action is *per se* ordered to an end in order to properly determine the object of an action. See also *ST* I-II.1.3.3, where Thomas states that a movement does not receive its species from that which is its end accidentally, but only from that which is its *per se* end.

32. Technically, the proximate end would be self-defense, and a higher (or more remote) end would be saving one's life.

33. This example of self-defense does not specifically include the step of judging by higher principles (ends) to which the intention is ordered, but this step is also important. The intention of self-defense is ordered to proper love of self, which is ordered to love of God. The intellect must judge that mortally wounding the other is also in accord with proper love of self and love of God for the act to be moral.

34. Although Thomas believes that the object comes from the intended end, he nonetheless notes that the intended end is not always the same as the object that is chosen (*ST* I-II.18.6). He uses the distinction between the interior and the exterior act to explain how what humans interiorly intend is not always what they exteriorly do (*ST* I-II.19 is devoted to the interior action, and *ST* I-II.20 is devoted to the exterior action). The more prudent the person, the more perfectly the exterior action will correspond to the interior action. The prudent person takes proper counsel and judges correctly.

35. Long, *The Teleological Grammar of the Moral Act*, describes this process in the following way: "A thing is said to be *per se* ordered to the other either if the achievement of one thing is absolutely required for the achievement of the other or simply by nature tends toward the achievement of another" (27–28). Note how the first condition he makes (absolutely required) is an act of counsel and the second condition (tends toward the achievement of another) is an act of judgment.

36. Because the object of the action is what best describes the essence, Thomas will sometimes state that the object is from the higher (remote) end and sometimes from the intended end. (For passages where the object is from the higher end, see *ST* I-II.18.6; 18.6.2; 75.4, and II-II.23.8 for a closely related case. For passages where the object is from the intended end, see *ST* I-II.1.3.3; 60.1.3; *Disputed Questions on Evil*, 8.1.14. For many more passages illustrating both of these points, see Pilsner, *The Specification of Human Actions in St. Thomas*, 219 and 222.) Sometimes the best description of the essence of the act is the remote end, for example, when one steals a minor amount (proximate end) in order to commit adultery (remote end). Sometimes the best description is from the proximate end, for example, when one murders (proximate end) in order to satisfy greed (remote end). In the first case, adultery is the more fundamental description of the action because it more appropriately describes what is happening in the situation. The person is committing adultery, and in the process of performing the action he steals something. In the second place, murder is the more fundamental description. See also the comments by Jensen, *Good and Evil Actions*, 21–22.

37. See *Catechism of the Catholic Church*, §1756; 1 Cor 6:9–10; *Gaudium et Spes*, §27; *Veritatis Splendor*, §78–81.

38. The object refers to the substance of the action. Circumstances do not refer to the substance of an action but are accidents. An intention can refer to either. If the action is in accord with the proximate intention, then the intention refers to the substance as causing the species of the action. If the proximate intention does not conform to the action because of a defect in the intellect, then it is an accident: a circumstance.

39. Sometimes the word "circumstance" is used in a less precise sense and can refer to certain aspects of the situation that do affect the object of the act. When used in this less technical sense, the circumstances can make an otherwise good act into an evil act.

40. I am assuming that there is no realistic way for the parents to attain the moral and spiritual resources to raise their children. The way this object is affected by the situation is that the parents intend the end of personally raising and educating their child. However, upon taking counsel, they realize that personally raising their child is impossible, so they must judge by the higher law of the spiritual welfare of their child in general. Hence, they determine that the best action is to give up their child for adoption.

SIX.   The Transforming Power of Grace

1. *The Way*, a 2010 movie written and directed by Emilio Estevez and starring his father, Martin Sheen, traces the spiritual (and physical) journey of several pilgrims along this route.

2. Thomas argues that as long as humans know a particular effect and know that there is a cause of this effect, they will not be completely happy until they know the essence of the cause. Since humans know the effects of God (creation) and know that God is the cause, they cannot be perfectly happy until they know the essence of God (*ST* I-II.3.8).

3. See Eph 1:5–6; 1 Jn 3:1; Jn 1:12–18; and *Catechism of the Catholic Church*, §§1996–99. Although grace is inherently Christological as merited by Christ, it was extended by God to Adam and Eve and to other humans who came before the Incarnation. Hence, simply because it is given through Christ's death and resurrection does not mean that it only affected those who came after Christ.

4. The heresy of Pelagianism denied the necessity of grace to be saved.

5. Thomas makes a distinction between grace within humans and grace as the love of God itself. The second type of grace is a special type of love "whereby He draws the rational creature above the condition of its nature to a participation of the divine nature" (*ST* I-II.110.1).

6. Cf. 1 Cor 3:16 and 6:19; Rom 5:5.

7. *ST* I-II.110.1.

8. See *ST* I-II.110.2, where Thomas makes a distinction between the grace by which humans are transformed by God bestowing on them "certain forms and powers" and the grace by which God moves humans to the "acquisition of the supernatural good."

9. See 2 Pt 1:4 and 1 Jn 3:1–3. See also *ST* I-II.110.4, where Thomas states that because the habit of grace is a participation in divine nature, it makes the soul like divine nature through a certain "regeneration" or "re-creation."

10. Thomas notes that good is placed in the definition of virtue with reference to its fitness to either essential nature or participated nature (*ST* I-II.110.3.2). The theological virtues are good as being in accord with participated divine nature (*ST* I-II.62.1.1).

11. See *ST* I-II.62.1.1, where Thomas makes a distinction between acting according to participated nature and acting according to essential nature.

12. For more explanation on how humans participate in divine nature through grace, see Rziha, *Perfecting Human Actions*, 78–92 and 142–54.

13. Sometimes the participation is not directly in the thing that has the perfections by nature but rather in an intermediary with the perfections that it obtained from something that has those perfections by nature. For example, the emotions can participate in the wisdom of the intellect that participates in the divine wisdom. However, ultimately, all participated perfections must come from something that has the perfections by nature. Divine wisdom is wisdom by nature. In all cases of a participated perfection, the perfection can be traced to something that has that perfection by nature. Nearly all arguments for God's existence are based on this principle.

14. Thomas uses the analogy of water participating in the heat of the fire to explain how habitual (sanctifying) grace perfects the soul. Water, by its own power, cannot heat anything, but with the superadded form of heat it can heat things (*ST* I-II.109.1).

15. See *ST* I-II.109; 110.4; II-II.8.1; III.62.2.

16. Thomas states: "Man must reach his ultimate end by his own operations. Now, each and every thing operates in accord with its own form. Therefore, so that man may be brought to his ultimate end by his own operations, a form must be superadded to him from which his operations receive a certain efficacy in meriting his ultimate end in advance" (*SCG* III.150).

17. The heresy of Monothelitism argued that Christ had only one will: a divine will and not a human will. This heresy was condemned at the Third Council of Constantinople because Christ would not be fully human if he did not have a human will.

18. Thomas states: "According to the Philosopher (*Metaph.* i, 2), what is "free is cause of itself." Therefore he acts freely, who acts of his own accord. Now man does of his own accord that which he does from a habit that is suitable to his nature: since a habit inclines one as a second nature. If, however, a habit be in opposition to nature, man would not act according to his nature, but according to some corruption affecting that nature. Since then the grace of the Holy Ghost is like an interior habit bestowed on us and inclining us to act aright, it makes us do freely those things that are becoming to grace, and shun what is opposed to it" (*ST* I-II.108.1.2).

19. Although grace is an external principle of good actions, nonetheless, to the extent it causes actions that are freely consented to by humans, it is called "cooperating grace" (*ST* I-II.111.2).

20. *ST* I-II.110.2.

21. Thomas notes that by divine power humans are able to merit eternal happiness. The merit of eternal happiness extends not only to the end but also the means. Hence, every act stemming from grace merits an increase in grace (*ST* I-II.114.8).

22. See *ST* I-II.112.1.2 for how the sacraments can instrumentally cause grace by the power of the first cause: God.

23. Some people first receive sanctifying grace when they make an act of faith and love. For these people, God must first infuse grace into them in order for them to perform these actions. Although the grace comes before the action in terms of nature, in terms of time they are simultaneous (*ST* I-II.113.7 and 8). For example, if someone without access to baptism comes to faith and love of Christ, they perform this action by the power of the grace that is infused into them at the same moment as the action. This act would be considered to be a baptism of desire.

24. See *ST* I-II.62.3, where Thomas states, "The theological virtues order man to supernatural happiness in the same way as by the natural inclination man is ordered to his connatural end." Sanctifying grace must also be followed by inclinations since for every form there is an inclination. Sanctifying grace is a form within the human soul and is followed by an inclination (see *ST* I.5.5).

SEVEN. Law

1. Ex 20:12. For an extremely deontological passage that shows the external punishment of those who do not obey their parents, see Dt 21:18–22.

2. One of the things that this commandment required was for children to care for their parents when their parents needed their aid. However, at least some members of the Jewish community saw this law as removing their freedom to use their resources in other ways. For example, in Mk 7:11–13, Jesus reprimands them by noting, "If a man says to his father or his mother, 'whatever I have that would help you is Corban (that is to say, given to God),' you no longer permit him to do anything for his father or his mother, thus invalidating the word of God by your tradition which you have handed down." However, if you look at the obedience passages in Proverbs, the system is much more teleological, as obedience is the first step toward wisdom (Prv 1:8; 6:20; 23:22).

3. This definition is taken from Aquinas's definition that law is an ordinance of reason for the common good (the true happiness of all), made by a proper authority, and promulgated (*ST* I-II.90.1–4).

4. Thomas notes that a true law must be in accord with right reason, for it belongs to reason to rule and measure acts by directing things to an end (*ST* I-II.90.1). Although formally caused by the reason, as a promulgated command, law is efficiently caused by the will.

5. Cf. *ST* I-II.97.3.

6. See *ST* I-II.95.1.

7. *ST* I-II.19.4.3; 95.2; *Disputed Questions on Evil*, 2.4. Although no humans in this life have direct knowledge of the eternal law, nonetheless, all humans to the extent that they know the first indemonstrable principles of practical reason have some knowledge of the eternal law (Cf. *ST* I-II.93.2).

8. One of the primary themes of the papacy of Pope Benedict XVI was that faith is the antidote to relativism. See, for example, *Caritas in Veritate*, §§1–5, which notes the necessity for charity and freedom to be guided by the truths of the Christian faith in order to overcome moral relativism.

9. See Ex 20:2–7; Dt 5:6–21; and *Catechism of the Catholic Church*, §§1961–64.

10. The grace of the Holy Spirit perfects the mind to reason correctly from natural principles and perfects the will to love the proper laws and actions. It also gives supernatural principles (held by faith) and supernatural power to understand and reason from these principles (the Holy Spirit's gifts of understanding, science, wisdom, and counsel). Furthermore, the Holy Spirit moves the will to desire the proper laws and actions, even when the human does not have all the counsel needed to make a good decision. Because

the assistance of the Holy Spirit allows humans to judge by means of God's wisdom (the eternal law), and God always knows the correct laws for the correct circumstances, the new law of grace allows humans to most perfectly perform the correct action.

11. See also Rom 12–15; 1 Cor 12–14; Col 3–4; and Eph 4–5.

12. The term "tradition" refers to teachings and practices divinely revealed by the Son and passed down to the present age through the Church. There are also other traditions within the Church that are not divinely revealed and can be changed without changing the essence of the Faith.

13. Not all elements of Church teaching are part of the new law. Only those elements that are part of the essence of the faith are part of the new law. Other elements of Church teaching are an application of the faith to a particular situation. These applications are human laws. Certain Church teachings are part of the new law because God gave teaching power to the apostles (Mt 16), and they passed this power down from bishop to bishop to the current bishops and pope. Hence, the bishops and pope, guided by the Holy Spirit, give the authentic interpretation of scripture and tradition and also the natural law. Many of the teachings found in the *Catechism of the Catholic Church* and in papal encyclicals are examples of this type of teaching. The Church teaches with the authority of Christ (see *Catechism of the Catholic Church*, §§2032–38).

14. Since God works through secondary causes, it is the job of all who guide children and beginners in the moral life to help these people progress beyond the stage of doing good actions only out of fear of punishment or desire for a reward to doing good actions because they love God and others. To help children make this transition, parents, teachers, and mentors must serve as good examples, give the reasons behind their laws (to show that the laws lead to happiness), and be consistent in enforcing the laws. Likewise, Jesus serves as a good example, shares the divine plan with us, and consistently challenges us to be good. He also gives us the Holy Spirit to guide and move us.

15. Aquinas believes that humans have a natural inclination to natural happiness (*ST* I-II.5.8; 62.3; I.83.1.5) and, correspondingly, to all those things that are necessary to attain it (*ST* II-II.122.4; 155.2; I-II.2.8), such as perfection of the body and all the powers of the soul (*ST* I-II.4.5). In fact, he notes that "each and every power of the soul is a type of form or nature and has a natural inclination to something. Wherefore, each and every power desires by the natural appetite that object which is suitable to itself" (*ST* I.80.1.3). For example, the intellect is naturally ordered to know the true, the will to love the universal good, the irascible appetite to the arduous good, and the concupiscible appetite to the moderation of the delectable (*ST* I-II.85.3; cf. I.81.2; I-II.94.2.2).

16. However, in reference to the third commandment, it would be very difficult to determine the number of days between Sabbath rest without divine revelation.

17. Thomas notes that the first principles of natural law are self-evident. He then notes that although the principles of natural law are self-evident in themselves, they are not necessarily self-evident to everybody. Thomas continues by stating that a principle is self-evident in itself (*per se nota*) if its predicate is contained in the notion (*ratio*) of the subject (*ST* I-II.94.2). For example, in the statement, "a coffeemaker is a machine that makes coffee," if one understands what a coffeemaker is, he also understands that it is a

machine that makes coffee. The notion (*ratio*) of the subject contains each of its four causes. In other words, to understand the subject is to understand its *formal, material, efficient*, and *final cause*. In relation to the self-evident first principles of natural law, the relevant cause is the final cause. Because God created humans ordered to particular actions, human nature is naturally inclined to its proper actions. Consequently, a complete understanding of human nature includes an understanding of the various different natural inclinations, just as an understanding of a coffeemaker includes an understanding of its proper action: making coffee. Hence, any propositions that state humans are naturally inclined to a proper end are self-evident in themselves, even if they are only self-evident to the wise (those that understand the end to which humans are inclined). In other words, natural law principles are only self-evident to those that understand the teleological nature of humanity. Unless this teleological structure is at least implicitly understood, the first principles of natural law will not be self-evident and recourse to natural law arguments will be futile. See Rziha, *Perfecting Human Actions*, 201–6, for more about how the natural law is known. See also Steven Jensen, *Knowing the Natural Law*, 121–26, for a discussion of how natural law precepts are *per se nota*.

18. In *ST* I-II.94.2, Thomas gives the following list of natural laws: (1) good is to be done and pursued, and evil is to be avoided; (2) human life is to be preserved; (3) humans should procreate and raise and educate children; (4) humans should know the truth about God and live in society. The order of this list is based upon the order of discovery—i.e., in the order of how knowledge is obtained. Thomas moves from what is first apprehended (to do good), to the most general natural inclinations (found in all beings—to exist), to those specific to humans—to know the truth and live in society. The order in the list that I give is based upon the order of nature and moves from the highest inclinations (to happiness), to the lowest (those things necessary for physical life).

19. Because of the unity of the human person, the complete contradiction of a lower inclination often results in the impairment of the entire person. For example, because the soul works through the body, the destruction of health also results in the inability of the intellect to seek the truth.

20. See *ST* I-II.91.3 and 95.2 and 3.

21. See this Martin Luther King, Jr., quotation found in his "Letter from a Birmingham Jail": "How does one determine whether a law is just or unjust? A just law is a manmade code that squares with the moral law or the law of God. An unjust law is a code that is out of harmony with the moral law. To put it in the terms of St. Thomas Aquinas: An unjust law is a human law that is not rooted in eternal law and natural law. Any law that uplifts human personality is just. Any law that degrades human personality is unjust. All segregation statutes are unjust because segregation distorts the soul and damages the personality. It gives the segregator a false sense of superiority and the segregated a false sense of inferiority. Segregation, to use the terminology of the Jewish philosopher Martin Buber, substitutes an 'I it' relationship for an 'I thou' relationship and ends up relegating persons to the status of things." King goes on to give other examples of unjust laws, such as the law against aiding a Jew in Nazi Germany (289–302).

22. See Phil 2:2 and following. After encouraging all to be of one heart and mind, Paul states, "Humbly regard others as more important than yourselves, each looking out not for his own interests, but for those of others." Paul then says to imitate Christ, "who though he was in the form of God . . ."

23. Work refers to any activity for the common good that perfects the person. For this expanded definition of work, see John Paul II, *Laborem Exercens*, §§1–3.

24. See Leo XIII, *Rerum Novarum*, §§4–20, and Pius XI, *Quadragesimo Anno*, §§116–26, for the Catholic Church's teaching on socialism.

25. Although it would be wrong for a government to own all the means of production (socialism), the government has a duty to promote the employment of its citizens through appropriate programs. See John Paul II, *Laborem Exercens*, §§16–18, and *Centesimus Annus*, §48.

26. See *ST* I-II.99.2.2, which states that divine law aids the soul not only in things in which human reason is insufficient, but also in areas where human reason is impeded. In other words, divine law is also needed when the divinely revealed truth could be known by natural reason, but for various possible reasons (e.g., sloth, lack of intelligence, lack of time to contemplate, etc.), humans are unable to come to this knowledge on their own (cf. *ST* II-II.2.4). See also Benedict XVI, *Deus Caritas Est*, §28. In speaking of the necessity of Catholic social thought, he states, "The State must inevitably face the question of how justice can be achieved here and now. . . . The problem is one of practical reason; but if reason is to be exercised properly, it must undergo constant purification, since it can never be completely free of the danger of a certain ethical blindness caused by the dazzling effect of power and special interests. Here politics and faith meet. Faith by its specific nature is an encounter with the living God—an encounter opening new horizons extending beyond the sphere of reason. . . . faith liberates reason from its blind spots and therefore helps it to be ever more fully itself. Faith enables reason to do its work more effectively and to see its proper object more clearly."

27. Brad Gregory, *The Unintended Reformation*, 198, traces the beginning of rights language back to the early canonists who sought to safeguard human dignity against both political and spiritual leaders that failed to rule in accord with eternal law. From canon law this language eventually migrates to various political documents over the centuries that also sought to safeguard certain liberties. Some examples of these documents are the Magna Carta (1215), the English Bill of Rights (1689), and the U.S. Bill of Rights (1791). Nonetheless, widespread use of "rights language" is a more recent phenomenon.

28. See *Pacem in Terris*, §§1–45. Earlier popes have used rights language when speaking of freedoms and obligations, such Leo XIII, who argues that humans have a right to private property (*Rerum Novarum*, §§5–15). However, rights language was not widely used until John XXIII.

29. See *Pacem in Terris*, §§4–10 and 37–38.

30. Since they often do not consider the unborn child a person, their right to an abortion does not seem, in their view, to violate the rights of another human.

31. See *Pacem in Terris*, §§11–38, for a long list of natural rights.

32. Although these are called "rights," they are not earned by human nature but bestowed because humans are adopted children of God.

EIGHT.   Virtue

1. Aristotle notes: "It is from the same causes and by the same means that every virtue is both produced and destroyed, and similarly every art; for it is from playing the lyre that both good and bad lyre-players are produced. And the corresponding statement is true of builders and of all the rest; men will be good or bad builders as a result of building well or badly. For if this were not so, there would have been no need of a teacher, but all men would have been born good or bad at their craft. This, then, is the case with the virtues also; by doing the acts that we do in our transactions with other men we become just or unjust, and by doing the acts that we do in the presence of danger, and being habituated to feel fear or confidence, we become brave or cowardly. . . . This is why the activities we exhibit must be of a certain kind; it is because the states of character correspond to the differences between these. It makes no small difference, then, whether we form habits of one kind or of another from our very youth; it makes a very great difference, or rather all the difference" (*Nicomachean Ethics*, 2.1 [1103]).

2. See, for example, Cessario, *The Moral Virtues and Theological Ethics*, 34–37.

3. *Metaphysics*, bk. 5 (1022b). See also *Nicomachean Ethics*, 2.5 (1106a).

4. A disposition exists even when it is not being actively used. For example, Kate might have the habit of being good at cooking even when she is not cooking. Consequently, Thomas notes that a habit is in one sense an act in that it perfects the powers of the soul, and in another sense it is in potency to further acts (*ST* I-II.49.3.1). Elsewhere Thomas speaks of a habit as being a medium between the potency of the soul and its proper actions (*ST* I.87.2).

5. See Cessario, *The Moral Virtues and Theological Ethics*, 47. See also Aristotle, *Nicomachean Ethics*, 3.2 (1104b–1105a).

6. I borrowed this example from Jensen, *Living the Good Life*, 70–71. In his analogy, he also notes that when old habits are transformed into new ones, the grass grows back up on the "old habit path" making it again difficult to cross.

7. See *ST* I-II.54.3.

8. See Rziha, *Perfecting Human Actions*, 130–40, for more detail on why humans need habits for their natural inclinations to be perfected. I explain how humans are naturally inclined to habits for three reasons: they are in potency to act, they need to be determined to a particular type of action, and several powers must be perfected by repetitive actions to perform actions ordered to the ultimate act of happiness.

9. Thomas states: "Hence, it is evident that virtues perfect us so that we follow in due manner our natural inclinations, which belong to the natural right. Wherefore to every definite natural inclination there corresponds a special virtue" (*ST* II-II.108.2).

10. In distinguishing between the different levels of dignity, Thomas notes that humans with the highest level of dignity are led to the good, not by others, but by themselves. The second level of dignity refers to those who are led to the good by others, but they still freely choose it. The third level of dignity refers to those who require coercion in order to be good, and the last level refers to those who cannot be directed to the good even with coercion (*Commentary on the Letter of Saint Paul to the Romans*, chap. 2, lect. 3). In other words, the highest level of dignity refers to those who are virtuous and hence able to know

and love the good by their own power. Others can know and love the good but need the guidance or motivation of others (external principles).

11. Although powers apart from reason are determined to one thing, reason is a power that compares several things, and thus the rational appetite (the will) may be moved by several apprehended goods (*ST* I.82.2.3). In other words, although the will by necessity adheres to the last end (happiness), the intellect can compare many goods that can be ordered to the end of happiness. Consequently, provided that these goods are not necessarily connected to happiness, the will does not adhere to any of them by necessity.

12. Inasmuch as a nonrational being acts, it will perform its proper action. It can, however, be prevented from performing its proper action by an outside force.

13. Thomas states: "According to the Philosopher (*Metaph*. i, 20), what is 'free is cause of itself.' Therefore he acts freely, who acts of his own accord. Now man does of his own accord that which he does from a habit that is suitable to his nature: since a habit inclines one as a second nature. If, however, a habit be in opposition to nature, man would not act according to his nature, but according to some corruption affecting that nature" (*ST* I-II.108.1.2).

14. Thomas states: "The will, of course, is ordered to that which is truly good. But if, by reason of passion or of bad habit or disposition, a man be turned away from that which is truly good, he acts slavishly, in that he is diverted by some extraneous thing, if consideration be given the will's natural order itself" (*SCG* IV.22.2).

15. See *ST* I-II.52.3, where Thomas notes, "If the intensity of the act corresponds in proportion to the intensity of the habit, or even surpasses it, every such act either increases the habit or disposes to an increase thereof."

16. An example of not acting with intensity in our relationship with God might involve going to daily Mass. If you were in the habit of going to daily Mass, but you skipped a few days, the habit would probably remain but would be weaker. If you skipped a lot of days, the habit could be completely destroyed. If you begin to see Mass as a burden, and your love from both the will and the emotions for Mass decreases, the habit may be decreased even if you go, because this is an act of lower intensity.

17. If humans fail to perform acts of faith, hope, and love, these virtues will be weakened. Furthermore, as I will explain in chapter 10 on sin, a single mortal sin can destroy the habit of charity.

18. Humans do not have two intellects, rather there is one intellect that is sometimes ordered to operation and sometimes ordered to knowledge for its own sake. The distinction is made because when the end of the intellect is speculative, it "thinks" differently than when its end is practical. Likewise, there are different virtues corresponding to the two types of "thinking."

19. For example, children (the effect) are of the same nature as their parents (the cause). Another example might be the carpenter who makes a desk. It would seem that the desk is not like the carpenter, but it is like the intellectual form (blueprint) within the mind of the carpenter.

20. For more arguments for God's existence, see *ST* I.2.3, where Aquinas gives five arguments for God's existence. The basic line of reasoning in all of Aquinas's arguments is

that an effect participates in its cause. Whenever there is something that has a perfection by participation, the perfection must ultimately come from something that has that perfection by nature. The being that has all perfections by nature is God.

21. Technically, judgment by higher truths is not an additional action of the intellect. It is actually another case of understanding (step 2), where knowledge is compared to higher truths.

22. See Rziha, *Perfecting Human Actions*, 193–230, for a detailed explanation of how the different acts of the intellect are perfected by the intellectual virtues.

23. Thomas notes that to understand is to penetrate into the essence of a thing, since the object of the intellect is what a thing is. However, there are many different kinds of things hidden within a thing. For example, under accidents are hidden the substantial reality, under words lie their meaning, under effects are their causes, etc. All of these things require the light of understanding to penetrate to the underlying reality. The stronger the light of understanding, the deeper it can penetrate into the essence of things and their principles (*ST* II-II.8.1).

24. Thomas holds that *synderesis* is a natural habit that is found to some extent in all humans. In other words, once humans understand the terms of the most fundamental principles of natural law, they are able to understand these principles. For example, if humans understand what "good" truly means, it is self-evident that humans should do good and avoid evil (*ST* I-II.94.6; 99.2.2; II-II.47.6.1). However, just as some principles of the speculative intellect are also self-evident and others require growth in virtue to understand them, so also other principles of natural law require growth in the virtue of practical understanding (*synderesis*) to properly understand them. Cf. *ST* I-II.90.1.2; 94.2.

25. Chapter 15, specifically devoted to prudence, will designate subvirtues that perfect each of the steps. See also *ST* II-II.48 and 51.

26. In cases of abuse or neglect of children, even this inclination can be corrupted.

27. See *ST* I-II.61.2 for more on the cardinal virtues.

28. *ST* I-II.63.4. See also *ST* I-II.58.4–5.

29. See *ST* I-II.61.1–2.

30. In *ST* I-II.62.3, Thomas states, "The theological virtues order man to supernatural happiness in the same way as by the natural inclination man is ordered to his connatural end." See also *ST* I-II.62.1; 110.4.1; *Scriptum Super Sententiis*, bk. 3, distinctio 23, q. 1, art. 4C; *Disputed Questions on Virtue* 1.10; and *Truth*, 14.2, in reference to faith.

31. See *ST* I-II.62.3 and *ST* II-II.17.8 to see how Thomas compares faith, hope, and charity to the inclinations to understand the truth and to love oneself and others.

32. The way I am using this distinction is less sophisticated than the way Thomas uses it. Thomas makes a distinction between love of friendship (*amor amicitiae*) and love of concupiscence (*amor concupiscentiae*) in *ST* I-II.26.4, where he notes that love of friendship is love of another person, while love of concupiscence is love of a good willed for either oneself or the other person. Consequently, because love of concupiscence also refers to the good willed to others, it is a broader category than the term "love of use" as I am using it. Also, love of friendship can refer to love of oneself—the key is that a person is loved rather than a good (loved either for one's own sake or for the sake of another).

However, much of the time when Thomas uses the term "love of concupiscence," he does contrast it with love of friendship in a way similar to the way I use the term "love of use" (see, e.g., *ST* I-II.27.3).

33. It is not necessary that every act of love of use develops into a deep intimate friendship, but it is necessary that every human loves others for their own sake. In order to function in society, humans must have love of use for many different people, including doctors, teachers, storekeepers, etc. However, although humans in this life cannot develop an intimate friendship with every person that they encounter, they must nonetheless love these people for their own sake and make their natural needs their own. Justice and charity perfect our ability to have love of friendship of others.

34. In *ST* II-II.17.8, Thomas notes, "The first love of God pertains to charity, which adheres to God for His own sake; while hope pertains to the second love, since he that hopes intends to obtain possession of something for himself." See also *ST* I-II.66.6.2; II-II.17.3 and 17.6. Although hope perfects the natural inclination to love oneself, because it is supernaturally infused, when talking of hope Thomas generally emphasizes the element of trust in God's assistance more than the self-love aspect of hope. Cf. *ST* II-II.17.7.

35. See *ST* I-II.65.2–3. See also Rziha, *Perfecting Human Actions*, 174–80, which shows how Thomas makes a distinction between *formally* and *materially* following eternal law. To formally follow eternal law, humans must have charity, i.e., they always intend to do God's will even if what they think is God's will is wrong. However, to materially follow God's will, humans must not only have charity but also the infused cardinal virtues so that they not only have good intention, but they also choose actions in conformity with God's wisdom.

36. See Aristotle, *Nicomachean Ethics*, 2.2 (1104).

37. Anorexia nervosa is generally considered to be a psychological disorder. However, the word is particularly well-suited to describe the vice of not having enough desire for food, since those with this disorder find food repulsive. In the context of morality, I am using this word to refer to those who through habit (either through their own fault or the fault of others) have a lack of desire for food, and certainly not to the disease we know today as anorexia.

38. There is an analogical mean for faith (between opinion and science) and hope (between despair and presumption), but not a real mean.

39. For the Holy Spirit's gifts of understanding, knowledge, wisdom, and counsel, see chapter 9, table 9.1.

NINE.   Guidance from the Holy Spirit

1. See Pinckaers, *Sources of Christian Ethics*, 404, on how the gifts of the Holy Spirit give a spiritual instinct that perfects the rational instinct of humans.

2. *ST* I-II.68.2. In addition, the theological virtues of faith and hope, by their nature, are imperfect. In the next life, faith will be replaced by direct knowledge of God, and hope is not necessary when complete unity with God exists. Charity remains in the next life, but even it is perfected.

3. Because the gifts and infused virtues are necessary for salvation, they flow from sanctifying grace. However, there are other gifts, called "gratuitous graces," that perfect humans to help others grow in love of God. These gifts are not found in everyone, but they also perfect the ability of humans to be moved by the Holy Spirit. The gifts mentioned in 1 Corinthians 12—prophecy, the ability to teach, the ability to perform miracles, the ability to speak in tongues, and others—are examples of gratuitous graces. These are not found in all but are distributed by God for the sake of the Church. See *ST* I-II.111.1.

4. See also Prv 2:2–11.

5. See *Catechism of the Catholic Church*, §308, which notes, "The truth that God is at work in all the actions of his creatures is inseparable from faith in God the Creator. . . . Far from diminishing the creature's dignity, this truth enhances it. Drawn from nothingness by God's power, wisdom, and goodness, it can do nothing if it is cut off from its origin, for 'without a Creator the creature vanishes.' Still less can a creature attain its ultimate end without the help of God's grace."

6. *ST* I.105.5. Thomas notes that God causes created agents to act by being the end for which they act, by causing the act itself, and by giving them form through which they act. In reference to humans, God as good is the end of human actions; God is the cause of all human actions; and God causes the human nature through which humans act. Cf. Rziha, *Perfecting Human Actions*, 57–66, for a detailed account of how God moves creatures to their actions as the efficient, exemplary, and final cause of their actions.

7. See *ST* I.105.3 for Aquinas's explanation of how God moves the intellect. The phrase "God gives the intellect the power to understand," which is found both in this sentence in the text and in the article by Aquinas, can be misunderstood and can give the impression that God creates the intellect and then leaves it alone. The proper understanding is that God is constantly giving the intellect the power to understand, as a first cause moves a second cause. Thomas further explains how God moves things in the disputed questions of *On the Power of God*, when he states, "Therefore God is the cause of everything's action inasmuch as he gives everything the power to act, and preserves it in being and applies it to action, and inasmuch as by his power every other power acts" (3.7).

8. See *ST* I.105.4.

9. Thomas also likes to use the analogy of an injured leg with a limp to illustrate the relation between God and humans in evil actions. The soul (the first cause) causes the act of limping (defective walking) but not the limp (the defect), which is caused by the injury in the leg. See *ST* I-II.79.2 and *SCG* 3.10.

10. Although all three of these cause defects in human actions, ignorance and disordered emotions excuse wrongdoing or diminish it. Hence, moral fault is found primarily in the act of the will. See *SCG* 3.10.

11. Every action has some goodness to the extent that it exists. Being is convertible with goodness. In other words, if something has being, then it must have some goodness, even if the amount of goodness is extremely minute.

12. Because even evil actions have some goodness in them, God can use even evil actions to bring the universe to its proper perfection. The greatest case of all is the crucifixion of Christ, where the evil act of killing an innocent man became the means of redeeming all. As Romans 8:28 notes, "All things work for good for those who love God."

13. John Paul II, *Laborem Exercens*, §§5–7, makes a distinction between the objective and subjective character of work. The objective character of work refers to how it transforms creation for the sake of the common good. The subjective character refers to how it perfects the worker. Of these two characteristics of work, John Paul states that the subjective is the more important. God does not need humans to bring creation to perfection (the objective value); rather, he allows them to enter into his plan solely for their benefit (the subjective value).

14. *SCG* IV.21.5. Here is the full text: "Of course, this is the proper mark of friendship: that one reveal his secrets to his friend. For, since charity unites affections and makes, as it were, one heart of two, one seems not to have dismissed from his heart that which he reveals to a friend; and so our Lord says to His disciples: 'I will not now call you servants but friends: because all things whatsoever I have heard of My Father I have made known to you' (Jn 15:15). Therefore, since by the Holy Spirit we are established as friends of God, fittingly enough it is by the Holy Spirit that men are said to receive the revelation of the divine mysteries."

15. For more on how the Holy Spirit moves humans to participate in eternal law, see Rziha, *Perfecting Human Actions*, 274–80.

16. Humans can only love something to the extent that it is known by the intellect. Nonetheless, the will does not love the image in the intellect but the thing itself. Hence, through charity, the will loves God himself, despite the fact that the knowledge of God is incomplete. In heaven, when humans know God as he is, the love of God can be increased even more.

17. Thomas explains that connatural wisdom is where humans judge divine things based on an inclination infused by the Holy Spirit (*ST* I-II.64.1; 68.4–5; II-II.45.2; 97.2.2).

18. See *ST* I-II.106.1; II-II.45.2.

TEN.   Sin, Temptation, and Vice

1. See *ST* I-II.71.6.

2. Sin is a lack of goodness in the moral realm when it should exist. Consequently, only the lack of moral perfection within a human act is a sin. The absence of many other types of perfections, such as those that must be attained gradually, those not in the moral realm (e.g., good eyesight), and those not suitable to human nature, do not result in sins. Something is only a sin if there is a lack of goodness that should exist in a freely chosen action, such as when a student chooses to cheat on a test. The student chooses the good of getting a good grade, but not the greater good of learning the material and honestly expressing this knowledge.

3. See *ST* I-II.79.1 and 2.

4. *ST* I-II.79.1.

5. An action must be ordered to God if the person knows about God. If the person does not know about God or has a false conception of God, then the action must be ordered to the highest good the person does understand.

6. See *Catechism of the Catholic Church*, §1855, which defines mortal sin in the following manner: "Mortal sin destroys charity in the heart of man by a grave violation of God's law; it turns man away from God, . . . by preferring an inferior good to him."

7. See *ST* I-II.88.1. Thomas further notes that mortal sins can only be repaired by the grace of God, since the order to the end is gone. However, with venial sins, charity continues to order the person to God, so that through the repetition of loving actions (caused by grace), the sin can be repaired.

8. She still retains some culpability for getting drunk, but she had no reason to believe that drunkenness would lead to passionately kissing the other man.

9. See *Catechism of the Catholic Church*, §1858; Ex 20:2–17; Dt 5:6–21; Mk 10:19; 1 Cor 6:9–10.

10. In a malicious person, the intellect and will can choose to commit evil actions without the promptings of the disordered emotions. Hence, the disordered intellect and will by themselves can also be causes of sinful actions. However, these are not cases of temptation since in terms of moral agency the intellect and the will are who the person is. Temptation refers to enticement from something outside of the intellect and will.

11. Thomas states that the devil cannot directly move the will or enlighten the intellect. Hence, the devil is not a direct or sufficient cause of sin (*ST* I-II.80.1). Although the devil cannot move the intellect and will, it can move bodily powers since bodily powers have a natural aptitude to be moved locally by a spiritual nature. Since sense knowledge and the emotions are in both the body and the soul, the devil can cause the imagination of sinful objects and incite the emotions to desire sinful things (*ST* I-II.80.2). Ultimately, the devil is only the occasional and indirect cause of sin (*ST* I-II.80.4).

12. An important theme in the Gospel of John is that the divine Son continues his mission even after he ascends into heaven. He continues his mission through the Holy Spirit. Just as the Son works through human flesh so that humans can see God (Jn 1:1,14), so also the Holy Spirit works through the followers of Jesus (Jn 14:26; 15:26–27; 16:12–15; 17:20–22; 20:19–23).

13. *The Rule of St. Benedict*, 7.44. The *Rule* states, "The fifth step of humility is that a man does not conceal from his abbot any sinful thoughts entering his heart, or any wrongs committed in secret, but rather confesses them humbly." Because of practices like this, the custom of frequent confession evolved in the monasteries and the communities that surrounded them. The laity living around the monastery saw the spiritual benefits of frequent confession and desired these benefits for themselves.

14. See Catechism of the Catholic Church, §§1457–58; §1458 states: "Without being strictly necessary, confession of everyday faults (venial sins) is nevertheless strongly recommended by the Church. Indeed the regular confession of our venial sins helps us form our conscience, fight against evil tendencies, let ourselves be healed by Christ and progress in the life of the Spirit."

15. If the confession of many venial sins will keep others from receiving the sacrament, then venial sins should be confessed in moderation. Although all venial sins should be covered in the examination of conscience, it may be prudent to confess only the four or five worst sins.

ELEVEN.   Completing the Map to Happiness

1. On earth, the natural inclinations lack the ability to sufficiently cause good actions for two reasons. First, by nature humans are in potency to many actions and need habits to determine their inclinations to these habits (see *ST* I-II.50.6). If they do not have the habits themselves, then the good habits of others are necessary to guide them to their proper action. Furthermore, original sin has corrupted the natural inclination that man has to virtue (*ST* I-II.85.1 and 2). Second, because of their social nature, humans need the help of others to be perfected (*ST* I-II.4.8); hence, even without original sin there would be the need for others to motivate and guide humans to good actions.

2. Of course, God's power is still necessary to move and guide them to perform actions by means of the powers of the soul perfected by virtues.

3. On both the natural and supernatural level, there is an order of causality moving from nature (or its perfection in grace) to happiness (natural or eternal). However, on the natural level, the earlier elements also normally precede the later ones in time. In other words, humans must be directed and motivated by human law to perform many good human actions before they become virtuous. (Keeping in mind that virtues do not develop in all areas simultaneously; there will often be some cases where motivation by human law is necessary to perform the good actions.) On the supernatural level, grace, the theological virtues, and the infused cardinal virtues are infused simultaneously in terms of time.

4. Recall from chapter 7 that the divine law contains within it the content of both the natural and human law. Hence, whenever parents and other authority figures guide humans with grace to good actions, they are guiding them in accordance with the divine law.

5. Because this training is so important for the long-term stability of society, God commands children to honor their father and mother so that they may have a long life in the promised land (Ex 20:12).

6. *Gaudium et Spes*, §53.

7. Ibid; §§57–59 provide principles for the proper development of culture.

8. Kant argued that all should follow the categorical imperative with a good will. The imperative is this: "So act as if your maxims should serve at the same time as universal law for all rational beings" (*Grounding for the Metaphysics of Morals*, 279–80).

9. Other simple systems, such as emotivism (always follow your emotions) or situationalism (always do the loving thing in a situation), have some truth but again neglect important elements of the moral life. The emotions must be perfected by virtues before they are trustworthy. Situationalism neglects the role of law in guiding humans to loving actions.

10. Thomas notes that animals judge which act is to be chosen by instinct. Humans are likewise determined by nature to the ultimate end of happiness. In other words, humans are not free to choose whether or not they want to be happy; they are naturally inclined to this end. However, the means of achieving this end can vary in humans because human reason is able to determine many possible actions that are ordered to many dif-

ferent understandings of happiness. Consequently, freedom comes from the ability to know different ways of attaining happiness and choosing one or more of them (*ST* I.83.1; I-II.10.2).

11. See Rziha, "The Thomistic Roots of Modern Papal Teachings on Freedom as Found in the Writings of Leo XIII," for more on the relation between freedom and law, virtue, and grace as stated by Pope Leo XIII and also sources of these views in the writings of Thomas.

12. John Paul II, in *Veritatis Splendor*, distinguishes authentic freedom from a false or artificial freedom (§§87, 89, 95, 99, 101; see also §§4, 13, 32). This distinction can also be found in the Vatican II document *Gaudium et Spes*, §17. Leo XIII in 1888 especially develops this distinction between true and false freedom in the encyclical *Libertas Praestantissimum*. The entire encyclical is devoted to explaining the proper view of freedom. Although he uses different terminology, Servais Pinckaers has written the most comprehensive work on the distinction between true and false freedom. He calls true freedom "freedom for excellence" and false freedom "freedom of indifference" (see Pinckaers, *Sources of Christian Ethics*, chaps. 14–17). I am greatly indebted to him for his insights on freedom.

13. Like most views, there is some truth in the understanding of artificial freedom. On earth, humans do have the ability to choose evil. On earth, humans never apprehend any good as being good in every way and can therefore always reject it. See *ST* I-II.10.2, where Thomas notes that the only thing that the will must by necessity choose is the universal good (God). However, on earth, God is never known perfectly. Hence, humans can reject him.

14. Although the will by necessity must choose the infinite good in heaven (because it is naturally inclined to this), this is perfect freedom because it fulfills the natural inclinations. In other words, in heaven you will finally have the happiness you always desired (see *ST* I-II.10.2).

15. See Jn 8:32–34 and Rom 6:20.

16. The reason I picked these three views is that they are contrasted in John Paul II's encyclical *Veritatis Splendor*, §§40–41.

17. Pinckaers argues that this type of "obligation-based" morality can be traced back to William of Ockham. Ockham believed that God was absolutely free. Ockham thought God by his absolute power could change any of the laws that he had revealed to humans. For example, he could even make hating God a good thing. Since Ockham did not see anything inherently good in the laws that God made, the only reason that humans had for following these laws was God's coercive power (see Pinckaers, *Sources of Christian Ethics*, chaps. 10–12, and chap. 14).

18. These theologians were involved in the probabilist controversy. The different parties in this controversy noted that laws do not apply to every situation. They then argued about whether or not a person had to follow the law based upon how "probable" it was that the law applied to his or her situation.

19. In *Veritatis Splendor*, §§36–40, John Paul II makes a distinction between genuine autonomy and false autonomy. Genuine autonomy recognizes that humans are self-ruling because they draw their ability to rule from divine wisdom. False autonomy disregards the

participation of human reason in divine wisdom and instead "posits a complete sovereignty of reason in the domain of moral norms regarding right ordering of life in this world" (§36). When I speak of autonomy in this section, I am equating it with false autonomy. Perhaps the greatest advocate of this understanding of autonomy was Kant, who believed that for an action to be moral it must stem from an autonomous will (see Kant, *Grounding for the Metaphysics of Morals*, 285–86). See also Kant, "What Is Enlightenment?" 462–67.

20. See also Rhonheimer, *Natural Law and Practical Reason*, chap. 5, who uses the term "participated autonomy" in the same way that I am using the term "participated theonomy." For a distinction between a Christian understanding of autonomy as theonomy and a secular understanding, see Kasper, *Theology and the Church*.

21. See Rziha, *Perfecting Human Actions*, 261–68, for more on the relationship between freedom and participation in God's knowledge and love within human actions.

TWELVE.   Faith

1. See Pinckaers, *Sources of Christians Ethics*, chap. 12, for an explanation of how both Catholics and Protestants tended to separate faith from morality.

2. The Vatican II constitution on divine revelation, *Dei Verbum*, §§3, 4.

3. Thomas states that in cases of knowledge, the intellect is moved to assent by the object itself. However, when things are not known with certainty, "the intellect assents to something, not through being sufficiently moved to this assent by its proper object, but through an act of choice, whereby it turns voluntarily to one side rather than to the other: and if this be accompanied by doubt or fear of the opposite side, there will be opinion, while, if there is certainty and no fear of the other side, there will be faith" (*ST* II-II.1.4). See also *De Veritate*, §14.1; cf. *ST* II-II.2.9.2.

4. The intellect can accept a principle as being true in two ways. One way is by deriving it from self-evident propositions or deriving it from previously demonstrated conclusions. The second way is by the will choosing to assent to the proposition. Since the principles of faith are supernatural and therefore cannot be derived from self-evident propositions, the will must choose to hold these propositions as true on account of the authority of God.

5. In responding to the statement that faith is foolish, Thomas states that the imperfect nature of our intellect takes away the basis of this difficulty. He continues, "For if man of himself could in a perfect manner know all things visible and invisible, it would indeed be foolish to believe what he does not see. But our manner of knowing is so weak that no philosopher could perfectly discover the nature of even one little fly. . . . If one were willing to believe only those things which one knows with certitude, one could not live in this world. How could one live unless one believed others? How could one know that this man is one's own father? Therefore, it is necessary that one believes others in matters which one cannot know perfectly by oneself. But no one is so worthy of belief as is God, and hence they who do not believe the words of faith are not wise, but foolish and proud" ("The Apostles' Creed," 5).

6. Since angels know things immediately, it is appropriate for them to immediately be given the grace of divine knowledge upon showing their love of God.

7. See *ST* II-II.2.3, and 1 Cor 13:12.

8. Since intelligible forms are abstracted from phantasms in the senses and the imagination, in the case of prophecy, God can either reveal himself through sensible images or by imaginary forms (*ST* II-II.173.2).

9. Thomas states: "The knowledge which we have by natural reason contains two things: images derived from the sensible objects, and the natural intelligible light, enabling us to abstract from them intelligible conceptions. Now in both of these, human knowledge is assisted by the revelation of grace" (*ST* I.12.13). Cf. *ST* I.111.1; II-II.173.2.

10. See *Dei Verbum*, §§7–10.

11. In the early Church, people were required to profess the Creed before being baptized. As Christianity differentiated itself from other faiths, more and more articles were added to the Creed. So although at the beginning it was merely a profession of belief in the three persons in the Trinity (distinguishing Christianity from the other religions of the time), over time other articles were added, such as the phrase "creator of heaven and earth" to describe the Father. This addition distinguished the Christian faith from Gnosticism, which did not believe God created the material world. For more on early Christian creeds, see Kelly, *Early Christian Creeds*. Kelly begins with the New Testament and shows the development of creeds in the first centuries of the Church.

12. It is not enough just to hear about the articles of the Faith. They must be presented in an intelligible way so that they do not contradict the natural inclination to know the truth. Faith perfects knowledge; it does not destroy it.

13. The Ten Commandments are the obligations of the Mosaic covenant. The structure of this covenant is similar to other covenants of the time period between a king and a vassal. A common feature of these covenants is a statement about how the vassal was to be faithful to the king and the king alone. This statement would be followed by a list of stipulations defining what being faithful meant. So also the Ten Commandments begin with a statement to be faithful to God alone. This statement is followed by a list of other commands defining what it meant to be faithful to God. See Hillers, *Covenant*, 48–54.

14. Schmidt, *Everything Is Grace*, 311.

15. Virtues seek the mean between excess and defect, as explained in chapter 8.

16. See also Pinckaers, who argues that faith is at the center of the moral life in *Sources of Christian Ethics*, 114–20.

17. See Rziha, *Perfecting Human Actions*, 232–36, for more on how faith perfects the different acts of the intellect.

THIRTEEN. Hope

1. *Spe Salvi*, §2. See also §7: "through faith, in a tentative way, . . . there are already present in us the things that are hoped for: the whole, true life. . . . Faith draws the future into the present, so that it is no longer simply a 'not yet.' The fact that this future exists changes the present."

2. Thomas notes: "The first love pertains to charity, which adheres to God for His own sake; while hope pertains to the second love, since he that hopes, intends to obtain possession of something for himself" (*ST* II-II.17.8).

3. See *ST* II-II.17.6.3 and 17.7. Thomas notes: "Now the object of hope is, in one way, eternal happiness, and, in another way, the divine assistance."

4. See Aquinas, *On Hope*, in *Disputed Questions on Virtue*, I.1. I am grateful to Tom Osborne for directing me toward this passage. Tom explained the distinction by stating, "The divine help, which is the means by which beatitude is hoped, is the formal object of hope, and the enjoyment of God is the material object."

5. *ST* II-II.18.2 states that the principal object of hope is "eternal happiness as being possible to obtain by the assistance of God."

6. See *ST* II-II.17.3, where Thomas states, "He can hope for another eternal life, inasmuch as he is united to him by love, and just as it is the same virtue of charity whereby a man loves God, himself, and his neighbor, so too it is the same virtue of hope, whereby a man hopes for himself and for another."

7. *Spe Salvi*, §28.

8. Paul gives a good example of hope when he states, "If only we suffer with him [Christ] so that we may also be glorified with him. I consider that the sufferings of this present time are as nothing compared with the glory to be revealed for us" (Rom 8:17–18).

9. Cf. Aquinas, *Commentary on the Letter of Saint Paul to the Romans*, 8.3, where he further breaks filial fear down into initial fear and holy fear.

10. Christ states: "And do not be afraid of those who kill the body but cannot kill the soul; rather, be afraid of the one who can destroy both soul and body in Gehenna" (Mt 10:28).

11. Fear, like all emotions, is necessary to keep the body alive. Consequently, in general worldly fears are good. They are only evil if they cause someone to lose rationality.

12. See Dt 28:15–69 for an excellent example of God using servile fear to motivate the Israelites to do good actions.

13. In the New Testament, the traditional concept of hell can be derived from a number of different passages that can be interpreted in a more deontological or a more teleological way. One of the more common images of hell is that of fire. For example, in Matthew 25:41, Jesus states, "Depart from me, you accursed, into the eternal fire prepared for the devil and his angels." In Mark 9:43, Jesus notes it is better to lose one of your hands than to go to Gehenna, the unquenchable fire (cf. Mt 5:28; 10:28; 18:19; Jn 15:6; Jas 3:6). In other places hell is presented simply as a place of eternal punishment (Mt 25:46; 2 Thes 1:9).The fire images can be interpreted in more deontological manner as causing external punishment, or they can be interpreted in a more teleological manner as showing what happens to things that are cast off, such as garbage (Mk 9:43), chaff (Mt 3:12; Lk 3:17), and unfruitful vines (Jn 15:6). The idea is that just as all of these discarded things are separated from the good things that are kept, so also the unrighteous are unhappy as separated from God.

14. Thomas states: "For there cannot be anything less to be hoped for from Him than Himself, since His goodness, whereby He imparts good things to His creatures, is no less than His essence" (*ST* II-II.17.2).

FOURTEEN. Charity

1. *ST* II-II.23.6.

2. Thomas notes: "If what gives a thing its species is removed, the species is destroyed, and that thing cannot remain the same; . . . Now hope takes its species from its principal object . . . eternal happiness as being possible to obtain by the assistance of God. Since then the arduous possible good cannot be an object of hope except in so far as it is something future, it follows that when happiness is no longer future, but present, it is incompatible with the virtue of hope" (*ST* II-II.18.2). Love of use of God will remain, but it will no longer be hope.

3. See Jn 15:15, where Jesus says, "I no longer call you slaves, because a slave does not know what his master is doing. I have called you friends, because I have told you everything I have heard from my father." Jesus is giving us the opportunity to make the Father's goals our own goals through our knowledge and love.

4. Another way that love is divided into types by Aquinas can be found in *ST* I-II.26.3: "We find four words referring in a way, to the same thing: viz. love [*amor*], dilection [*dilectio*], charity [*caritas*] and friendship [*amicitia*]. They differ, however, in this, that 'friendship,' according to the Philosopher (Ethic. viii, 5), 'is like a habit,' whereas 'love' and 'dilection' are expressed by way of act or passion; and 'charity' can be taken either way." He goes on to note that love is any inclination toward the good in either the will or passions. Dilection is only in the will formed by the judgment of the intellect and not in the passions, and charity expresses a further perfection to love.

5. As the believer progresses in the spiritual life, God will often remove the gift of emotional love to make sure that the person is loving God for who he is and not because of the pleasure received. This time of "spiritual dryness" is also called "the dark night of the soul."

6. The term "friendship" here refers to the authentic friendship where friends are united by sharing their significant needs and goals. However, the term "friendship" can also refer to other types of relationships, such as a friendship based on pleasure (corresponding to love of use and emotional love) or based on a common interest (corresponding to either love of use or friendship). For example, a friendship based on pleasure might refer to people who hang out with others solely because they attain pleasure from their interactions. These types of friends do not really know each other at a deep level, nor do they make the other's needs and goals their own. Friendship based on a common interest is when people share a common interest in a job, a favorite cause, or a favorite sports team, for example. Both of these types of friendship can coexist with true friendship, just as for the virtuous person, emotional love and love of use coexist with love of friendship. See Torrell, *Christ and Spirituality in St. Thomas Aquinas*, 46–50, on these different types of friendship.

7. Thomas notes that love of friendship consists of both benevolence, when humans love someone so as to wish good to them, and the communion that results from the mutual love of friends (*ST* II-II.23.1). Elsewhere, Thomas describes how the union comes about by stating, "To the extent that the things which belong to a friend the lover judges

to be his own, the lover seems to be in the beloved as made the same as the lover. But conversely, to the extent that he wills and acts for his friend as for himself, as regarding his friends as the same as himself, in this manner, the beloved is in the lover" (*ST* I-II.28.2).

8. See Phil 2:2–11: "Complete my joy by being of the same mind, with the same love, united in heart, thinking one thing. . . . humbly regard others as more important than yourselves, each looking out not for his own interests, but also everyone for those of others. Have among yourselves the same attitude that is also yours in Christ Jesus. Who, though he was in the form of God . . ."

9. Although God is loved for his own sake, this love always includes the benefit of happiness since God creates humans to find happiness in him.

10. See Rziha, *Perfecting Human Actions*, 163–73, for more on how charity causes humans to share in the eternal law, God's divine plan.

11. See 1 Jn 4:7–16, and *ST* II-II.24.3. Although God is already in all creatures by essence, power, and presence, he can be in humans in a special way as the object known is in the knower and the object loved is in the lover.

12. See Mt 11:29–30, and Rom 10:28–30.

13. St. Teresa of Calcutta is famous for saying, "We cannot do great things, only small things with great love."

14. See *ST* I-II.65.2, where Thomas states that there are acquired virtues without charity, but only those virtues that produce good works in proportion to a supernatural last end are truly and perfectly virtues. Charity is essential for any virtues to produce works in proportion to eternal happiness.

15. See 1 Cor 13:1–4.

16. Thomas notes that charity is not the essential form but the efficient cause ordering an infused virtue to its proper end (*ST* II-II.23.8).

17. *ST* II-II.23.2.

18. *ST* II-II.24.9.

19. God has given humans everything, and it is impossible to give God more than he deserves. Nonetheless, because among the virtues only charity attains God himself, it is possible to speak of going beyond the love of justice in giving of our lives to God.

20. Benedict XVI explains the difference between justice and charity by stating, "Charity goes beyond justice, because to love [charity] is to give, to offer what is 'mine' to the other; but it never lacks justice, which prompts us to give the other what is 'his,' what is due to him by reason of his being or his acting" (*Caritas in Veritate*, §6). See also *ST* II-II.31.1.3.

21. Phil 2:3–8 (emphasis added). See Pinckaers, *Sources of Christian Ethics*, 130, for how Paul considers humility to be essential for having the virtues of faith and charity. Cf. Mt 23:12; Lk 14:11 and 18:14; Eph 4:2; Jas 4:10, for other passages on the necessity of humility.

22. Thomas covers humility in the section on temperance (*ST* II-II.161). He defines humility as "a proper amount of love for glory." However, within scripture and Catholic tradition, humility, as the virtue that counters pride, has been given a more fundamental role than merely a virtue perfecting the emotions (as in Aquinas). Augustine, for example,

notes that humility allows humans to be guided by love of God because it gives humans the ability to be subject to God. On the other hand, Augustine notes that pride is an excessive love of self—where one considers one's own soul as a kind of end in itself (*City of God*, 14.13). Consequently, following the example of Paul, Augustine, and Gregory the Great, I have placed humility as a virtue that corresponds to charity.

23. St. Gregory the Great notes that the all-powerful Son, for the purpose of teaching humility, became small and even suffered for our sake. Because the origin of our fall was the pride of the devil, the humility of God is the instrument of our redemption (*The Morals of the Book of Job*, 34.54).

24. See Jn 15:13–15: "No one has greater love than this, to lay down one's life for one's friends. You are my friends if you do what I command you. I no longer call you slaves, because a slave does not know what his master is doing. I have called you friends, because I have told you everything I have heard from my father."

25. For example, in talking about her role in salvation history, Mary humbly states, "My soul proclaims the greatness of the Lord, . . . for he has looked with favor on his lowly servant. From this day, all generations will call me blessed. The Almighty has done great things for me and holy is his name" (Lk 1:46–49).

26. *The Morals of the Book of Job*, 23.22–24; 34.50–51; see also 27.76, where Gregory notes that if a virtue is removed from humility, it is no longer fed by charity. Because of the importance of humility, Gregory elsewhere notes that God will allow people to be tempted, and even to sin, so that they will grow in humility. He notes that Christians upon committing an evil act consider themselves weak, causing their good acts to be even holier. He continues by noting that virtuous people apply evil temptations to a good purpose (34.44–45).

27. See, for example, Mt 23:12: "Whoever humbles himself will be exalted."

28. Thomas treats prayer under the virtue of religion, which is a subvirtue of justice (*ST* II-II.83). Justice is the virtue perfecting the will to give other humans and God their due. Religion and prayer give God the honor he deserves (*ST* II-II.83.3). Although giving God due honor is a very important aspect of prayer, I am treating prayer as a communication with God that flows from faith and manifests charity. Because I am treating prayer in this way, it more properly fits under the virtue of charity than justice.

29. See *Dei Verbum*, §2.

30. For more on the necessity of interior communication with God in order to properly love God through external actions, see Chautard, *The Soul of Apostolate*.

31. Traditionally, prayer has been categorized into one of five categories: adoration, petition, intercession, thanksgiving, and praise (*Catechism of the Catholic Church*, §§2623–49). All of these five types of prayer express charity or hope. Because humans adore God by loving his goodness, adoration especially manifests charity. Petition is the type of prayer where humans ask God for particular gifts, especially the forgiveness of their sins. This type of prayer especially manifests hope, because humans are trusting in the divine assistance. Nonetheless, charity causes humans to hope in God all the more. Intercession takes place when humans pray for others. Humans pray for others because they love them out of their love for God. Thanksgiving manifests charity because, when

humans give thanks, they express their love for God, who is good and the source of their gifts. Finally, praise expresses charity as humans show their love of God by glorifying God because of his divine goodness.

32. These five ways of showing love are borrowed from Chapman, *The Five Love Languages*. Although through the years my students and I have thought of other ways of showing love, I have found that these five ways from Chapman are fairly comprehensive and familiar to the students.

33. Spending the day thinking about the bad features of someone will cause loving actions to be done with significantly less intensity.

34. A common theme among the Church Fathers was the necessity of prayer to grow in virtue. For example, a common quotation attributed to St. Ephraem the Syrian states, "Virtues are formed by prayer. Prayer preserves temperance. Prayer suppresses anger. Prayer prevents the emotions of pride and envy. Prayer draws into the soul the Holy Spirit, and raises man to Heaven."

35. Thomas specifically notes that the merciful person has a compassionate heart for another's unhappiness (*ST* II-II.30.1).

36. Because of the primarily deontological nature of the Old Testament, one might think that God's mercy was always equated with forgiving the Israelites when they broke the covenant. This is one way that God's mercy was spoken of in the Old Testament. However, even more frequently the term "mercy" in the old covenant simply refers to the fact that God blessed the Hebrew people—usually with the covenant blessings. See, for example, 1 Chr 17:13, where God's mercy is upon the descendants of David, whose lineage will rule forever. See also the many places where God's mercy is a synonym for the covenant blessings and given to those that followed the law (Ex 29:6; Num 14:19; Dt 5:10).

37. Thérèse of Lisieux explains that though some have great gratitude that God in his mercy forgives their sins, she sees the mercy of God even more perfectly in that he kept her from sinning in the first place (*Story of a Soul*, 84).

38. Thérèse of Lisieux states in reference to God's mercy: "How much more does Your Merciful Love desire to *set souls on fire* since Your Mercy *reaches to the heavens*. O my Jesus, let me be this happy victim; consume Your holocaust with the fire of Your Divine Love!" (*Story of a Soul*, 181; emphasis in the original).

39. See Benedict XVI, *Caritas in Veritate*, §57, where he states that "a particular manifestation of charity and a guiding criterion for fraternal cooperation between believers and non-believers is undoubtedly the *principle of subsidiarity*, an expression of inalienable human freedom. Subsidiarity is *first and foremost a form of assistance to the human person via the autonomy of intermediate bodies.* Such assistance is offered when individuals or groups are unable to accomplish something on their own, and it is always designed to achieve their emancipation, because it fosters freedom and participation through assumption of responsibility" (emphasis added). The context of this quote is the notion that the individual is fulfilled in loving relationships. The principle of subsidiarity recognizes that humans are fulfilled in this way by giving them opportunities to give of themselves to others and to receive the love given to them (reciprocity). This unity especially takes place in intermediate communities that foster freedom and participation.

40. St. Teresa of Calcutta said, "The greatest disease in the West today is not TB or leprosy; it is being unwanted, unloved, and uncared for. We can cure physical diseases with medicine, but the only cure for loneliness, despair, and hopelessness is love. There are many in the world who are dying for a piece of bread, but there are many more dying for a little love. The poverty in the West is a different kind of poverty—it is not only a poverty of loneliness but also of spirituality. There's a hunger for love, as there is a hunger for God" (*A Simple Path*, 79).

41. On the other hand, even if they have good intentions, members of an organization that are prideful and fail to truly love will alienate others and hinder their ability to be happy.

42. See *ST* II-II.31.3.

43. In explaining how structures of sin are conquered, St. John Paul II states, "Thus one would hope that all those who, to some degree or other, are responsible for ensuring a 'more human life' for their fellow human beings, whether or not they are inspired by a religious faith, will become fully aware of the urgent need to change the spiritual attitudes which define each individual's relationship with self, with neighbor, with even the remotest human communities, and with nature itself." John Paul goes on to note that structures of sin are conquered through solidarity (*Solicitudo Rei Socialis*, §38).

44. See St. John Paul II, *Solicitudo Rei Socialis*, §42, and *Centesimus Annus*, §57, for more on the preferential option for the poor.

45. Benedict XVI explains this virtue in the following way: "*Charity goes beyond justice*, because to love is to give, to offer what is 'mine' to the other; but it never lacks justice, which prompts us to give the other what is 'his,' what is due to him by reason of his being or his acting." By the standards of justice, all of my superfluous goods already belong to the poor, who require these goods to be truly happy. The only goods that are "mine" are my necessities, which charity drives me to share with others (*Caritas in Veritate*, §6).

46. *Evangelii Gaudium*, §265.

47. John Paul II notes the link between charity and preaching the gospel when he encourages people "to love, assimilating deeply Christ's ardent desire 'that all people may be saved' (1 Tim 2:4); to let ourselves be loved, letting him use us according to 'his ways which are not our ways' (cf. Is 55:8) so that every man and woman on earth may come to know him and be saved." In the same letter he states, "No one, however, can invoke Jesus and believe in Him, unless they are told about him, and they hear his name (cf. Rom 10:14–15). Hence the supreme command which the Master gave to his disciples before he returned to the Father: 'Go . . . teach' (Mt 28:19); 'Preach . . . , he who believes and is baptized will be saved' (Mk 16:16)" (*Message for World Mission Sunday*, 1997).

48. *Evangelii Gaudium*, §264. Francis continues: "We need to implore his grace daily, asking him to open our cold hearts and shake up our lukewarm and superficial existence."

49. Pope Francis states, "An evangelizing community gets involved by word and deed in people's lives; it bridges distances, it is willing to abase itself if necessary, and it embraces human life, touching the suffering flesh of Christ in others. Evangelizers thus take on the

'smell of the sheep' and the sheep are willing to hear their voice. An evangelizing community is also supportive." (*Evangelii Gaudium*, §24).

50. See Ez 3:17–21: "If I [the Lord] say to the wicked man, You shall surely die; and you do not warn him or speak out to dissuade him from his wicked conduct so that he may live: that wicked man shall die for his sin, but I will hold you responsible for his death."

51. *The Rule of St. Benedict*, §53.

52. Ibid.

53. See Conway, "Strangers in Our Midst." For a Catholic understanding of tolerance, see Ulrich Lehner, *The Catholic Enlightenment*, 47–73.

54. For an example of hospitality, Trudy writes about the people of Le Chambon, France, who took Jews into their homes during the Nazi occupation (see "Strangers in Our Midst").

55. Thomas states, "This is the proper mark of friendship: that one reveal his secrets to his friend. . . . Therefore, since by the Holy Spirit we are established as friends of God, fittingly enough it is by the Holy Spirit that men are said to receive the revelation of the divine mysteries" (*SCG* IV.21).

56. There are a number of places that the beatitudes could be analyzed within this work. In the *Summa Theologiae*, Thomas links a beatitude to each virtue and analyzes it within the context of the virtue. Augustine links each beatitude to a gift of the Holy Spirit and a petition of the Our Father. For example, humility (being poor in spirit) is linked to fear of the Lord; meekness to piety; sorrow to knowledge; justice to fortitude; mercy to counsel; purity to understanding; and peace to wisdom (Augustine, *The Lord's Sermon on the Mount*, 13–21). Augustine divides the Our Father into seven petitions, which he links to the first seven beatitudes. The first beatitude is linked to the first petition, and so forth (ibid., 125–27). The links between the beatitudes, the petitions, and gifts can sometimes be a little contrived. In this work, because I wanted to take into consideration the context of the beatitudes as the first terms of the new covenant (Mt 5–7), I have decided to analyze them all together under the virtue of charity.

57. See Mt 5:43–48, which states that humans must "love your enemies, and pray for those who persecute you, that you may be children of your heavenly father. . . . So be perfect, just as your heavenly father is perfect." See also Mt 6:24–34, which notes that God must be sought above all other things: "Seek first the kingdom [of God] and his righteousness." Finally, see Mt 7:21–29, which notes the necessity of doing the will of the Father to be saved.

58. Note how several of the obligations of the beatitudes are closely related to the following dispositions of love in 1 Corinthians 13:1–13. The disposition from 1 Corinthians is followed by the similar beatitude in parentheses. Love is not pompous (blessed are the poor in spirit), not quick tempered (blessed are the meek), does not rejoice over wrongdoing (blessed are those who mourn), does not brood over injury and bears all things (blessed are the merciful), and endures all things (blessed are those who are persecuted).

59. Thayer, *Thayer's Greek-English Lexicon of the New Testament*, 386. The first word of the Psalms, *'ashre*, is also a word that can be translated as either "blessed" or "happy." See Nowell, *Pleading, Cursing, Praising*, 2. She states, "The first word of the Psalter is "happy,"

in Hebrew *'ashre*. From its first word this little book of 150 song-prayers promises to tell us how to be happy—truly deeply happy." The same can be said of the of the beatitudes— they teach us how to be truly deeply happy. One might even call them the "happies" rather than the beatitudes.

60. Paul states: "The Spirit itself bears witness with our spirit that we are children of God and if children, then heirs of God and joint heirs with Christ, if only we *suffer* with him so that we may also be glorified with him" (Rom 8:16–17; emphasis added).

61. See chapter 19 herein for more on unjust anger.

62. See Romans 8:28: "We know that all things work for good for those who love God."

63. See *ST* II-II.27.4.

64. Thomas considered peace to be an effect of charity. He states that peace requires concord and "concord, properly speaking, is between one man and another, in so far as the wills of various hearts agree together in consenting to the same thing." He also notes that peace includes unity within the appetites of a person (*ST* II-II.29.1).

65. See *ST* II-II.161.3.

66. Gregory the Great, *Morals on the Book of Job*, 32.46.

67. Ibid., 32.45. Gregory gives many other examples in addition to these.

68. Ibid., 34.48: Gregory notes that pride causes a person to lose the "eye of faith" by which he judges the goodness of deeds. The prideful person considers the deeds of all others to be displeasing, but his own deeds to be good.

69. Sir 10:15. See also *ST* I-II.84.2, where Thomas notes that pride is the beginning of all sins because it corrupts the intention that humans have to their proper end. See also Gregory the Great, *Morals of the Book of Job*, 34.48. Gregory notes that pride attacks all the virtues and turns what appears to be virtue into vainglory.

70. See Lv 18:26–29: "You, . . . must keep my statutes and decrees forbidding all such abominations by which the previous inhabitants defiled the land; otherwise the land will *vomit* you out also for having defiled it. . . . Everyone who does any of these abominations shall be *cut off* from among his people" (emphasis added). Breaking the laws of God results in the loss of the promised land. To be "vomited" is a synonym for being "cut off." People are "cut off" when they break a covenant with God, just as the animal that is killed in the sealing of the covenant is cut. See also Lv 20:22 for other examples of being spewed forth from the land. See Gen 9:11, 17:14; Ex 9:15, 12:15–19, 30:33, 31:14; Lv 7:20–27; Ps 37; and Is 53:8 for a few of the 200 or so passages about how people who break the covenant are "cut off."

71. See Lewis, *The Screwtape Letters*, 56: "Indeed, the safest road to Hell is the gradual one—the gentle slope, soft underfoot, without sudden turnings, without milestones, without signposts."

72. See *ST* II-II.35.1. Since it is sorrow, it is a vice against joy.

73. See 1 Jn 4:20: "If anyone says, 'I love God,' but hates his brother, he is a liar; for whoever does not love a brother whom he has seen cannot love God whom he has not seen. This is the commandment we have from him: whoever loves God must also love his brother."

74. Sometimes it is essential to cause discord with another in order to bring about a greater good. For example, people might have to fight others who are corrupt or make unjust laws. (By fighting, I do not necessarily mean physical fighting.) See *ST* II-II.37.

75. *ST* I-II.39.1. See also Jn 17:20–23 for Jesus's call that all be united.

76. Other examples could include parents using drugs in the presence of their children or parents participating in morally wrong business practices. By these actions parents teach their children that sinful actions are acceptable.

77. Christ notes the seriousness of this sin when he states, "Whoever causes one of these little ones who believe in me to sin, it would be better for him to a have a great millstone hung around his neck and to be drowned in the depths of the sea" (Mt 18:6).

FIFTEEN.   Prudence

1. See *ST* II-II.47.6 and 47.7.

2. *ST* II-II.53.3. Cf. *ST* II-II.48.1.

3. The shrewd person has an aptness to discover the middle term (*ST* II-II.49.4). Thus, the shrewd person determines whether or not the major (universal) and minor (singular) premises have two identical terms that allow a conclusion to be derived from them.

4. *ST* II-II.49.5. If the universal and particular premises do not have an identical middle term or a conclusion cannot be logically drawn from the premises, then the means cannot be chosen because it is not proportional to the end (cf. *ST* II-II.64.7).

5. Although prudence determines the means, it does form more particular goals that are ordered to a higher intended goal. For example, in seeking the goal of helping the poor, prudence might first help the intellect determine the goal that a certain amount of money will be given to the poor. The intellect then must determine the best way to attain this amount of money.

6. Humans must not just ask, "Does this fulfill what I want to do?" (the proximate end) but also, "Is this what I should be doing?" (the ultimate end).

7. Aquinas states: "Cognitive habits differ according to higher and lower principles: thus in speculative matters wisdom considers higher principles than science does, and consequently is distinguished from it; and so must it be also in practical matters. Now it is evident that what is beside the order of a lower principle is sometimes reducible to the order of a higher principle. . . . Now it happens sometimes that something has to be done which is not covered by the common rules of actions, for instance in the case of the enemy of one's country, when it would be wrong to give him back his deposit, or in similar cases. Hence, it is necessary to judge of such matters according to higher principles than the common rules, according to which *synesis* judges: and corresponding to such higher principles it is necessary to have a higher virtue of judgment, which is called *gnome*" (*ST* II-II.51.3).

8. See *ST* II-II.47.8.

9. Thomas states that foresight and caution are important parts of prudence (*ST* II-II.48.1; he defines these virtues in 49.6 and 49.8).

10. Thomas notes that precipitation exists whenever someone is rushed into action by the impulse of his will or passion and does not take good counsel (*ST* II-II.53.3).

SIXTEEN.   Justice: Part One

1. Sometimes these people really do lose something that they have a natural right to have, and they deserve to have whatever they lost reinstated. Thomas considers restitution, the restoring of a thing unjustly taken, to be an essential part of justice (*ST* II-II.62).

2. Benedict XVI affirms these two sources when he states, "Justice [is the virtue] which prompts us to give the other what is 'his,' what is due to him by reason of his *being* or his *acting*" (*Caritas in Veritate*, §6; emphasis added).

3. Confirming that justice meets both the natural needs of others and compensates humans for their actions, *Gaudium et Spes*, §67, gives the following requirements for a wage to be just: "Finally, remuneration for labor is to be such that man may be furnished the means to cultivate worthily his own material, social, cultural, and spiritual life and that of his dependents [meeting natural needs], in view of the function and productiveness of each one [the type of work and productivity of the worker], the conditions of the factory or workshop, and the common good."

4. The understanding of justice as a divine attribute also changes based on the moral system. In the primarily deontological system of the Old Testament, God's justice was seen in two ways: (1) Justice was the divine attribute of God, causing him to reward faithfulness to the covenant and to punish transgressions of the covenant; (2) God was also just by being faithful to the covenant promises that he established. However, in a teleological system with a wise and loving God, the justice of God is more about his love of humans and the recognition that God created humans to enter into a loving relationship with the Trinity. See, for example, St. Thérèse of Lisieux, who notes that in the past to say that God is just meant that God expected a perfect following of his laws or else he would punish the human. She notes, however, that with a greater understanding of God's love, his justice means that he takes into consideration the weakness of humans and gives them his love (*A Story of a Soul*, 180).

5. Objects of both the emotions and the will have varying degrees of goodness. The amount that these appetitive powers should be attracted to these objects should vary with the amount of goodness in the object. The greater the good, the more the powers should be attracted to it. For example, emotional love of another human should be greater than emotional love of a plant. Likewise, fear of something that hurts the soul should be greater than fear of a spider. An emotional response that is either too intense or not intense enough comes from vice. The things that the will loves also have varying degrees of goodness. Those persons and things with greater goodness should be loved more than those things with less goodness. All things should be loved the proper amount, and both too little and too much love of something results in a vice. Consequently, justice perfects the will to attain the mean.

6. Benedict XVI, *Caritas in Veritate*, § 35. Aquinas makes a similar distinction between general justice (*ST* II-II.58.6), commutative justice (*ST* II-II.61.1), and distributive justice (*ST* II-II.61.2). General justice refers to the relation between the individual and the common good. Since, for Thomas, just laws are ordered to the common good, he also refers to general justice as legal justice. Since the end of the 1800s, the Catholic Church has been writing social encyclicals that emphasize the obligations of individuals to the common good, which has been called "social justice." (But the term "social justice" does not appear in a social encyclical until *Quadragesimo Anno* in 1931.) *Quadragesimo Anno* refers to social justice as the virtue where all members of society act for the needs of the common good (§§57, 58, 71, 74, 88, 110, 126). For example, it states, "The public institutions themselves, of peoples, moreover, ought to make all human society conform to the needs of the common good; that is, to the norm of social justice" (§110).

7. Catholic social teaching emphasizes that the community exists for the sake of the individual. However, because humans are created in the image of the Trinity, the individual is fulfilled by acting for the community. See Benedict XVI, *Caritas in Veritate*, §§53–55.

8. See, for example, *Caritas in Veritate*, §40, which encourages investments that help the poor but condemns "the speculative *use of financial resources* that yields to the temptation of seeking only short-term profit, without regard for the long-term sustainability of the enterprise, its benefit to the real economy and attention to the advancement, in suitable and appropriate ways, of further economic initiatives in countries in need of development."

9. Social justice requires that the needs of the poor be given precedence over the needs of others. See John Paul II, *Sollicitudo Rei Socialis*, §42, and *Centesimus Annus*, §57.

10. Piety toward our nation can also be called "patriotism."

11. See *ST* II-II.82 for more on acts of devotion: 83 for more on prayer, 84 for more on adoration, 85 for more on sacrifice, and 88 for more on vows and promises.

12. The communal aspect of worship is necessary for a variety of reasons. First, by worshipping within a community, each succeeding generation can be brought into the ceremony, preserving the faith of the people. Second, a community has the resources to provide priests and others who devote their lives to the project of making worship as proportional to the excellence of God as possible. Third, the community is united by worship in fulfilling the natural and supernatural inclinations that humans have toward unity.

13. Aquinas notes in *ST* I-II.26.3: "We find four words referring in a way, to the same thing: viz. love (*amor*), dilection (*dilectio*), charity (*caritas*) and friendship (*amicitia*). They differ, however, in this, that 'friendship,' according to the Philosopher (Ethic. viii, 5), 'is like a habit,' whereas 'love' and 'dilection' are expressed by way of act or passion; and 'charity' can be taken either way." For more on the love of friendship, see Schwartz, *Aquinas on Friendship*.

14. See *ST* I-II.4.8.

15. Friendship can be an important element of fraternal correction. Often when helping to correct the vices of others, it is insufficient to simply tell others to change their lifestyles: they will often be unable to make the changes even if they believe you. To truly help

someone become more virtuous, it is often essential to enter into a long-term loving relationship with the person.

16. Pope Francis notes in *Laudato Si'*, §47, that "when media and the digital world become omnipresent, their influence can stop people from learning how to live wisely, to think deeply and to love generously. . . . Today's media do enable us to communicate and to share our knowledge and affections. Yet at times they also shield us from direct contact with the pain, the fears, and the joys of others and the complexity of their personal experiences. For this reason . . . a dissatisfaction with interpersonal relationships" can occur.

17. See St. John Paul II, *Sollicitudo Rei Socialis*, §§27–29. John Paul speaks of superdevelopment: "An excessive availability of every kind of material good for the benefit of certain social groups, easily makes people slaves of 'possession' and of immediate gratification, with no other horizon than the multiplication or continual replacement of the things already owned with others still better."

18. See *Gaudium et Spes*, §70: "Investments, for their part, must be directed toward procuring employment and sufficient income for the people both now and in the future." Catholic social thought is very clear about the fact that investments can help others, but it also notes that investments done solely for profit or for improper speculative purposes are wrong. See note 8 in this chapter.

19. See Lk 21:1–4: the story of the poor widow's gift.

20. See *Centesimus Annus*, §§34–36. John Paul II makes a distinction between artificial and authentic needs and how although the free market is often good at satisfying authentic needs, it can also encourage the creation of false needs and can be driven by these false needs. John Paul notes that drugs and pornography are examples of false needs. He also notes that the market often fails to fulfill authentic needs, and that humans need to make lifestyle changes where "the quest for truth, beauty, goodness, and communion with others for the sake of common growth are the factors which determine consumer choices, savings and investments." He goes on to note the obligation that humans have to give even from their necessities (*Centesimus Annus*, §36).

21. See Leo XIII, *Rerum Novarum*, §46. This desire of the Church that all accumulate some property does not apply to members of religious communities, who are spiritual signs of the lack of personal property in the full inheritance.

22. See the Letter of James: "Behold, the wages you withheld from the workers who harvested your fields are crying aloud, and the cries of the harvesters have reached the Lord" (Js 5:4).

23. John Paul II in *Laborem Exercens*, §9, speaks of the necessity of work for human and societal fulfillment and the corresponding virtue of industry that perfects humans to perform work.

24. There is a threefold good of work: it produces goods that are necessary for society to function (the objective value), it perfects workers by making them more like God (the subjective value), and it unites humans by making them share a particular goal and action. See *Laborem Exercens*, §§5–6.

25. *Caritas in Veritate*, §48.

26. Ibid.

27. See ibid.: Benedict explains the defect as the desire for "total technical dominion over nature, because the natural environment is more than raw material to be manipulated at our pleasure; it is a wondrous work of the Creator containing a 'grammar' which sets forth ends and criteria for its wise use, not its reckless exploitation."

28. See ibid.: Benedict explains the excess as "considering nature an untouchable taboo. . . . This position leads to attitudes of neo-paganism or a new pantheism."

29. *Laudato Si'*, §159.

30. Ibid., §§49, 51, 139, and 158.

31. Ibid., §§3, 230.

32. Ibid., §138.

33. Ibid.

34. Mt 6:24. See also Eph 5:5, which states, "Be sure of this, that no immoral or impure or greedy person, that is, an idolater, has any inheritance in the kingdom of Christ and of God." See also Col 3:5, which explicitly calls greed idolatry.

35. Ex 20:4–5. See also Ex 34:10–17 for a similar passage.

36. Several of the Byzantine emperors in the eighth century outlawed icons (images of Christ and the saints), defaced and destroyed them, and forced local bishops to accept this view. In 787, the Second Ecumenical Council of Nicaea declared that, following tradition, the holy images (icons) should be venerated. For as often as the Lord, Mary, and the saints are seen in artistic representations, humans are lifted up in memory of them. These representations should be given reverence (which is explicitly distinguished from worship given to God alone) because honor paid to the image passes on to that which is represented.

37. See chapter 1 for more on how humans use sense knowledge when they think.

38. Even if humans do not look at images of God, they still have a sensual image or word in their mind that represents him, because this is the way that humans think.

39. In the dispute over whether or not holy images should be venerated, St. John of Damascus argued that the prohibition of icons challenged the Christian belief in the incarnation of Christ. In other words, God became human so that humans could come to physically sense God though the image of Christ. So although the Old Testament forbids the worship of graven images, by graven images it refers to the worship of pagan gods. Theodore of Studium further developed John's arguments by noting that an image is necessary to represent a concrete person. Without images our knowledge of Christ is only abstract and not personal. See Wilken, *The First Thousand Years*, 302–5.

40. See Ex 25:10–22 and Nm 4:4–15 for how they were to venerate the ark of the covenant. In reference to the temple, see 1 Kgs 6:22–35 and Ez 40–41. See Nm 21:4–9 and Jn 3:14–15 for how the image of a serpent on a pole represented Christ. *Catechism of the Catholic Church* emphasizes the Christological dimension of sacred images, when it states, "The sacred image, the liturgical icon, principally represents Christ. It cannot represent the invisible and incomprehensible God, but the incarnation of the Son of God has ushered in a new 'economy' of images" (§1159).

41. See St. John Paul II, *Dies Domini*, "The Lord's Day—as Sunday was called from Apostolic times—has always been accorded special attention in the history of the Church

because of its close connection with the very core of the Christian mystery. In fact, in the weekly reckoning of time Sunday recalls the day of Christ's Resurrection. It is *Easter* which returns week by week, celebrating Christ's victory over sin and death, the fulfilment in him of the first creation and the dawn of 'the new creation' (cf. *2 Cor* 5:17). It is the day which recalls in grateful adoration the world's first day and looks forward in active hope to 'the last day,' when Christ will come in glory (cf. Acts 1:11; 1 Th 4:13–17) and all things will be made new (cf. Rev 21:5)."

42. See Acts 20:7 and 1 Cor 16:12. Cf. Jn 20:19–29 for how Christ appeared to the apostles after the resurrection on a Sunday.

43. Thomas notes that humans have a "natural inclination to set aside a certain time for each necessary thing, such as refreshment of the body, sleep, and so forth. Hence . . . man sets aside a certain time for spiritual refreshment, by which man's mind is refreshed in God" (*ST* II-II.122.4.1).

44. In the past, most people participated in servile labor (bodily labor), so servile labor was prohibited on Sunday (see *ST* II-II.122.4.3). This rest was essential for the physical and spiritual well-being of most humans. However, today, many people do not perform bodily labor, but they still need to avoid their normal job in order to participate in the foretaste of the full inheritance found in the celebration of Sunday. For example, my job of teaching students is not manual labor, but I should attempt to avoid preparing for class on Sunday.

45. See Mk 2:27–28 and Mt 12:9–14 for examples of how Jesus changed the interpretation of the Sabbath to include doing charitable activities.

46. See *Catechism of the Catholic Church*, §§2184–87, for more on resting on Sunday.

47. Note the way that the third Eucharistic Prayer expresses this truth: "Grant that we, who are nourished by the Body and Blood of your Son and filled with his Holy Spirit, may become one body, one spirit in Christ. May he make of us an eternal offering to you, so that we may *obtain an inheritance with your elect*" (emphasis added).

48. If Catholics intentionally miss Mass without a serious reason, they commit a mortal sin. See *Catechism of the Catholic Church*, §2181.

49. Holy days of obligation vary with each country and sometimes even within a country. However, in the United States the holy days of obligation are Christmas, the feast of Mary, the Mother of God (Jan.1), the Ascension (in some dioceses), the Immaculate Conception (Dec. 8), the Assumption (Aug. 15), and All Saints' Day (Nov. 1).

50. See *Gaudium et Spes*, §74: "Yet people who come together in the political community are many and diverse, and they have every right to prefer divergent solutions. If the political community is not to be torn apart while everyone follows his own opinion, there must be an authority to direct the energies of all citizens toward the common good, not in a mechanical or despotic fashion, but by acting above all as a moral force which appeals to each one's freedom and sense of responsibility."

51. As we saw in chapter 9, the Holy Spirit's gifts, and the guidance of the Holy Spirit, are also necessary for these supernatural inclinations to cause divine actions of knowing and loving.

52. See *Catechism of the Catholic Church*, §§2207–13, for more on the relation between the family and society.

53. See John Paul II, *Laborem Exercens*, §19, and *Evangelium Vitae*, §86.

54. John Paul II notes that just wages can either come from a "family wage—that is a single salary given to the head of a family for his work, sufficient for the needs of the family without the other spouse having to take up gainful employment outside the home—or through other social measures such as family allowances or grants to mothers devoting themselves exclusively to their families" (*Laborem Exercens*, §19).

SEVENTEEN.   Justice: Part Two

1. See *Catechism of the Catholic Church*, §§2263–66; and *ST* II-II.64.7, where Thomas states that one act can have two effects: one intended and one unintended consequence. The saving of one's life is the intended effect, and the killing of the unjust aggressor is the unintended consequence.

2. To help people make moral decisions, the principle of *double effect* was developed over the last several centuries to assist people in determining the proper object in difficult situations. I do not use the principle of double effect because it is mostly effective in a deontological methodology and is less helpful in a teleological system. In other words, good prudence is always better than the principle of double effect. Nonetheless, it can help people make good decisions by aiding them in forming good intentions, taking good counsel, and judging properly.

Each of the steps of the principle of double effect correspond to steps within the human action. The first step of the principle of double effect (*an evil act cannot be intended*) corresponds to steps 3 and 4 of the human action (understanding the end and intention). The second step of the principle of double effect (*the intended good effect must be greater than or equal to the foreseen evil effects*) corresponds to step 7 of the human action (judgment). The third step (*the intended good effect must not be achievable without the evil effects*) corresponds to step 5 of the human action (counsel). The fourth step (*the good effect must be at least as immediate as the evil effect*) makes sure that only one action is taking place, also corresponds to judgment. Thus, the principle of double effect is valuable in some situations because it walks the person through the steps of the human action (as anyone with prudence would do). However, in a prudent person, the acts of taking counsel and judgment are concerned with far more than just the points considered by the principle of double effect. For example, researching the situation in counsel means far more than just determining if the only way to cause the good effect is by causing an evil effect. Consequently, the principle of double effect will always be limited to a particular type of action, and even in these situations, it will not always be accurate because it does not take into consideration *all* aspects of a situation or judge by *all* higher principles. Thus, although the principle of double effect is helpful, it should never be seen as a substitute for prudence. See Long, *The Teleological Grammar of the Moral Act*, 63–82, for a further critique of the principle of double effect.

3. A first-century Church manual called the *Didache* (*The Teaching of the Twelve Apostles*), 172, states, "You shall not murder a child by abortion nor kill that which is born." See also St. John Paul II, *Evangelium Vitae*, § 61, for some second-century Christian documents that note the evil of abortion.

4. John Paul II in *Evangelium Vitae* states: "Therefore, by the authority which Christ conferred upon Peter and his Successors, in communion with the Bishops—who on various occasions have condemned abortion and who in the aforementioned consultation, albeit dispersed throughout the world, have shown unanimous agreement concerning this doctrine—I declare that direct abortion, that is, abortion willed as an end or as a means, always constitutes a grave moral disorder, since it is the deliberate killing of an innocent human being. This doctrine is based upon the natural law and upon the written Word of God, is transmitted by the Church's Tradition and taught by the ordinary and universal Magisterium" (§62).

5. There are other morally allowable ways of treating the ectopic pregnancy, which are debated by ethicists. I recommend that you read Kaczor, "The Ethics of Ectopic Pregnancy."

6. United States Conference of Catholic Bishops, *The Ethical and Religious Directives for Catholic Health Care Services* (2009), §47.

7. Cf. *Catechism of the Catholic Church*, §§2309–10.

8. Ibid., §2267.

9. Benedict Ashley and Kevin O'Rourke note that life is a gift from God and to reject the gift is to also reject the giver. They go on to note that all modern arguments for suicide stem from the modern notion of absolute autonomy, which misunderstands true freedom. Humans do not create themselves but are part of a society that has its origin in God (Ashley and O'Rourke, *Health Care Ethics*, 415–16).

10. In other words, humans are more like God when they take care of the young, the helpless, the sick, and the suffering. Hence, those that require the aid of others are just as essential to God's plan as those taking care of them.

11. Kheriaty, *The Catholic Guide to Depression*, chap. 4, which is on depression and suicide.

12. Ibid., 96–99.

13. *Catechism of the Catholic Church*, §§2282–83.

14. St. John Paul II in *Evangelium Vitae*, §65, defines euthanasia as "an act or omission which of itself and by intention causes death, with the purpose of eliminating all suffering."

15. If the treatment is not life-sustaining, then it can be rejected as long as rejecting it does not interfere with the fulfillment of a person's divine calling (vocation in the general sense). For example, suppose someone is in great pain and is given a drug to control the pain. This treatment is not life-sustaining. It can be rejected as long as the pain does not keep the person from performing one's proper actions. In essence, the underlying principle is that humans are required to do whatever is necessary to fulfill their vocation, i.e., their mission within the divine plan.

16. John Paul II, *Evangelium Vitae*, §65.

17. This obligation assumes that there is a reasonable way to obtain the treatment. For example, suppose a poor person in an undeveloped country gets a sickness that is easily curable by medical treatment in the United States. However, this form of medical treatment is not available in the undeveloped country. The poor person cannot be expected to come to the United States for treatment.

18. See John Paul II's address in 2004 to the participants at the international congress "On Life-Sustaining Treatments and the Vegetative State." He states: "I should like particularly to underline how the administration of water and food, even when provided by artificial means, always represents a natural means of preserving life, not a medical act. Its use, furthermore, should be considered, in principle, ordinary and proportionate, and as such morally obligatory, insofar as and until it is seen to have attained its proper finality, which in the present case consists in providing nourishment to the patient and alleviation of his suffering." In other words, only if the food and water are not attaining their proper goal of sustaining and comforting the patient should they be removed.

19. See Congregation for the Doctrine of the Faith, "Responses to Certain Questions of the United States Conference of Catholic Bishops Concerning Artificial Nutrition and Hydration": "When stating that the administration of food and water is morally obligatory in principle, the Congregation for the Doctrine of the Faith does not exclude the possibility that, in very remote places or in situations of extreme poverty, the artificial provision of food and water may be physically impossible, and then *ad impossibilia nemo tenetur*. However, the obligation to offer the minimal treatments that are available remains in place, as well as that of obtaining, if possible, the means necessary for an adequate support of life. Nor is the possibility excluded that, due to emerging complications, a patient may be unable to assimilate food and liquids, so that their provision becomes altogether useless. Finally, the possibility is not absolutely excluded that, in some rare cases, artificial nourishment and hydration may be excessively burdensome for the patient or may cause significant physical discomfort, for example resulting from complications in the use of the means employed."

20. *Catechism of the Catholic Church*, §2265, states, "Legitimate defense can be not only a right but a grave duty for someone responsible for another's life, the common good of the family or the state."

21. A human's being consists of not only his substantial being (his being flowing from human nature), but also his accidental being (e.g., his size, gender, habits, relations to others, etc.). For example, Joe is not just a human being, but a human male with particular virtues, talents, gifts, etc. Because humans participate in the one act of God through their work, their work is also a part of their being. In other words, one way of answering the question of "Who are you?" is by explaining what work you do. Since work transforms and perfects creation, the perfections in creation become an extension of a person's being.

22. For other arguments for the right to private property, see *Rerum Novarum*, §§6–14.

23. See Pius XI, *Quadragesimo Anno*, §§44–47; *Gaudium et Spes*, §§69–71; and St. John Paul II, *Centesimus Annus*, §§30–34.

24. The universal destination of goods is a higher principle than the right to private property since the first cause is always greater than the secondary cause. See John Paul II,

Laborem Exercens, §14; Paul VI, *Populorum Progressio*, §§22–26; and the Pontifical Council for Peace and Justice, *Compendium of the Social Doctrine of the Church*, 176–81.

25. Acts 2:44–45.

26. A common business activity that violates the common good is "speculative use of financial resources that yields to the temptation of seeking only short-term profit, without regard for the long-term sustainability of the enterprise, its benefit to the real economy and attention to the advancement, in suitable and appropriate ways, of further economic initiatives in countries in need of development" (Benedict XVI, *Caritas in Veritate*, §40).

27. In fact, it is often necessary for a business to make a profit for the sake of the common good. See Benedict XVI, *Caritas in Veritate*, §§46–47, where Benedict stresses the importance of businesses in developing nations making a profit that is directed toward the achievement of human and social ends.

28. See *Catechism of the Catholic Church*, §2405, and Lk 12:13–21.

29. For further explanation of how living a life of evangelical poverty leads to happiness, see Dubay, *Happy Are the Poor*.

30. See Augustine's "Letter to Proba," 376–400. In this letter, Augustine notes that there are only two valid reasons for owning property: to take care of the necessities of life and to help your friends (and he clarifies that by friends he means everyone, including enemies).

31. They could also give their money to the Church, but since religion is a natural need, I am considering money given to support the Church to be a necessity of life (like buying food or shelter). The Church does serve as an organization that helps the poor, especially by providing education, so money given to the Church for this purpose would be a proper use of extra wealth.

32. See *Catechism of the Catholic Church*, §2408, and *ST* II-II.66.7.

33. *Catechism of the Catholic Church*, §2446. The *Catechism* quotes John Chrysostom: "Not to enable the poor to share in our goods is to steal from them and deprive them of life" (*Hom. In Lazaro*, 2.5).

34. To determine a just wage, the following things should all be considered: the needs of the employee (to raise a family in a dignified manner and acquire property), the state of the business, the effect on the common good, and, last of all, the contribution that an employee makes to a business. See *Gaudium et Spes*, §67.

35. See Leo XIII, *Rerum Novarum*, §§43–45, for an example of unjust labor contracts. Leo notes that a contract that pays unjust wages is unjust, even if it has been agreed upon by both parties. They are unjust because "there underlies a dictate of natural justice more imperious and ancient than any bargain between man and man, namely, that wages ought not be insufficient to support a frugal and well-behaved wage earner."

36. *Catechism of the Catholic Church*, §§2410–11.

37. Think of the example of the rich young man in Matthew 19 who is unable to follow Jesus because he is too attached to his material goods.

38. Another significant element of Catholic social thought is the critique of economic systems, such as socialism and capitalism. *Unbridled* capitalism, which makes profit the exclusive norm and ultimate end of economic activity, is wrong because it goes against the universal destination of goods (e.g., the amount paid to a worker cannot be solely

determined by supply and demand, the needs of the worker must also be considered). Likewise, complete socialism, which removes the right to private property, is also unacceptable, for it does not recognize the human effort put into the creation of goods (see *Catechism of the Catholic Church*, §§2424–31). Both of these systems violate a proper understanding of human freedom as noted in this book. Socialism removes the ability of humans to freely use their resources to serve God and others; unbridled capitalism is based on an artificial freedom to do whatever one wants with his or her possessions.

39. *Catechism of the Catholic Church*, §§2439–41.

40. If there is grave need, a truth that destroys the reputation of others can be prudently revealed. For example, if someone is sexually abusing children, this knowledge should be made available to the parents of all children who could even possibly be in danger. The judgment by the higher truth of protecting children causes the object of the action to be protecting children and not destroying another's reputation.

41. For example, regularly informing your neighbor that he is overweight is generally not conducive to loving relationships.

42. *Catechism of the Catholic Church*, §§2482–83.

43. See Pius XI, *Quadragesimo Anno*, §136: "All created goods under God should be considered as mere instruments to be used only in so far as they conduce to the attainment of the supreme end [God]." . . . "The sordid love of wealth, which is the shame and great sin of our age, will be opposed in actual fact by the gentle yet effective law of Christian moderation, which commands man to seek first the Kingdom of God and His justice."

44. In other words, in the modern era, nearly everyone is exposed to an excessive amount of material goods (either owned by themselves or others). As long as people are contemplating the goodness of these goods that they love, they have some happiness. However, these goods will never bring the true happiness found in loving God and others.

45. See, for example, Mt 6:21; Lk 12:13–15; Eph 5:5; Prv 14:30; and Col 3:5. See also Jas 5:1–6, which compares the greed that causes people to pay unjust wages to murder.

46. See *Gaudium et Spes*, §72, and *Populorum Progressio*, §21.

47. See Lk 21:1–4; 16:19–30; 12:13–21; and 6:20.

EIGHTEEN.   Temperance

1. In *Evangelii Gaudium*, §6, Pope Francis is critical of Christians "whose lives seem like Lent without Easter." While noting that people have real reasons to be sorrowful, he exclaims that the message of Christianity is one of great joy!

2. See 1 Thes 5:16 and Phil 4:4, where Paul exhorts the inhabitants of these cities to rejoice always.

3. See *ST* II-II.141.3. John Murphy explains temperance in this way: "[Temperance] is the moderator of all pleasures, especially pleasures connected with the two great functions of organic life, namely the preservation of the individual through the use of food and the preservation of the race through sex" (*The Virtues on Parade*, 97).

4. See *ST* II-II.142.1.

5. See *ST* II-II.155.

6. On the other hand, I have had many students over the years with anorexic tendencies. Because their emotions have been trained to despise food, they receive no joy from eating. They must force themselves to eat and even go to the opposite extreme of eating too much in order to attain the mean of desiring the proper amount of food.

7. I am distinguishing moral drunkenness from legal drunkenness. Legal drunkenness is defined by a certain blood alcohol level. In most states, one can be legally drunk and still retain the use of his or her reason. Moral drunkenness is indicated by the impairment of reason.

8. Keep in mind that just as there are degrees of drunkenness, there are degrees of voluntariness. Cf. *ST* I-II.77.7 and II-II.150.4.

9. See *ST* II-II.150.2.

10. Fisher, "The Drive to Love," 90–92. Although I find the neurobiological results of the studies done by Fisher and her colleagues to be very helpful in explaining the relation between the body and soul, I do not endorse any of the conclusions that she draws from her studies.

11. Ibid., 101. See also an interview done on the *CBS Early Show*, July 19, 2010. Fisher states, in reference to brain scans of people experiencing romantic love, "We found activity in a brain pathway that is exactly the same brain pathway that becomes affected when you're profoundly addicted to cocaine and nicotine."

12. See Greenfield, *The Private Life of the Brain*, 94–96. Greenfield notes that emotional states can be "caricatured" by the use of drugs. She also notes that drugs cause emotional pleasure, but this pleasure is a "hoax." Although drugs can cause an "artificial" emotional response, a similar response takes place in humans who have a chemical imbalance. The chemical imbalance can cause emotions such as sorrow or fear within a human, even though there is no sense knowledge of an experienced evil (for sorrow) or a distant evil (for fear). This can happen in cases of depression.

13. Although some emotion-enhancing drugs (such as caffeine) can make people more productive and pleasant, in the end they can become a "crutch" that people resort to instead of exerting the effort to stimulate and form their emotions in natural ways. Nonetheless, because caffeine does not normally remove freedom, prudent use of it can sometimes be a great good, and, out of charity toward others, many people should drink their coffee.

14. There may be other exceptions. For example, some people may be able to form the vice of lust through a single sexual encounter. See Fisher, "The Drive to Love," 103, for the chemical effects within the brain caused by the sexual act.

15. See Pinckaers, *Sources of Christian Ethics*, chap. 5.

16. See John Paul II, *Love and Responsibility*, 171–72: "Only the chaste man and the chaste woman are capable of true love. For chastity frees their association, including marital intercourse, from that tendency to use a person . . . and by so freeing it introduces into their life together and their sexual relationship a special disposition to 'loving kindness. . . . Chastity is the sure way to [marital] happiness.'"

17. Murphy explains: "The heart filled with impurities has little room to love, whereas the pure and clean heart is large enough to encompass everyone in the world. Lust would have us turn social powers back toward ourselves, and if the vice becomes a habit, the soul falls prey to a kind of slavery of the body" (*The Virtues on Parade*, 114).

18. For an insightful book on the importance and nature of leisure, see Pieper, *Leisure, the Basis of Culture*.

19. See *Gaudium et Spes*, §61: "May this leisure be used properly to relax, to fortify the health of soul and body through spontaneous study and activity, through tourism which refines man's character and enriches him with understanding of others, through sports activity which helps to preserve equilibrium of spirit even in the community, and to establish fraternal relations among men of all conditions, nations and races."

20. Pinckaers, *Passions and Virtue*, 119–23, speaks of the virtue of sports and its importance in physical, emotional, and spiritual growth.

21. See ibid., 58–63, for more on the virtue of humor. Pinckaers notes that Aquinas referred to this virtue as *eutrapelia*, the midpoint between having no sense of humor and buffoonery.

22. When I use "technical terminology," I like to say that they are looking at others through "love goggles."

23. St. Thérèse of Lisieux, *Story of a Soul*, 222–23. Thérèse tells the story of her response to a sister she did not emotionally love: "There is in Community a Sister who has the faculty of displeasing me in everything, in her ways, her words, her character, everything seems very disagreeable to me. And still she is a holy religious who must be very pleasing to God. Not wishing to give in to the natural antipathy I was experiencing, I told myself that charity must not consist in feelings but in works; then I set myself to do for this Sister what I would do for the person I loved the most. Each time I met her I prayed to God for her, offering Him all her virtues and merits . . . I wasn't content simply with praying very much for this Sister who gave me so many struggles, but I took care to render her all the services possible, and when I was tempted to answer her back in a disagreeable manner, I was content with giving her my most friendly smile, and with changing the subject of the conversation. . . . One day at recreation she asked in almost these words: 'Would you tell me, Sister Thérèse of the Child Jesus, what attracts you so much towards me; every time you look at me, I see you smile?' Ah! What attracted me was Jesus hidden in the depths of her soul."

24. Acts 2:13–15.

25. Mk 10:1–12.

26. Mt 5:27–28. To simply be tempted to have lustful thoughts is not a sin. It only becomes a sin when one judges that the thoughts are wrong and continues to dwell on them. There is a joke that explains this point. A man was in the confessional confessing that he had committed the sin of lust by having lustful thoughts. The priest asked if he entertained the thoughts. The man replied, "No, Father, they entertained me."

27. See Paul VI, *Humanae Vitae*, §§11–12.

28. Monogamy is required because of the limitedness of humans on earth. The degree of love of friendship required for marriage is so intense that the spouses must take on all

of each other's goals, desires, suffering, needs, and property. In other words, in imitation of the Trinity, they only perform one action, each in their respective way. On earth, humans are too limited to have this kind of knowledge and love of more than one other person. In the full inheritance, when all humans can know and love each other perfectly, then they can all be permanently united within the one act of God.

29. Although many actions have a natural meaning, they can still be used in a way that is contrary to their natural meaning. Both acts and words can be used to deceive others.

30. Even those who take a vow of celibacy desire to express their undying love of others. Their religious lifestyle is a sign of the permanent love which all humans will have for each other in the full inheritance.

31. See Paul VI, *Humanae Vitae*, §§11–12: "Nonetheless, the Church, calling men back to the observance of the norms of the natural law, as interpreted by its constant doctrine, teaches that each and every marriage act must remain open to the transmission of life. . . . That teaching often set forth by the magisterium, is founded upon the inseparable connection . . . between the two meanings of the conjugal act: the unitive meaning and the procreative meaning."

32. This is further seen by the fact that circumcision was a sign of God's promise to make Abraham's descendants numerous (Gn 17).

33. See Mk 10:1–12 and Eph 5.

34. Although the grace of God uniting humans to each other is available to all who are married, humans can reject it and stop loving each other.

35. For biblical passages against homosexual actions, see Rom 1 and 2, and 1 Cor 6:9–10.

36. See Smith, *Humanae Vitae*, for a detailed study showing why the Catholic Church has always condemned contraception.

37. Even if a person cannot be a biological parent, they must still be a spiritual parent to others around them.

38. In the ancient Jewish tradition, couples would abstain from sex whenever they were performing a special activity for God, such as when priests ministered in the temple or men were involved in war.

39. In 1853, the bishops of Amiens, France, asked whether those who abstained on certain days to avoid pregnancy should be corrected, especially if they had a serious reason. The Sacred Penitentiary replied, "Those spoken of in the request are not to be disturbed, provided that they do nothing to impede conception." See Brian W. Harrison, "Is Natural Family Planning a Heresy?" *This Rock* 16, no. 2 (2005): 12–16.

40. Generally, a woman is only fertile for five to six days per cycle.

41. See *Catechism of the Catholic Church*, §§2373–79.

42. See Mt 5:31–32; 19:3–9; Mk 10:1–9; Lk 16:18; 1 Cor 7:10–11; and Eph 5:21–33. See also *Catechism of the Catholic Church*, §§2382–85.

43. See *Catechism of the Catholic Church*, §2383.

44. As noted by St. Paul, "Love is patient, . . . it does not brood over injury . . . it endures all things" (1 Cor 13:4–7).

45. The positive influence of stability on relationships is not found only in marriage. The Benedictine monks also take a vow of stability, and it was from them that I first learned the importance of stability in growing in friendship and holiness as a community.

46. Christ refers to himself as the bridegroom (Mt 9:15; 25:1–13; Mk 2:19).

47. John Paul II, *The Jeweler's Shop*, 64–66.

48. See ibid., 88, where Adam sums up the point of the play by stating, "Sometimes human existence seems too short for love. At other times it is, however, the other way around: human love seems too short in relation to existence—or rather too trivial. At any rate, every person has at his disposal an existence and a Love. The problem is: How to build a sensible structure from it?"

49. If humans dress and act modestly, then they are not liable if someone looks at them as an object of lust.

50. Traditionally, the season of Lent has been used as a time to increase the virtues of temperance and fortitude.

NINETEEN.   Fortitude

1. See *ST* II-II.123.5 and 6.

2. See *ST* II-II.124.

3. Although the magnanimous person sets his goals high, he is not prideful because he believes that he can attain his goals by the power of God working within him. He is actually very humble.

4. See Jn 3:13–22; Mt 21:12–13; Mk 11:15–17; and Lk 19:45–46 for examples of Jesus using just anger to cleanse the temple.

CONCLUSION

1. Mt 11:30.

BIBLIOGRAPHY

Aquinas, Thomas. "The Apostles' Creed." In *The Catechetical Instructions of St. Thomas Aquinas*, translated by Joseph B. Collins, 3–68. New York: Joseph P. Wagner, 1939.

———. *Commentary on Aristotle's De Anima.* Translated by Kenelm Foster and Sylvester Humphries. Notre Dame, IN: Dumb Ox, 1994.

———. *Commentary on the Letter of Saint Paul to the Romans.* Translated by Fabian Larcher. Lander, WY: The Aquinas Institute for the Study of Sacred Doctrine, 2012.

———. *Commentary on the Nicomachean Ethics.* Translated by C. I. Litzinger. Chicago: Regnery, 1964.

———. *Disputed Questions on Virtue.* Translated by Ralph McInerny. South Bend, IN: St. Augustine's Press, 1999.

———. *On the Power of God.* Translated by the English Dominican Fathers. Westminster, MD: Aeterna, 2015.

———. *Quaestiones Disputatae de Veritate.* [English translation: *Truth.*] Translated by R. Mulligan, J. McGlynn, and R. Schmidt. Chicago: Regnery, 1952–1954.

———. *Saint Thomas Aquinas, Disputed Questions on Evil.* Translated by J. Oesterle. Notre Dame, IN: University of Notre Dame Press, 1983.

———. "Sermon on the Lord's Prayer" and "Sermon on the Sacraments." In *The Aquinas Catechism*, edited by Ralph McInerny, 103–60 and 253–70. Manchester, NH: Sophia, 2000.

———. *Summa Contra Gentiles.* Translated by A. Pegis and V. Bourke. Notre Dame, IN: University of Notre Dame Press, 1975.

———. *Summa Theologica.* Translated by Fathers of the English Dominican Province. New York: Benzinger Brothers, 1947.

———. *Truth.* Translated by R. Mulligan, J. McGlynn, and R. Schmidt. Chicago: Regnery, 1952–1954.

Aristotle. *Metaphysics*. Edited by W. D. Ross. Oxford: Oxford University Press, 1924.

————. *Nichomachean Ethics*. In *Introduction to Aristotle*, translated by W. D. Ross, 327–581. New York: Random House, 1947.

Ashley, Benedict, and O'Rourke, Kevin. *Health Care Ethics: A Theological Analysis*. Washington, DC: Georgetown University Press, 1997.

Augustine. *The City of God*. Translated by Marcus Dodds. Peabody, MA: Hendrickson, 2009.

————. *Confessions*. Translated by Henry Chadwick. New York: Oxford University Press, 2008.

————. "Letter to Proba." In *Saint Augustine: Letters*. Vol. 2, *(83–130)*, 376–400. Washington, DC: Catholic University of America Press, 2010.

————. *The Lord's Sermon on the Mount*. Translated by John Jepson. Westminster, MD: The Newman Press, 1948.

Benedict of Nursia. *The Rule of St. Benedict in English*. Edited by Timothy Fry. Collegeville, MN: The Liturgical Press, 1982.

Benedict XVI. *Caritas in Veritate*. San Francisco: Ignatius, 2009.

Bourke, Vernon. "The Role of Habitus in the Thomistic Metaphysics of Potency and Act." In *Essays in Thomism*, edited by Robert E. Brennan, 103–9. New York: Sheed and Ward, 1942.

Boyd, Craig. "Participation Metaphysics, The *Imago Dei*, and the Natural Law in Aquinas' Ethics." *The New Blackfriars* 88 (2007): 274–87.

Bradley, Denis. *Aquinas on the Twofold Human Good: Reason and Human Happiness in Aquinas' Moral Science*. Washington, DC: Catholic University of America Press, 1997.

Brennan, Robert E. *Thomistic Psychology—A Philosophic Analysis of the Nature of Man*. New York: Macmillan, 1941.

Catechism of the Catholic Church. Washington, DC: United States Conference of Catholic Bishops, 1997.

Cavanaugh, T. A. *Double-Effect Reasoning: Doing Good and Avoiding Evil*. New York: Oxford University Press, 2006.

Cessario, Romanus. *The Moral Virtues and Theological Ethics*. Notre Dame, IN: University of Notre Dame Press, 1991.

Chapman, Gary. *The Five Love Languages: The Secret to Love that Lasts*. Chicago: Northfield, 2010.

Chautard, Jean-Baptiste. *The Soul of Apostolate*. Trappist, KY: The Abbey of Gethsemani, 1946.

Congregation for the Doctrine of the Faith. *Dignitas Personae*. 2008.

————. "Responses to Certain Questions of the United States Conference of Catholic Bishops Concerning Artificial Nutrition and Hydration." *Origins* 30 (2007): 242–45.

Conway, Gertrude. "Strangers in Our Midst: From Tolerance to Hospitality." In *Philosophy of Education: Introductory Readings*, 4th ed., 210–22, edited by William Hare and John Portelli. Alberta, Canada: Brush Education, 2013.

Cyprian of Carthage. *On the Lapsed*. In *Ante-Nicene Fathers*, Vol. 5, edited by Alexander Roberts, James Donaldson, and A. Cleveland Coxe. Peabody, MA: Hendrickson, 2004.

Dewan, Lawrence. "Wisdom as Foundational Ethical Theory in Thomas Aquinas." In *The Bases of Ethics*, edited by William Sweet, 39–78. Milwaukee, WI: Marquette University Press, 2000.

DeYoung, Rebecca Konyndyk, Colleen McClusky, and Christina Van Dyke. *Aquinas's Ethics: Metaphysical Foundations, Moral Theory, and Theological Context*. Notre Dame, IN: University of Notre Dame Press, 2009.

Di Blasi, Fulvio. *God and the Natural Law: A Rereading of Thomas Aquinas*. Translated by David Thunder. South Bend, IN: St. Augustine's Press, 2006.

Didache (The Teaching of the Twelve Apostles). In *Early Church Fathers*, edited by Cyril Richardson, 171–82. New York: Simon & Schuster, 1996.

Dubay, Thomas. *Happy Are the Poor: The Simple Life and Spiritual Freedom*. San Francisco: Ignatius, 2002.

Escrivá, Josemaría. *Christ Is Passing By*. New York: Scepter, 2002.

Fabro, Cornelio. *La nozione metafisica di partecipazione secondo S. Tommaso d' Aquino*. Milan: Vita e Pensiero, 1939.

Fisher, Helen. "The Drive to Love: The Neural Mechanism for Mate Selection." In *The New Psychology of Love*, edited by R. J. Sternberg and K. Weis, 87–115. New Haven, CT: Yale University Press, 2006.

Francis, [Pope]. *Evangelii Gaudium (The Joy of the Gospel)*. Translated by the Vatican. Boston: Pauline Books and Media, 2013.

———. *Laudato Si': On Care for Our Common Home*. Translated by the Vatican. Huntington, IN: Our Sunday Visitor, 2015.

Francis of Assisi. *Francis and Clare: The Complete Works*. Edited by Regis Armstrong and Ignatius C. Brady. Mahwah, NJ: Paulist, 1986.

Gallagher, David. "The Will and Its Acts (Ia-IIae, qq. 6–17)." In *The Ethics of Aquinas*, edited by Stephen Pope, 67–89. Washington, DC: Georgetown University Press, 2002.

Gilson, Etienne. *Christian Philosophy of St. Thomas Aquinas*. Notre Dame, IN: University of Notre Dame Press, 1994.

Greenfield, Susan A. *The Private Life of the Brain: Emotions, Consciousness, and the Secret of the Self*. New York: Wiley and Sons, 2000.

Gregory, Brad. *The Unintended Reformation: How a Religious Revolution Secularized Society*. Cambridge, MA: Harvard University Press, 2012.

Gregory the Great. *Morals on the Book of Job*. Translated by the Members of the English Church. Oxford: Baxter Printer, 1844.

Guardini, Romano. "Truth and the Eucharist." In *Preparing Yourself for Mass*, 179–84. Manchester, NH: Sophia Institute Press, 1993.

Hillers, Delbert R. *Covenant: The History of a Biblical Idea*. Baltimore: Johns Hopkins University Press, 1969.

Hittinger, Russell. *First Grace: Rediscovering the Natural Law in a Post-Christian World*. Wilmington, DE: ISI Books, 2003.

Jenkins, John. *Knowledge and Faith in Thomas Aquinas*. Cambridge: Cambridge University Press, 1991.

Jensen, Steve. *Good and Evil Actions: A Journey through Saint Thomas Aquinas*. Washington, DC: Catholic University of America Press, 2010.

———. *Knowing the Natural Law: From Precepts and Inclinations to Deriving Oughts*. Washington, DC: Catholic University of America Press, 2015.

———. *Living the Good Life: A Beginner's Thomistic Ethics*. Washington, DC: Catholic University of America Press, 2013.

John of St. Thomas. *The Gifts of the Holy Spirit*. New York: Sheed and Ward, 1951.

John XXIII. *Pacem in Terris*. In *Catholic Social Thought: The Documentary Heritage*, edited by David O'Brian and Thomas Shannon, 131–62. Maryknoll, NY: Orbis, 1992.

John Paul II. *Centesimus Annus*. In *Catholic Social Thought: The Documentary Heritage*, edited by David O'Brian and Thomas Shannon, 439–80. Maryknoll, NY: Orbis, 1992.

———. *Evangelium Vitae*. Boston: Pauline Books and Media, 1995.

———. *The Jeweler's Shop*. Translated by Boleslaw Taborski. San Francisco: Ignatius, 1992.

———. *Laborem Excercens*. In *Catholic Social Thought: The Documentary Heritage*, edited by David O'Brian and Thomas Shannon, 352–92. Maryknoll, NY: Orbis, 1992.

———. *Love and Responsibility*. San Francisco: Ignatius, 1993.

———. *Man and Woman He Created Them: A Theology of the Body*. Translated by Michael Waldstein. Boston: Pauline Books and Media, 2006.

———. "On Life-Sustaining Treatments and Vegetative State: Scientific Advances and Ethical Dilemmas." *National Catholic Bioethics Quarterly* 4 (2004): 573–76.

———. "The Problem of the Will in the Analysis of the Ethical Act." In *Person and Community: Selected Essays*, translated by Theresa Sandok, 3–22. Peter Lang: New York, 1993.

———. *Sollicitudo Rei Socialis*. In *Catholic Social Thought: The Documentary Heritage*, edited by David O'Brian and Thomas Shannon, 395–436. Maryknoll, NY: Orbis, 1992.

———. *Veritatis Splendor*. Boston: Pauline Books and Media, 1993.

Kaczor, Christopher. "The Ethics of Ectopic Pregnancy: A Critical Reconsideration of Salpingostomy and Methotrexate." *The Linacre Quarterly* 76, no. 3 (2009): 265–82.

Kant, Immanuel. *Foundations of the Metaphysics of Morals*. In *Kant Selections*, edited and translated by Lewis White Beck, 235–89. New York: Macmillan, 1998.

———. "What Is Enlightenment?" In *Kant Selections*, edited and translated by Lewis White Beck, 426–67. New York: Macmillan, 1998.

Kasper, Walter. *Theology and the Church*. New York: Crossroad, 1992.

Kelly, J. N. D. *Early Christian Creeds*. London: Continuum, 2006.

Kheriaty, Aaron. *The Catholic Guide to Depression*. Manchester, NH: Sophia Institute Press, 2012.

King, Martin Luther, Jr. "Letter from a Birmingham Jail." In *A Testament of Hope: The Essential Writings and Speeches of Martin Luther King, Jr.*, edited by James Washington, 289–302. New York: HarperCollins, 1991.

Lehner, Ulrich. *The Catholic Enlightenment: The Forgotten History of a Global Movement*. New York: Oxford, 2016.

Leo XIII. *Libertas*. Kansas City, MO: Angelus, 2006.

———. *Rerum Novarum*. In *Catholic Social Thought: The Documentary Heritage*, edited by David O'Brian and Thomas Shannon, 14–39. Maryknoll, NY: Orbis, 1992.

Lewis, C. S. *The Screwtape Letters*. New York: Macmillan, 1982.

Lombardo, Nicholas. *The Logic of Desire: Aquinas on Emotion*. Washington, DC: Catholic University of America Press, 2010.

Lonergan, Bernard. *Grace and Freedom: Operative Grace in the Thought of St. Thomas Aquinas*. New York: Herder and Herder, 1971.

Long, Steven. "Obediential Potency, Human Knowledge, and the Natural Desire for God." *International Philosophical Quarterly* 37 (1997): 45–63.

———. *The Teleological Grammar of the Moral Act*. Ave Maria, FL: Sapientia, 2007.

MacIntrye, Alasdair. *After Virtue*. Notre Dame, IN: University of Notre Dame Press, 1984.

———. *Three Rival Versions of Moral Inquiry*. Notre Dame, IN: University of Notre Dame Press, 1990.

Mattison, William C. *Introducing Moral Theology: True Happiness and the Virtues*. Grand Rapids, MI: Brazos, 2008.

McInerny, Ralph. *Aquinas on Human Action*. Washington, DC: Catholic University of America Press, 1992.

Melina, Livio. *Sharing in Christ's Virtues*. Translated by William May. Washington, DC: Catholic University of America Press, 2001.

Moore, Scott. "Hospitality as an Alternative to Tolerance." *Communio* 27 (Fall 2000): 600–608.

Murphy, John. *The Virtues on Parade*. Milwaukee, WI: Bruce, 1959.

Nowell, Irene. *Pleading, Cursing, Praising: Conversing with God through the Psalms*. Collegeville, MN: Liturgical Press, 2013.

O'Collins, Gerald. *The TriPersonal God: Understanding and Interpreting the Trinity*. New York: Paulist, 1999.

Oesterle, J. A. *Ethics: The Introduction to Moral Science*. Englewood Cliffs, NJ: Prentice-Hall, 1958.

Paul VI. *Humanae Vitae*. Boston: St. Paul Books and Media, 1968.

Pieper, Joseph. *The Four Cardinal Virtues*. Notre Dame, IN: University of Notre Dame Press, 1966.

———. *Leisure, the Basis of Culture*. Translated by Gerald Malsbary. South Bend, IN: St. Augustine's Press, 1998.

Pilsner, Joseph. *The Specification of Human Actions in St. Thomas Aquinas*. Oxford: Oxford University Press, 2006.

Pinckaers, Servais. *Morality: The Catholic View*. Translated by Michael Sherwin. South Bend, IN: St. Augustine's Press, 2001.

———. *Passions and Virtues*. Translated by Benedict Guevin. Washington, DC: Catholic University of America Press, 2015.

———. *Sources of Christian Ethics*. Translated by T. A. Noble. Washington, DC: Catholic University of America Press, 1995.

Pius XI. *Quadragesimo Anno*. In *Catholic Social Thought: The Documentary Heritage*, edited by David O'Brian and Thomas Shannon, 42–80. Maryknoll, NY: Orbis, 1992.

Pontifical Council for Peace and Justice. *Compendium of the Social Doctrine of the Church.* Washington, DC: United States Conference of Catholic Bishops, 2004.

Rhonheimer, Martin. *Natural Law and Practical Reason.* Translated by Gerald Malsbary. New York: Fordham University Press, 2000.

Rziha, John. *Perfecting Human Actions: St. Thomas Aquinas on Human Participation in Eternal Law.* Washington, DC: Catholic University of America Press, 2009.

———. "The Thomistic Roots of Modern Papal Teachings on Freedom as Found in the Writings of Leo XIII." *Nova et Vetera* 13 (Spring 2015): 585–600.

Schmidt, Joseph. *Everything Is Grace: The Life and Way of Thérèse of Lisieux.* Frederick, MD: Word Among Us Press, 2007.

Schmidt, Robert. *The Domain of Logic according to Saint Thomas Aquinas.* The Hague: Martinus Nijhoff, 1966.

Schwartz, Daniel. *Aquinas on Friendship.* Oxford: Oxford University Press, 2007.

Shanley, Brian. "Divine Causation and Human Freedom in Aquinas." *American Catholic Philosophical Quarterly* 72 (1998): 98–122.

Sherwin, Michael. *By Knowledge and By Love: Charity and Knowledge in the Moral Theology of St. Thomas Aquinas.* Washington, DC: Catholic University of America Press, 2005.

Smith, Janet. *Humanae Vitae: A Generation Later.* Washington, DC: Catholic University of America Press, 1991.

Teresa of Calcutta [Mother Teresa]. *A Simple Path.* New York: Random House, 1995.

Thayer, Joseph. *Thayer's Greek-English Lexicon of the New Testament.* New York: American Book Company, 1889.

Thérèse of Lisieux. *Story of a Soul.* Translated by John Clarke. Washington, DC: ICS Publications, 1996.

Torrell, Jean Pierre. *Christ and Spirituality in St. Thomas Aquinas.* Washington, DC: Catholic University of America Press, 2011.

United States Conference of Catholic Bishops. *The Ethical and Religious Directives for Catholic Health Care Services.* Washington, DC: USCCB, 2009.

Vatican II. *Dei Verbum.* In *Vatican Council II: The Conciliar and Post Conciliar Documents,* edited by Austin Flannery, 750–65. Collegeville, MN: Liturgical Press, 1975.

———. *Gaudium et Spes.* In *Vatican II: The Conciliar and Post Conciliar Documents,* edited by Austin Flannery, 903–1001. Collegeville, MN: Liturgical Press, 1975.

———. *Lumen Gentium.* In *Vatican II: The Conciliar and Post Conciliar Documents,* edited by Austin Flannery, 350–423. Collegeville, MN: Liturgical Press, 1975.

Westberg, Daniel. *Right Practical Reason.* Oxford: Clarendon, 1984.

Wilken, Robert Louis. *The First Thousand Years: A Global History of Christianity.* New Haven, CT: Yale University Press, 2012.

Wippel, John. *Metaphysical Thought of Thomas Aquinas: From Finite Being to Uncreated Being.* Washington, DC: Catholic University of America Press, 2000.

———. "Thomas Aquinas and the Axiom 'What Is Received Is Received according to the Mode of the Receiver.'" In *Metaphysical Themes in Thomas Aquinas II,* 113–22. Washington, DC: Catholic University of America Press, 2007.

Wojtyla, Karol. *See* John Paul II.

INDEX

abortion, 244–45
actions. *See* human actions
almsgiving, 203
anger, 282–83
annulment, 275
apostasy, 180, 181
Aquinas, Thomas
  on charity, 194, 213, 316nn34–35, 325n7
  on faith, 322n3, 322n5
  on freedom, 320n10
  on friendship with God, 141
  on God, 289n7
  —as cause of human actions, 146, 294n15, 317nn6–7, 317nn9–10
  on gifts of the Holy Spirit, 133
  on grace, 307nn8–11, 308n14, 308n16
  on happiness, 297n10, 298nn18–20
  on hope, 324nn2–6
  on human actions, 68, 215–16, 302n8
  —determining goodness, 304n25, 306n36
  on human nature, 21, 28, 291nn27–29, 292n37, 293n2
  on love, 290nn13–14, 325n4
  on law, 309nn3–4, 309n7, 310n17, 311n18
  on prudence, 216, 332n7
  on sin, 148

  on virtues, 125, 313nn9–10, 314nn13–15, 315nn30–32
Aristotle
  on habits, 114, 313n1
  on happiness, 46
  on hylomorphism, 17
artificial birth control, 266–73
artificial reproduction, 273–74
atheism, 181
autonomy, 169

beatitude. *See* happiness
beatitudes, 59, 206–9
Benedict XVI
  on Catholic social thought, 312n26, 328n39, 334n8, 341nn26–27
  on the environment, 233
  on hope, 183, 185
  on justice, 333n2
Benedict of Nursia, 205, 319n13
beneficence, 202
body (human), 17–18, 22–24, 28–39
  as related to soul (*see* soul)

capital punishment, 247
caution, 221
cell phones, 231

353

JOHN RZIHA is professor of theology at Benedictine College and author of *Perfecting Human Actions: St. Thomas Aquinas on Human Participation in Eternal Law.*

Printed in the USA
CPSIA information can be obtained
at www.ICGtesting.com
LVHW021506120823
755043LV00008B/345